ASIAN FORMS *of the* NATION

NORDIC INSTITUTE OF ASIAN STUDIES

Studies in Asian Topics

ASIAN
FORMS
of the
NATION

edited by
Stein Tønnesson
and Hans Antlöv

CURZON

The Nordic Institute of Asian Studies (NIAS) is funded by the governments of Denmark, Finland, Iceland, Norway and Sweden via the Nordic Council of Ministers, and works to encourage and support Asian studies in the Nordic countries. In so doing, NIAS has published well in excess of one hundred books in the last twenty-five years, most of them in co-operation with Curzon Press.

Nordic Council of Ministers

Nordic Institute of Asian Studies
Studies in Asian Topics, No. 23

First published in 1996 by Curzon Press Ltd.,
St. John's Studios, Church Road
Richmond, Surrey TW9 2QA

ISBN 0–7007–0403–5 [Hardback]
ISBN 0–7007–0442–6 [Paperback]

ISSN 0142–6208

© Nordic Institute of Asian Studies 1996

British Library Catalogue in Publication Data
A CIP catalogue record for this book
is available from the British Library

Printed in Great Britain by
Biddles Ltd, Guildford and King's Lynn

Contents

Figures

Maps

CHAPTER ONE

Asia in Theories of Nationalism and National Identity

Stein Tønnesson and Hans Antlöv

There have been five main variants of nationalism, states a recent study, defining the 'five roads to modernity' as the English, French, Russian, German and American. They 'set the examples followed by the rest of the planet'.[1] The inclination of many scholars has been to assume that the formation of nations in Asia and Africa, sometimes even in the pioneering Latin America, has been a distorted reflection of the European precedents. Over the last ten to fifteen years, however, the scholarship on nationalism and national identity has gone through a process of sophistication and globalization. The national phenomenon outside Europe is being studied more intensely than before, and non-European scholars are taking up positions in the theoretical debate.[2] It has become more common to discover the particular forms that nations have taken in Africa, America and Asia, and compare them to the several European varieties. The purpose of the present book is to make this into a lasting trend and ensure that Asia becomes unavoidable in the general debate. The chapters are built on papers from a workshop on 'Comparative Approaches to National Identity in Asia', held at the Nordic Institute of Asian Studies in May 1994, with Benedict Anderson as keynote speaker. This first chapter has been written subsequently and is meant to serve as an introduction.

---

1. Liah Greenfeld, *Nationalism. Five Roads to Modernity*, Cambridge: Harvard University Press, 1992, p. 23.

2. See Select Bibliography, pp. 348–352.

Asia, we contend, has its own national forms, which are no mere reflections of European or American models. We shall not argue that there is something specifically Asian about these forms but that each Asian nation, just like the European and American ones, has its own individual character that is not exactly identical to any other but which may still be fruitfully compared with others. It is true that nationalism emerged in eighteenth- and nineteenth-century Western Europe and in the Americas. It was here that the principle of national sovereignty first developed, with its emphasis on representative institutions, a centralized administration, fixed borders, popular identification with the state through education, national festivals, compulsory military service and a public jurisdiction. These general features characterize the universally applicable principle of the 'nation-state', a principle which did indeed spread from Europe to the rest of the planet. Stateless societies, tributary political hierarchies and monarchic states have all but disappeared from the globe. In order to be successful in the new global marketplace, it is important for a state to develop and maintain a collective 'we-feeling' among its citizens, and a sense that the state belongs to them. If the citizens do not identify with the state, its authority may erode, and territories with little effective authority cannot attract investments and generate growth. The irony of the world today is that globalization undermines the sovereignty of each individual state while at the same time making it increasingly important for a state, in order to be competitive in the global market, to obtain the strong dedication from its citizens that sovereign nation-states have been particularly apt at achieving. We define the term 'nation-state' broadly as *a state which the great majority of the citizens identify with to the extent of seeing it as their own,* and we see 'nationalism' as *an ideological movement for attaining or maintaining a nation-state.*[3] What, then, is a 'nation'? This is the most difficult question, and one that has already been answered in many different ways. We shall abstain from offering another definition here, and just quote two influential ones below.

---

3. Anthony D. Smith defines nationalism in a way that does not require a programme for the creation of a fully independent state: 'a movement for attaining and maintaining autonomy, unity and identity on behalf of a population deemed by some of its members to constitute an actual or potential 'nation',' Anthony D. Smith, *National Identity*, London: Penguin, 1991, p. 73. We prefer to restrict the term to movements aiming at full, independent statehood. On the other hand, Smith suggests a far more restrictive definition of 'nation-state' than ours, but then he considers the term 'nation-state' to be a misnomer, and in his latest book starts to use 'natio*nal* state' in the wider sense of our term.

Why should we be particularly interested in *Asian* forms of the nation? Apart from a normative obligation to overcome eurocentrism, and the obvious need of Asians – and Asianists – to study nationalism in 'their' part of the world, there are also two more scholarly reasons. First, existing theory needs to be tested against non-European cases. If a theory cannot explain the Asian evidence, then it is not globally applicable. By examining Asian cases, it may be possible to test the explanatory range of theories established from Europe. A preparatory step in this direction will be to examine how some of the most sophisticated established theoreticians have tried to incorporate Asia in their theoretical frameworks. A further step will be to single out some of the most salient controversies within existing theory and see to what extent Asian cases sustain one or the other view.

Second, from an inductive perspective, we may consider some basic features distinguishing Asia from Europe, and see if these features can engender fruitful questions leading to new theoretical insights. In this way we may be able to formulate new theory that can also inform the study of nationalism in Africa, the Americas and Europe.

Asia in Three Important Theories

Since the 1970s a number of fine scholars have launched innovative theories about how national identities are formed in various kinds of interplay between politics, historical memory and cultural construction. These are theories that go beyond political philosophy and treat nationalism as a social phenomenon, in much the same way as with religions.[4] From the many authors we have selected three for special scrutiny, all of whom have adopted a global approach: Ernest Gellner, Benedict Anderson and Anthony D. Smith. Our purpose is to examine the implications of their theories for the understanding of nationalism and national identity in Asia.

The foundation of Ernest Gellner's argument, as presented in his *Nations and Nationalism* (1983), is a distinction between the agrarian and industrial stages of human history. He denies the existence of nationalism in agrarian societies, situates the nationalist phenomenon primarily in the early stages of industrialization, and believes that it may fade away in more

---

4. Bruce Kapferer even proposes that nationalism *is* a religion since 'the nation is created as an object of devotion'. Bruce Kapferer, *Legends of People, Myths of State: Violence, Intolerance, and Political Culture in Sri Lanka and Australia*, Washington: Smithsonian Institution Press, 1988, p. 1.

'mature, homogeneous' industrial societies. In agrarian societies there was always a cultural gulf between the rulers and the ruled. High (literary) and low (non-literary) cultures existed simultaneously, with the high cultures being normally larger than any individual state, and the low cultures generally much smaller: almost everything in an agrarian society thus 'militates against the definition of political units in terms of cultural boundaries'.[5] Industrial society, by contrast, requires a homogeneous system of education that merges high and low culture, either by imposing the high culture on the population or by upgrading a low culture to a high culture. It is during this homogenization process that nationalism is generated. Gellner suggests a typology of nationalisms built on a model combining three inputs: distribution of power, access to education, and ethnic (low cultural) division. In agrarian societies only the powerful have access to education, thus ethnic division does not present a problem. But when the cultural homogenization required by industry sets in, uneven access to power and education between groups that lend themselves to ethnic demarcation creates a problem. This, in turn, gives rise to national-ism and determines its form. If some groups have little access to both power and education, they will form their own nationalisms in opposition to their rulers. This is Gellner's first model, called 'Habsburg' or 'Balkan', which he finds has been emulated in twentieth-century Africa south of the Sahara. If the powerless get access to education and are able to coalesce into an ethnic majority within a culturally divided society, one gets the 'classical liberal Western nationalism' of the Italian or German kind (no non-European example is mentioned). If the powerless are better educated than the powerful, but represent a minority without a specific homeland, one gets Gellner's third type, 'diaspora nationalism' of the Jewish (and overseas Chinese and Indian) kind.

Is this model applicable to Asia? Gellner's thinking is built mainly on the experience of the Christian and Islamic civilizations, but he draws other parts of Asia into his discussion. Asia figures prominently in the chapter where he demonstrates how agrarian societies preclude nationalism. One of his low-culture examples is the Himalayan peasant, who can move freely be-tween caste, clan and village identities but can never assume a national one.[6]

5. Ernest Gellner, *Nations and Nationalism*, Oxford: Blackwell, 1983, p. 11. A collection of Gellner's later essays about nationalism can be found in his *Encounters with Nationalism*, Oxford: Blackwell, 1994.

6. Gellner, *Nations and Nationalism*, pp. 12-13.

This example is discussed in Chapter 8 of this volume by Graham E. Clarke, who explains the continuing resilience of non-national identities in Himalaya by topographical obstacles to inter-valley communication. The Himalayan peasant may not, perhaps, be all that typical of pre-modern societies, but Gellner also tries to demonstrate the non-national character of Asian high cultures: the Islamic, the Hindu and the Confucian. In passing he concedes, however, that at least two of them form partial exceptions to his rule. Islamic culture is an exception because the distinction between high and low culture was already blurred at the agrarian stage: Islamic society was therefore 'ideally prepared' for the merger 'required' in the age of industry. Confucian high culture was also an exception because it was so closely linked to one individual state; it thus anticipated 'in that way, but that way only' the modern linkage of state and culture.[7] The pre-nationalist linkage between state and culture in China forms the point of departure for Torbjörn Lodén in Chapter 10 where he discusses whether the Chinese are finally about to liberate themselves from an age-old quest for political unity.

When Gellner leaves the agrarian societies, and explains how high and low cultures merge during the transition to industrial society, only one of the major high cultures, the Islamic, remains distinctly in focus. Gellner develops the point of how 'unique' this culture has been in allowing for a swift merger between high and low culture. Islam has thus lent itself easily to be used as an idiom for modern national identities, at least in those nations which are differentiated by Islam, or a variant of Islam, from other nations. Gellner's view here is markedly different from the general assumption that Islam has hampered the development of nationalism by offering a wider, alternative framework of identity.

One weakness of Gellner's book is his lack of precision as to when the transition from agrarian to industrial society occurred in the various parts of the world. His readers may be left with the assumption that twentieth-century African and Asian nationalism is a kind of delayed repetition of what happened in Europe when it was industrialized. Researchers working from such an assumption might look for Asian Balkans, Germanies and Jews, with little prospect of improving their understanding of either Asia or the nationalist phenomenon. But Gellner has virtually nothing to say about industry, or the needs of economic enterprise, as such. His chapter on 'industrial society' deals almost uniquely with culture. He simply assumes

---

7. For the Islamic exception, see Gellner, *Nations and Nationalism*, p. 76; for the Confucian, *ibid.*, pp. 15, 80, 141.

that educational – and hence cultural – homogenization reflect industrial need. Gellner seems, implicitly, to *define* industrial society as a society with a standardized system of education.[8] This identification of industry and school prevents him from taking into account the homogenizing capacity of standardized systems of education in pre-industrial China, Korea, Japan and Vietnam; it also prevents him from taking full account of how Western-style teaching in (non-industrialized) European colonies influenced local nationalism. Despite these weaknesses Gellner's theory may still inspire fruitful questions concerning the friction between the Islamic community as a whole and each Islamic nation, and also concerning some of the current cultural processes of educational standardization in the industrializing countries of Pacific Asia. Perhaps the main point we can learn from Gellner is the crucial role that ethnic inequalities in access to education have had in determining the form of each nationalism, hence nation.[9] The applicability of Gellner's theory to Asian cases, however, is limited by his lack of appreciation for the way in which the international state system has compelled societies everywhere, with little regard for whether or not they were industrial, to seek integration through nationhood.[10] Gellner's causal model is built on imbalances within *each single* (but loosely defined) industrializing society. International factors such as the role of European colonialism, or American and Soviet inspiration, are not included in his model. They are of tremendous importance in Asia.

Our second theoretician, Benedict Anderson, does much to rectify the second flaw in Gellner's model by launching a sophisticated *diffusionist* theory. He deals with the spread of nationalism from the Americas and Europe and its adaption in the rest of the world. The spread of nationalism

---

8.   Gellner holds that in industrial societies the monopoly of legitimate education is 'more central than is the monopoly of legitimate violence'. Industrial society has a 'school-transmitted culture, not a folk-transmitted one'. Moreover, 'The agrarian age of mankind is a period in which some can read and most cannot, and the industrial age is one in which all can and must read', *Nations and Nationalism*, pp. 34, 36, 77.

9.   For a statement in support of Gellner's emphasis on mass education (but with no mention of how Gellner ties it to unequal ethnic access), see Anthony D. Smith, *Nations and Nationalism in a Global Era*, Cambridge: Polity Press, 1995, pp. 91-92. On the importance of colonial school systems, see Benedict R.O'G. Anderson, *Imagined Communities: Reflections on the Origin and Spread of Nationalism*, London: Verso, 1983 (2d ed. 1991), pp. 119ff., 126f.

10.   For a richly documented analysis of this process, see Jan Aart Scholte, 'The International Construction of Indonesian Nationhood, 1930-1950', in Hans Antlöv and Stein Tønnesson (eds), *Imperial Policy and Southeast Asian Nationalism, 1930–1957*, London: Curzon Press, 1995, pp. 191-226.

from Europe was also the preoccupation of Elie Kedourie, a leading scholar of nationalism in the 1960s, but whereas Kedourie described the contaminating influence of the nationalist *idea* as such, Anderson tries to track down a radical overall change of human consciousness of which nationalism is but one expression. Notably, the change of consciousness involved entirely new concepts of time and space.

In his *Imagined Communities*, first published in 1983 and revised and expanded in 1991, Anderson argues that the nation is a cultural construct, not in the sense of building on historical tradition but in that of being collectively imagined by all those going to the same kinds of school, viewing or listening to the same media, sharing the same mental map of the nation and its surrounding world, or visiting the same museums. There is thus nothing immanent or original about the nation: it is a construct, similar everywhere, only using different symbols, but it always considers itself as antique: it creates its own narrative, imagining itself as 'awakening from sleep'.

Whereas Gellner (like us) has found it best to abstain from a formal definition of the term 'nation', Anderson defines it as '*an imagined political community – and imagined as both inherently limited and sovereign.*'[11] He uses the word 'imagine' as almost synonymous with 'see' or 'visualize', and does not imply a 'false consciousness'. That a community is 'imagined' does not mean it is 'imaginary'. All communities larger than villages (where people meet face-to-face are imagined. In pre-nationalist societies there were two main larger cultural systems: the religious community and the dynastic realm. The religious communities were not territorial but were held together by sacred languages, and the dynastic realm was linked to a dynasty, not to an ethnic group or nation. The prevailing concepts of time and space were concrete, complex and rooted in nature, and built around sacred or dynastic centres. At this juncture new and far more rigid concepts of time and space were disseminated. The idea emerged that history is a chain of causes and effects, and peoples got histories attached to a designated homeland. A new consciousness linking an abstract, empty, homogeneous and chronological time to the fate of a people living within a rigidly demarc-ated, mapped geographical space, was spread through *print capitalism*: book publishing and newspapers. Where Gellner's focus was on education, that of Anderson is on the media.

---

11. Anderson, *Imagined Communities*, p. 6.

Like Gellner, Anderson offers three, but different, types of nationalism: *creole*, *linguistic* (or vernacular) and *official*. In his view, these were the three models shaped in America and Europe, and which became available to people in other places from about the second decade of the nineteenth century. Twentieth-century nationalism in Asia and Africa – 'the last wave' in Anderson's pre-Gorbachev terminology – could draw on more than a century of human experience and three earlier models of nationalism.[12] Notice how his terminology 'activates' those at the receiving end: models become 'available' and the Asians and Africans 'draw on' earlier models. Sometimes he uses the verb 'pirate'. The emulators do not necessarily copy only one model but can draw on lessons from all of them to create their own blend.

When revising *Imagined Communities* in 1991, Anderson regretted that he had overestimated the emulative capacity of the local nationalists in the colonies and underestimated the active role of European colonial adminis-trations in shaping the framework for the last-wave nations.[13] But apparently he did not regret having disregarded the impact of pre-national conditions, or traditions, in the various parts of Asia and Africa on each national form. His emphasis on modern 'imagining' led him to downplay the limits as to what *could be imagined* by a significant number of people in each specific place. It is easier to imagine a new kind of community if it resembles one that has already been imagined by one's parents or teachers. Each nation therefore tends to become a mixture of borrowed models and local inherited imaginings. Together they form what Benedict Anderson once described as a 'unique amalgam' which gives each nation its individuality. Admittedly, when Benedict Anderson used the term 'unique amalgam', it was not about a 'national individuality' but about *Javanese* conceptions of politics. He saw Javanese political culture as having its own distinctive character, radically different from the European one: 'I in no way assume that Javanese con-ceptions about politics are, in their separate elements, peculiarly Javanese – although I do believe that, in their totality, they form a unique amalgam.'[14]

How can it be that Benedict Anderson, with his strong background in Southeast Asian studies, should place so much emphasis on the 'pirating' of

---

12. *Ibid.*, p. 140.

13. *Ibid.*, p. 135.

14. 'The Idea of Power in Javanese Culture' can be read together with an autobiographi-cal introduction accounting for the author's change of perspective in Benedict Anderson, *Language and Power, Exploring Political Cultures in Indonesia*, Ithaca: Cornell University Press, 1990 (quote from p. 19).

Western models and downplay the impact of local political culture in the formation of Asian nation-states? There are two likely reasons. First, the purpose of *Imagined Communities* was not primarily to account for the difference among nations, but to explain the rapid spread of the nationalist principle over the last 200 years. Thus he had to emphasize what nations have in common. Second, Benedict Anderson's main background was in the study of a society that did *not* become a separate nation (the Javanese), whereas in *Imagined Communities* he was trying to account for the imagining of nations such as Indonesia, a larger, more heterogeneous and entirely modern community. Anderson's book could hardly have been written by someone with a background in the study of China or other Confucian societies.

Our third scholar, Anthony D. Smith, is today's main spokesman of the view that modern nations have ancient ethnic origins and were not invented or imagined. In 1971 he wrote a critical overview of the then prevailing theories on nationalism and, against the background of de-colonization, followed up in 1983 with a book on nationalism in the Third World. In 1986 he completed a larger study of the ethnic origins of nations, in which he asks what it is that has allowed some historical ethnies to survive while others have disappeared (his term 'ethnie' refers to pre-nationalist ethnic groups).[15] The most obvious survivors are those (aristo-cratic) ethnies which have been able continuously to sustain a royal dynasty or a succession of dynasties recruited from the ranks of one ethnic group. But Smith is mainly preoccupied with such ethnies which survived without their own state. He finds that the most resilient ones were those that had a communal salvation religion with its own rites, liturgies, customs, sacred language and texts, and an organized priesthood (Jews, Armenians). Other important features of surviving ethnies were: a fixed homeland, a high degree of autonomy, a high degree of hostility from surroundings, memories of heroic battles, sacred centres, sacred languages and scripts, special lifestyles and especially historical records and a historical outlook.[16] These, by the way, are exactly the kind of features that nationalists have tried to discover, invent or pirate from others. Smith has continued to emphasize the importance of religion, myths and ethno-history in his further reflections on

---

15. Anthony D. Smith, *Theories of Nationalism*, New York: Holmes & Meyer, 1971 (2nd ed. 1983); *State and Nation in the Third World*, Brighton: Harvester Press, 1983; *Ethnic Origins of Nations*, Oxford: Basil Blackwell, 1986.

16. Smith, *Ethnic Origins of Nations*, p. 124.

the current resurgence of nations, summed up in his introductory volume *National Identities* (1991) and his *Nations and Nationalism in a Global Era* (1995).

To begin with, Smith shares with Gellner and Anderson the view that nationalism and the nation-state are modern; he distances himself from 'perennialist' or 'primordial' theories. But he insists that nations have roots in pre-modern ethnic communities. Instead of emphasizing the break between agrarian and industrial society, he establishes the historical 'genealogy' of modern nations, the most cohesive of which were formed around an 'ethnic core'. Nationalist leaders have had to embed their image of the nation in such historical myths and symbols that could have the deepest resonance in the popular imagining, and it is precisely this historical embeddedness which has given nationalism its force.

Smith makes a subtle distinction between the pre-modern *ethnie* and the modern nation. *Ethnies* are 'named units of population with common ancestry myths and historical memories, elements of shared culture, some link with a historic territory and some measure of solidarity, at least among their elites'. A *nation*, by contrast, is 'a named human population which shares myths and memories, a mass public culture, a designated homeland, economic unity and equal rights and duties for all members'.[17] There are five changes that have, so to speak, transformed ethnies into nations: the inclusion of the whole people (masses), the constitution of a 'legal-political community', legitimation through nationalist ideology, integration in the international system, and the delimitation of a national territory.

Unfortunately, Smith does not, like Gellner and Anderson, offer a theory to explain these changes, elucidate the emergence of modern nations or account for the spread of the nationalist principle, but he suggests a typology of modern nations based on the 'routes' they have followed to the status as national states. Basically there are two routes: one from above – incorporation of the population by agents of the state (France is the main European example, Thailand and Japan are obvious ones in Asia)[18] – and one from below – the formation of a new state by an ethnie through separation or unification (Ireland and Italy are two European examples;

---

17. Smith, *Nations and Nationalism in a Global Era*, pp. 56-57. See also his *National Identity*, p. 14. In Smith's *Ethnic Origins of Nations*, p. 97, he defined *ethnies* as 'clusters of population with similar perceptions and sentiments generated by, and encoded in, specific beliefs, values and practices.'

18. Smith, *Nations and Nationalism in a Global Era*, p. 41. A succinct summary of Smith's two routes can be found in *National Identity*, p. 123.

Asian examples include Burma, Sri Lanka, Pakistan and Bangladesh). In his latest book, Smith reluctantly adds a third 'plural' type to cover the United States of America, but he is not happy with it since it does not satisfy his basic criterion for a really national nation-state: that it has an ethnic core. He is therefore forced to argue that even the United States is built around a core of English emigrants, that the Hindu community forms the core of the Indian nation, and that Islamic communities do the same in many Islamic states.[19] Smith seems to prefer having only two types, and to see 'plural nations' as not quite nations at all. If we ignore Smith's reluctance, and include his residual category as a national type of its own, we shall end up with the same three models as proposed by Benedict Anderson, although with different names. Anderson's linguistic/official/creole are called ethnic/civic/plural by Smith.

How does Smith incorporate Asia in his typology? Where Gellner combines knowledge of Europe and modern Islam, Smith knows Europe, Africa and the ancient cultures of the Middle East. But Gellner and Smith have also made efforts to include examples from the Americas and from South, Southeast and East Asia. In an introduction from 1983, Smith cites as an 'important reason' for reorienting the study of nationalism away from its exclusive concern with 'modernization' the need to 'move away from the dominant Eurocentric outlook'.[20] However, when Smith moves 'outside the West' – to quote a recurrent expression – he uses his two Western routes, bureaucratic incorporation and vernacular mobilization, as his matrix and distinguishes two sub-categories of bureaucratic incorporation: the *imperial* and the *colonial*. His Asian examples of transformation from *empire* to nation through bureaucratic incorporation are China, Japan, Persia and Turkey.[21] The *colonial* route, in which the nation was 'defined, in its boundaries and character, by the colonial state', is also supplied with four Asian references (Iraq, India, Burma and Indonesia), yet what Smith has to say about this route seems to be based mainly on the African experience and is not really relevant for Asia: 'Truly, colonial nationalisms are still-born; they are imitative "nationalisms of the intelligentsia", unable to forge real nations.'[22] The distinction between an imperial and a colonial route seems

19. Smith, *Nations and Nationalism in a Global Era*, p. 41.
20. Smith, *Theories of Nationalism*, p. xi.
21. Smith, *National Identity*, pp. 100ff.
22. *Ibid.*, p. 108.

questionable, as far as Asia is concerned. As demonstrated by Thongchai
Winichakul in Chapter 3 of this volume, the non-colonized Siam behaved in
a similar way towards the people in the Lao border zones as did the French
from the other side. On the other hand, as Christopher Goscha shows in
Chapter 4, there were colonized territories where the nationalists did not, in
the end, accept the political space created by the colonial power, and instead
followed an 'imperial route'.

Smith often just adds Asian examples of features that are also well
illustrated in Europe or the Middle East. He has not entirely left the habit of
the 1960s and 1970s to lump Africa, Latin America and Asia together under
the flawed category of 'the Third World'. Nor has he completely overcome
the older habit of subsuming all Asians under categories established on the
basis of phenomena in the border zone between Europe and Asia. In
National Identity he first seems to endorse Kohn and Plamenatz's classic
distinction between a 'Western' civic-territorial and an 'Eastern' ethnic-
genealogical model of the nation, with the Western as rational and the
Eastern as mystical but, when returning to the matter in a chapter on types
of nationalist ideologies, he soundly observes that both models can be
found both in the East and the West.[23] In Chapter 5 of this volume,
however, Peter van der Veer seems to confirm the basic difference between
the secularized nationalism of Western Europe and the religiously defined
nationalisms in the formerly colonized world. This makes considerable
sense for someone studying Hindu nationalism or Singhalese Buddhism,
and also for students of some versions of political Islam, but less so,
perhaps, for those who study the more secular nationalisms in black Africa,
East Asia – or in the Indian Congress Party.

Perhaps the main criticism that one can direct against Smith is that he
elevates the ethnic nation – the nation built around one ethnic core – to a
pre-eminent form, and that he exaggerates the collective pervasiveness of
ethnic and national identities. They are more pervasive in some periods
than others, and some are more pervasive than others. Smith's contention
that the Indonesian nation is built around a Javanese ethnic core is as
questionable as his view that the United States is a nation whose emotional
pervasiveness relies on the original foundation myths of a white puritan

23. *Ibid.*, pp. 11-15, 80-81. See also *Theories of Nationalism*, p. xi, and *Nations and Nationalism in a Global Era*, p. 77. For a vigorous critique of Kohn's distinction, see Partha Chatterjee, *Nationalist Thought and the Colonial World. A Derivative Discourse*, Minneapolis:
University of Minnesota Press, 1986 (reprinted 1993), pp. 2ff.

Anglo-Saxon core.[24] While Benedict Anderson's theory fits well with the Indonesian experience, Smith's theory goes well with the Vietnamese. The main appeal of Anthony D. Smith's historical and ethnic approach is that it allows us to see Asians as having their own national forms, based on distinct historical memories. The modernist theories of Gellner and Anderson imply, each in their own way, that Asians have merely repeated what Europeans had done before. Most European and North American authors have understood nationalism outside Europe as a derivation or modification of the European experience. Nationalism in the former colonies is perceived as *anti-colonial* and the non-colonized parts of the non-European world – China, Japan, Thailand, Afghanistan, Iran, Ethiopia, even Turkey – are often left out of the discussion. Smith is not devoid of these fallacies but this is not due to his basic approach. It is rather the recent mode to disregard history and see it as a pure construct which has reinforced the view of Asians as mere emulators: anti-colonial and post-colonial leaders have just been 'inventing traditions' the same way nationalists used to do in Europe.

Does Asia Fit Our Theories?

We shall now depict the main theoretical approaches more broadly, and ask to what extent they are useful for students of Asia. Among the most controversial issues in existing theory are the *role of history and tradition* and the *typology* of nations.

THE ROLE OF HISTORY AND TRADITION

To put the debate about the role of tradition in a proper perspective, it may be useful to draw a distinction between *modernist, post-modernist* and *ethno-culturalist* approaches. They have different consequences for the way Asian national forms are interpreted.

The *modernist* approach has two versions: one 'diffusionist' (Elie Kedourie, Benedict Anderson), and one 'functionalist' (Gellner). Both see nationalism as a modern phenomenon; no national identities existed before the American and French Revolutions. Modern forms of state surveillance, industrial production and capitalist marketing depend upon the homo-

---

24. For the Javanese as the dominant ethnie of Indonesia, see Smith, *Theories of Nationalism*, p. 217; *National Identity*, pp. 110, 114. For the United States, see *National Identity*, pp. 149-150; *Nations and Nationalism in a Global Era*, pp. 41, 107f., 119.

genization or partitioning of inconsistently organized societies into a standardized system. The origins of colonial nations, then, can be traced to social and political changes in the nineteenth and early twentieth centuries, more specifically Western education, new social classes, political liberalization, and increased mobility. The modern nation-state not only represents popular sovereignty but also registers and disciplines its citizens through laws and education. There is something irresistible about the process of modernization in which nationalism destroys or encapsulates myriads of local cultures and creates 'the modern society'. The modernist approach sees history as a number of 'roads to modernity'. In one version, the road goes onwards to transcend the nation and create a global culture.

A prominent protagonist of the modernist view is the socialist historian Eric Hobsbawm. He sees nationalism as having played a progressive role in an earlier historical phase when populations fought for freedom from autocratic and imperial rule, but later taking on a reactionary role in dividing communities which ought to stick together.[25] From this perspective, Hobsbawm compares Western and Third World nationalisms in a way that reveals the poverty of rigid modular thinking. First he says that Third World nationalisms were modelled on the standard liberal Western form, then that in practice they differ from the model since they have failed to live up to it, and, as an afterthought, he adds that most Western nationalisms have failed on this score too. Thus the Western and the Third World nationalisms resemble one another in their failure to fit the standard liberal form.

Benedict Anderson's theory can be said to form a bridge between the modernist and the *post-modernist* approaches. His term 'imagined community' and his emphasis on the persuasive power of the media has suited post-modernists well. They reject 'objective' history, and see history as a narrative, being told and retold continuously. There is no real 'past' out there to decide what history looks like. People's view of history is formed by the imaginative power and narrative capabilities of those who dominate the media. Post-modernist theory has done much to dissipate the idea of a national history. According to the post-modernist, the nation exists only by virtue of a constant creation and recreation of symbols and imaginations such as maps and flags, language and myth, enemies and constitutions. Nationalism is commonly portrayed as a force representing and mobilizing

25. Eric Hobsbawm, *Nations and Nationalism since 1780*, Cambridge: Cambridge University Press, 1990, p. 164.

a whole. But as any ideology, it is contested even within the nation it imagines, in the sense that some people would prefer a local, a global or a rival national identity. There is a constant fluidity in nationalist symbols and culture, whether we choose to call them polyphonic, subaltern, fragmented, local, or gendered.

One problem with the post-modernist approach is its disregard of historical facts. Only the narrative matters. Nations are thus in danger of losing the little that modernists have left of their history. National histories are discounted from the 'development stages' of the modernist school to just stories, told by nationalists and believed by manipulated audiences. Another problem is the inability of post-modernists to explain the forcefulness of national sentiments. We are told that these are based on pure constructs, and that we must critically deconstruct 'ethnicity', 'nation' and 'culture'. But while the post-modernist deconstructs, people build their lives on intensely felt identities. In the post-modernist perspective, ethnic groups and nations lose not only their history; they also lose any reason for being as pervasive as they are, and they lose their future. Indeed, many post-modernists – and modernists, too – predict that nations will disappear during the present globalization process. This seems quite unlikely, although it is true that global media and communications are opening new space for 'deterritorialized' identities that supplement and challenge the national ones.[26]

The *ethno-culturalist* approach roots nationalism in pre-modern ethnies or polities. An ethnie becomes a nation by acquiring its own sovereign state (Germany, Poland, Cambodia), or a dynastic state establishes a bureaucratic culture into which its subjects are absorbed (China, France). In some cases it works both ways (Norway, Korea, Vietnam). The defining features of the ethnie/nation can be language, religion, customs, a 'homeland' with symbolic places, or a shared history. Such qualities have long been embedded in the popular imagination as signs of difference. The contents of tradition have changed, and sometimes radically, but there have still been strikingly continuous patterns of demarcation between the We and the Other.

A balanced ethno-culturalist approach is attractive from the Asianist's point of view because it allows us to approach the continent from the angle of its own history. We start from the ethnic groups and political entities which we know from written records of past centuries and see how they

---

26. See David Morley and Kevin Robins, *Spaces of Identity: Global Media, Electronic Landscapes and Cultural Boundaries*, London: Routledge, 1995.

have been transformed into nations through confrontation and incorporation of ideas coming from Europe in the nineteenth and twentieth centuries.

One sees the difference between the three approaches in the understanding of the term 'tradition'. In 1983, Eric Hobsbawm and Terence Ranger launched *The Invention of Tradition,* a book title which, like *Imagined Communities,* became an academic catch-word. In his preface to the book, Hobsbawm defines invented traditions, in short, as 'responses to novel situations which take the form of reference to old situations, or which establish their own past by quasi-obligatory repetition.'[27] He is careful to distinguish between invented and genuine traditions: 'Where the old ways are alive, traditions need be neither revived nor invented' and goes on to claim that the element of invention is particularly clear in the ways that history has been used to forge 'that comparatively recent historical innovation, the "nation", with its associated phenomena: nationalism, the nation-state, national symbols, histories and the rest.' According to Hobsbawm, their 'novelty is no less novel for being able to dress up easily as antiquity'.

Paradoxically, this proposition from a historian embedded in the tradition of progressive socialism has become a crucial element in the postmodernist reinvention of history as a set of narrative fragments. Anthony D. Smith acknowledges of course that modern nations have created a whole set of new traditions, but he emphasizes that, in order to maintain themselves, even new traditions must be 'culture-specific', i.e. address themselves to a group which already sees itself as a group.[28] The relationship between new traditions and ancient group identities is taken up in Chapter 9 by Mikael Gravers who examines the 'mythistory' of the Karen in eastern Burma. Smith has made frequent use of the Karen as example of a durable, vibrant *ethnie* without a state of its own.[29] Gravers seeks an explanation for the pervasiveness of Karen identity, and turns to a concept which is also used by Smith: *authenticity.* However, Gravers chooses a different point of departure. Smith starts with the historical ethnie. Authenticity attests, according to Smith, to 'the originality, the self-generating nature, of a given

27. He also offered a longer definition: 'a set of practices, normally governed by overtly or tacitly accepted rules and of a ritual or symbolic nature, which seek to inculcate certain values and norms of behaviour by repetition, which automatically implies continuity with the past.' Eric Hobsbawm and Terence Ranger (eds), *The Invention of Tradition,* Cambridge: Cambridge University Press, 1983, pp. 1-2.

28. Smith, *Nations and Nationalism in a Global Era,* p. 24.

29. Smith, *Theories of Nationalism,* p. 217; *Ethnic Origins of the Nation,* pp. 114, 212; *National Identity,* pp. 7, 111, 124, 134.

culture-community'.[30] Gravers does not stress originality but begins with the nationalists. He is interested in how they *authenticate* a (new or old) tradition. They can do it by invigorating a mythical past focusing on religion, invoking historical events, or emphasizing linguistic and other properties. Some Karen have simply written their own history, and found ways of making it known to other Karen. But these efforts must constantly refer to images, stories or memories that the target group hold dear, and which distinguish this group from others. Gravers' study of the Karen seems to support the view that this is how their identity was formed, but it would perhaps be possible to interpret the Karen case differently. Actually, we know little about the Karen self-perception and their view of the Burman Other in the pre-modern period. The Karen identity could perhaps be portrayed as invented by missionaries and British census officials. An argument along this line has been made for the Montagnards in central Vietnam by Oscar Salemink.[31]

The modernist and post-modernist approaches encourage the understanding of the national phenomenon by emphasizing the kaleidoscopic fluidity of identities and by highlighting connections between national imaginings and certain historical processes of the nineteenth and twentieth centuries. To the extent, however, that these approaches deny the nation a history and a future, they are unlikely to be accepted by Asianists. To understand contemporary Asia it is necessary to take a synthetic approach, one that restores to the nation its history and future, while also taking full account of the shifts that national and other identities have gone through historically – and might be subject to in the future.

This is not meant to rehabilitate the efforts of nationalist historians seeking the roots of their nations in certain essential features of the past, be they physical, linguistic or religious. The modernists and post-modernists are right to emphasize that no cultural essentials can explain the presence of any specific nation-state. Every single cultural element can be replaced with another without breaking the historical continuity of a certain ethnic or national identity. Thus assertions that there existed a kind of 'Indian essence' before the arrival of the British should be met with scepticism. There were many different and highly compartmentalized communities on

30. Smith, *Nations and Nationalism in a Global Era*, pp. 66ff., 146.

31. Oscar Salemink, 'Primitive Partisans: French Strategy and the Construction of a Montagnard Ethnic Identity in Indochina', in Antlöv and Tønnesson, *Imperial Policy and Southeast Asian Nationalism*, pp. 261-293.

the South Asian peninsula. What brought them together and made them feel a common identity was their subjection to British rule. The main fallacy of the ethno-culturalist approach is its logical tendency towards concreteness: to look for an essential cultural difference. Such attempts have proved unsuccessful everywhere, even in the case where one might most expect success: i.e. in the Japanese *Nihonjinron* literature, which seeks to prove the existence of uniqueness based on 'race', culture, social structure and psychological predisposition.[32]

A nation needs to be kept alive through continuous transformation and reconstruction of its constitutive myths. Such myths change over time, and the borders between ethnic and national identities move. How this has happened in the Japanese case is demonstrated by Tessa Morris-Suzuki in Chapter 2 through her wonderful metaphor of a 'dance of identities'. A national history can be properly understood only when seen in relation to other national histories, and, even more, to non-national histories cutting across the constantly moving borderlines between various communities which, by nature, are all *imagined* to the extent that they are more than local. Both nations and other communities have different but interlinked histories, and are also likely to have different but interlinked futures.

At any point in time, diverging images of the past can be used to shape political entities, all of which are on the same heuristic level. Every nation has several possible national histories. A Hindu-nationalist version of the Indian past is not necessarily more false – or true – than a secular image of the same past, but the former may be more powerful in the hands of agitators. One promising route of inquiry is to look at the several possible nations which could have emerged from a given ethnie or political formation, and then ask why one of them won out. Thomas Hylland Eriksen, a student of the multicultural nations of Mauritius and Trinidad and Tobago, has tried to do this also for his native Norway.[33] Despite the fact that Norway and Sweden were both under the same crown between 1814 and 1905, Norwegians never saw themselves as Swedes. Thus integration with Sweden was not an option. But integration with Denmark was. In the late eighteenth and early nineteenth centuries, many members of the Norwegian social elite were of Danish origin or had been educated into

32. Harumi Befu, 'Nationalism and *Nihonjinron*', in Befu, *Cultural Nationalism in East Asia*, pp. 107-135.
33. Thomas Hylland Eriksen, *Ethnicity and Nationalism: Anthropological Perspectives*, London: Pluto Press, 1993, p. 92

a Danish-Norwegian identity. In the mid-nineteenth century there was also a movement in all three Scandinavian countries aiming at the creation of a common Scandinavian identity. The fact that the purely Norwegian identity eventually became predominant cannot be explained only by strong ethnic roots, but must be ascribed to historical events and processes during the nineteenth century itself. This was the period when the Norwegian national identity became strongly embedded in the population and linked to the ideal of a separate Norwegian state. This was also the period when a certain version of the Norwegian past was used to forge the modern nation.

In their search for a national history, nationalists must justify separate political institutions and provide a sense of profound meaning to the people at large. In Chapter 11, C.W. Watson highlights the role of Western-educated elites in a process with a different outcome in the highly compart-mentalized politics of colonial Malaya. Here a pan-Malaysian identity was shaped during the process of decolonization. There was no strong nationalist movement in British Malaya, and no clear idea of what a Malay(si)an nation might look like. More than other nations, Malaysia is still today undergoing a construction process in which the outcome remains uncertain.

Just like Europe, Asia seems both to fit and not to fit the rival theories concerning the role of history and tradition. But some Asian nations lend themselves more easily than others to one or the other view. In some places, notably in East Asia, nationalists have not found it difficult to root national identity in pre-modern ethnies. It has been easy to find cultural practices and historical records which could be reinterpreted and used to sustain and disseminate the idea of a nation with its own homeland and history. Many students of such nations will prefer an ethno-culturalist approach. In other cases, such as India and Indonesia, the historical reinterpretation came closer to 'invention of tradition', and thus it may be tempting to eschew A.D. Smith's insights and apply modernist or post-modernist viewpoints. But if we look at each nation in isolation, using only the approach that seems to fit it best, we may lose many possible insights. What we would like to suggest is to try out all three approaches on every Asian nation, preferably in a comparative perspective.

THE TYPOLOGY OF NATIONS

Basically, a nation has three constitutive elements: ethnie, state and territory. The most common typologies are derived from the respective weight that each of these elements has had in defining the nation. If an ethnic group forms its own state, you get *ethno-nationalism;* if a state uses its bureaucracy to mobilize a single national culture, you get *official nationalism;* finally if the inhabitants of a certain territory secede from a larger state or colonial power, and form a new multi-ethnic state with a joint national ideology, you get *plural nationalism.* We would like, now, to see if we can use these three types (derived from Anderson and Smith) to map the Asian forms of the nation. The typology is constructed on the basis of the *routes* that states and ethnies have followed to nationhood.

The first route, the creation of a new state on ethno-religious grounds, has been of little importance in East and Southeast Asia, but more so in South Asia. One might add Buddhist Burma to this category since it was separated from India in 1937, and the main examples of ethno-religious separation are also located in the former British colonies of South Asia: Sri Lanka (Buddhist with Hindu and Islamic minorities) and Pakistan and Bangladesh (Islamic). Their cultural difference from India is religious, the difference between Bangladesh and Pakistan linguistic (and territorial). As yet, there has been no case of successful ethno-religious separation in East or Southeast Asia, although the exclusion of Singapore from Malaysia in the mid-sixties and the war for Cambodia's liberation from Vietnamese dominance in the nineteen-eighties had ethno-religious elements. In several countries, there are ethnic movements aiming at independence, such as the Christian Karen in Burma and the Islamic Moros in the Philippines. The two occupied territories East Timor and Tibet could also be counted in this category. We might add that the movement for formal Taiwanese independence is to some extent motivated by ethnic difference between those who lived on the island before Japan lost its colonies in 1945, and those coming from the mainland to take over. Both groups are Han Chinese, but they speak different tongues.

The second route, the broadening of an existing state into nationhood (official nationalism), is the route which was followed by Japan and transformed Siam into Thailand. Other monarchies have tried this route, but failed. The Chinese empire was hampered by the fact that the Ch'ing dynasty was Manchu, not Han; it succumbed to revolution in 1911-12. Official nationalism in Korea was halted by Japanese conquest and assimilation policies, and the Lao, Khmer and Viet kingdoms were put under French tutelage. The French imposed a new larger political space, French Indochina, on the local monarchies and built a new, centralized state structure. Not until 1940, when French power was challenged by Japanese occupation and indigenous revolutionary forces, did the colonial administration in earnest promote the authority of the local monarchs, and only in Cambodia did official nationalism meet with some degree of success. Official nationalism has also been one of the routes leading to the construction of Malaysia, where the position of head of state rotates between the rulers of each federated state. The route of official nationalism is still open to the monarchies of Bhutan and Brunei, and is being actively pursued in Nepal, despite the 1990 revolution.

The third route, anti-colonial liberation, leading to the creation of a plural state in a political space demarcated by European imperialism, has characterized those parts of South and Southeast Asia where the colonial states did not converge with any former dynastic realm. This route, which was paved by the colonial regimes, has been taken by India, Burma, Indonesia, the Philippines and Malaysia. Indeed, it seems that all successful plural nations in this world have developed through a process of colonization and anti-colonial liberation. In all of these multi-territorial and multi-ethnic states, the lesser dynastic realms of the past have been either abolished or deprived of sovereignty, sometimes by the colonial, sometimes by the post-colonial regime. For such states it has been more difficult to authenticate 'mythistories' than for the nations following the first or second route. India, Burma, Indonesia and the Philippines are the Asian nations that can best be compared to the plural Americas and also to nation-building efforts in Africa. The post-colonial governments have found various ways of trying to overcome the fragmented character of their states, and mobilize a cohesive national identity: India through federal democracy and a softly Hinduist secularism; Burma through military socialism and violent suppression of separatist minority movements; Indonesia through *Pancasila* ideology, belief in 'one God', economic growth, and a highly politicized army. The attempts to construct first a Malay and then a multi-ethnic Malaysian nationhood are discussed by C.W. Watson in Chapter 11, and by Shamsul A.B. in Chapter 12. The self-denigrating character of national self-perception in the Philippines is richly documented and explained in Chapter 7 by Niels Mulder.

The three types thus seem to fit a significant part of the Asian experience, although several national projects have followed more than one trajectory. But what about China? It has actually taken a fourth route: class struggle or social revolution. One reason why this route has not been taken seriously in studies of nationalism in Europe may be that Europeans travelling it have all pretended, or hoped, to transcend nationalism.[34] In East and Southeast Asia social revolution (with the Soviet Union as its model) should be seen as perhaps the main route to nationhood. In China, an armed revolutionary movement led by a party under Han Chinese leadership was able to forge an alliance with ethnic minorities in waging a class war against a rival Han Chinese nationalist movement, leading to the establishment of a radical 'People's Republic' within the former borders of the Ch'ing dynastic realm. This provoked the creation of a counter-republic in Taiwan, and expanded the Chinese diaspora, cutting its ties with the mainland for more than three decades.[35] The overlapping Chinese identities resulting from these traumatic experiences, and their relation to the ideal of a unitary state, are discussed by Torbjörn Lodén in Chapter 10. Social revolutionary movements in Korea, Vietnam, Laos and Cambodia have also been able to establish, albeit only temporarily in Cambodia, states based on an ideology of class struggle. In the Laotian and Vietnamese cases, the revolutionary parties were able to build lasting alliances with ethnic minorities in the strategically important highlands, and later to integrate them, to some extent with a separate status, in their socialist nation-states.

Can New Theory Come out of Asia?

Let us now single out some factors that distinguish the formation of Asian nations, and look for new insights. Apart from the importance in Asia of social revolution as a fourth road to nationhood, there are a number of differences between Asia and Europe, such as the greater cultural variation of Asian societies; the role of religion in separating Asian nations from each other; the hierarchic character of many Asian societies; the establishment in Asia of what we may call 'civilizational nations'; and, Asia's relationship to Europe. We shall discuss these differences and, in the end, take up two

---

34. The social democratic nations of northern Europe have to some extent followed this route. Their royalty and officialdom were unable to incorporate the population in the nation. Instead, broad social movements forced their way into the institutions, reforming them and taking over the leadership while making various kinds of compromises with the ruling classes.

35. A lucid analysis of Chinese *class nationalism*, inspired by a study by Abdullah Laroui of intellectual elites in the Islamic world, can be found in Fitzgerald, 'The Nationless State', pp. 82ff. For a thorough analysis of the impact of Marxism on national thinking in China and Japan, see Germaine A. Hoston, *The State, Identity, and the National Question in China and Japan*, Princeton: Princeton University Press, 1994.

innovative ideas to be derived from this book: a theory of *national space* and a theory of *nations-of-intent*.

Asia is a cultural mosaic.[36] Europe has had many variants of nationalism, but virtually all of them belong to the same Christian culture, with Greek and Roman antiquity as a shared frame of reference, and the Islamic world as the closest Other. The divisions between the Orthodox, Catholic and Protestant Churches are divisions within one shared civilization. Asia has a greater cultural variety, with four major belief and morality systems (Hinduism, Confucianism, Buddhism, Islam), a range of popular beliefs, and zones where they blend with Christianity, with global humanism, and with one another.[37] It is difficult – and perhaps too early – to say what this cultural diversity has had to say for the forms that nations take in Asia. But if Smith is correct in assuming that new traditions are able to establish themselves only to the extent that they take up elements which people can identify as belonging to 'their own past', then Asian nations may well, at least in some respects, be moving away again from the European models – perhaps also from each other. Perhaps the global standardization of the national form which took place as an effect of European imperialism, and which led to a global conflict between two main 'Western' forms during the Cold War, does now give way to a cultural diversification also of national forms. A growing self-confidence in many parts of Asia is likely to reduce the attraction of Western models. It seems to us that the religious revival of the last few decades, the attempts to establish anti-Western Islamic nations, the resurgence of Hindu nationalism, and the growing discussion about 'Asian values' all point in the direction of more rather than less diversity of national forms. All of this seems to contradict the trend towards a 'global culture'. Globalization and diversification are happening at the same time, a fact that inevitably leads to friction.

One result of Asia's greater cultural variety is that religious factors have played much the same divisive role that vernacular languages have played in Europe. What Benedict Anderson calls the standard linguistic or vernacular model is difficult to find in Asia, and this confirms that Asians

---

36. Grant Evans (ed.), *Asia's Cultural Mosaic: an Anthropological Introduction*, New York: Prentice Hall, 1993.

37. Denys Lombard's impressive work, *Le carrefour javanais: Essai d'histoire globale* (3 vols), Paris: École des Hautes Études en Sciences Sociales, 1990, moves backwards in history, pealing off Javanese culture like the layers of an onion: Western impact, maritime experiences, Islamization, Chinese heritage, and remnants of the concentric Hindu kingdoms.

have not just pirated European models, but have based the image of their nation on the differences that they themselves consider most important. National languages, such as Mandarin Chinese and Bahasa Indonesia have, of course, been crucial means of integration and assimilation, but (with the notable exception of the struggle for Bangladesh) one has not seen ethnic mobilization on the basis of a linguistically defined vernacular culture except where this has also been religiously defined. Smith's insistence on the importance of the pre-modern ethnie is applicable to Asia only if we define the Asian ethnie in religious terms. There is little doubt that the interaction between *official nationalism* and *religious nationalism* will continue to be a recurrent theme in the development of many Asian nations, and that further studies of the relationship between religion and nation will be crucial to improving our theories of nationalism. This volume's main contributor in this field is Peter van der Veer, who deals with the (ab)use of the Rama cult by Hindu nationalists. It might be fruitful to compare the struggle between the Indian state and Hindu nationalism with the vaguely monotheistic compromise which was reached by Indonesian nationalists in 1945 concerning the national status of Islam. In the Netherlands Indies, the Islamic faith had been seen as the main sign of difference between *inlanders* on the one side, Europeans and Chinese on the other. The first nationalist movements were clearly Islamic in character. Still, a compromise was reached whereby a faith subscribed to by 90 per cent of the population was given a status as just one of several authorized religions. This solution has survived for fifty years. Indeed Suharto's regime has legitimated the political function of the military by the constant need to defend the nation against two major internal evils: communism and Islamic fundamentalism. Indonesia, unfortunately, is not discussed in this book.

In the future, there is likely to be an upsurge of studies of the relationship between religions, nationalism and the capitalist spirit in Asia. Gellner made the intriguing prediction in 1983 that under modern conditions, Islam's 'capacity to be a more abstract faith, presiding over an anonymous community of equal believers, could reassert itself'.[38] Perhaps the most long-lasting effect of political Islam's resurgence will be precisely to link up states and peoples emotionally, thus finally creating the more solid national identity which so many military and socialist leaders have failed to arouse in the past.

---

38. Gellner, *Nations and Nationalism*, p. 41.

The prevailing strength of hierarchic thinking has had a profound influence on national forms in Asia. Nationalism in both Asia and Europe, to be sure, has been associated with egalitarianism and a call for social justice. Indeed, one of the main nationalist aims has been to increase the power of 'the people' in relation to groups enjoying privilege and authority by virtue of hierarchic structures. The strength of Asian communism testifies to the appeal that egalitarianism has had in Asia. But Asian hierarchies have shown greater resilience than in Europe, not to speak of the Americas. Indeed many national leaders take pride in the values embedded in a society where every individual knows his or her proper place. This lies behind the current attempts to define an 'Asian democracy'. The difference between a self-consciously hierarchic society and an egalitarian immigrant community is sharply analysed by Bruce Kapferer in his *Legends of People, Myths of State* where he compares the fiercely egalitarian Australia with the rigidly compartmentalized Singhalese society.[39] The Sri Lankan case demonstrates how tragic the implications can be when a dominant, hierarchically organized ethnic group tries to culturally monopolize a nation-state which was meant to accommodate more than one ethnic group. In some Asian societies, resurrected social hierarchies have thus entered into a violent conflict with the national idea. In large states like India and Indonesia, the more historically embedded hierarchic principles and the bureaucratic structures of the modern state have lived side by side, from time to time in a state of tension. Only in a few places, like Singapore and Taiwan, has the nation got a meritocratic hierarchic form. This has no doubt been facilitated by the Confucian heritage.

One important aspect of Graham Clarke's analysis of Himalaya in Chapter 8 is his focus on the tension between strictly hierarchic local societies and national institutions draped over the old structures without breaking them up. Why are ethno-religious hierarchies so resilient in much of Asia? According to Louis Dumont and Bruce Kapferer, hierarchy is an intrinsic part of South Asian perceptions of person, society and nation. There is thus little scope for an egalitarian nationalization of the Indian or Sri Lankan populations. Will this remain so, or is it something that will change with their further integration in the global marketplace? Or will the hierarchies transcend the nation and manifest themselves in the social networks of the global village? We shall not try to answer these questions, which are connected to the issue of whether or not the Indian and Chinese

---

39. Kapferer, *Legends of People, Myths of State*.

states can survive in the next century, or if they will disintegrate and give way to globally oriented networks.

A conspicuous difference between the state systems of Asia and Europe is the presence in Asia of what we may call 'civilizational nations': India and China – maybe Japan. Western Europe has not had such a nation since the fall of the Third Reich, but Russia may be seen as a civilizational nation representing the Slavic-Orthodox world. Iran has civilizational aspirations, and the USA plays this role in 'the West'. But the main continent for civilizational nations is Asia. If we look at Samuel Huntington's controversial division of the world into seven major civilizations, we shall find that the Western one is divided into some thirty states, the Slavic-Orthodox into ten, the Latin American into well over twenty, the African into more than thirty-five, and the Islamic world west of the Indus into twenty-seven, whereas Asia east of the Indus has four civilizations (Islamic, Hindu, Confucian and Japanese), half the world's population but only twenty-three states.[40] The Islamic world does not have a civilizational nation although several have aspired to become one, but the other three civilizations have. As suggested by Torbjörn Lodén in Chapter 10, rather than comparing India and China to individual European nations, we may compare them to Europe as a whole, and ask what led Asians to form civilizational nations when civilizations elsewhere split up into multiple states.

Prasenjit Duara has used Chinese and Indian history to attack the modernist theory of nationalism in a way that must please A.D. Smith.[41] Duara rejects Levenson's famous theory of high-culturalism as the prevalent kind of Chinese identity before the age of nationalism. According to Duara, the high-culturalist version of China lived side by side with a concept of an exclusive Han political community. This latter concept was accentuated by the Jin and Mongol invasions of the twelfth century, and again by the Manchu invasion in the seventeenth. This fits well with what Torbjörn Lodén has to say, but as far as India is concerned, Duara does not

40.   Samuel P. Huntington, 'The Clash of Civilizations', *Foreign Affairs*, vol. 72, no. 3, Summer 1993, pp. 22–49. A recent article by Ravinder Kumar, 'L'Inde: "Etat-Nation" ou "Etat-civilisation"?', *Herodote*, no. 71, 1993, pp. 43–60, is in itself an expression of the Indian self-perception of being something more than just a nation-state, but whereas we use the term 'civilizational nation' about nations who see themselves as representing the values of something bigger than themselves but smaller than the whole of humanity, Kumar asserts that there really existed a precolonial panindian 'subtle confederation' which is now being represented by the Republic of India as a 'civilizational state'.

41.   Prasenjit Duara, 'Bifurcating Linear History: Nation and Histories in China and India', *Positions*, vol. 1, no. 3, 1993, pp. 779-804; and *Rescuing History from the Nation: Questioning Narratives of Modern China*, Chicago: University of Chicago Press, 1995.

obtain support from Peter van der Veer in Chapter 5 of this volume. Duara claims that India has been characterized by a Brahmanic universalism, and a kind of politicized religious community which existed as an ideal for several rulers. Thus India was a kind of historical community although it was not unified under one state. In his description of the politicized Hindu community, Duara builds on a seminal article by Sheldon Pollock that is criticized by Peter van der Veer.[42] Van der Veer is suspicious of Pollock's use of the *Ramayana* epic to construct a kind of historical precedent for the Hindu 'othering' of Muslims, but he does not address the larger question of whether there was such a thing as an Indian identity or community before the construction of the Raj. What made India into a nation-state in our wide definition of the word was not racial, religious or linguistic unity, but the inclusive idea of an Indian civilization with a great peninsular geo-body. But the civilizational, inclusive strand of Indian nationalism has all along been challenged by regional and religious opposition groups. Hindu national-ism, which relates to Indian civilizational nationalism in the way that ethnic-based Han nationalism relates to Chinese high-culturalism, has resurged in the 1980s and 1990s, and represents a threat to the cohesion of the Indian federation, perhaps greater than Sikh and Muslim separatism, whose strength to some extent reflects the degree of Hinduization of Indian politics.

Hindu nationalism is also discussed in Chapter 6 by Arild Engelsen Ruud, who argues for the importance of understanding religious practices in their social context before analysing how they are used politically. Ruud introduces the concept of 'regional culturization' and argues that the recent reintroduction by Hindu nationalists of 'traditional Hindu feasts' to the Bengali countryside has been a way of promoting the status of certain groups threatened by urbanization, rural transformation and the policies of the dominant Marxist party. Whereas, on the all-Indian level, the Hindu nationalist Other is an impure Muslim, the real Other in Bengal is a low-caste Marxist. But Hindu nationalism is also a vehicle for promoting regional Bengali interests. When Bengali identity was promoted in the late colonial period by writers and politicians such as Tagore, Subhaschandra Bose and Vivekananda, it was not evenly distributed. It was appropriated by the high-caste, well-mannered elite of Calcutta, the *bhadralok*, who have continued to see themselves as the most civilized Bengali and indeed, by virtue of their Bengaliness, as also the most Indian (i.e. most civilized) in

---

42 Sheldon Pollock, 'Ramayana and Political Imagination in India', *Journal of Asian Studies*, vol. 52, no. 2, 1993, pp. 261-297.

the whole of the peninsula. Precisely because the Bengali elite sees itself as particularly Indian, it has not been inclined to separatism. Hindu nationalism has established its presence in West Bengal by becoming a kind of 'stand-in motive' for the promotion of caste status and regional interests.[43] Bengalis who vote for the Hindu nationalist parties do it out of local concerns, most notably from resentment over lost status. Hindu nationalist activists feel that there may be a way back to the lost civilization and prosperity of the Bengal of the past. Arild Engelsen Ruud shows how concerns about caste status and regional identities can manifest themselves in a nationalist form.

It is important not to forget that Gandhi's nationalism was not so much aimed at the creation of a nation-state; he rarely talked about an Indian nation. Nationalism was patriotism, in defence not of a nation, but of a moral order derived from ancestral loyalty and communal integrity. His mission was to recreate the sense of an Indian civilization, regenerating its people and creating the conditions for an autonomous moral growth.[44] In contrast to the strong unitary China of Sun Yat-sen, Chiang Kai-shek and Mao Zedong, Gandhi's India was more of a diffuse but moral plurality.

Japan is so different from the rest of East Asia that Huntington may be right to classify it as a civilization of its own. Smith sees Japan as 'without doubt the most successful case of modernizing nationalism' in any empire outside the West: 'Meiji political nationalism created the modern Japanese nation on the basis of aristocratic *(samurai)* culture and its ethnic state, while also utilizing those demotic peasant traditions that could be integrated into the ruling imperial system.' But he notes how defeat in World War II deprived the Japanese nation of some of its mystique, and doubts if *nihonjinron* can prove a durable base for Japanese national identity.[45] Still, it seems utterly unlikely that the Japanese will give up their deep sense of a separate identity. Nothing can better demonstrate the prevailing strength of Japanese separateness than the recent internal urge for 'internationalization'.[46]

---

43. 'Stand-in motive' *(vikarierende motiv)* is a notion conceived by the Norwegian historian Jens Arup Seip. Stand-in motives or stand-in arguments are, he says, 'sent out like heralds to the public, not in order to announce the genuine motives, but to divert attention from them. National emotions are a typical stand-in motive' (translation by ST). Jens Arup Seip, 'Nasjonalismen som vikarierende motiv', in *Fra embedsmannsstat til ettpartistat og andre essays,* Oslo: Universitetsforlaget, 1963, pp. 78-85 (quote from p. 79).

44. Bhikhu Parekh, 'Ethnocentricity of the Nationalist Discourse', *Nations and Nationalism*, vol. 1, no. 1, 1995, p. 39.

45. Smith, *National Identity,* pp. 105-106.

However, in Chapter 2 of this volume Tessa Morris-Suzuki further de-mystifies the Nipponese experience by demonstrating that the Japanese state has resorted to the same kinds of assimilation policies as other official nationalisms. She investigates three Japanese peripheries, not those acquired at the turn of the century and lost in 1945 (Taiwan, Korea, Manchuria and the Kuriles), but peripheries remaining within Japan today. By looking at the Japanese state's approach to the Ainu people of northern Hokkaido, the population of the Ryukyu Islands, and the descendants of European settlers on the Ogasawara (Bonin) Islands, she finds that the intensity of 'Nippon-ization' has varied with the state's relations to external powers. In periods of relative safety, the minorities have been allowed, even encouraged, to be different, whereas in periods of a perceived external threat, they have been subjected to deliberate assimilationist policies.

In conclusion, it seems to us that the study of nationalism in Asia requires a theory of the civilizational nation, and that this may inspire the study also of Russia and the United States, as well as the futile attempts to shape a common European, Pan-American or Islamic identity. From such a theory would come a world map with five civilizational nations: China, India, Japan, Russia and the United States, and five overlapping, politically divided regions: Latin America, Africa, the Islamic world, Southeast Asia (with Australia and New Zealand), and Europe (also with Australia and New Zealand). This means, of course, that Asia as a whole does not exist either as a culture, civilization or a potential political unit. It is just a geographical area, and a term used in some kinds of discourse where a mythical 'West' is the Other.

The final difference between all of Asia on the one side and Europe on the other is obvious but still important to keep in mind: all Asian nations have been deeply influenced by their relationship to Europe, or rather to 'the West' as a whole. This is something Asia shares with Africa. To understand the historical impact of Europe and the United States on Asia, one should try to imagine the effects it would have on terrestrial humanity if pale-skinned human beings from a group of foreign planets, with an extremely advanced technology, started to arrive in ever-increasing numbers. Some would want to trade with us, others to teach us their religion, and yet others to study our customs. Some would be brutal, others

46 See Mahathir Mohamad and Shintaro Ishihara, *The Voice of Asia: Two Leaders Discuss the Coming Century*, Tokyo: Kodansha International, 1995.

treat us with respect, but they would all be convinced of their own inherent superiority. Thus they would try to teach us their ways of doing things, while establishing protectorates over the weakest of our states, dividing the earth into rival spheres, and building bases in strategic places. Whenever we refused to trade with them or take their sound advice, they would use airborne gunships to shell our cities. After some initial resistance we would submit ourselves to their power, but gradually a new generation would grow up with an extra-terrestrial education, and this generation would want to liberate the globe, catch up with the foreign planets, and launch protest movements, strikes and guerrilla wars to fight extra-terrestrial imperialism.

The formation of Asian national identities has happened in the shadow of European (including Russian) and US domination, and the memory of colonial subjugation remains a crucial element in the national self-perceptions of many Asians. This memory consists not only of an enemy image, but also contains a kind of admiration for the former colonial master. As demonstrated by Niels Mulder in Chapter 7, this is striking in the memory that Filipinos have of US colonialism.

For a long time the West has been the Significant Other, and this has provided Asian nationalisms with a basic ambivalence, which is still alive, not least in discourses about democracy. On the one hand the nationalists have aimed at liberation from Europe, hence separation. On the other hand they have seen their only chance of achieving this aim in learning Western ways and being recognized by Western powers as sovereign nations with a role to play in global politics. In order to obtain recognition of the right to difference, they have had to become similar.

This ambivalence needs to be carefully researched with a double approach analysing both the quest for difference and the urge for similarity. When interpreting national symbols one must look both for their standard form (the square flag, the annotated anthem, the published Constitution, the printed emblem) and for the little elements of local difference. Just as the various Vietnamese and Korean dynasties tried to distinguish them-selves from their model in the Middle Kingdom by adopting norms, rituals and symbols as equal as possible to those of Beijing – sometimes even more equal than the model itself – but still with a few significant differences, many twentieth-century nationalist movements have demonstrated their independence through norms, rituals and symbols strikingly similar to those cherished in London, Paris, Washington and Moscow, but still with some local flavour. The first sentences in Ho Chi Minh's Declaration of

Independence in 1945 were direct translations from the American Declaration of Independence and the French Declaration of Man and the Citizen, but he singled himself out by wearing the simple clothes of a local peasant. The independence rally was organized in a way bearing close resemblance to the *Grande Féderation* of 1790, with the addition of microphones and automobiles, but Ho Chi Minh read out his speech under a parasol reminiscent of the ones used to shield the emperor's mandarins from excessive sunshine.[47] So far there has been little research into the ambivalent relationship between similarity and difference in nationalist ritual.

There is no doubt that Asian nations have been formed in the image of American and European modular forms, to use Benedict Anderson's expression, but this is only one side of the coin. On the other are the limitations imposed by, and the usage made of local culture. There is something to be learnt from the Bengali Subaltern intellectual Partha Chatterjee, who attacks the idea that Indian national identity was imagined uniquely through the lens of the colonial power, and asks: If non-Western nationalists could choose only between certain forms of already imagined communities, what then was there left to imagine?[48] He challenges Benedict Anderson by broadening the question of identity from the political to the 'private' sphere and arguing that identities were also formed and kept alive in homes and social networks where Europeans had no access.

Chatterjee concedes that the British established the religious, caste, linguistic and ethnic categories that are used in modern India, and acknowledges the role of these categories in the formation of Indian national identity. Still he rejects the idea that 'India' is an entirely modern creation, and argues: 'The more nationalism engaged in its contest with the colonial power in the outer domain of politics, the more it insisted on displaying the marks of "essential" cultural differences so as to keep out the colonizer from that inner domain of national life and to proclaim its sovereignty over it.'[49] This 'essential' inner or spiritual domain of culture was never colonized, he claims, and although it was developed in response to Western imperialism, it was always Indian and never European. In the inner domain, the nation was already sovereign. Furthermore, Chatterjee ventures to disrupt the unifying aspiration of Indian nationalism, and

47. Stein Tønnesson and Hans Antlöv, *Nations-of-Intent in Southeast Asia: Indonesia, Vietnam and Malaya, 1945-1948*, manuscript in preparation, NIAS.
48. Partha Chatterjee, *The Nation and Its Fragments*, Princeton: Princeton University Press, 1993, p. 5.
49. *Ibid.*, p. 26.

argues that there are different co-existing national voices or 'fragments' – among women, peasants, elite, castes, outcasts – each with its separate discourse.

When the national idea entered Asia it could not be implemented without mediation, hence transformation, by indigenous agencies in particular social settings. There were existing and alternative ideas with which European-style nationalism interacted and intermixed. The interlinkage between 'inner' and 'outer' domains has been demonstrated by Chatterjee, and more recently by Bhikhu Parekh who contends that 'to treat non-Western nationalisms as if they were nothing more than imitations of the European original is to display not only an ethnocentric bias but also an unacceptable degree of intellectual ignorance'.[50] Parekh, Chatterjee, and also several of the authors contributing to this volume argue that the nationalist ideas were invested with local qualities, meanings and nuances which could not be found in Europe. People had their own views on what constituted a legitimate social order, and such views could not be ignored by the modernizing leaders of the anti-colonial struggles.

What Thongchai Winichakul writes about the mapping of Siam in Chapter 3 is instructive. It demonstrates how the encounter between two types of geographical knowledge led one to be subsumed under the other. The Siamese court did not conceive of its power sphere as a carefully measured and demarcated territory with border lines around it, but as an influence radiating outwards and gradually decreasing the further away from the royal centre one got. There were, then, wide border zones where local kings and villages could have multiple loyalties. Thongchai Winichakul demonstrates how, in the matter of a few decades, the Western concept reframed the minds of the Siamese court, leading to a race for the abolition of multiple loyalties and the demarcation of a national territory. The new concept was based on Western cartography. It served the interests of the Siamese court in a new international context, and its victims were those tributary kingdoms and villages who could no longer uphold relations with more than one superior authority. The road to the modern Thai nation-state was thus opened by the replacement of a personalized hierarchic structure with a mapped royal territory. The British and French presence led the Siamese king to change his way of relating to his lands in much the same way that European monarchs did following the Peace of Westphalia, but far more quickly. The change increased the court's power in the

---

50. Bhikhu Parekh, 'Ethnocentricity of the Nationalist Discourse', p. 45.

outlying regions of the kingdom. This in turn created a need to invest the population of these regions with a Thai identity. The Thai geo-body was demarcated and needed to be filled with a shared culture. This, then, is when the need arose in Bangkok to define Thainess by assembling the elements of a national tradition.

Thongchai's contribution is a programmatic example of a new theoretical insight derived at least in part from Asia: the role of *national space*. One of the less noticed chapters in Benedict Anderson's *Imagined Communities* is the one where he tries to demonstrate how nationalism was linked to a complete change in the concept of *time*. The new chapter he added about *space* in the 1991 edition (which was inspired by Thongchai's doctoral thesis) is already part of a trend.[51] Not only Thongchai but also Christopher Goscha, Graham E. Clarke and Tessa Morris-Suzuki deal with matters of space in this volume.[52] Morris-Suzuki links space with time by remarking how a contemporary spatial difference between the Ainu and the population of the central Japanese islands, through the influence of modern evolutionary thinking, was translated into an idea of a temporal span between historical stages. The Ainu were seen as underdeveloped survivors of an earlier period in the history of Japanese society. Through proper education they could be brought up to their compatriots' current stage of development, and become full members of the Japanese nation.

As has been shown by Norbert Elias, Michel Foucault and others, the ordering and division of space was one of the main premises of modern society. Segmented notions of territorial sovereignty in pre-modern Asia had to give way to the crude divisions of modern political maps. The territorial patriotism inspired by the image of such maps was, even to Anthony D. Smith, an 'entirely novel' phenomenon.[53] Ancient Asian maps and frontiers have been much studied, and a French anthology has ventured to trace the emergence of the Vietnamese space by examining the Dai Nam empire's concept of its borders up to the colonial period.[54] What Thongchai has done is to insert a study of Asian frontier concepts in the contemporary debate about nationalism and the formation of the nation-state.

---

51. Anderson, *Imagined Communities*, ch. 10 (1991 edition).

52. See also Steven Grosby, 'Territoriality: The Transcendental, Primordial Feature of Modern Societies', *Nations and Nationalism*, vol. 1, no. 2, 1995, pp. 143-162.

53. Smith, *National Identity*, p. 107; *Ethnic Origins*, p. 93. See also Smith, 'States and Homelands: the Social and Geopolitical Implications of National Territory', *Millennium*, vol. 10, no. 3, 1981, pp. 187-202.

With the introduction of the map, radical changes occurred not only in the perception of the dynastic realm and its borders, but also in the ideas of an ethnic homeland, the old symbiosis between a piece of earth and 'its' community.[55] The homeland turned from being the image of a physical landscape around a sacred spot or centre to becoming a flat form drawn on a piece of paper. It is not altogether easy to link up Thongchai's 'map theory' with the 'homeland theory' of A.D. Smith; Smith accentuates the myths of the ethnie whereas Thongchai refuses to recognize any concept of ethnic 'Tai-ness' and studies only the frontiers of the Siamese dynastic realm. The question of an original or ethnic T(h)ai-land is without relevance, he thinks, since an ethnic identity represents no more than a binary opposition between Self and Other, and thus changes meaning from one situation or relationship to the next. The sacred centres were not symbols of either Tai- or Thai-ness, but elements in the pre-nationalist religious and royal conceptualization of geography. For A.D. Smith the homeland is the land that surrounds the places most crucial to an ethnie's myths or memory, its *lieux de mémoire*. Thongchai also emphasizes the role of sacred centres in the pre-modern spatial concepts of Siam, but does not see them as 'ethnic'. These contrasting views on the ethnicity of sacred centres mirror the difference referred to above between Levenson's view of imperial China as merely high-culturalist and Duara's insistence that there was also an old concept of ethnic Han Chineseness. This difference of interpretation points to the need for further studies into the relationships between 'ethnicity', concepts of sacred centres or 'homelands', and courtly perceptions of the geographical range of royal power.

Just as in Siam, the pre-colonial states in Himalaya had no concept of a demarcated territory. In Chapter 8, Graham E. Clarke emphasizes the obstacle that Himalaya's mountainous topography has represented to the forging of national identities. States were kept together by the ritual power of their royalty. With the modern rivalry between the British, Russian and Chinese empires, the competing and flexible *mandala* states were frozen into mapped 'Princely States' or 'Himalayan Kingdoms'. Cartographers, anthropologists and linguists established borders and ethnic categories. Presumed

54. P.B. Lafont (ed), *Les frontières du Vietnam: Histoire des frontières de la péninsule indochinoise*, Paris: L'Harmattan, 1989. See also Thongchai Winichakul, *Siam Mapped: A History of the Geo-Body of a Nation*, Honolulu: University of Hawaii Press, 1994, p. 17, where he refers to what Edmund Leach has written about the Burmese territory.

55. Smith, *Ethnic Origins*, p. 28.

'peoples' were given organic names, and so the 'Gurkhas', 'Baltis' and 'Ladhakis' were defined, either as pure inventions or as projections of a dominant kingroup. The result is still there today: an ethnic hierarchy of various tribes and peoples occupying different and distinct territories.

Morris-Suzuki attacks historians for investigating pre-national times with contemporary national territories as frames of reference. The national geo-body is read back into history. We have a long way to go before we can liberate the human past from the nationalist straitjacket, which is so intimately linked to the construction of the modern historical discipline as such. Perhaps this liberation of the past can be more easily undertaken from the perspective of areas where the modern political spaces are not congruent with pre-modern dynastic realms, such as in peninsular Southeast Asia. Braudelian historical studies such as Anthony Reid's and Denys Lombard's are basic contributions in this direction.[56]

A de-nationalized approach to pre-national history may also facilitate the discovery of how political spaces other than the dominant national one have continued to play a role in the nationalist era. Christopher Goscha has studied the relationship between two rival political spaces on the Southeast Asian mainland: Annam/Vietnam and Indochina. In Chapter 4 of this volume he tries to explain why the colonial territory did not provide a successful matrix for the local nationalism, but in the end had to give way to the separate nation-states of Vietnam, Cambodia and Laos. Goscha starts with a presentation of how the French, through roads, railways, maps, schoolbooks, and imaginary travels, tried to create an Indochinese space with a concomitant political identity. Within the Indochinese Union, however, the French also maintained the dynastic realms of the Nguyen dynasty in the imperial capital Hue, as well as the Cambodian and Lao principalities. With French encouragement, many young Viet migrated to Laos and Cambodia to take up administrative positions and commercial functions. This stimulated an all-Indochinese outlook among many educated Viet, but few Lao or Khmer came to share this outlook, and it conflicted with the more narrow perspective of those Viet who remained attached to the Dai Nam kingdom and to the eastern lowlands inhabited by ethnic Viet. This latter space (shaped like an S or a dragon on the map) was variably called An Nam, Viet Nam and other names. Goscha demonstrates how the

---

56. Anthony Reid, *Southeast Asia in the Age of Commerce, 1450-1680*, vol. 1, *The Lands Below the Winds*, vol. 2, *Expansion and Crisis*, New Haven: Yale University Press, 1988 and 1993. Lombard, *Le carrefour javanais*.

vacillation between the narrow and the wider Viet outlook provoked heated discussions both on the conservative and communist side of Indochinese colonial politics in the 1920s and 1930s, and remained a dilemma for the revolutionary leaders in 1945.[57]

Why did all of the Netherlands Indies become one nation-state after World War II while French Indochina split into three? This question was raised by Benedict Anderson in his *Imagined Communities* and has been thoroughly discussed by David F. Henley,[58] but Christopher Goscha also brings a number of new elements to illuminate the issue. Anderson has focused on the language factor: the use of Vietnamese writing *(quoc ngu)* in Indochina, but of Malay (rather than Javanese) in Indonesia. Both Henley and Goscha suggest that the French Indochinese Union was created too late and did not last long enough to become effectively imbued in the popular imagination. Another reason mentioned by Henley is that the French retained the various monarchies in Indochina whereas the Dutch reduced the sultanates in Java to almost nothing.

We would like to add that the numerical superiority of the Viet in Indochina, and the Viet immigration into Laos and Cambodia, are likely to have made Viet domination more threatening to the Lao and Khmer than the possibility of Javanese domination to the peoples of Sumatra, Kalimantan and Sulawesi. Then also Java consists of a Javanese east, a Sundanese west and a cosmopolitan Jakarta. And we remember Gellner's point on the role of education: since this was the main road to nationalism, the ethnic composition of colonial schools and universities was crucial. In French schools and universities, the Viet were in a great majority as compared to Khmer, Lao and others. The students in Dutch schools and universities were more evenly recruited. They could thus more easily join together in a desire for Indonesian independence. In the early 1920s,

---

57. Christopher Goscha, *Vietnam or Indochina? Contesting Concepts of Space in Vietnamese Nationalism, 1887-1954*, Copenhagen: Nordic Institute of Asian Studies, NIAS Report no. 28, 1995, takes his richly documented analysis all the way up to the creation of General Vo Nguyen Giap's 'Indochinese battlefield' during the 'First Indochina War'. When the first war (1945-54) is called the 'Indochina War' and the second (1964-75) 'the Vietnam War', the reason is not that Laos and Cambodia were kept out of the second, but that the Indochinese federal project had been given up both by France and the Vietnamese communists by 1950, at least officially.

58. David E.F. Henley, 'Ethnographic Integration and Inclusion in Anticolonial Nationalism: Indonesia and Indochina', *Comparative Studies in Society and History*, vol. 37, no. 2, April 1995, pp. 286–324.

intellectuals of Sumatran Minangkabau origin effectively blocked all plans for creating a separate Javanese nation.

Finally, we should be open to the possibility that A.D. Smith may find good arguments in the Indochinese experience: because of their historical defence line against the Han Chinese with their Middle Kingdom, the Viet are likely to have had a stronger 'ethno-national' identity than the Javanese well before the construction of the colonial states. It is difficult to estimate the strength of eighteenth- or nineteenth-century ethnic sentiments since we lack reliable sources. But this should not lead us to exclude the possibility that twentieth-century Vietnamese nationalism, and also its Cambodian reflection, actually do feed on ethnic identities which have been passed on from generation to generation, and which have been repeatedly accentuated through contact and conflict with the Chinese, Thai and other local Others. To the Viet, the Chinese have for a long time been the main Other; for the Khmer the Other were the Viet in the east and the Thai in the west. Goscha quotes the conservative Annamese nationalist Pham Quynh as saying in 1931: 'Indochina has never existed and will never exist ... the Annamese nation is a reality that dances before the eyes.' As Henley has emphasized, there were those, at the beginning of the twentieth century, who envisaged a purely Javanese nation, but has anyone since then declared that Indonesia has never existed and will never exist, or that the Javanese nation is a reality that dances before the eyes?

In Chapter 12, Shamsul A.B. is also preoccupied with rival and overlapping national identities but his form of identity is rooted neither in history nor religion, language or ethnicity as such, nor even in the present, but in visions of the future called 'nations-of-intent'. The term 'nation-of-intent' was first used by Robert Rotberg in an African context, and is now further conceptualized by Shamsul.[59] A nation-of-intent is a vision of a territorial entity, a set of institutions, an ideal-type citizen and an identity profile that a group of 'social engineers' have in mind and try to implement. It will often be an idealistic form shared by a number of people who identify themselves not only with one another, but with a whole nation whose other members they hope will join their vision. A nation-of-intent can be the idea of a statesman wishing to unite different groups under his government's authority, of an opposition party, a separatist group, a religious or other community. The notion of nations-of-intent highlights the subjective and

---

59. Robert Rotberg, 'African Nationalism: Concept or Confusion?', *Journal of Modern African Studies*, vol. 4, no. 1, 1967, pp. 33-46.

changeable aspects of nationhood and opens up the possibility of several co-existing or competing identity forms within the same nation. The difference between Shamsul's concept and Anderson's 'imagined community' is that the latter has to be imagined by those who are part of it before it can be said to exist, whereas the nation-of-intent is not yet being imagined, at least not in the intended form, by the great majority of its constituents. A further difference is that the nation-of-intent remains open to change, i.e. through conceptual merger with other nations-of-intent. In Malaysia, a rivalry between various nations-of-intent is taking place beneath the surface of UMNO-dominated politics. Prime Minister Dr. Mahathir Mohamad's official nation-of-intent is embodied in his Vision 2020. By then he wants to have created a 'united Malaysian nation' out of the present mixture of 52 per cent 'Malays' (including non-Muslim 'tribal groups'), 37 per cent 'Chinese' and 11 per cent 'Indians'. But, as Shamsul demonstrates, this vision is contested by other nations-of-intent. This unresolved contest, he says, gives various groups in Malaysia the possibility to articulate their image of the nation's future form.

The nation-of-intent concept allows us to look closer at how identity forms are spread and transformed into fully fledged imagined communities, how legends and myths are rephrased, and how they are used to generate passion. The mobilization of popular sentiments will, we believe, be a key issue in future research. Theoretical works on nationalism have mainly dealt with the origins and causes of nationalism, and with establishing a relevant typology. Every author on nationalism makes an obligatory remark about the unbelievable forcefulness of nationalist sentiment, and Benedict Anderson is preoccupied throughout his writings with the sacred intensity of nationalist feelings, but few venture into a more dedicated exploration of what it is that generates the passion.[60]

The notion of nations-of-intent may serve two purposes. One is to open the scholar's eyes to the role of future images in the past. In situations of political fluidity, the nations-of-intent of certain national leaders have deeply influenced the course of history. We need to know what these leaders have been hoping for, or have expected, in order to understand what they did. The second purpose is to expand civil society in Asia and provide it with a conceptual tool to tackle the national and international future.

---

60. A lucid commentary on Anderson's attempts to account for the sacredness of nationalism can be found in Gopal Balakrishnan, 'The National Imagination', *New Left Review*, no. 211, 1995.

The construction of Asian national forms is still going on. There is no inevitable process leading to a standard universal, or Asian, form. New kinds of knowledge channelled through new types of media allow the dissemination of various nations-of-intent. There will still be a need to refer to familiar historical themes, symbols, myths or memories in order to get one's message through. It thus also seems quite likely, if not inevitable, that many nations-of-intent will continue to resemble the most familiar forms. But a new self-confident Asia may also, perhaps, develop new variants of nationalism, thus setting examples which may later be followed by the rest of the planet.

Map 1: Japan's frontier islands.

CHAPTER TWO

The Frontiers of Japanese Identity

Tessa Morris-Suzuki

Historians of Japan become accustomed to dealing with slippery concepts. They wrestle with definitions of development, modernization and Westernization; they worry over the application of concepts like feudalism, fascism and democracy to the Japanese experience. But in all this the one term which seldom appears to need discussion is the word 'Japan'. Japan seems real and self-explanatory: as Delmer Brown once put it, a 'natural region' whose isolation and climatic uniformity accounted for the early rise of national consciousness.[1] In the words of a more recent study, 'the surrounding ocean serves as a protective moat' shielding Japan both from invasion and migration, so that since the third or fourth century AD there has been 'very little infusion of other ethnic groups, resulting in a contemporary population that is fundamentally homogeneous'.[2]

It is only recently that a few Japanese historians – notably Amino Yoshihiko[3] – have started to pull at the threads which hold together this vision of a cohesive national fabric, and have shown how readily those threads, when teased, unravel. The purpose of this chapter is to take the process of unravelling a little further by considering the problem of Japan's frontiers. I shall begin from the rather obvious observation that Japan in its

1. Delmer M. Brown, *Nationalism in Japan: An Introductory Historical Analysis*, Berkeley: University of California Press, 1955, pp. 6–7.

2. Louis D. Hayes, *Introduction to Japanese Politics*, New York: Paragon House, 1992, pp. 4–6.

3. See, for example, Amino Yoshihiko (trans. G. McCormack), 'Deconstructing "Japan"', *East Asian History*, no. 3, June 1992.

present form is a modern artifact, whose frontiers were drawn in the middle of the nineteenth century and have been a source of contention for much of the twentieth. The 'moat' which surrounds Japan is in fact dotted with lines of stepping stones: small islands which have acted as zones of continuous economic and cultural interchange. The drawing of modern frontiers cuts across these zones and encloses within the Japanese state at least three groups whose language and history had very little in common with those of, say, Tokyo or Osaka: to the north, some 19,000 Ainu who inhabited Hokkaido, Southern Sakhalin and the Kurile archipelago; to the south, a quarter of a million Okinawans who inhabited the Ryukyu archipelago; and to the southeast, the tiny but extraordinarily cosmopolitan population of the Ogasawara (Bonin) Islands. (When Japan obtained control of the Ogasawaras, they had a population of seventy-one whose places of origin included Britain, the United States, Spain, Germany, Hawaii and Guam.) Looking at the story of these groups – societies which suddenly found themselves stranded on the margins of a modern state – can tell us a good deal about the nature of the state itself. The policies of assimilation which were used to turn the people of the frontier into Japanese citizens involved a sharpening of the official definition of what it meant to be Japanese. But that definition itself was not constant or stable. Instead, as we shall see, it was contextual and changing, shaped both by circumstances within Japan and by the nature of relations between the Japanese state and the societies of the periphery.

The questions raised by reflecting on the frontiers of Japan, however, go further than the bounds of Japanese studies. They touch upon the whole way in which we deal with space in history. The modern practice of history writing developed side by side with the rise of the nation-state, and the study of history in schools and universities has largely meant the study of national histories (above all of the history of one's own nation). In the writings of E.P. Thompson as much as G.R. Elton, of Inoue Kiyoshi as much as Ueyama Shumpei, history is a vision of the forces which have moulded national society. The nation therefore casts a long shadow backwards on our vision of the past, and channels our perceptions into a particular spatial framework. In my bookcase, I have a volume on the history of Thailand since the tenth century, which, considering the repeated political and culture realignments within the space we now label 'Thailand', seems only a little more bizarre than its neighbour on the shelf, a history of the Soviet Union from palaeolithic times to World War II. The use of the nation-state as the framework for understanding the past, in other words, imposes important biases on our understanding of history.

From several thousand years ago until very recent times, a wide variety of socio-political structures existed side by side. These ranged from empires, through state-organized societies of various shapes and forms, to small societies which operated without elaborate political structures. (Examples of the last include both Ainu society and the small, anarchical community created by settlers on the Ogasawara Islands.) It is only in the past fifty years, since the breakup of the European empires, that the nation-state has emerged as the universal and uniform vessel for the management of human affairs. Projecting the outline of the nation-state backwards upon history, and treating history as the life-story of the nation (whether told from the perspective of the rulers or the ruled) encourages us to focus on particular sorts of social structure: the relatively centralized, hierarchical, politically articulated societies which are the most obvious predecessors of the modern nation.

When we write the history of the nation, we almost inevitably begin by looking for commonalities and generalizations. To write the history of Japan is to establish a set of unifying factors – a description of the shared geography, technology, religious and cultural traditions – which gives the subject 'Japan' its form and its historical life. Having set up this large spatial structure, the historian then goes on to examine the way in which the structure has changed over time. There is, perhaps, a logical connection between an interest in complex social structures and an interest in structural change. Large socio-political systems seem by their nature more prone to dramatic, revolutionary transformation than small systems. The balancing act required to keep their many articulated parts in harmony is a complicated one, and they are susceptible to innovation, convulsion and sudden collapse. In small societies, by contrast, change may more readily be negotiated within existing structures. The small, non-state society, therefore, is not only less likely to generate the types of written and archaeological evidence which provides grist to the historian's mill, but is also perhaps less likely to generate those radical social and cultural changes with which the historian's mind likes to grapple.

But the focus of the historical gaze is also determined by the division of labour in modern academia. During the nineteenth century the study of small societies, whose non-written cultures could only be grasped by first-hand experience, was marked out as the realm of the anthropologist. The questions posed by anthropologists were not, by and large, questions about historical change, but rather about those enduring social regularities which came to be defined as 'culture'. The politics of academia therefore produced a vision of a world divided in two: on the one hand, there were large, complex 'historical' societies which participated in the processes of evolution culminating in 'modernity'; on the other, there were the small, static, 'primitive' societies whose destiny was to be swallowed up by modernity's relentless advance.

The eye of the historian, therefore, tends to look for change over time rather than diversity across space. Histories of seventeenth- and eighteenth-century Japan are much more likely to speak about social and economic developments within a supposedly integrated system than they are to speak about social and economic differences between one area and another, let alone between Japan and its small, semi-dependent neighbours. The underlying argument of this chapter is for a better balance in history writing between sensitivity to temporal change and sensitivity to spatial diversity. Just as anthropologists have found a growing need to make their work 'historical', so there is a need for historians to develop a greater awareness of the complex way in which a multiplicity of social systems – including small non-state societies as well as larger states and empires – have co-existed, interacted and overlapped with one another.

Three Views of the World

Let us begin with three views of the world as it appeared from various perspectives in the period which, in European history, is labelled the 'early modern' age. One is a view from the north: that is, from the perspective of Ainu society. The Ainu did not keep written records, but some fragments of their world view can be recaptured from their treasury of legends and from the language they used to describe themselves and others. In the eighteenth and nineteenth centuries, a number of Ainu-Japanese vocabularies were compiled for trade and diplomatic purposes and, as Kikuchi Isao has shown, we can use these to draw interesting conclusions about the Ainu sense of place. Like many identity groups, the Ainu saw themselves simply as ordinary people: the word 'Ainu' is the word for 'human being'. Ainu society itself, however, was subdivided into regional groups called *kur* or *utar*, which might loosely be translated as 'clan', and the same words were used to describe small neighbouring societies like the Uilta and Nivkh of

Sakhalin (who were designated *Rebunkur*, 'Clans of Beyond the Sea', as opposed to the Ainu *Yaunkur* or 'Clans of the Land'). But there was also another category of society – the large social groups which the Ainu called *shisham*. Initially applied to the Japanese (also referred to as *Yaunshisham*, 'Neighbours of the Land') this word also came to be used as the name for Russians and, in the nineteenth century, for American whalers (*Fuureshisham* or 'Red Neighbours', presumably because of the colour of their hair).[4] *Shisham* is a word with neutral or even perhaps positive overtones, literally meaning 'great and nearby'.[5] This reflects the open attitude of the Ainu to strangers – an attitude not uncommon in small societies which, like the Ainu, rely heavily on trade. The Russian explorer Krusenstern was echoing a much-repeated sentiment when he described the Ainu as showing 'neither fear nor backwardness' in their encounters with strangers but as having a hospitality and courtesy which 'make me consider the Ainos [*sic*] as the best of all the people that I have hitherto been acquainted with'.[6]

Until the middle of the seventeenth century the Ainu had some reason to welcome Japanese traders. Although contacts with the Neighbours from the Land were always turbulent and sometimes violent, trade relations flourished during the fifteenth and sixteenth centuries with Ainu exchanging furs, fish, hunting hawks and a variety of goods from the Asian continent for Japanese swords, cooking vessels and lacquer ware. Many Ainu households acquired treasured collections of high-quality Japanese metal and lacquer goods which would have been far beyond the reach of the average Japanese farm family. After the establishment of the Tokugawa Shogunate in 1603, however, trade came under new forms of control. The domain of Matsumae (in southern Hokkaido) tightened its grip over commerce with the Ainu, creating a monopoly which enabled its representatives to demand exorbitant prices for Japanese goods. In the eighteenth century, merchants licensed by Matsumae started to establish more permanent bases in Ainu territory, setting up fisheries in which they often employed Ainu as semi-slave labour.

The changing relationship looked, from the Ainu perspective, like an increasing Japanese disregard for the basic human etiquette of commercial

4. Kikuchi Isao, *Hoppōshi no naka no Kinsei Nihon*, Tokyo: Kokura Shobō, 1991, pp. 90–96.

5. *Ibid.*, p. 94.

6. A.J. von Krusenstern, *Voyage Round the World in the Years 1803, 1804, 1805, and 1806*, vol. 2, Amsterdam and New York: N. Israel/Da Capo Press, 1968, pp. 76, 83.

exchange. In Ainu oral tradition, this seems to be expressed in a sense of betrayal by people who had once been trusted. A famous ballad, for example, tells how a Japanese merchant tried to steal the wife of the god Oina, in the process killing her infant son. The ensuing revenge by Oina on the Japanese is seen by some as an allegorical description of the Shakushain War, the large-scale Ainu uprising against Japanese incursions into their territory which occurred in 1669. But the cry of Oina's wife to her captors suggests a wider consciousness of a souring in the relationship between the Ainu and the Neighbours of the Land: 'I had heard the Japanese called honourable people, people with truly good hearts, but how evil your hearts must be!'[7]

Next, a view from 'the metropolis', or at least from the standpoint of the relatively educated urban section of the Japanese population. Until the middle of the eighteenth century most ordinary people in Japan would have had little cause to reflect on their identity as *'Nihonjin'* (Japanese). The word *kuni* ('country') when it was used, more often referred to the local region or domain than to Japan as a whole. Even in the early nineteenth century, travellers were warned that, once outside their own region they were in 'enemy territory', and guidebooks found it necessary to advise the visitor to strange provinces not to laugh at local customs or accents.[8]

Amongst intellectuals, however, the sudden expansion of contacts with the outside world in the sixteenth century had stimulated curiosity about Japan's place in the world – a curiosity which was not extinguished by the tight controls on foreign trade imposed from the mid-seventeenth century onwards; and, as the social commentator Tokutomi Sohō was later to argue: 'the concept "foreign nations" brought forth the concept "Japanese nation"'.[9] A fascinating expression of this gradually emerging sense of nationality can be found in the illustrated guides to the 'Peoples of the World' which appeared in Japan from the late sixteenth century onwards. The first examples were incorporated into decorative screens which included maps of the world copied from imported Western sources. Intriguingly, these screens faithfully reproduced the Western schema by which nations are presented as contiguous blocks of bold primary colours,

7. Quoted in Shinya Gyō, *Ainu Minzoku to Tennōsei Kokka*, Tokyo: San-Ichi Shobō, 1977, p. 242.
8. See Constantine N. Vaporis, 'Caveat Viator: Advice to Travellers in the Edo Period', *Monumenta Nipponica*, vol. 44, no. 4, 1989, esp. pp. 461 and 478.
9. Quoted in R. H. Myers and M. R. Peattie eds., *The Japanese Colonial Empire 1895–1945*, Princeton: Princeton University Press, 1984, p. 64.

separated by clearly defined borders. Yet their designers do not seem to have made a clear association between political nationhood and the colours represented on the map: Japan is typically partitioned into several differently coloured blocks, representing the long-vanished provinces of the Nara period (645–794 AD).[10] The ethnic groups presented on these screens were at first depicted in a style which suggests meticulous copying of a European prototype, but as time went on the iconography became 'Japanized' and the imagery vividly inventive. One *Bankoku Sōʒu* (Chart of All the Nations) produced in 1640, depicts forty different ethnic groups, each illustrated by a man and woman wearing national dress. Japan, represented by a splendidly armoured samurai and his wife, occupies pride of place in the top right-hand corner, and is followed by China, Tartary, Taiwan and a variety of Southeast Asian countries such as Java, Sumatra, Annam and Tonkin. Further down the chart come India and several European countries, ending with some rather speculative depictions of 'Americans' and 'Africans'.[11]

Before the late eighteenth century, however, most Japanese visions of the world outside were influenced as much by China as by the West. The widely-circulated *Wakan Sansai Zue* (Illustrated Japanese-Chinese Encyclopaedia) of 1712 borrowed much of its information from a Chinese prototype, the Illustrated Encyclopaedia of 1609, but supplemented this with knowledge gathered by Japanese scholars from Dutch merchants and other sources. The Encyclopaedia divided the world beyond Japan into two parts: 'foreign countries' (*ikoku*) who used Chinese characters and chopsticks, and 'outer barbarians' (*gai-i*), who wrote horizontally and ate with their hands.[12] In the first category come China, Korea, Chinra (Chedju Island, in fact long since absorbed by the Korean kingdom), Mongolia, the Ryukyu Kingdom, Ezo (the land of the Ainu), Tartary, the land of the Jurchens, Taiwan, Cochin and Tongking.[13] The second group includes some readily recognisable regions such as Malacca, Siam, Luzon, Spain, Java, Jakarta (*Jagatara* – treated separately from Java), Bengal and Holland. Interspersed amongst them are less familiar places, including the Land of the

10. See Muroga Nobuo, 'Atarashii Sekai no Ninshiki: Nanban Sekaizu Byōbu', in *Daikōkai Jidai no Nihon 5: Nihon kara Mita Ikoku*, Tokyo, Shōgakukan, 1978.

11. Torii Ryūzō, *Kyokutō Minʒoku*, vol. 1, Tokyo: Bunka Seikatsu Kenkyūkai, 1926, pp. 122–124.

12. *Wakan Sansai Zue*, vol. 1, Tokyo: Nihon Zuihitsu Taisei Kankōkai, 1929, p. 217; see also Torii, *Kyokutō Minʒoku*, 130.

13. *Wakan Sansai Zue*, pp. 202–216.

Pigmies, the Land of Giants and the Land of the Bird People.[14] Each country is both illustrated and described, sometimes in considerable detail. The sections on Korea, Ezo and the Ryukyu Kingdom, for example, not only provide several paragraphs on national history and customs but also include a sample vocabulary of the local language. The feeling conveyed by this work is of a world made up of concentric circles of increasing strangeness, stretching almost infinitely outwards from a familiar centre. Holland's position as one of the last countries to be described – just before the Land of Dragons and the place inhabited by creatures with six legs and four wings – indicates, perhaps, that it represented the most distant and strangest people of whom the Japanese were clearly aware.

This vision of the world as a series of concentric circles was, of course, drawn from the Chinese *hua-i* (in Japanese, *ka-i*) model of the world, in which barbarism (*i*) increases the further one moves away from the settled and civilized centre (*ka*). In the Illustrated Japanese-Chinese Encyclopaedia there seems still to be some ambiguity as to whether Japan or China is to be regarded as the centre. It is true that China is listed as a 'Foreign Country', while Japan does not appear at all in the description of the peoples of the world. Other sections of the Encyclopaedia, however, contain much more information about Chinese geography than they do about the geography of Japan.

By the end of the eighteenth century, however, Japan's place in the order of things had become more confident. The *Chinsetsu Kidan Ehon Bankokushi* (Illustrated Strange Tales and Wonderful Accounts of the Countries of the World) of 1772 (revised in 1826) begins with Japan, before working its way gradually outward to such places as the Land of People with One Eye and the Land of People with One Leg. Japan, while still illustrated by a picture of a samurai, is now represented by a distinctly urbanized samurai encountering a group of geisha in a city street. The author, without undue modesty, lists nobility and instinctive moral rectitude as being among the defining characteristics of the Japanese: 'even if they do not know the five [Confucian] virtues, they still keep to the true path'. The most important characteristic of Japaneseness, however, and the one discussed at greatest length, is a sensitive appreciation of the beauties of poetry. [15] This description seems to reflect the influence of the emerging

14. *Ibid.*, pp. 217–246.
15. See Torii, *Kyokutō Minzoku*, p. 139.

ideas of the Nativism, propagated by scholars like Motoori Norinaga (1730–1801), in which Japanese identity was defined in terms of spontaneous virtue and creativity, as opposed to the rigidity and sterility attributed to Chinese learning.

Lastly, a view from the south. The intellectual life of the Ryukyu kingdom, like the intellectual life of Japan, was deeply influenced by China, and absorbed the same *ka-i* model of the global order. Indeed, as its power expanded in the fifteenth and sixteenth centuries, the kingdom constructed its own miniature version of the Chinese system, exacting tribute from outlying islands such as the Yaeyama, to the south of the main Okinawan Island. Within this order, however, Ryukyuan scholars were conscious of their kingdom as a small country poised in the most delicate of strategic locations. On the one hand, Ryukyuan writings reveal familiarity with and respect for the power of their larger neighbours. The songs of the classical *Omoro sōshi* (including material dating from the twelfth to early seventeenth centuries) praise local cities by comparing them to the splendours of the Japanese cities of Kyoto and Kamakura, and the sixteenth-century king Shō Shin's achievements are listed as including the 'emulation of the system of the imperial palaces of China, [in which] blue stones have been carved to make the balustrades which span the lower section of the palace. This is a sign of prosperity which was not seen in ancient times.' Better still, Shō Shin had succeeded in having Ryukyu's tribute missions to China increased from triennial to annual events: an achievement which not only brought increased trading profits into the kingdom but also marked a satisfying recognition by the great Ming empire of the Ryukyus' significance.[16]

At the same time, however, the kingdom's social elite were aware and proud of their special place as a crossroads of East Asian trade. A fifteenth-century inscription commissioned by King Shō Taikyū describes his realm as 'the anchorage of all the nations', an archipelago whose small size is made up for by its position on the intersecting sea-roads from north (Japan and Korea), west (the Ming empire) and south (the many lands of Southeast Asia). The Ryukyus 'gather together all that is best from the three kingdoms of Korea, they serve as a balancing wheel to the Great Empire of Ming, and stand at the mouth of the Region of the Sun [Japan]'.[17] Though it might

16. Mitsugu Sakihara, *A Brief History of Early Okinawa Based on the Omoro Sōshi*, Tokyo: Honpō Shoseki Press, 1987, p. 166.

17. Quoted in Higashionna Kanjun, *Ryūkyū no Rekishi*, Tokyo: Kyōhundō, 1966, pp. 68–70.

lack military or political power, the kingdom could still envisage itself as possessing a special commercial hold over a vast geographical area: 'Kyoto and Kamakura/ Java and the South Seas [literally 'southern barbarians']/ China and Miyako/ Let them all serve our king', ran one verse from the *Omoro sōshi*.[18]

This sense of strategic importance – of balancing the competing pressures and demands of larger neighbours – was a source both of pride and of considerable unease. After the invasion of the Ryukyus by the Japanese domain of Satsuma in 1609, the kingdom was forced into the particularly invidious position of maintaining its traditional tributary relationship with China while at the same time trying to satisfy the injunctions of a new and more assertive tributary overlord, Satsuma, and through it indirectly the Japanese Shogunate.

The Ka-I Order and the Logic of Difference

The path which led to the redefinition of Ainu and Ryukyuans as 'Japanese' was shaped by two forces. The first was the force of Japan's changing relationship with China; the second, the force of the encounter with the European powers. Although the relationship with China and the relationship with Europe were in many ways interconnected, the logic of these forces often pulled in different directions.

The steady decline of the power of China encouraged Japan's elite to redraw the traditional *ka-i* view of the world so that Japan itself would be the pre-eminent *ka*, the civilized centre of its own miniature world order.[19] This required a restructuring of relations between inside and outside, placing the societies on the Japanese periphery in a subordinate, tributary relationship modelled on the relationship between the Chinese empire and its 'barbarian' periphery. The foundations of the new order were laid down at the beginning of the Tokugawa period, when the domain of Matsumae was granted a monopoly over trade with the Ainu, and Satsuma's invasion subordinated the Ryukyu kingdom to its control.

The symmetry between north and south was not perfect. In the south, Satsuma posted its officials in the Ryukyu capital, Shuri, and claimed the right to regulate the kingdom's trade and taxation system. Part of the tax in

18. Quoted in Sakihara, *A Brief History of Early Okinawa*, p. 177.

19. See, for example, Ronald P. Toby, *State and Diplomacy in Early Modern Japan*, Princeton: Princeton University Press, 1984, pp. 217–219.

kind levied on Ryukyu agriculture was transferred to Satsuma, becoming an important source of the domain's income, and regular tribute missions from the Ryukyus were sent, not simply to Satsuma but to the Shogun's seat of government in Edo.

Until the early eighteenth century, the Shogunate itself took little interest in these visits, but from about 1708 onwards the central government began to recognize them as a crucial legitimating symbol of its claim to stand at the pinnacle of a hierarchical world order whose focal point was Edo.[20] In the north meanwhile, the domain of Matsumae showed little desire to intervene in the life of the Ainu, and allowed its appointed officials (and later, licensed merchants) to trade and exploit as they wished. Matsumae levied no tax on the Ainu, but creamed off a substantial portion of the profits of trade. Although Ainu elders made annual ceremonial visits to the Lord of Matsumae's castle – visits which the domain interpreted as being tribute missions – they did not make the long journey to the shogunal capital.

The common cornerstone of the *ka-i* edifice, however, was the logic of difference. The relationships with the Ainu and the Ryukyu kingdom were important precisely because they represented the subordination of foreign people to Japanese dominion. Everything about the relationship, therefore, had to be structured in such a way as to magnify the exotic character of the peripheral societies. In Matsumae domain, the Ainu families who had lived side by side with Japanese settlers in the southern tip of modern Hokkaidō were gradually driven out into 'Ezochi' – Ainu territory. Ainu were forbidden to learn Japanese or wear characteristically Japanese articles of clothing such as straw sandals and straw raincoats, and were discouraged from engaging in farming. (The Ainu economy was largely based on hunting and fishing, but Ainu women also cultivated small plots of millet and vegetables. Among the measures used by Matsumae to suppress this was a prohibition on the sale of seeds to the Ainu.)[21]

In the relationship between Satsuma and the Ryukyu kingdom, the most important celebration of difference was the tribute mission to Edo. Each mission was an extravagant and elaborately staged dramatization of the logic of *ka-i*. The large Ryukyu contingent, including merchants, scholars and craftspeople as well as government officials, travelled in

20. See Kamiya Nobuyuki, *Bakuhansei Kokka no Ryūkyū Shihai*, Tokyo: Kokura Shobō, 1990, pp. 249–251.
21. See, for example, Mogami Tokunai, *Ezo Sōshi*, in *Hokumon Sōsho*, vol 1, Tokyo: Kokusho Kankōkai, 1972, p. 315.

procession from Satsuma to Edo, flanked by an armed guard of Satsuma warriors. Ryukyu officials were given precise instructions about their dress and conduct for these occasions. A decree of 1709, for example, stated that they were to carry long swords, dress in brocade and bring with them 'Chinese style' weaponry. Their equipment, above all, must be 'of the sort used in a foreign court, so that they cannot be mistaken for Japanese'.[22]

The sense of difference was inscribed in the Japanese popular imagination not just by ceremonial events like the tribute missions to Edo, but also by travellers' accounts of the exotic 'world outside' published from the early eighteenth century onwards. Images of difference presented by early travellers were often copied word for word by other writers, creating a stock repertoire of distinctions between centre and periphery. Descriptions of the Ainu almost always began with comments about hairstyle, clothing, jewellery and the facial tattooing common amongst Ainu women. As David Howell observes, in Tokugawa society differing hairstyles were one of the most obvious marks of status, and the only people who did not bind or shave their hair were members of certain outcaste groups. The flowing locks and beards of the Ainu were therefore the visible sign of a people beyond the realms of the existing social order.[23] After detailed discussions of clothing and footwear, the accounts generally went on to discuss the Ainu diet. To Japanese observers it was striking that the Ainu grew no rice (though they bought it in considerable quantities from Japanese merchants), that they took their meals at irregular times, and that they ate deer and bear as well as salmon and a variety of other fish.

Japanese travellers' tales, as much as those of their eighteenth-century European counterparts, are often supercilious in their descriptions of the 'barbarians'. The illiteracy of the Ainu and their ignorance of the Confucian sages aroused particular contempt. On the other hand, Ainu skill at diving for shellfish was remarked upon, as was their use of poisoned arrows for hunting. Matsumae domain, in fact, made strenuous efforts to discover the secrets of Ainu arrow poisons, and several Japanese visitors to the region

---

22. Quoted in Kamiya, *Bakuhansei Kokka no Ryūkyū Shihai*, p. 255; for an important discussion of this logic of difference, see also Kikuchi Isao, 'Kyōkai to minzoku', in Arano Teiji *et al.*, *Ajia no naka no Nihonshi*, vol. 4, Tokyo: Tokyo Daigaku Shuppankai, 1992.

23. David Howell, 'Ainu Ethnicity and the Boundaries of the Early Modern Japanese State', *Past and Present*, 142, February 1994, p. 88; see also Kikuchi Isao, 'Kinsei no okeru Ezokan to "Nihon Fūzoku"', in Hokkaidō Tōhoku Shi Kenkyū kai (ed.), *Kita kara no Nihonshi*, Tokyo: Sanseidō, 1988, pp. 206–229.

seem to have studied Ainu herbal medicine in the hope of finding new cures to familiar maladies.[24]

In accounts of Okinawa, the narrative often began with a retelling of the legend (apparantly propagated from the early seventeenth century onwards) which identified the kings of Ryukyu as descendants of the Japanese warrior Minamoto no Tametomo, thus offering an official justification for Satsuma's invasion of the kingdom in 1609. They then described the ranks of Ryukyu nobility, commenting particularly on the clothes and headgear which distinguished each rank. (The unusual hats worn by the Ryukyu nobility figured prominently in the iconography of difference.) As in the case of the Ainu, the hairstyles, jewellery and tattoos of Ryukuan women attracted comment. The many ceremonies marking the seasons of the year and the stages of human life in the Ryukyu kingdom were recorded in detail. Descriptions of events like the celebration of New Year, when children played special ball games and demonstrated their agility on home-made seesaws, give a picturesque flavour to accounts of life in the 'South Seas'. The songs and dances of the archipelago were often discussed at length, as were the local cremation practices, including the Ryukyuan practices of washing and arranging the bones of the deceased after cremation. Although some similarities with Japan were noted – houses looked similar, and the literate sections of the Ryukyu population used the Japanese phonetic syllabary – the overall impression is very much of 'different country', though not of a place whose exoticism would put it in the outer circles of barbarism.[25]

The Nation-State and the Logic of Assimilation

Japan's growing contact with the European powers from the late eighteenth century onwards, on the other hand, exposed the country to the pressures of a quite different world order: an order based upon European notions of nationhood. The imperial nations of Europe, of course, had their 'barbarian peripheries', but these were not arranged in concentric circles round the

---

24. See Sakakura Genjirō, *Ezo Zuihitsu* (1739), in *Hoppō Mikōkai Kobunsho Shūsei*, vol. 1, Tokyo: Sōbunsha, 1979, p. 73; for other descriptions of Ainu society see Mogami, *Ezo Sōshi*; Arai Hakuseki, *Ezo Shi* (1720) in *Hoppō Mikōkai Kobunsho Shūsei*, vol. 1, Tokyo: Sōbunsha, 1979.

25. See, for example, Morishima Chūyō, *Ryūkyū Dan* (1790), and Anon., *Ryūkyū Kaigo* (1850), both reproduced in *Edoki Ryūkyū Mono Shiryō Shūran*, vol. 4, Tokyo: Honpō Shoseki KK, 1981.

metropolis: they were far-flung maritime empires, linked to the mother country by the invisible webs of world-wide shipping routes. From the Japanese point of view, what was new about this was not the notion of a frontier itself: Japan was full of frontiers, well-marked and well-guarded lines separating domain from domain, or (in the case of Matsumae) separating the Japanese-settled area from Ainu territory. Rather, it was the idea of the frontier as a single, unequivocal line marking the boundary between one nation and another, instead of the idea of a series of frontiers marking gradually increasing degrees of difference.

Japan's first important encounter with this European order occurred in the north, as Russian traders, soldiers and missionaries extended their influence from Kamchatka into the northern Kurile Islands. By the 1740s there were trading posts and churches on the northern island of Shumshu, and local Ainu were rapidly being Russified: adopting Western dress, Russian names and Orthodox Christianity. Japan's response to this challenge was predictable. To protect the northern border from Russian encroachment, it was clearly necessary that the Ainu should be redefined as Japanese. In the words of the famous geographer Honda Toshiaki (1744–1821), who advocated the Japanese colonization of the Kuriles, Sakhalin and Kamchatka: 'we must establish a mutual frontier between Japan and other countries and create a fortress to withstand foreign enemies'.[26] The form which this Japanization of the periphery should take was a source of lively debate in scholarly circles. While some writers focused narrowly on the strategic significance of the region, others (including Honda's student, the explorer Mogami Tokunai) advocated the large-scale agricultural development of Ainu territory, and suggested that the Ainu themselves should be taught the Japanese language, encouraged to adopt Japanese styles of dress and diet, and instructed in the arts of farming.[27]

The ideas of men like Mogami had some impact on the thinking of the central government. As the Russian threat intensified, Ainu territory was placed under direct Shogunal control (the east of modern Hokkaido together with the southern Kuriles was transferred to Shogunal rule in 1799, and the west together with southern Sakhalin in 1807). The initial government instructions drawn up for running the territory spoke of the need to encourage the Ainu to 'turn into Japanese' (*wajin ni henka suru*) by gradually encouraging them to live in Japanese houses, to abandon their

26. Kaiho Mineo, *Kinsei no Hokkaidō*, Tokyo: Kyōikusha, 1979, p. 129.
27. Mogami, *Ezo Sōshi*.

Figure 1: Ainu being forcibly persuaded to 'improve their customs'.

Source: Matsuura Takeshirō, *Kinsei Ezo Jinbutsushi*, reprinted in Hanazaki Kōtei, *Shizuka na Taichi: Matsuura Takeshirō to Ainu Minzoku*, Tokyo: Iwanami Shoten, 1993.

uncivilized habits of meat eating, to cut their hair in Japanese style, take up farming and study the Japanese language.[28] Many of these measures however, proved in practice to be beyond the financial and administrative resources of the Shogunate, and assimilation policies, as they were put into effect, concentrated very much on outer appearances. Strenuous (though not entirely successful) efforts were made to persuade Ainu men to cut their beards and tie up their hair in a style that would define them as *hyakusho* ('commoners' in the Tokugawa status system).[29] Some traditional ceremonies were suppressed, and a number of Ainu communities, particularly those near the border with Russia, were induced to adopt the traditional Japanese farmer's dress of cotton jacket and straw sandals. In several areas, Japanese officials organized public ceremonies to 'celebrate the improvement of customs' (*kaizoku no gi*), at which cooperative Ainu were paraded in their new costume, treated to Japanese-style banquets and sometimes presented with 'assimilation medals' (*kaizoku pai*).[30]

28. Takakura Shinichirō, *Shinpan Ainu Seisakushi*, Tokyo: San-Ichi Shobō, 1972, p. 139.

29. On the meaning of *hyakusho* see Yoshihiko Amino, 'Emperor, Rice and Commoners', (trans. G. McCormack) *Japanese Studies*, vol. 14, no. 2, September 1994, pp. 1–12.

30. Takakura, *Shinpan Ainu Seisakushi*; see also Kikuchi, *Hoppōshi*, pp. 11–13.

Two points about these policies are particularly interesting. The first is the acknowledgement that people could be 'turned into Japanese': that is, that national identity was a matter of following certain customs, rather than an immutable matter of race. The second is the form of 'Japaneseness' which was imposed upon the Ainu. At a time when writers like Motoori Norinaga were developing a particular image of Japan-as-opposed-to-China (an image which emphasized spontaneity and natural appreciation of beauty), the official version of Japan-as-opposed-to-Ainu was still surprisingly Chinese. That is to say, it followed the Chinese *ka-i* formula in stressing outer appearances and etiquette as the main distinctions between civilization and barbarism, and, where it addressed issues of personal ethics, it did so mainly in Confucian terms.[31] One of the few Japanese works to be translated into the Ainu language for the purposes of moral instruction was, curiously enough, a handbook of Confucian ethics generally attributed to the Japanese scholar Muro Kyūsō, but which was itself actually Muro's translation of a work by the Sinophile Ryukyuan scholar Tei Junsoku.[32]

A sense of the encroaching presence of the Western powers influenced eighteenth-century Japanese views of the world to the west and south, as well as to the north. In 1785 the astronomer Hayashi Shihei produced his Illustrated Outline of the Three Countries (*Sankoku Tsūran Zusetsu*), the first attempt to define Japan's position in relation to its neighbours, Korea, the Ryukyu kingdom and the Ainu. Unlike the screen-painters of the early Tokugawa period, Hayashi coloured his map in a way that defined Japan as a single unit, clearly distinguished from its neighbours, and in the process firmly defined the Ryukyus and Ainu territory as foreign countries. Hayashi not only advocated the Japanization of the Ainu but also discussed the climate and fertility of the then uninhabited Ogasawara Islands, and argued that they should be colonized by Japan.[33] However nothing came of this, and Hayashi was soon after imprisoned for his temerity in publishing his views on the need for stronger Japanese maritime defences.[34] It was only in the north that the threat from Europe seemed close enough to warrant practical action, and even there efforts at assimilation were dropped as the

---

31. On the importance of visible symbols as markers of identity, see Howell, 'Ainu Ethnicity', p. 87.

32. Takakura, *Shinpan Ainu Seisakushi*, p. 356.

33. See *Hayashi Shihei Zenshū*, vol. 2, Tokyo: Daiichi Shobō, 1979, pp. 77–79.

34. Grant K. Goodman, *Japan: the Dutch Experience*, London: Athlone Press, 1986, pp. 213–215.

Russian menace receded. In 1821 control of the northern frontier was returned to Matsumae domain, and the bewildered Ainu were promptly ordered to stop wearing Japanese clothes and abandon their efforts to learn the Japanese language.[35]

Modernity, Civilization and Assimilation

A comprehensive effort to 'Japanize' the periphery began only after Japan's wholehearted entry into the modern world order in the mid-nineteenth century. In 1855 Japan and Russia completed the first of many attempts to define their mutual border, and in 1869, the year after the Meiji Restoration, the Land of the Ainu was incorporated into the new state under the name 'Hokkaidō'. Uncertainty over the Ogasawara Islands – and the small community of American, European and Pacific Islander colonists who had made their home there since the 1830s – continued until 1875 when Britain quietly removed the plaque which had been erected to claim the islands as its colony in 1827.[36] Although the multinational Ogasawarans did not readily fit the emerging Meiji images of the ethnic nation-state, practical expediency overcame ideology, and by the mid-1880s, when large-scale migration from Japan to the islands began, the first settlers had all been enrolled in the family registers (*koseki*) which at that time served as the official criterion of Japanese nationality.[37] Control of the Ryukyus was more contentious and caused serious strains in Japan's relationship with China. In the end, however, neither the Ryukyu kingdom itself nor China had the strength to resist the demands of the self-assertive Meiji government: in 1879, the last king, Shō Tai, was forced to abdicate and the Ryukyu kingdom became Okinawa Prefecture.

Once the outlines of the state had been defined, there followed a period of cultural colouring in: an attempt to blend the societies of the periphery into the official image of a united and centralized nation. But the Japanese

---

35. Takakura, *Shinpan Ainu Seisakushi*, pp. 280–281.

36. The original plaque, with a statement on the back renouncing Britain's claim to the islands, is held in the Australian National Library, Canberra. A claim to the islands had also been made on behalf of the United States by Commodore Perry in 1853, but this was dropped in the 1860s.

37. The *koseki* system was introduced in 1872. It was not until 1899 that the Japanese Citizenship Law provided a legal framework for the definition of Japanese nationality and the conditions for naturalization; on the naturalization of the Ogasawarans, see Yamagata Ishinosuke, *Ogasawarato Shi*, Tokyo: Tōyōdō 1906, p. 367.

society to which the people of the periphery were to be assimilated was itself in the midst of rapid and profound change. The idea of civilization which inspired the Meiji government's *mission civilizatrice* was no longer the Chinese notion of *ka*, with its emphasis on order and outward propriety, but rather the Western-inspired version of civilization for which Meiji scholars were obliged to invent a Japanese translation: *bunmei*. Unlike *ka*, *bunmei* was a dynamic concept, laden with overtones of progress. Its basis was not harmony and hierarchy but *production*: the ability to create material wealth which would release the human spirit from the bonds imposed on it by nature. In the words of its most famous Japanese theorist, Fukuzawa Yukichi, the attainment of *bunmei* involved successive stages of development. First the 'primitive' stage in which 'neither dwellings nor supplies of food are stable' and 'man ... cowers before the forces of nature'; next the 'semi-developed' stage where 'daily necessities are not lacking, since agriculture has been started on a large scale', but where people only 'know how to cultivate the old', not 'how to improve it'; and finally the stage of full civilization where, on the basis of material abundance, 'today's wisdom overflows to create the plans of tomorrow'.[38]

In relation to *bunmei*, Japan found itself again in much the same position as it had in relation to *ka* in the early seventeenth century. Once more it was relegated to the periphery of civilization, faced with the task of creating anew its own local world order in which it could constitute itself as the centre. In the seventeenth century, this had involved turning the societies of the frontier into tributary foreign states; now it involved turning them into parts of the civilized nation-state. For, as Fukuzawa comfortingly pointed out, civilization was a relative thing, and if Japan looked 'uncivilized' when compared to the Western great powers, the Japanese 'can be called civilized' when compared with the Ainu.[39]

This shifting vision of the world order had three crucial consequences for Meiji assimilation policy. In the first place, it meant that assimilation went far beyond the outward forms of clothing, hairstyles or even language, to transform the texture of daily life and work. Its central element now was a restructuring of the relationship between humans and nature, imposing on the periphery an idealized image of a society of hard-working, small-scale peasant farmers. In 'Japan proper', the traditional pattern of *de*

---

38. Fukuzawa Yukichi (trans. David A Dilworth and G. Cameron Hurst), *An Outline of a Theory of Civilization*, Tokyo: Sophia University Press, 1973, pp. 13–14.

39. Fukuzawa, *An Outline*, p. 14.

facto ownership of land by individual peasant families had been given a new gloss of civilization by a Land Tax Ordinance of 1873, which conferred *de jure* property rights on farmers and imposed on them a uniform duty to pay a monetary land tax. This now became the standard of civilization for the periphery. In Hokkaido, the government (advised by Horace Capron, a former US Secretary of Agriculture who had played an important role in the opening up of the American west) embarked on a plan for the large-scale colonization and agricultural development of the island. The Ainu – a dwindling minority in their own country – lost their traditional hunting and fishing grounds, which became the property of the Japanese state or were transferred to the private ownership of colonists from Japan proper.

The main instrument for the assimilation of the Ainu was to be the Former Natives Protection Law (*Kyūdojin Hogo Hō*) of 1899, whose philosophical foundations were made plain by a government representative during the parliamentary debates on the bill:

> The former natives of Hokkaidō, known as 'Ainu', are our fellow imperial subjects. However, with the opening up of Hokkaidō, entrepreneurs from Japan proper (*naichi*) have begun to acquire land and develop ventures, and under the laws of the survival of the fittest the former natives have become pressured and lost their living space. The future consequences of this situation can be imagined by all. That our fellow imperial subjects should fall into such distress is not in accord with the benign sentiments of the imperial will, and therefore this law has been proposed.[40]

Under the law, Ainu families were to be given 2 to 5 hectares of farm land together with grants of seed and tools. The land could not be sold without official permission, and was to be confiscated by the government if it was not farmed within fifteen years. At the same time, the financial assets of Ainu communities were placed under government control and used as the state deemed fit to meet the 'welfare' needs of the Ainu.

Not surprisingly, the law served none of its stated purposes. As an assimilation measure, it failed because it marked the Ainu out as different: people who could not be relied upon to act as proper citizens without government guidance. As a welfare measure, it failed because the plots of land provided were often too small to be viable, and because notions of individual small-scale farming were at odds with the traditional structure of the Ainu community. In many cases, plots were rented out to Japanese

---

40. See Hokkaidō Utari Kyōkai (ed.), *Ainu Shi: Shiryō Hen*, vol. 3, *Kingendai Shiryō*, part 1, Sapporo: Hokkaidō Utari Kyōkai, 1990, p. 88.

settlers on long-term leases at low rents, while their Ainu owners went to seek work in the rapidly growing towns or the coastal fisheries. This, ironically enough, turned some Ainu into 'absentee landlords', and ensured that they experienced a final round of dispossession in the land reforms introduced after World War II by the democratizing forces of the Allied occupation.[41]

To the south, in the newly created prefecture of Okinawa, the course of events was initially very different. The Ryukyu archipelago had a substantial and fairly prosperous ruling class, many of whom had close emotional ties to China. Having offended the Chinese by the destruction of the kingdom, the Japanese government was wary of provoking further conflict by too obvious a policy of Japanization. Although Matsuda Michiyuki, the official in charge of the establishment of Okinawa Prefecture, warned Okinawans that they would 'experience the same situation as the American Indians and the Ainu' if they did not 'change their old attitudes', little was done at first to enforce such change.[42] The officialdom of the old kingdom was replaced with a new superstratum of Japanese administrators, but the traditional form of communal land-holding was retained and Okinawans were neither given the right to elect members to the new Japanese parliament (opened in 1890) nor required to serve in the new conscript army.

During the late 1890s, however, this policy of 'preserving old customs' (as it was called) underwent a dramatic change. The overwhelming victory of Japan in its war with China (1894–95) removed Japanese inhibitions about offending the Chinese, and the strains of maintaining the traditional tax system in an age of rapid economic change provoked protests from local taxpayers. The establishment of a new order was marked by the introduction of the Okinawa Prefecture Land Reorganization Law (*Okinawa Ken Tochi Seiri Hō*), passed in the same year as Hokkaido Former Natives Protection Law, and serving the same basic purpose of replacing communal with private land ownership. The tradition by which the village controlled farm land, and had the power to redistribute it from time to time between inhabitants, was replaced by a system of individual property rights vested in the heads of households, while the numerous Okinawan taxes in kind were replaced by a single monetary land tax.[43] This removed some of the arbitrary and oppressive aspects of the old regime, but (like the Japanese Land Tax

---

41. Hokkaidō Utari Kyōkai, *Ainu Shi*, p. 861.

42. Okinawa Ken (ed.), *Okinawa Ken Shi*, vol. 1, Tokyo: Gannandō Shoten, 1977, p. 237.

43. *Ibid.*, pp. 80–83.

Ordinance itself) opened the way to the rapid consolidation of farm holding in the hands of landlords, many of whom, in the Okinawan context, were Japanese merchants.

Because it reached so deeply into everyday life – imposing national uniformity on a wide range of economic, social and cultural institutions – the Meiji assimilation process forced the state to confront complex problems of defining standards. A second major consequence of the vision of *bunmei*, indeed, was the emergence of a much more ambitious and totalizing vision of 'Japaneseness' than had existed in the Tokugawa period. Tokugawa efforts to assimilate the Ainu, for example, had been accompanied by some attempts to teach them Japanese, but these had been sporadic and largely left to the initiative of local officials. In the Meiji period, by contrast, the institutionalized enforcement of Japanese as the national language was a central element of assimilation. As the Okinawan education authorities observed in 1901:

> The educational level of this prefecture has become equal to that of other prefectures. There has been progress in the development of a sense of national citizenship and in exterior appearances such as the clothing of boys and girls. However, there are still some areas in which there is a sense of foreignness and underdevelopment compared with other prefectures. Not only many uneducated people, but also some schoolchildren and people who have completed general education speak the local dialect, and even when they speak normal language (*futsūgo*), their intonation and pronunciation sounds odd.[44]

But the enforcement of 'normality' requires a definition of what was normal. The idea that a single, recognisable norm of Japanese behaviour should exist in all areas of human life was widespread, not just amongst officials but also amongst sections of the population in the periphery itself. The *Ryūkyū Shimpō* (Ryukyu News), a journal established by young Okinawan intellectuals in the 1890s, advised its readers that their aim should be 'to become like the people of other prefectures in tangible and intangible ways, for better and for worse, from A to Z. In graphic terms, we might say that when they sneeze, they should sneeze like people from other prefectures.'[45] The Meiji state did not go so far as to propose a uniform Japanese way of sneezing but it did succeed in imposing order on many aspects of the existing regional

---

44. Okinawa Ken, *Okinawa Ken Shi*, vol. 4, p. 99.

45. Quoted in Ōta Masahide, *Minikui Nihonjin: Nihon no Okinawa ishiki*, Tokyo: Simul Press, 1969, p. 23; see also Alan S. Christy, 'The Making of Imperial Subjects in Okinawa', *Positions: East Asia Cultures Critique*, 1, 3, Winter 1993.

diversity of Japanese culture, including the multiplicity of regional dialects which existed throughout the country. Efforts to enforce the use of 'normal language' in Okinawa and amongst the Ainu were accompanied by heated debates about the relative merits of the Kyoto or Tokyo dialects, or of various forms of artificial *lingua franca*, as the official form of 'standard Japanese' – debates which were ultimately won by those who favoured the Japanese of the Tokyo middle classes.[46]

Social standardization was imposed, both on the people of the frontier and the people of the various Japanese regions, through the education system and through military training. Conscription, which was introduced to Okinawa in 1898 (thirteen years ahead of parliamentary representation) not only fostered a uniform ideology of loyalty to the emperor, but also brought together people from all over the country, helping to create a sense of the nation as community and to accelerate the spread of standard Japanese as the common means of communication.

Time, Space and Difference

But the perhaps most interesting implication of the notion of *bunmei* was the way in which it allowed difference to be transposed from the realm of space to the realm of time, so that 'foreignness' increasingly came to be reinterpreted as 'underdevelopment'. Fukuzawa's vision of a series of stages of development allowed the unfamiliar features of Ainu or Okinawan society to be perceived as remnants from a more primitive stage of human history. As a result, the frontier areas, which had once been seen as having their own distinctive sets of foreign customs, now began to be homogenized in the popular mind into a uniformly backward periphery. As one Governor of Okinawa remarked in the early twentieth century, it was the Prefecture's misfortune to be regarded 'in the same light as the recently developed area of Hokkaido', with the result that 'any attempt to reform an institution or improve a regulation is always rejected by citing the example of Hokkaido.'[47] Even the cosmopolitan Ogasawarans, who were at first allowed to have a bi-lingual education in English and Japanese, came to be regarded as an obstacle to development as the islands were opened up to colonization from other parts of Japan. In some cases they were even sent off to the mainland

---

46. See Nannette Twine, *Language and the Modern State: The Reform of Written Japanese*, London and New York: Routledge, 1991, ch. 8.

47. Quoted in Ōta, *Minikui Nihonjin*, pp. 27–28.

to have their 'lifestyle elevated and their customs improved'.[48] So the vision of a world made up of concentric circles, where foreignness increased the further one moved from the centre, came to be replaced by a vision of a single nation where 'development' and 'modernity' diminished the further one moved from the capital towards the geographical extremities.

The transfer of difference from geography ('foreignness') to history ('backwardness') was encouraged by early-twentieth-century academic research on the societies of the periphery. Inspired by the evolutionary sciences of the West, scholars like the archaeologist and ethnographer Torii Ryūzō (1860–1953) demonstrated links in material culture between the Ainu, Okinawans, and the earliest Jōmon inhabitants of the main Japanese islands. The pioneering anthropologist Koganei Yoshikyo (1858–1944) took this hypothesis one step further, suggesting (on the basis of his study of skeletal remains) that the Ainu were direct descendants of the earliest inhabitants of Japan. Though this genetic link remained a topic of controversy, the idea that Ainu culture reflected the material culture of an earlier stage of Japanese history was widely accepted. Hayashi Yoshishige's researches into Ainu farming methods, for example, led him to the conclusion that the Ainu, 'being a static hunter-gatherer people', had preserved the Japanese agricultural techniques of 1,500 years ago 'almost unchanged to the present day'.[49]

Meanwhile the famous ethnographer Yanagita Kunio (1875–1962) was eagerly pursuing links between the folk practices of Okinawa and those of various parts of Japan. As one recent reappraisal of Yanagita's work points out, Yanagita began by emphasizing the diversity of social forms within the Japanese archipelago, seeing different areas and different social structures as having their own particular histories. From the late 1920s onwards, however, his approach shifted to one that defined difference increasingly as a product of time rather than space. The central areas of Japan now came to be seen as representing the most modern forms of Japanese society, and the periphery as containing survivals of more ancient linguistic and social structures.[50] So Okinawan culture could be represented as an anthropological

48. Tokyo Fu (ed.), *Ogasawarato Sōran*, Tokyo: Tokyo Fu, 1929, p. 190.

49. Hayashi Yoshishige, *Ainu no Nōkō Bunka*, Tokyo: Keiyūsha, 1969, p. 3.

50. Fukuta Ajio, 'Shoki Yanagita Kunio no kenkyū to gendai minzokugaku', in Amino Yoshihiko ed., *Rekishigaku to Minzokugaku*, Tokyo: Furukawa Shobunkan, 1992, pp. 135–156; for this concept of centre and periphery see particularly Yanagita Kunio, 'Katatsumuri Kō' in *Teihon Yanagita Kunio Shū*, vol. 18, Tokyo: Chikuma Shobō, 1963; Yanagita Kunio, "Kyōdo seikatou no kenkyūhō", in *Teihon Yanagita Kunio Shū*, vol. 25. Tokyo. Chikuma Shobō, 1964; see also Christie, 'Making of Imperial Subjects', p. 623.

treasure-house whose contents revealed 'the shape of things as they were in the beginning', and as they had once been throughout the entire Japanese archipelago.[51] All of this gave substance to idea, not simply that the Ainu and the people of the Ryukyu Islands were Japanese now, but that they had *always been* Japanese, only Japanese marooned in some earlier phase of human history.

The transfer of difference from the dimension of space to the dimension of time was closely linked to the emerging sense of ethnicity as the chief criterion of nationhood. In Tokugawa Japan, as we have seen, constructions of identity were built around notions of manners and customs, rather than of blood. European racial theories, however, were enthusiastically studied and adopted by Japanese scholars in the Meiji era, and by the beginning of the twentieth century Japanese national identity was increasingly being linked to the idea of an organically united Japanese 'Volk' (*minzoku*). The concept of *minzoku*, which gained widespread currency in Japan in the first two decades of the twentieth century, allowed a convenient blurring between the cultural and genetic aspects of ethnicity, while emphasizing the organic unity of the Japanese people. As Thongchai Winichakul (writing of the Thai experience) observes, the definition of the geographic boundaries of the modern nation gave birth to the image of the nation as a 'geo-body', possessing a primordial integrity and life of its own.[52] In the Japanese context, the vision of the peripheral societies as remnants of the Japanese past provided a convenient means of reconciling visible cultural difference with the ideological construction of the nation as a united 'body' (*kokutai*) made up of a single *minzoku*.

A somewhat similar process seems to have accompanied the development of modern nationalism in some European countries. Late medieval English descriptions of the Welsh, Scots and Irish, for example, depict them as alien and bizarre, 'as if Nature were amusing herself in private with greater licence in the most distant regions than in public near the centre of the world'.[53] With the emergence of the British as an imperial nation, however, the view from 'the centre of the world' shifted: by the mid-nineteenth century Whig history had redefined the Celtic fringe (and the

---

51. See Okinawa Ken, *Okinawa Ken Shi*, vol. 1, pp. 692–699.

52. Thongchai Winichakul, *Siam Mapped: A History of the Geo-Body of a Nation*, Honolulu, University of Hawaii Press, 1994.

53. William Caxton, *The Description of Britain*, modern English edition by Marie Collins, New York: Weidenfeld and Nicolson, 1988 (original published in 1480), p. 162.

Scottish highlands in particular) as a region trapped in a primitive stage of evolution likened to that of American Indians, its people 'kept... far behind the Saxon' by insufficient exposure to 'the civilizing influence of the Protestant religion and the English language'.[54]

To return to our starting point, the imagining of national communities is an imagining across time as well as across space: a process by which certain people and events are defined as belonging to 'our' past, and others are excluded. The way in which the history of 'Japan' is usually written leaves the people of the frontier with a very attenuated past: a prehistory, perhaps, as part of the complex ethnic mix which made up the 'Japanese' people, but little sense of a continuing participation in a regional interplay, with constantly shifting boundaries and identities, between the large societies of Japan, China and Korea and the smaller societies of the Ryukyus, Taiwan, the Ainu, Uilta, Nivkhs and others. More often than not, the societies of the frontier seem to fall through the cracks between the imagined history of nation-states, ending up in obscure monographs of 'special interest' ethnography.

The problem was interestingly demonstrated in 1993 when the Japanese national broadcaster NHK took the bold step of presenting a dramatized version of seventeenth-century Ryukyu history as its main historical drama of the year. *Ryūkyū no Kaze* (entitled in English 'Dragon Spirit') was its first attempt to present the history of the frontier in the format of Japanese TV drama, but the series in the end was criticized by Okinawan scholars for focusing too much upon the royal court and its connections to Japan, and was relatively unpopular with the general Japanese viewing public because it contained too many unfamiliar names and 'foreign' words.

The production of *Ryūkyū no Kaze*, however, is a sign that in the 1990s the changing shape of the world system is yet again forcing redefinitions of 'Japaneseness'. International links between ethnic minorities and indigenous peoples in various parts of the world are encouraging a revival of regional identity amongst Ainu and Okinawans. The collapse of Cold War tensions is recreating lost historical links between the Ainu and the 'Clans Beyond the Sea' in Sakhalin,[55] and between Okinawans and the Chinese part of

54. Thomas Babington Macaulay, *The History of England*, edited and abridged by Hugh Trevor-Roper, London: Penguin, 1986 (original published in 1848–61), p. 365.

55. See, for example, 'Getting Back Our Islands', *Ampo*, vol. 24, no. 3, 1993, pp. 7–9.

their historical heritage. At the same time, the growing number of foreign workers in Japan and of marriages between Japanese and foreigners is creating quite new challenges to the attempt to construct Japan as a racially or linguistically homogeneous nation.

By retracing the historical interplay between shifting definitions of 'Japan', 'Ainu' and 'Okinawan', one can help to open up space for a rethinking of the nature of the nation. In particular, I hope that this process emphasizes the modernity and the transient nature of those national frontiers which so often restrict our historical vision. Rediscovering history, not as the biography of the nation-state but as a dance of identities between many contiguous social forms, re-emphasizes the importance of spatial difference, as well as temporal change, in the making of the modern world. And as we become more conscious of the many gradations of that spatial difference, that world as a whole starts to look just a little different.

CHAPTER THREE

Maps and the Formation of the Geo-Body of Siam

Thongchai Winichakul

Most studies on nationalism have suggested that the elements that define nationhood can be found in language, ethnicity, significant cultural traits, or a political unity. They are regarded as the essential common elements which constitute the identity of a nation. More recently, following the influential works by Anderson, Gellner, and Hobsbawm and Ranger,[1] the essentialism of the national identity is fundamentally denied. Many have turned to focus on how those elements were invented, and helped in creating the imagined nationhood. So far, none of them has paid attention to the most obvious constitutive element of a nation-state, namely its territory, as if it were merely a non-effective container of those essential elements. Supplemental to those attempts, therefore, this essay asks a similar question – how a nation is created as such an entity.[2] But it argues in a dissimilar way that nationhood was literally 'formed' by the demarcation of its body, the territoriality of a nation. The case is Siam in the late nineteenth century.

---

1. Benedict Anderson, *Imagined Communities*, London: Verso, 1983; revised edition, 1991. Ernest Gellner, *Nations and Nationalism*, Ithaca: Cornell University Press, 1983. Eric Hobsbawm and Terrence Ranger (eds), *The Invention of Tradition*, Cambridge: Cambridge University Press, 1983.

2. This article is an abridged version of Thongchai Winichakul, *Siam Mapped: A History of the Geo-body of a Nation*, Honolulu: University of Hawaii Press, 1994. It contains the main concepts and propositions. The clarification of its methodology and implications is added, especially at the beginning and in the final remarks. Needless to say, it is in no way a substitute for the book.

The essay does not deny the attempts to explain the imagined nation by ethnicity, language or tradition. Nor does it propose that territoriality solely constitutes nationhood. Yet the attention to the 'body' and its 'form-ation' here is vital to our theoretical concepts and methodology in several ways. First of all, nationalism survives by the belief in the particular identity of a nation. Those recent studies on the construction of such an identity try to explain how particular elements were invented, composed, and their importance elevated ideologically. But to identify an identity, either in an essentialist way or to the contrary, is to define it. Definition, according to an Oxford dictionary, means 'clearness of outline; making or being distinct in outline'.[3] Spatially speaking, defining anything is to draw a line to demarcate the domain of such an entity, which differentiates it from others simultaneously. More precisely, to define is to mark the clear 'out-line' which can differentiate one thing from its proximity. In this sense, the construction of a national identity is also, and always, a spatial operation. Again, this does not mean that geography is most important. Rather, the creation of nationhood is a process of constructing the domain of a national entity, of demarcating the clear out-line of it, thereby creating the body of a nation.

Second, in explaining the construction of nationhood, most studies simply identify what the elements that constitute an identity are. They rarely identify the limits of such an identity, where the proximate ethnicity, language, or tradition are no longer considered belonging to such a nation. In other words, they explain the positive identification of nationhood in the non-essentialist way. The spatial perspective suggested above, on the contrary, seeks to explain the construction of the element which identifies where one nationhood begins and ends, differentiating what it is as well as what it is not. The 'form-ation' of the geo-body of Siam demarcated the positive (what is Siam) as well as the negative (what is not Siam).

Third, the spatial terminology and discourse, such as position, boundary, domain, field and body, have been favoured by many post-modernist and feminist theories for some time.[4] Yet only a few fields of geography, such as architecture and urban geography, have been taken seriously in cultural studies. Political geography has not, and no geography has appeared yet in the recent studies on nationalism. Instead of applying

---

3. A.S. Hornby, *Oxford Advanced Learner's Dictionary of Current English*, Oxford: Oxford University Press, 1974, p. 226.

4. Edward Soja, *Postmodern Geographies*, London: Verso, 1989.

the spatial perspective to study the usually favourite subjects like ethnicity or language, the study of the territoriality of a nation here is to make a literal proposition of the ideas described above. It is to recognize the significance of political geography as parts of everyday culture. In turn, this study is at the conjuncture between history, political geography, anthropology and critical theories.

Last but not least on the concept of this essay, a nation-state and nationalism are a modernist project originating from the West. The essay does not argue that Siam existed as a nation before its encounter with European colonialism. Nor does it suggest, however, that nationhood was simply thought out, or imagined into being, as if it were a grand idealistic design of the imagination. It will show that the idea of nationhood never simply spread from the West to the rest of the world without the mediation, hence transformation or localization, by indigenous agency in particular cultural settings. Moreover, since nationhood was by no means the first or the only kind of imagined community, a nation was formulated amidst the confrontation with the existing 'imagined' community. Nationhood was a discursive construct, the material effect of a shifting discourse which defined the existence of a community, in this case from a kingdom to a nation.

The Geo-Body

The territory of a nation is not just a profane part of the earth's surface. It is a constitutive element of nationhood which generates plenty of other concepts and practices directly related to it: for example, the concept of integrity and sovereignty; border control, conflict, invasion and war. It defines and has some control over many other national affairs, such as the national economy, products, industry, trade, education, administration, culture and so on. Unarguably, the territory of a nation is the most concrete feature of nation for the management of nationhood. It is the most solid foundation, literally and connotatively, of nationhood as a whole. For a theoretical geographer, it is the territoriality of a nation.[5] For people of a nation, it is a part of SELF, a collective SELF. It is a nation's *geo-body*.

5. Robert D. Sack, *Human Territoriality: Its Theory and History*, Cambridge: Cambridge University Press, 1986, pp. 19-20, 216, 'Territoriality [is] the attempt by an individual or group to affect, influence or control people, phenomena, and relationships, by delimiting and asserting control over a geographic area ... [It is] a rather complex strategy [and] the device through which people construct and maintain spatial organization'.

Geographically speaking, the geo-body of a nation occupies a certain portion of the earth's surface which can be objectively identified. It seems to be concrete to the eyes and having a long history as if it were natural, and independent from technology or any cultural and social construction. Unfortunately, that is not the case. The study shows that the geo-body of a nation is merely the effect of modern geographical knowledge and its technology of representation, a map. The geo-body, the territoriality of a nation as well as its attributes such as sovereignty and boundary, are not only political but also cultural constructs. They were formulated on the soil where the indigenous spatial discourse had existed long before. The study emphasizes how the new geographical discourse displaced the existing indigenous concepts of space, through the innumerable meetings of the two kinds of knowledge, which generated conflicts, confrontations, miscommunication, serious and humorous misunderstandings.

Geographies and Maps

It goes without saying that the empires and kingdoms in pre-modern Southeast Asia, probably not unlike others in the world, did not have the same kind of boundary as a modern state does. This was not due to lack of expertise or techniques, but to the fact that the concept of such a boundary did not exist. This does not mean, however, that there had been no knowledge of geography, no maps, or no limits of a country. Only that they were of other kinds.

As Joseph Schwartzberg has studied extensively, the pre-modern cartographic tradition in Southeast Asia was rich. Yet the research into this subject, especially on Siamese maps, is disappointingly inadequate, resulting in the lack of our knowledge of it.[6] The best known traditional maps from the region and from Siam in particular are the 'Three-world' cosmographic maps.[7] It is also well known how the architecture of a city and palace in the Hindu-Buddhist tradition is cosmographic in spirit.[8] The map of pilgrim-

---

6. See the chapters by Joseph Schwartzberg in David Woodward and J.B. Harley (eds), *The History of Cartography*, vol. 2, Book 2, *Cartography in the Traditional East and Southeast Asian Societies*, Chicago: University of Chicago Press, 1994, esp pp. 839-840. His detailed study of most of the maps I mention below and more is fascinating and far better than any studies so far.

7. *Ibid*, pp. 720-737.

8. Robert Heine-Geldern, *Conceptions of State and Kingship in Southeast Asia*, Data Paper no. 18, Cornell Southeast Asia Program, Ithaca: Cornell University, 1956.

age is another kind of religious map which is based on a particular belief system of the relationship of sacred shrines in various places. The places, shrines and their relations have meanings like alphabets and words have in a particular grammar. In real terms, it mostly covers the areas beyond the nation-states today. Some shrines are even located in heaven.[9] The geography of Buddhist legends was also well known in the Buddhist countries in Southeast Asia. It usually defied the actual geography in order to show the genealogy of Buddhism in Suwannaphum, the mainland Southeast Asia. An eighteenth-century Thai map, for example, whose original could be a century older, shows what is northern Thailand as adjacent to Jambudipa, the name of the original homeland of Buddhism, without Burma in between. Sri Lanka in the same map was on the opposite side from Jambudipa but closer to the Malay peninsula.[10] According to this knowledge, the Buddha was born in the mythological land of Jambudipa, not in a Himalayan city north of India today. Theravada Buddhism in the region came directly from the two genuine origins of the religion, namely the Buddha's Jambudipa and Sri Lanka. This kind of geography cannot be understood, or the map can be misunderstood without knowing its grammar, i.e. the Buddhist legends.[11]

The notion of a country was also possibly expressed in a non-secular geographical term, like China was believed to be the centre of the world while other countries were in the islands around the middle kingdom. In the mainland Southeast Asian traditions, a kingdom was a federation-like realm under local spirits, whose power was appropriated by, or conferred upon, or subjugated to the power of the overlord and his spirit.[12] 'Siam' could also be

9. For the geography of a pilgrimage, see Charles F. Keyes, 'Buddhist Pilgrimage Centers and the Twelve-year Cycle: Northern Thai Moral Orders in Space and Time', *History of Religion*, vol. 15, no. 1, 1975, pp. 71-89. See Schwartzberg's analysis of another pilgrimage map, the religious route map as he calls, in Woodward and Harley (eds), *History of Cartography*, vol. 2, book 2, pp. 777-784.

10. See Thongchai, *Siam Mapped*, figure 2 and pp. 25-28.

11. Frank E. Reynolds, 'Buddhism as a Universal Religion and as a Civic Religion', in Bardwell L. Smith (ed.), *Religion and Legitimation of Power in Thailand, Laos and Burma*, Philadelphia: Anima Books, 1978, pp. 194-203. See also Winai Pongsripian, 'Traditional Thai Historiography and its Nineteenth Century Decline', PhD thesis, University of Bristol, 1983, pp. 69-82.

12. For more on the indigenous conception of the realm in Southeast Asia see David P. Chandler, 'Maps for the Ancestors: Sacralized Topography and the Echoes of Angkor in Two Cambodian Texts', *Journal of the Siam Society*, vol. 64, part 2, July 1976, pp. 170-187; H.L. Shorto, 'The 32 Myos in the Medieval Mon Kingdom', *Bulletin of the School of Oriental and African Studies*, vol. 26, no. 3, 1963, pp. 572-591.

expressed in a cosmographical sense rather than in political-geographical terms.[13]

It does not mean that a non-cosmographic, profane map of the earth surface was non-existent in Siam.[14] Definitely, it is a technology most cultures knew, using it to construct, for example, military maps. The map of a Buddhist legend and the cosmographic notion of a kingdom as described above are evidence of the synthesis of the cosmographic/religious space and the topographic/profane earth. Yet different cultures had different traditions of maps and map-making. The Mercator earth and its legacy is the modern European product. Likewise, a Siamese topographical map before modern geography was a chart full of symbols showing relations of places, distances, landscapes, and so on. But there was no scale, coordinates or arithmetic abstraction. To read it one has to understand its grammar. Several of these maps may not look accurate to our eyes, but they were used in battles, in travels, in recording land donations and perhaps in navigating the sea-trade in the region.[15]

Modern geography from the West was a different kind of knowledge. It has a long history of shifts, turns and development from Ptolemy, the medieval T-O map, to Mercator and the modern mapping. Since the late eighteenth century, in Europe it has been indispensable to the modernist project of nationalism and nation-state. Undoubtedly it played a prominent role in colonialism. Not only was the political conquest by the West a new page of world history; also colonialism brought modern geography as it was in the nineteenth century and the nation-based political geography into contact with the indigenous knowledge of geography and political community. Dissemination and exchange of knowledge, confrontations and displacements ensued. Literally, colonialism created a new face of the globe.

---

13. See Thongchai, *Siam Mapped*, pp. 34-35, and figure 6.

14. Schwartzberg calls them 'geographical maps', in contrast to the cosmographic ones, which include secular route maps, maps of localities and nautical maps.

15. Victor Kennedy studies a strategic or logistical map in 'An Indigenous Early Nineteenth Century Map of Central and Northeast Thailand', in Tej Bunnag and Michael Smithies (eds), *In Memoriam Phrya Anuman Rajadhon*, Bangkok: the Siam Society, 1970, pp. 315-348 and maps; Lorraine Gesick examines another map which is part of the documents on land donations to temples in southern Siam in 'Reading Landscape', *Journal of the Siam Society*, vol. 73, part 1+2, 1985, pp. 157-161; I make comments on a coastal chart in *Siam Mapped*, figure 4 and p. 29. Schwartzberg also discusses all of them in Woodward and Harley (eds), *History of Cartography*, vol. 2, book 2, pp. 763-766, 784-785 and plate 36.

The Non-bounded Siam and Its Margins

Siam, like other kingdoms in Southeast Asia, was a hierarchical con-
glomeration of towns and cities whose supreme overlord acquired sacred
power endowed in various places, objects and rituals, such as the throne, the
palace, regalia, the white elephants, the coronation, and so on. But his
(rarely her) control over the towns within the realm was uneven, usually
waning with distance from the centre. Each town (*muang* in Thai) governed
a certain area, mainly within its walls and the adjacent areas only,
particularly the travelling paths and the passages through the jungles,
mountains, and between towns. The limits of a town might be marked only
sporadically at certain intervals, or there would be an agreement that the
limit was at some specific point, or at the distance a guard could patrol.
Above all, the markings might not be connected since not all areas needed
to be marked. In other words, though a town had its territorial limits, its
boundary was quite different from a modern boundary, and a town was
usually not bounded. The limits might even be left vague or open between
two friendly towns.[16] Moreover, the limits of a town might or might not
connect with those of another town. The areas beyond the authority of any
town were virtually the 'ungoverned', or 'jungle' or 'uncivilized' (*pa, thuan*
in Thai). A pre-modern realm of a kingdom was a patchy territory full of
hierarchically sovereign units. As its limits were marked by the frontier
towns, the realm of a kingdom was usually not bounded either.

On the western frontier of Siam, the long ranges of mountainous
jungles had been left unoccupied. Siam and Burma were arch-rivals of
comparatively equal strength, and the mode of warfare at that time was
basically to plunder and to depopulate the frontier towns of the enemy. This
led both sides to abandon the area between their frontier towns as a natural
buffer. For Siam a *khetdaen* (the term now used to translate boundary) was
not necessarily connected or joined with the Burmese ones. It was the limit
within which the authorities of a country could exercise their power. On the
other hand the areas left over became a huge corridor between the two

---

16. For more about the frontier and boundary of a town see Gehan Wijaywardene, 'The
Frontier of Siam', in Craig J. Reynolds (ed.), *National Identity and Its Defenders*, Clayton,
Victoria: Monash University, 1992, pp. 157-190. The article, supposedly arguing against
my propositions, elaborates that a pre-modern town in Siam (and Lanna) knew its limits,
and boundaries were not unknown. As a matter of fact, that is also what I proposed. But
my point is that the indigenous concepts of territorial limit and boundary were different
from the ones of modern geography (Thongchai, *Siam Mapped*, ch. 3). Nonetheless, his
misreading leads to a useful elaboration which confirms my propositions.

Map 2: Non-bounded Siam and its margins.

countries; that is, a thick horizontal line on the earth's surface between the two sovereignties. But the corridor itself was without sovereignty. In other words, the boundary of sovereignty was inside the border, or the border extended beyond the boundary. The two sovereignties did not interface. If we draw up a modern political map of the region as the British and the French tried to do in the nineteenth century, there would be a huge belt on the earth's surface, in which elephant catchers were allowed to trespass but not the authorities of either side. The concepts and practices related to this kind of boundary were also different from the modern ones. To look after a *khetdaen* of this kind, for example, a frontier town had to post guards to protect certain passages through the corridor with great care. But the areas under guard, and the marking of the *khetdaen* were determined by local authorities, not by the central court who did not really care where it was. Between arch-rivals, moreover, the *khetdaen* was regarded a secret. The attempt at an inquiry or request for demarcation, as the British did in the 1820s-1840s might be seen as a weird or even a hostile act. Apart from that, local authorities of the frontier towns regularly sent spies to observe the enemy's activities. They sought for the opportunity to attack and plunder the enemy's town if it was within reach. None of these activities was necessarily ordered or needed sanction from the centre.[17]

The situation on other frontiers was different. The areas between Siam/Lanna and Upper Burma, and the ones along the Mekong were composed of plenty of large and small tributary states and chiefdoms. A tributary was not a colony. It was not occupied nor was it directly controlled by the overlord. It was an autonomous state. But within the context of pre-modern hierarchical relations among kings, a tributary was an inferior state, whose king paid submission to the overlord. Consequently, he had to comply with the overlord's demands, otherwise he would be punished severely. But there was no territorial annexation. A tributary normally retained its own monarch, administration, its own circle of dependencies, its military force, etc. A tributary king retained his sovereignty though he recognized the supremacy of the overlord. To put it bluntly, the sovereignty of different lords hierarchically piled up the same political territory. It is hardly surprising, therefore, that Siam always claimed that Cambodia and the northern Malay states, for example, belonged to Siam, while studies from the tributaries' points of view always find the opposite.[18]

Unlike a modern sovereign nation-state, whose existence means being independent from any foreign intervention, and having equal status with other states, a tributary state existed by submitting itself to one or usually several overlords to avoid punishment from any of them. The multiple

---

17. See Thongchai, *Siam Mapped*, ch. 3.

18. See David P. Chandler, *A History of Cambodia*, Boulder: Westview Press, 1983; and R. Bonney, *Kedah 1771-1821: the Search for Security and Independence*, London: Oxford University Press, 1971.

submissions would balance the power of the interested overlords, who might impose their 'protection' at will. The practice of multiple submissions was recognized even among the overlords who, many times, demanded of a tributary that it submit itself to all of them. The overlords shared supremacy. As a result, a tributary could be regarded by numerous overlords as belonging to their spheres. Territorial sovereignty in this sense was not exclusive. The realm of a tributary state was under the sovereignty of its ruler as well as hierarchically under the sovereignty of his superiors. Our modern notions of independence and exclusive sovereignty did not at all apply.

The areas between Siam and Upper Burma and between Siam and Vietnam were under multiple sovereignty. This situation was well known to the local Lao and Thai people as *muang song fai fa* or *muang sam fai fa* ('a town under two overlords'; 'a town under three overlords'). If we draw up a modern political map of the region as the British and the French tried to do in the nineteenth century, the boundaries of the superior states, Burma, Siam and Vietnam in particular, would be overlapping or blurred.[19] The concepts and practices for peaceful resolution among the overlords and for the survival of the smaller states in the pre-modern polity appeared as time-bombs when they were to be translated into the diplomatic practices of the modern international era.

In modern political geography, a state occupies a piece of the earth's surface determined by demarcated boundaries around it. Any doubts regarding a boundary must be resolved. Otherwise it could lead to serious conflicts between nations. But in a country which is not a tiny island, no one can see its geographical body. First, it is impossible simply because of the size. Second, even from a satellite view, the demarcation lines that go through mountains, jungles, seabeds and deserts are hardly identifiable. What is it then that makes the geo-body of a nation alive in our imagination and makes our discourse about it sensible? The answer: the map. Our conception of the nation with its finely demarcated body comes from nowhere else than the political map. A modern nation-state *must* be imaginable in mapped form; otherwise the geographical discourse of a nation would not work. Unfortunately, under the regime of modern geography, disconnected, disjoined or overlapping boundaries are unthinkable and unacceptable. They must be changed. The boundary of the

---

19. More details in Thongchai, *Siam Mapped*, chs. 4 and 5.

modern kind must replace the indigenous geographical discourse and practices if a nation is to be conceivable in modern geographical terms.

'Boundary Clashes'

Modern geography was a powerful science in the hands of Europeans journeying to the East from the sixteenth century to nineteenth-century colonialism. Geographical inquiries, surveys and map-making were parts of the colonial advance and the main tasks of many diplomatic and exploratory missions. Key colonial officials were map-makers. Map-making was encouraged and rewarded with promotion.[20] Unfortunately, in the case of Siam, map-makers had to rely on oral information from native people who might not be able to tell them where the limits of a country were. Even the native elite might have only a scant knowledge of the margins because such was not their concern.

When the British conquered southern Burma (Tenasserim) in 1826, they urged Siam to demarcate the boundary between the British-held and Siamese territories. For the Siamese court, a boundary demarcation was not a matter of concern. If the British really wanted to know their boundary, the court replied, they could ask the old inhabitants in the area. And that was it. Let the British do the demarcation if they feel the need.[21] Likewise, since the British wanted it, the king of Chiangmai, then a tributary north of Siam, allowed them to demarcate a border all by themselves in 1834, using information from local people.[22] On the other hand, the ruler of Nakhonsithammarat, a Siamese city on the Malay peninsula looking after the Malay states on behalf of Bangkok, was once angry at the British for their repeated requests about the boundary between Siam and Kedah.[23] The British were furious in their turn because Siam appeared to be un-

---

20. It is not difficult to find maps done by Europeans. They normally incorporated maps in their books about Asia, and mostly with a discussion about geography. For a discussion about European-made maps of Siam and Indochina in the nineteenth century see Larry Sternstein, '"Low" Maps of Siam', *Journal of the Siam Society*, vol. 73, part 1+2, Jan+July 1985, pp. 132-156. For European-made maps of Southeast Asia see Robert Fell, *Early Maps of Southeast Asia*, Singapore: Oxford University Press, 1988. For map-making for promotion, see Larry Sternstein's article above and 'Low's Description of the Siamese Empire in 1824', *Journal of the Siam Society*, vol. 78, part 1, 1990, pp. 9-34.

21. *The Burney Papers*, Bangkok: Vajiranana National Library, 1910-1914, vol. 1, pp. 154-155.

22. *Ibid.*, vol. 4, part 1, pp. 221-241.

23. *Ibid.*, vol. 3, part 1, p. 151.

cooperative. Soon they learned that Siam had been annoyed by their repeated requests for boundary demarcation. But neither side quite understood the other's ideas.

Two decades later, the British were still urging that the boundary be demarcated. Siam finally agreed, for unknown reasons. It appears that in the period when their relations were amicable, from 1826 to the early 1840s, Siam was uncooperative. But when relations became strained, the Siamese court suddenly agreed to settle the boundary. The demarcation did not work smoothly, however. In most cases, disagreements were due to the simple fact that there had never been any boundary of the British kind before. In the traditional corridors, Siam now demanded a boundary/ *khetdaen* which would keep both countries apart to prevent any collision. In other areas where trespassing between various realms had been allowed without hindrance, the British practice of border control, posting military guards along the 'lines' and checking travellers, posed a grave concern to Siam.[24]

In one incident in 1846, the British protested that a number of Siamese guards had entered into British territory, erecting a post to claim the area for Siam. They also charged the Siamese court with complicity in this action. The British took the matter seriously, analysing the reasons behind Siam's aggressive move and concluding from their rationality in international politics that Siam no longer feared Burma so they no longer wanted the British to balance Burmese power. But actually, in that case, the Siamese court did not even know what their guards had done. The territorial claim *per se* was not yet a matter of the court's concern. An investigation finally found that the trouble-making guards had not in fact made any claim; they did not even discuss the matter with their boss or among themselves. The alleged boundary mark turned out to be '[a] heap of stones together with a small wooden house for religious purpose on top of them'.[25] It was likely that the guards did travel into British territory. But they did so as part of a customary spying mission, which was never meant to claim any territory. Candidly, the guards argued that they could not look after an area as far away as that since it was three days travel from their houses. Obviously, the British rationality in international politics was misplaced.

---

24. *Ibid.*, vol. 4, part 1, pp. 132, 160-161, 196-199.
25. *Ibid.*, vol. 4, part 1, pp. 188-192.

Battles over the Ambiguous Space

These are examples of what happened when different discourses of boundary confronted each other. But these were also moments when a new kind of boundary was presented and established in the field of signification in which the Siamese also participated. Semiotically speaking, the confrontations made the notions of 'boundary' and 'khetdaen' in Thai ambiguous. On the one hand it referred to the indigenous *khetdaen*. But on the other hand, the modern kind of boundary asserted itself as an alternative meaning of *khetdaen*. Ambiguity and possible shifts of meaning could happen at every moment the terms were translated, either in actual translation from Thai into English and vice versa, or in any communication in which the two notions were put forward in the same semantic field, such as boundary negotiation or map-making. The shifts occurred at various moments in favour of the more powerful discourse. We may say that incidents of the kind just cited, and in any forms of communication about boundary, were loci of modern geography and geo-body in the making.[26]

The multiple sovereignty of a tributary state and the overlapping margins were equally ambiguous to the modern-minded Europeans. They caused several misunderstandings and conflicts between Europeans and native people, and even among Europeans themselves, who could argue for different policies based on different interpretations. For example, the question of whether Kedah, Perak and a few other Malay states were independent or not had caused complication of relations between the Siamese, the British and the Malay rulers in the first half of the nineteenth century. The British authorities at Penang, Singapore and in Calcutta were split into two factions because of conflicting interpretations and, thereby, policies.[27] One considered the Malay states independent; the other regarded them as under Siamese sovereignty. As discussed above, neither or both were correct.[28] The ambiguity caused by multiple sovereignty and overlapping frontiers became explosive when Siam and France contested the eastern bank of the Mekong in the late nineteenth century.

---

26. For more discussion about the displacement of the notion of boundary, see Thongchai, *Siam Mapped*, ch. 3. In ch. 2 of the book I discuss specifically the model of this politico-semiological displacement by taking the confrontation between Western astronomy and the indigenous astrology in Siam in the nineteenth century as the case.

27. Lennox A. Mills, *British Malaya 1824-1867*, London: Oxford University Press, 1966, pp. 30-39, 140-147, 150-153, 156-158, 167-172.

28. See Thongchai, *Siam Mapped*, pp. 87-92 for an interpretation of this ambiguity and its consequences, especially the role of tribute missions and gift exchange in defining the status of kings in hierarchical relations.

The ruling circle of Siam at the time – King Chulalongkorn and his brothers – were the first generation to have modern education and Western knowledge. Therefore, not only the French in Cochinchina but also their Siamese counterparts knew that their countries had never had a demarcated boundary. By that time, however, the Siamese rulers also desired to acquire modern civilization, meaning the Western one. They wanted to have their country bounded and mapped. By translating their traditional overlord perspective into modern geography, moreover, they established a wish to extend the territory of Siam to all of their traditional tributary states including the eastern bank of the Mekong, whose multiple submission had long been recognized by the Siamese.

Take Luang Prabang, a centre of the Lao kingdom, as example. In a private letter from the Thai king to a Thai advisor at the Luang Prabang court in 1888, the king realized that this major tributary submitted to more than one overlord. But he was afraid that the French might tempt the Laotian court to depart from Siamese protection. His instruction, therefore, specified in detail how to please the Lao rulers and make them suspicious of the French. Here is his self-conscious project:

> [We/Siam] must try to please them [Lao/Luang Prabang] describing the fact that Thai and Lao belong to the same soil ... France is merely the other, who looks down upon the Lao race as savages. Whatever the French do to please the ruler of Luang Prabang is merely a bait on the hook ... Although the Lao habitually regard Lao as 'we' and Thai as 'they' in cases where only the two peoples are considered, if they compare the Thai and the French, however, they may regard the Thai as 'we' and the French as 'they', naturally.[29]

Similar objectives were put forward in relation to other tiny chiefdoms closer to Vietnam. Siam realized the strong influence of Vietnam over those chiefdoms and the absence of Siam's. But the Siamese elite also realized that there was an opportunity to take over those towns because the French were busy putting down resistance in the newly colonized Annam and Tonkin.

To resolve the ambiguity of sovereignty in the area once and for all, the Siamese rulers used both military force and mapping, the same methods employed by the Europeans. The opportunity came in the 1880s when Chinese bandits, believed to have fled from the Taiping rebellion, increased their activities in what is today northern and central Laos. In a campaign

---

29. From Chiraporn Sathapanawattana, *Wikrittakan R.S.112 [The 1893 Crisis]*, Bangkok: Srinakharinwirot University (Prasanmit), 1980, pp. 411-412. The translation and emphases are mine.

allegedly to suppress these bandits from 1885 onwards, Siam took the opportunity to march through the entire ambiguous-but-desirable territory and made it part of the Siamese territory, unambiguously, for the first time. Politically this was done by establishing new local regimes under the supervision or direct control of Thai officials, instead of allowing local rulers to resume their rule after the conquest. Siam for the first time did not let the former tributaries be autonomous. Submission meant integration. Loyalist rulers were appointed with odd titles whose meanings had never appeared anywhere before, such as *Phra Sawamiphaksayamkhet* (Sir Loyalty-to-the-Siamese-Realm), *Phra Phithak-anakhet* (Sir Protector-of-the-Boundary), *Phraya Khumphon Phithakburanakhet* (Lord Commander-Protecting-the-Territorial-Integrity), *Phraya Khanthasema* (Lord Limit-of-the-Realm), *Phra Ratana-anakhet* (Sir Beautiful-Boundary).[30]

Map and Might

All the troops in the campaign were assigned with an important task – mapping. Every troop unit was ordered to provide protection and to facilitate the surveyors and mapping officials, most of whom were Europeans and headed by a British surveyor named James F. McCarthy.[31] Mapping officials urgently surveyed and made triangulations, trying to cover the areas claimed by Siam as fast as possible. McCarthy was himself actively involved in planning the military operations since the conquest became closely connected with his surveying task. His knowledge of the area was very useful for the military. He made several military recommendations, including the crucial one to take two specific Phuan towns in Laos in order to fulfil the desire to have Siam controlling as far as the Annamese cordillera.[32] These two towns later became the foci of military confrontation between Siam and France in 1892-93.

---

30. Chaophraya Surasakmontri, *Prawatkan chomphon chaophraya surasakmontri* [Autobiography of General Chaophraya Surasakmontri], Bangkok: Khurusapha, vol. 2, 1961, pp. 264, 389, and vol. 3, pp. 202-203, 263, 290, for example.

31. See the description of his own work in James F. McCarthy, *Surveying and Exploring in Siam*, London: Royal Geographic Society, 1900, also reprinted by White Lotus, Bangkok, 1994.

32. See Kennon Breazeale, *A Culture in Search for Survival: The Phuan of Thailand and Laos*, Monograph Series, no. 31, Yale University Southeast Asia Studies, New Haven: Yale Center for International and Area Studies, 1988, pp. 73-74, 89-92, 95-98, 116.

The relation between map and military force was remarkable. The desire of the force was to make the territory exclusive and map it. In actual practice, the operation of the force was planned and guided by the preliminary maps of particular areas anticipated or desired to be Siam's. Sometimes, mapping advanced one step ahead of the troops. Then the military followed, making the mapping proposal of the areas come true. In a sense, mapping spearheaded the conquest. Nevertheless, the sphere of Siam's influence had never been defined and in fact it was overlapping with the one of the Hue court, from 1885 under the French. A proposed exclusive margin and boundary therefore was a speculation. The survey and mapping were done alongside the military advance because only the latter could provide the authority under which mapping could be executed. In a sense, map anticipated the space; force executed it; map again vindicated it. Siam's exclusive margins were inscribed both on the earth's surface and on paper. Enthusiastically, McCarthy once wrote to the king that he should locate the boundary and map it. 'We, then, can know the land where we live', he wrote.[33] Mapping which had annoyed and frightened the Siamese court about half a century earlier, and by that time still frightened many local people, became an indispensable technology to decide and establish the geo-body of Siam.

On Siam's eastern borders, France had also begun mapping, as means of expansion. Preoccupied with the administration of the newly acquired Vietnam, the French started their alleged campaigns against the Chinese bandits two years later than Siam. As a great power at the time, ironically, they found the eastern bank of the Mekong just conquered by Siam. The French put forward their claims against Siam's. The French claims were all based on surveys and maps which had been underway around the same time as the Siamese one, i.e. before the appearance of French forces in the area.[34]

The Siamese had predicted the situation and instructed their troops to avoid any confrontation with the French, let alone fighting for any disputed territories. The confrontation at Thaeng (Dien Bien Phu) in 1888 is a splendid example of how a new kind of boundary was settled. In that incident, the Siamese and the French forces 'suppressed the bandits' along

33. Surasakmontri, [Autobiography], vol. 2, p. 372.

34. The chief surveyor for the French who later became a consul and a well known colonialist in Indochina was Auguste Pavie. See the description of his works in Auguste Pavie, *Mission Pavie Indo-Chine 1879-1895, geographie et voyages,* 7 vols., Paris: E. Leroux, 1900-1919.

their way until they confronted each other at Thaeng. At first, the commanders of both sides argued for their exclusive right for the town and ordered each other to pull out. They also proposed that their mapping officials should be allowed to move on to survey the territories occupied by the other. Perhaps they were aware that their claims were equally legitimate and their maps similarly poor. Finally they agreed to observe the status quo. That is, neither of them would move forward; but would let the conquered areas belong to the conquerors until negotiations in Bangkok could decide the matter. Although still without a boundary line, the sovereignty of the two countries now interfaced, as modern geography wanted, without a corridor or an overlapping margin.

The Franco-Siamese conflict between 1885 and 1893 was a military, political, and geographical one. What was at stake was not only the conquests and defeats, expansion and retreats of territory. But the confrontation and displacement of different kinds of geographical discourses were getting under way. However, in this struggle, the French and the Siamese were on the same side, that is, they were both agencies of modern geography. The true losers were those tributaries who might not realize until much later that a new kind of political space and territorial management had been established. Their customary strategy for survival, based on the concepts of hierarchical realms, no longer worked because such a strategic practice actually was the cause of the kind of ambiguities that led to conflict between modern states. To put it another way, the true loser was the traditional notion of territory, and modern geography was the true conqueror. No matter who won or lost in the military contest, the regime of modern geography and mapping prevailed.

But not all confrontations could be settled like the one at Thaeng. Actually most could not. The culmination of the crisis between Siam and France in 1893, when the French blockaded the Chao Phraya river with two gunboats ready to shell the Grand Palace in Bangkok, was in fact another strategic move resulting from plenty of minor confrontations along the contested areas, some of which caused deaths and casualties. The crisis ended by Siam's handing over most of the eastern bank of the Mekong to the French. In conventional Thai historiography, this crisis is known as the loss of Siamese territory to France. But I would say it was a contest of two conquering map-makers. The contest was anticipated and made possible by modern geography. The territory of Siam did not shrink but actually expanded, since it integrated huge areas of former tributaries whose realms had been more or less autonomous.

The Emergence of the Geo-Body

Alongside the conquest and later the defeat in the contest for the left bank of
the Mekong, Siam introduced a new administrative system to integrate all
those former tributaries which then became Siam's outlying provinces. The
basic aim was to bring them under the direct control of the Bangkok
government, thus establishing a new kind of territorial integrity. The new
system based on territorial divisions was in fact named Monthon Thesa-
phiban, meaning the protection of space.[35] It became a new mechanism to
establish a new kind of sovereignty according to the new geographical
vision of how Siam should be.

The new geographical desire was behind all the military expansionism,
the administrative integration, and of course the mapping operations, from
the very beginning to the final stages. It was a new discourse, a new
language of space by which the kingdom of Siam would be conceived and
represented. It became a mental frame for thinking and talking about the
country geographically. But since the reality did not yet exist, the new
geography provided the conceptual model of the geo-body of Siam.
Modern geography and maps anticipated it. They created Siam. Drafts and
sketches of the map of Siam were drawn before any survey finished, so the
troops could have a desirable realm in mind and could use it to argue
against the French who also had their version of the Siamese territory.
Modern geographical discourse of mapping turned both the Europeans and
the Siamese who submitted to its regime into its agency to establish all the
requisites such as the modern kind of boundary, the unambiguous and
exclusive sovereignty over a particular territory, and all the necessary
practices for the reproduction of knowledge. In order to realize the desire to
have the country mapped, the ambiguities necessary for the pre-modern
hierarchical polity now faced extinction. Many had died for the establishment of the mapped space. The true losers of territories were those former
tributary states, which were conquered and distributed among the regional
powers.

The new administrative system, and the operations of force and
mapping were methods of the concretization of the geo-body of 'We-Self'
for Siam. The so-called loss of Siamese territory was the other side of this
arrangement of the earth's surface by political geography. It was how the

---

35.   Tej Bunnag, *Provincial Administration of Siam 1892-1915*, Kuala Lumpur: Oxford
University Press, 1977.

adjacent domain of *They-Other* of Siam was marked. It set the limit of *We-Self*, where *We-Self* ended and *They-Other* began. All of them were different aspects of the same process of displacement by the modern geographical discourse of mapping, that is, the formation of the geo-body of Siam. Siam was the materialized effect of the new knowledge which anticipated and concretized it both on paper and on the earth's surface. The geo-body came into being not so much through the imagination or the act of 'thinking-out' as by the concrete confrontations and shifts of the discourse of how the political community called Siam should be delimited. The shifts took place materially in those innumerable moments when the ambiguities led to the displacement of meanings. The ambiguities and shifts left various traces: humorous and serious misunderstandings, miscommunication, mistranslations, protests, diplomatic contests and violent conflicts.

From then on, the map of Siam and the discourse of the geo-body of Siam became powerful representations of nationhood. They provided a new, modernist way of knowing and speaking of Siam. The holy kingdom of the Siamese kingship, which used to be manifest as a cosmographic or religious space, now became the mapped Siam. An enormous number of concepts, practices and behaviours relating to its geo-body followed. The violation of sovereignty, for example, has since then included any infringement on an inch of its territory, something which would have been considered insignificant or easily given away in the pre-mapped polity. Lives can become statistic numbers since those inches are worth sacrifice. A nation's territory is not a profane or fully secular space. In the transformation, some values attached to the traditional discourse of kingdom were transferred to the geo-body and the map of Siam, making them become more than the profane earth's surface: hence people's loyalty and attachment to the nation's geo-body. The sanctity of the royal kingdom as the extension of the royal body, the sacredness of the soil and the earth in indigenous beliefs, and its significance in the cosmographic sense, were bestowed upon such a profane scientific entity as a map.

On the other hand, the geo-body and the map of Siam have generated several symbols, meanings and values adding to the discourse on nationhood. The notion of Thainess, for example, can be understood spatially or in the mapping form. For years, communists were believed to be non-Thai or outsiders since Thai born in Thailand were assumed to have a religion and to be loyal to the monarchy. The anti-communist propaganda habitually depicted communism as a threat from the outside (see Figure 3). One of the government's major anti-communist forces was the border patrol police. Thai communists were believed to have been deceived by outsiders. Such a spatial notion of communism collapsed when the conflict became visibly domestic and thousands of students, many from affluent families, joined the communist struggle. In the same example, nonetheless, maps and the geo-body may have limitations in representing nationhood. The border patrol police usually operated well inside the Thai territory since it guarded against the enemy of Thainess, the communists, who happened to operate everywhere, including a university near the Grand Palace in Bangkok. The border patrol police was a major force called in to suppress the students gathering in that campus in October 1976. In this case, the domain of Thainess was abstract. It was not in actual fact coterminous with the geo-body. But the illusion was somehow maintained, partly by keeping the name border patrol police.[36]

Perhaps it is most important that, through semiological conjunctures, the geo-body, the map and another constitutive element of nationhood – history – have become the discursive foundation, temporally and spatially, of nationalism. That is the last subject of this essay.

The Geo-Body and History[37]

The Siamese nationhood emerged as a new entity, departing from all previous forms of imagined community. Its history, thus, does not date back to the times of the ancient kingdoms. Rather, it was formed and invented by the politico-semiological operations of modern geography and maps just over a hundred years ago. Of course, the conventional Thai history tells us otherwise. In it, the emergence of the Siamese geo-body was camouflaged by the historiography of the Franco-Siamese conflict, of the loss of territory, and of the reform of the provincial administration. As I have argued, all of them were parts of the making of the geo-body itself. In the conventional history, however, Siam had been a powerful but peaceful country in the region since its first kingdom at Sukhothai in the thirteenth century. Despite its fall to aggressive neighbours a few times, Siam was

---

36. These issues cannot be dealt with adequately here. Please see Thongchai, *Siam Mapped*, chs. 1, 7 and conclusion.

37. The argument under this section is from *Ibid.*, ch. 8.

always able to restore its independence and move forward to civilization and prosperity. Evidence of its success was its vast empire up to the nineteenth century, with the realm covering most of Laos and Cambodia today, parts of today's Burma, Yunnan and the northern Malay states. Under the threats of the British and especially the French colonial powers in the late nineteenth century, Siam painfully ceded about one-third of its former territory in order to save its independence and its heartlands which became Thailand today. Apparently in this historiography, the historic moment I have described in this essay was merely the latest one in a series of struggles for national independence and glory. It was anything but the emergence of the geo-body and nationhood.

The narrative of the conventional history is different from my account because it is based on three strategic assumptions. First, it assumes that the geo-body and the Thai nationhood were primeval. Thai history is the story of the ups and downs of the Thai territorial nation, amidst threats from powerful outsiders, namely China, Burma and the Europeans. Therefore the entire history can be highlighted and captured in a well-known historical atlas which basically tells a story of the changing size of the Siamese realm.[38]

Second, it assumes the context of modern international relations. Not only was the hierarchical relation between the overlords and the tributaries eliminated, but Siam in the nineteenth century also appeared as the victim of European colonialism, rather than a regional power in contest with the French, as suggested in my story. Seen in this context, metaphorically speaking, 'France adopted the ploys of the Wolf who, first, picks a quarrel with the Lamb, then jumps over and executes it.'[39] Siam becomes the Lamb rather than the Smaller Wolf, the losing contestant in the context of regional expansionism. It is clear that the French and Siam's relative positions and relationship could be seen quite differently in the two political contexts.

---

38. The famous atlas is in Thongbai Taengnoi, *Phaenthi phumisat prayok matthayomsuksa tonton lae tonplai* [Geographical atlas for junior and senior high schools], Bangkok: Thai-wattanaphanit, which was reprinted more than twenty times between 1963 and 1986, pp. 26-39. I discuss this atlas extensively in *Siam Mapped*, pp. 150-156 and figures 13-19.

39. This analogy was made by an influential Thai historian, Khachon Sukhabanij, see his collection *Khomun prawattisat samai bangkok* [Historical accounts of the Bangkok period], Bangkok: Srinakharinwirot University (Prasanmit), 1981, p. 244. It has been the standard view of the studies of the Franco-Siamese conflict. See, for example, David Wyatt, *Thailand: A Short History*, New Haven: Yale University Press, 1984, pp. 201-208.

Third, the conventional narrative always assumes Bangkok's point of view. This perspective is politically correct and acceptable only in the context set by the second assumption. One of the consequences of this assumption is the sanitization of the voices of the ultimate victims, those former tributaries and the indigenous political geography. In the Bangkok perspective, the annexation of former tributaries became the 'reform of provincial administration' over its outlying provinces; the expansion became the 'defence' of its territorial integrity; the resistance by some tributaries became the 'internal' conflict, as opposed to the European 'outsider' threat; and the successful 'reform' became an emancipation of those tributaries from slavery and semi-vassalage to begin self-government.[40] Indeed, if we merely change the point of view, the story of the administrative reform could be read very much like a history of colonization.

Consequently, the agony of losing the contest, losing the royal dignity, and the inability to transform the entire imperial desire into the mapped country, has been (mis)represented as the agony of losing Siamese territory, the victimization of Siam, and yet the glorious success of Siamese diplomacy to preserve the heartland and independence of the country. The three strategic assumptions above are crucial to reproduce and sustain such a representation. This is an irony since all of them – the primeval geo-body, the modern international context, and Bangkok's perspective – are products of the new political geographic discourse, and can exist only in relation to the mapped nation in one way or another. Yet they help to deny the history of the emergence of the geo-body in such a historic, though painful, moment. Indeed, only by (mis)representing the origin of the geo-body in the nineteenth century in such a way that the moment was merely another struggle to defend the independence of the nation, could the Thai past be cherished as a success.

Furthermore, the pain aggravated by the emergence of the geo-body may have shaped the entire history of Siam. Around the same time as the emergence of the geo-body, the new kind of Siamese history was formulated. As it turned out, the theme and the master plot of the new Thai history appeared very similar to the ones of the misunderstood history of the crisis in the 1890s. The usual narrative of Thai history is the story of the

---

40. This perspective, which has been the standard view of the studies of the so-called reform of administration in 1890s Siam, and the Bangkok-centric discourse is best represented by Tej Bunnag, *Provincial Administration of Siam, 1892-1915*, Kuala Lumpur: Oxford University Press, 1977. See especially the final paragraph of the book. This is discussed in Thongchai, *Siam Mapped*, pp. 144-148, 159.

struggles of a small but glorious, peaceful and courageous nation, against threats, subjugation and suffering, in order to establish itself firmly on that corner of the earth's surface which clearly belongs to it. This was definitely not the pre-nationalist past. Precisely speaking, the crisis of the late nineteenth century became an episode of the repetitive motif in the narrative of the nation. The question is whether the grand narrative of the nation's history helped to make the crisis conceivable in certain ways; or the ways the crisis was then comprehended by the Siamese elite had in effect shaped up the meanings of Thai history in the making, hence its themes, and plots.

The Siamese elite's agony in the crisis was indescribable. For several months after the crisis, the king himself was demoralized and lost interest in the country's affairs. He was sick and almost died, though eventually re-gaining his strength physically and politically. The crisis certainly left a scar in the elite's life and thinking. I would argue that the Bangkok elite extended their perspective, sentiment, and memory of the crisis retrospectively to other historical times. Unsurprisingly, they found the repetitive motif that eventually constituted the grand narrative of the Thai past. The emergence of the Siamese geo-body and the agony of its birth also became the defining moment of the new historical narrative of the nation Siam.

Final Remarks

Throughout this essay, it may seem that modern geography, maps and the geo-body are the only or the most significant elements that define nationhood. Why must there be such a single element that defines the totality of nationhood? Without the illusion of the singular, most significant identity, the essence, or the study of totality, the attempt here is just to make sure that geography, body and form are not underestimated or downgraded in favour of the customary stocks of historical study of nationalism, such as language, race, religion, class, political economy, and so on. We usually look beneath the surface to find the abstract essence of everything including national identity. But what we should be equally interested in is its surface, its form, its superficial and explicit constitution. For nationhood, the geo-body is indispensable. It is the conditionality that dictates any invented essence. Furthermore, as we have seen, its genealogy was not necessarily political or economic. This essay may exaggerate by focusing sternly on it while sanitizing any distraction such as economic or diplomatic history, and ethnicity. It by no means denies other elements.

It is quite common to discuss whether the proposition made in one study is applicable to other cases. Here one may doubt if the proposition of this essay, that maps created the geo-body of Siam in the nineteenth century, is applicable to other nations or true only for Siam which, according to a widely held belief, was unique due to its independence throughout the colonial period.[41] Just how credible is the proposition, even to Siam, since I have consciously disregarded some essential elements of the Siamese nation-hood such as the institution of the monarchy? Generally speaking, the proposition of this essay should be applicable to many cases of confrontation between European and other geographical outlooks in Asia, Africa and America. More specifically, my proposition may be difficult to accept even for students of Siam. That is because one has tended to exaggerate the degree of continuation from the pre-modern Siamese monarchy to the modern state of Thailand.

Most importantly, as I suggested initially, the main subjects of this study – geography, map, boundary, form and body – are the direct, literal application of the spatial perspective to study the formation or definition of nationhood. The ideas and methodology here should also be taken metaphorically in studying other constitutive elements of a nation. No matter what we think national identity essentially is, it is merely a discursive demarcation and construction of a domain whose distinctiveness is defined by certain discursive boundaries. In other words, not only the geo-body but everything else as well is 'mapped'.

The intellectual domain known as national history, for example, was also mapped. It is a domain of knowledge, a discursive field, whose establishment involved a differentiation from myth, fiction and other kinds of knowledge of the past. Its narrative, plots, subjects and other story elements, have filled up the anticipated temporal coordinates of the nation's life-story. The Thai past has been shaped by a new kind of historical knowledge which negotiated its place between the Western concept of history and the indigenous traditions of chronicles, folk-tales and religious stories. Ethnicity was discursively mapped too. The ideas of who are Thai and who are not, or who are the modern, civilized Thai and who are the primordial, authentic Thai, have been defined from time to time by certain ethnographic ideologies. In the late nineteenth and the beginning of the

---

41. See Prasenjit Duara's feature review of Thongchai, *Siam Mapped*, in *American Historical Review*, vol. 100, no. 2, 1995, pp. 477-479.

twentieth century, the spatio-ecology became a measure to categorize people: the wild or forest people, the villagers, the civilized city-dwellers, and the Westerners. Of course, each indicated its place in the temporal, progressive scale of civilization.[42]

National identity has as its basis the binary opposition of We-Self and Others. It does not represent an intrinsically national quality. Any constitutive element of nationhood is merely a discursive field whose meanings may change, hence shifting its limits and altering the national identity. A late-coming nation-state like Siam usually realized its nationhood through the creative transculturation between the West and the indigenous. The confrontation and tension between the changing Western influence and the transforming indigenous culture never end. Consequently, national identity is always unfixed, contradictory and ambiguous. The modern Siamese nation emerged and has survived through this tension, not by anti-colonial heroism as conventional history usually suggests. Let us celebrate the history of this creative confrontation.

---

42. I hope to clarify the ideas on how history and ethnicity were also mapped, spatially speaking, elsewhere. For ethnicity, see Thongchai Winichakul, 'The Other Within: Travel, Proto-ethnography, and Spatial Differentiation of People in Siam in the Late Nineteenth Century', to be published in Andrew Turton (ed.), *Civility and Savagery: the Differentiation of Peoples within the Tai Speaking Polities of Southeast Asia*, Oxford: Oxford University Press, forthcoming.

Figure 2: Vietnam in the grip of Japanese imperialism – caricature from Ho Chi Minh's newspaper, *Viet Nam Doc Lap*, 1 November 1941.

Two contrasting views of *They-Other*.

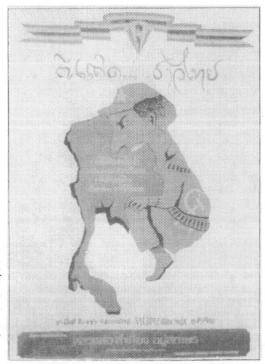

Figure 3: 'Wake up, Thai people' – caricature of the map-of-Vietnam devouring the map-of-Thailand, probably from the late 1970s (courtesy Conrad Taylor).

CHAPTER FOUR

Annam and Vietnam in the New Indochinese Space, 1887–1945

Christopher E. Goscha

Why could Javanese patriots declare an independent Republic of all of Indonesia in 1945, whereas their Vietnamese counterparts settled for just Vietnam?[1] The Vietnamese and Javanese had formed the cornerstones in the French and Dutch colonial projects, but in 1945 only the space created by the Dutch served as a valid framework for the emergence of an independent nation. Rather than seeing an Indochinese Republic on the map today, we have grown accustomed to the thin, S-like Vietnam. Its reality seems self-evident and 'natural', whereas the idea of an Indochinese nation seems somehow artificial and unreal.

Yet we often forget that the name 'Vietnam' was not as widely used by the Vietnamese prior to September 1945 as one may think today. In the years leading up to the August Revolution, some nationalists still wanted to see 'Dai-Nam' or 'Dai-Viet' resurrected, while others countered with 'An-Nam' or 'Indo-China'. This latter appellation gave away that even the spatial limits of this emerging nation were unclear. The Javanese were not the only ones tempted by the geographical patterns of the colonial model; Vietnamese nationalists of almost all political colours had been having Indochinese visions since the early 1920s. As a former cabinet minister in the short-lived Tran Trong Kim government of mid-1945 conceded decades

---

1. Benedict Anderson first posed this question in his *Imagined Communities*, London: Verso, 1991, pp. 120–133. David E.F. Henley takes it further in his 'Ethnographic Integration and Exclusion in Anticolonial Nationalism: Indonesia and Indochina', *Comparative Studies in Society and History*, vol. 37, no. 2, April 1995, pp. 286–324.

later: 'Had the French created Indochina twenty years earlier, we might
have declared an Indochinese government in 1945.'[2]

Only recently have the historians Vu Ngu Chieu and Stein Tønnesson
brought our attention to the semantic competition between the terms
'Vietnam', 'Annam' and 'Indochina' in their studies of the events leading up
to the August Revolution.[3] In this essay, I want to push these investigations
a little further by adding the idea of space, as Tessa Morris-Suzuki and
Thongchai Winichakul have done in the respective cases of Japan and Siam,
and by examining some of the questions raised by Benedict Anderson and
David Henley concerning the idea of Indochina. Rather than assuming the
Vietnam we see on the map today, I want to go back in time and space to
understand how French colonial policies interacted with and transformed
traditional Vietnamese notions of the geo-political landscape.[4] I shall thus
begin by reviewing briefly the Vietnam that existed on the eve of European
colonization. I will then concentrate on the period between the creation of the
Indochinese Union in October 1887 and the formation of the Democratic
Republic of Vietnam in September 1945.

From my sources emerges a central reflection on the contradiction
confronting nationalists caught between an ethnocultural identification with a
geo-political space known today as 'Vietnam' and an unprecedented, French
Indochinese realm which tempted them to think in wider geographical
terms. Whether communist or non-communist, all the nationalists under
study here agreed on the reality of a national 'body' (*un seul corps*) – to
borrow one famous patriot's precise term[5] – but they had more trouble
defining its geographical limits. Was it Vietnamese or Indochinese, or
something else? This question would trap many a patriot – not least the
conservative nationalist, Pham Quynh, and his communist counterpart, Ho
Chi Minh. Most studies of Vietnamese nationalism stress the uniqueness of

---

2. 'Bao Cao Nhan Dan Dai Viet, *Dong Phat*, no. 5966, 16 March 1945, p. 1 and Interview
with Hoang Xuan Han, 1 August 1993, Paris.

3. Stein Tønnesson, *The Vietnamese Revolution of 1945*, London: Sage Publications, 1991,
pp. 376–377, 393–94 and Vu Ngu Chieu, 'The Other Side of the 1945 Vietnamese Revolution between 1940 and 1946', PhD Thesis, University of Wisconsin-Madison, 1985, as
cited by Tønnesson, p. 289.

4. NIAS has published an extended version of this chapter, entitled *Vietnam or Indochina?
Contesting Concepts of Space in Vietnamese Nationalism, 1887–1954*, Copenhagen: NIAS
Report no. 28, 1995.

5. Nguyen Tinh [Nguyen An Ninh], 'Vers la Nation Indochinoise', *La Cloche Fêlée*, no.
14, 21 April 1924, p. 1.

Vietnamese identity, taking for granted both the space and its name. I want to get at the idea of 'Vietnam' by exploring the failure of contesting spatial and semantic concepts, notably 'Annam' and 'Indochina'.

Present convention holds that 'Vietnam' is preferable to 'Annam', since 'Annam' is considered pejorative. I accept this, for there is no doubt that the third syllable of the French word 'An-na-*mite*' could sting painfully in colonial encounters of a certain kind, just as the two Chinese characters, 'An-Nam' (Pacified South), could convey a humiliating sense of submission. The problem, however, is that prior to 1945 many Vietnamese nationalists actually used, and sometimes even preferred, the word 'Annam' and 'Annamese'. I am thinking of the famous poet and editor of the *Annamese Review*, Tan Da; the president of the fiercely anticolonial Vietnamese Nationalist Party (Viet Nam Quoc Dan Dang), Nguyen Khac Nhu; as well as Ho Chi Minh and Nguyen An Ninh.[6] These four patriots were obviously not French 'collaborators'; so it seems that the word 'Annam' did not always have pejorative connotations.

Thus, instead of discarding this term, it may be more useful to hold on to it momentarily as a way of locating breaks in the nationalist discourse, behind which competing ideas, such as 'Viet-Nam' and 'Indo-China', started contesting Annam's hegemony. This will allow me to understand why, especially when writing in *quoc ngu* (romanized script), the nationalists jumped suddenly from 'Annam' to 'Dai Viet', 'Nam Viet', 'Nha Nam', 'Nuoc Nam', 'Dong-Duong' (Indochina) and especially 'Viet-Nam', and then slid back to 'Annam' as if nothing had happened. I shall switch to the word 'Vietnam' in my text for the period from 1925, when this coupling – sometimes but not always used by the generation of the pioneering nationalist Phan Boi Chau (1867–1940) – began gaining pride of place in the minds of an expanding nationalist elite. But let us first return briefly to the pre-colonial period.

Contesting Patterns of Space

On the eve of French conquest, the linguistically homogeneous Viet inhabited the lowlands of the eastern part of the Indochinese peninsula from

---

6. Nguyen Khac Hieu [Tan Da], 'Kinh ngo cung Doc-gia chu vi', *An-Nam Tap Chi*, no. 14, July 1930, pp. 1–3; Nguyen Khac Nhu, 'Du Luan', *An-Nam Tap Chi*, no. 10, 1 March 1927, pp. 10–13; Nguyen Ai Quoc, *Le Procès de la colonisation française*, Paris, 1924; and Nguyen An Ninh, *Cao Vong cua Bon thanh Niên An-nam, Dan Uoc*, Saigon: Xua nay, 1926.

the Red River Delta to the Mekong Basin.[7] The term 'Viet Nam' (Yüeh Nan in Chinese) only appeared in an official sense in the early nineteenth century. Having unified territories running down the eastern coast of the Indochinese peninsula, the founder of the new Nguyen dynasty, Gia Long, sent a delegation to Beijing to gain recognition of his newly formed empire. Normally, the Chinese sovereign would have bestowed the official seal of 'An Nam Quoc Vuong' (King of the Pacified South) on his southern neighbour as a symbol of the tributary relationship that underpinned their relations. Gia Long broke with this tradition when he chose to refer to his empire as 'Nan-Yüeh' – pronounced by the Viet as 'Nam-Viet' (Southern Viet/Yüeh). Worried that the use of this term belied expansionist designs on Beijing's southern flank, the Chinese emperor reversed the word order to form the term 'Viet-Nam'. When Gia Long accepted this, the Chinese emperor changed the seal to read 'Viet Nam Quoc Vuong' (King of the Southern Viet Country), but continued to refer to his empire as 'An-Nam'. The Viet court was not satisfied with the new name either, and official usage of 'Viet-Nam' did not last long. In 1813, the court revived briefly the old term 'Dai Viet' (Greater Viet) and, in 1838, Minh Mang replaced the word 'Viet' with 'Nam' to refer to his rapidly growing southern empire as 'Dai Nam' (The Imperial State of the South). No one informed Peking, but Nguyen rulers used 'Dai Nam' until June 1945.

Not the French. They shared the Chinese preference for the word 'Annam', using it officially for the first time in the Treaty of Saigon in 1862, which turned the southern section of what they referred to as the Empire of Annam into a French colony, 'Cochinchine' (Cochinchina). Two decades later, the French divided the central and northern parts of the Empire into two protectorates: 'Annam' referred to the central part, while 'Tonkin' was the French phonetic reproduction of the Sino-Viet word 'Dong Kinh,' meaning eastern capital.[8] To refer collectively to all three spaces, the French borrowed the term 'Annam' from the expression 'Ancien Empire d'Annam'. Thus 'Annam' could mean either the central protectorate or the whole of the three eastern possessions. To the west, the French expanded their Indochinese colonial domain with a protectorate over Cambodia (1863) and a less clear one over Laos by the turn of the century. Together

---

7. For the sake of clarity, I shall use the terms 'Lao', 'Khmer' and 'Viet' when referring to ethnic groups, while I shall employ the terms 'Laotian', 'Cambodian' and 'Annamese/ Vietnamese' when speaking of nations.

8. V.A. Malte-Brun, *Géographie universelle Asie et Afrique*, Paris, 1874, p. 200 and J.M.J., *Dictionnaire annamite-français*, Tan Dinh: Imprimerie de la Mission, 1877, p. 263.

these five new units – Tonkin, Annam, Cochinchina, Cambodia and Laos – constituted the pentagonal structure of 'Indo-Chine Française'.[9] Usage of 'Dai Nam' or 'Viet-Nam' ceased.

New French delimitations required new indigenous formulations. Annamese geographers borrowed the term 'ky' from Minh Mang's 1833 administrative reforms to describe the French idea of a 'specific region, confine or geographical domain.' 'Cochinchina' thus became 'Nam [south] ky' in Annamese; 'Annam', 'Trung [central] ky', and 'Tonkin', 'Bac [north] ky'. Annamese continued to call Cambodia by its Sino-Viet radical: 'Cao-men', 'Cao-man', or 'Cao-mien', while they wrote Laos as 'Ai-Lao', 'Ai-Leo', or 'Leo'.[10] In French, each of these five constituents formed a 'pays' (a land), translated into Viet as 'xu'.

The term 'Indo-China' was not what it may seem today. English missionaries and linguists had first used this hyphenated coupling as early as 1811 to refer rather loosely to the Asia beyond India. The French geographer of Danish birth, K. Malte-Brun, joined in a decade later, transforming it into French as 'Indo-Chine' in order to pinpoint the space falling between the Bay of Bengal and the South China Sea and between the Malaccas and southern China.[11] The Viet word for Indochina, 'Dong-Duong', appears rarely in dictionaries published before the twentieth century. One renowned French-Annamese dictionary published in 1898 did not even list it, while another translated 'Dong-Duong' first as 'les mers orientales' and only secondly as 'Indo-Chine française'. This term can even

9. Yet the geographical term,'Indo-Chine' must not be confused with the political 'Indo-Chine française'. Malte-Brun wrote in 1874 that politically 'Indo-Chine' constituted seven distinct 'states': 1 l'Indo-Chine anglaise, 2 la Birmanie, 3 le Royaume de Siam, 4 l'Empire d'An-nam, 5 la Cochinchine française, 6 le Royaume du Cambodge, 7 les Etats indépendants de la Presqu'île de Malacca. V. Malte-Brun, *Géographie*, p. 192. However, when I use 'Indochina' in my text, I will be referring to 'Indochine française'. For reasons of clarity, I will not show the hyphen in 'Indo-China' or 'Viet-Nam' from this point.

10. Jean Bonet, *Dictionnaire annamite-français,* Paris: Imprimerie Nationale, 1898, Volume II, pp. 11, 197, 320, 411; F.M. Savina, *Dictionnaire tày-annamite-français,* Paris, 1910, p. 174; J.M.J. *Dictionnaire annamite-français,* p. 82; Dao Duy Anh, *Phap Viet Tu Dien,* Paris: Minh Tan, 1936, pp. 68, 205, 923.

11. *The Indo-Chinese Gleaner containing miscellaneous communications on the Literature, History, Philosophy, Mythology, [etc.] of the INDO-CHINESE NATIONS,* vol. I, Malacca: Anglo-Chinese Press, 1818–1821; John Leyden, *Comparative Vocabulary of the Barma, Maláyu and T'hái languages,* Serampore: Mission Press, 1810, pp. V et VII; Pierre Brocheux and Daniel Hémery, *Indochine. La colonisation ambiguë, 1858–1954,* Paris: La Découverte, 1995, chapter 1; and 'Extrait de la leçon inaugural de Lucien Bernot au Collège de France, 2 March 1979', *Lettre de l'AFRASE,* 2nd Semester 1992, p. 10. According to Bernot (who is French), Malte-Brun was *not* the first to use the word 'Indochine', but rather J. Leyden.

be found as an ancient name for 'Japan'.[12] By World War I, however, Annamese speakers were using this Sino-Vietnamese coupling, borrowed from the Chinese radicals – 'Dong' for the 'east' and 'Yang' for 'east of the ocean' – to translate the term 'Indo-Chine'. In the end, the Annamese grew accustomed to several words for identifying 'Indochine française', above all 'Dong-Duong' ('Indo-Chine'), 'Dong-Phap' (Oriental France), 'An-do-Chi-Na' (Sino-Annamese for 'India-China') and 'Dong-Duong thuoc Phap' (French Indochina).

Rethinking Space Together

The French did not create Indochina overnight. Once admirals had militarily subordinated traditional peninsular empires to French sovereignty, administrators had to organize vast territories covering much of the eastern part of the Indochinese peninsula. To plant the French flag was one thing, but to rule over 16 million people of diverse ethnic and religious backgrounds was another. The French had to give shape to their domain. Cartographers and diplomats were sent to the front lines to sculpt French Indochina. They negotiated an end to Annam's traditional pattern of relations with Siam and China and carefully plotted the outlines of the new colonial space. Most troubling to this process was obstinate Annamese resistance to dismantling the Dai Nam empire. By crushing this resistance, however, the French boxed themselves in, for such repressive action undermined their efforts to win the support of the very Annamese whose collaboration would be essential to the construction of French Indochina. They would be essential to filling positions in the administration and as manual labourers in the building of roads, railways and bridges. The French had to convince the Annamese that Indochina was a continuation of their history. One of France's top Asia hands, Jules Harmand, understood the need to 'associate' historic patterns of Annamese expansion with the colonial project. He wrote in 1885:

> The day that this race understands that its historical ambitions can, thanks to us, come to fruition in ways that it never before imagined; when [the Annamese] sees our aid allow him to take vengeance for the humiliations and defeats that he has never forgiven his neighbours; when he feels definitely superior to them and

---

12. J.F.M. Génibrel, *Dictionnaire Annamite-Française*, Saigon: Imprimerie de la Mission à Tan Dinh, 1898; J.M.J., *Dictionarium latino-anamaticum*, Tan Dinh: Typis Missionis, 1878, p. 214; Bonet, *Dictionnaire*, pp. 161, 197; and Interview with Hoang Xuan Han, 1 August 1993, Paris.

sees his domination expand with ours, only then will we be able to consider that the future of French Indochina is truly assured.[13]

In 1887, the French founded the 'Indochinese Union'. By 1907, cartographers and diplomats finished sculpting its major geographical outlines, while French representatives signed treaties with the Siamese Court defining a western border to complement the 1884 Franco-Chinese Treaty that had delimited the northern Indochinese border. In short, force, diplomacy and cartography had given geographical life to a French Indochinese colony. Legislation passed in 1911 sidelined the court at Hue by consolidating the governor general's power as ranking administrator, in charge of diplomatic relations, civil service, defence, budget and internal security. Further measures gave life to the word 'Indochina' by promoting public works projects, investments in industry, and communication systems. World War I delayed major projects, but from 1919 French colonization resumed with renewed vigour, and Franco-Annamese collaboration was an important component of this development. As Governor General Albert Sarraut asked in his famous speech to Annamese elites in April 1919: 'What do we want to do and how must we work together, French and Annamese, for the good of this wonderful Indochina and for the welfare of her populations?'[14]

The Annamese took Sarraut seriously that day, translating and commenting on his speech throughout the local press. His plans for developing a modern communications system, an industrial policy and educational projects convinced many Annamese that there was a future in building Indochina with the French. 'Modernization' was the key word. His predecessors had already connected Hanoi by rail to Kunming. It was extended southwards toward Vinh, Haiphong, and eventually down the coast. French engineers built a network of roads and highways throughout the Union, penetrating the rugged hills isolating Laos to connect silver mines along the upper Mekong to the port at Vinh and to clear thick forests in eastern Cambodia in order to truck rubber from plantations in the Mekong Basin to the port in Saigon. Shipping lines linked these ports to major trading centres in Hong Kong, Canton, Bangkok, Singapore and Marseilles. Many traditional notions of time and space fell by the wayside.

---

13. Cited by Paul Isoart, 'La création de l'Union indochinoise', *Approches Asie*, no. 11, November 1992, p. 54. All translations from French and *quoc ngu* are mine, unless otherwise noted.

14. Albert Sarraut, 'Discours prononcé le 17 avril 1919 au Van-Mieu', p. 1, dossier 12J-III-3, Archives Départementales de l'Aude.

The French needed the Annamese. Faced with overpopulation in Tonkin and northern Annam, they began shipping Tonkinese labourers to southern Indochina to clear the jungle and to labour on rubber plantations. In Cambodia, the Annamese population grew from 79,050 in 1911 to 140,220 in 1921. Of the 16 Indochinese bureaucrats working in the Town Hall of Phnom Penh in 1913, 14 were Annamese and 2 Cambodian. In the offices of the Commissariat at Battambang in 1915, 11 out of 21 bureaucrats were Annamese; in the 'résidence' of Kandal, 8 of 14; 13 out of 19 at Kompong Chhang-Pursat and so on.[15] The ratio of Annamese bureaucrats in Laos was even greater. Employed as civil servants, mechanics, carpenters or miners, the Annamese actually outnumbered the Lao in major urban centres. In 1937, for example, there were 10,200 Annamese living in Vientiane, but only 9,000 Lao.[16] As a French writer explained: 'Thanks to our roads and railways, we have opened Laos to outsider activities; the mountain barrier that had once protected it is now gone. Between Laos and Annam, the Pyrenees have now vanished.'[17]

The growing number of civil servants travelling between eastern and western Indochina underscóred the changing patterns of Annamese movement within the colonial domain. The French trained them, housed them and paid them regularly. Judged more dynamic and efficient than their Lao and Khmer counterparts, Annamese graduates filled a myriad of lowlevel positions as secretaries, interpreters, telegraph operators, veterinarians, postal clerks, customs officers, train conductors, etc. By the 1930s, thousands of Annamese held functionally important jobs within the French Indochinese bureaucracy and army. Given the relatively minuscule European population in Indochina, it would not be an overstatement to say that by the 1930s the Annamese were largely responsible, at the ground level, for the running of the Lao and Cambodian Indochinese bureaucracies. We can track this Indochinese reorientation in Annamese minds in bulletins left behind by

---

15. Alain Forest, *Le Cambodge et la colonisation française*, Paris: L'Harmattan, 1980, pp. 446, 460.

16. Nguyen Van Luyen, 'Van de … ', no. 257, p. 1; 'Enquête no. 1-A sur l'alimentation des indigènes, questionnaire destiné aux administrateurs,' p. 1 in Commission Guernut [CG], dossier [hereafter, d.] Laos, Province de Vientiane, carton [hereafter, c.] 96, Centre des Archives d'Outre-Mer [hereafter, CAOM] and Ministère des Colonies, Inspection géné-rale des Colonies, 'Utilité du remplacement par étapes des auxiliaires annamites de l'administration française au Laos par des Laotiens', 13 March 1936, pp. 3–6, in Nouveau Fonds [hereafter, NF], d. 2494/2, c. 287, CAOM.

17. Roland Meyer, *Le Laos. Exposition coloniale internationale, Paris 1931*, Hanoi: IDEO, 1931, p. 63.

civil servant associations called 'amicales'. The Association Amicale du Personnel Indigène des Résidences du Cambodge is a good example. Based in Phnom Penh, in 1933 the president was an Annamese, but Cambodians held the posts of vice president, secretary and they had a representative on the council. Five years later, the Khmer members had disappeared, voted out by the Annamese majority. This change was symbolized semantically, when the Amicale replaced the word 'indigène' with 'indochinois'.

This Indochinese-speak is noteworthy. To the French, 'indigène' referred to the subject races who originated from the area within the borders of Indochina; however, at another level, one could also use this word to distinguish between racial groups falling within the five geographical sub-divisions of Indochina (*les cinq pays*). Thus, both Annamese and Khmer were 'indigènes' of Indochina, but an Annamese had a harder time defining himself as an 'indigène' of Cambodia or Laos. He had to turn 'Indochinese' or become a 'French subject'. It was a complicated word game. Depending on his geographical position within the Indochinese realm, not only could the Annamese slip in and out of his 'Annamese' everyday garb, but he could also dress up in his 'Indochinese' best. It meant access to education and jobs, or it could mean passing before different colonial courts in the Indochinese realm.

An offshoot of the staffing of the Laotian and Cambodian civil services with literate Annamese was that the Annamese readership expanded westwards. Besides the newsletters disseminated by numerous 'Amicales', trucks or steamships delivered *quoc ngu* and French language papers to urban centres in Laos and Cambodia. An Annamese bureaucrat could purchase the *Tribune Indochinoise, Tin Tuc, l'Annam Nouveau* or *Phu Nu Tan Van* in Cambodian news-stands. *Quoc ngu* papers even spread their way across the Mekong to Annamese communities in northeastern Siam and into southern China, thereby transcending the formal boundaries of French Indochina. Annamese control of printing presses in Vientiane and Phnom Penh reinforced the Indochinese-wide nature of Annamese publishing.[18] An Annamese teacher edited the *Tin Lao* in Laos. The Phnom Penh based daily *Viet Kieu Nhot Bao* tapped into the expanding Annamese bureaucratic and trading communities in Cambodian urban centres by the late 1930s. This growing, literate Annamese population in Laos and Cambodia soon attracted the attention of publishers. The manager of the Indochinese Publishing House (Nha Xuat Ban Dong Duong) could proudly advertise

---

18. The *Cao Mien Huong Truyen* was the Vietnamese edition of the *Echo du Cambodge*.

that he sold his *quoc ngu* books in 'the major stores throughout Indochina', while more than thirty Annamese editors splashed the word Indochina – either 'Indochine', 'Dong Phap' or 'Dong Duong' – across the frontpages of their papers.

The colonial education system reinforced the penchant for Indochinese things. It was, after all, *une formation Indochinoise*.[19] This was symbolized best in 1911 when the governor general, Albert Sarraut, created an 'Indochinese University' in Hanoi with one of its aims being to form civil servants by redirecting Annamese attention away from its Chinese in-fluences. The French abolished the Confucian examination system and replaced it with a Western-style system. History and geography courses emphasized the reality of Indochina, its history, structure and functioning. Colonial educators commissioned Western-style maps of the five lands of Indochina and sent them to village schools throughout the Union. There was an eastern tilt in the French conception of Indochinese education, however, symbolized by the preponderant number of schools in Annam where there were very few Lao or Khmer students. Even in Laos and Cambodia, Annamese youngsters often outnumbered their Lao and Cambodian classmates in the 'Franco-Indigène' schools, the latter preferring the Renovated Pagoda Schools.[20]

Jean Marquet, author of the highly successful textbook *The Five Flowers: Indochina Explained*, was a fervent admirer of Annamese culture and a writer influential in developing the new education policy. Through the form of a fictive travelogue, Marquet explained in simple terms the history of French Indochina to his young Annamese readers.[21] Let us take a closer look at the Indochina across which the French 'were walking' (*faisaient promener*) their Annamese students.

Once upon a time, an ageing Annamese father gathered his five sons to explain the hard times his tea business was encountering. He informed them that he had consulted the proper genies for advice and had subsequently had a dream in which his sons handed him five different petals, which, when

19. Anderson, *Imagined Communities*, p. 124.

20. J. Loubet, Proviseur du Lycée Albert Sarraut, 'Enseignement en Indochine en 1929', Hanoi: IDEO, 1929, p. 6; Pascale Bezançon, 'La rénovation des écoles de pagode au Cambodge', Paris: Mémoire de Maîtrise, Paris VII, 1992; Anderson, *Imagined Communities*, p. 125 and Ministère des Colonies, Inspection des Colonies, no. 32, 20 June 1936, 'L'enseignement au Laos: Les écoles de pagode', pp. 11–12, d. 2495/2, c. 287, NF, CAOM.

21. Jean Marquet, *Les cinq fleurs. L'Indochine expliquée,* Hanoi: Direction de l'Instruction Publique en Indochine, 1928.

gathered, formed a unique flower. Marquet has his father-figure interpret this dream as a sign that his sons had to travel to the five lands (*pays*) of French Indochina in search of new aromatic leaves to boost the family business. He sends one son to Tonkin, another to Annam, and so on to Cochinchina, Cambodia and Laos. From this point, Marquet takes us on a spatial voyage with our five young Annamese through the looking-glass of French Indochina. But first we must stop over with the local village teacher for a quick geography lesson. The son who had been the best in this subject recites: 'French Indochina is formed by five wonderful departments: Cochinchina, Cambodia, Annam, Tonkin and Laos.' He then did the same for all the provinces and their capitals. With our map now firmly in mind, we can proceed down the newly built roads, railways, and canals. We discover *modern* factories, mines and plantations. We explore the most remote parts of Indochina as we ride with our Annamese explorers in cars, trains, steamships and even in an aeroplane for our return trip to Hanoi. In a matter of a hundred pages, we streak across this Indochinese wonderland, its history, its development and its future. Indeed, the aeroplane is symbolically most important, for it allows Marquet to drive home the modernizing influence of French colonialism and to highlight the spatial reworking of Indochina as a *French pilot* transports his young *Annamese passenger* from the *Cambodian* bush to *Hanoi*. Our Annamese traveller explains his Indochinese vision *during* their aeroplane ride. And hundreds of metres above the ground, the imagination knows no limits: 'I thought I was dreaming: I had just covered almost two thousand kilometres, crossed ten rivers and a thousand hills. In other words, thanks to a flying-machine, I had just passed over, within a few hours, all of Indochina.' In traditional Annamese travel terms, this was a record crossing. In a matter of hours, our imaginary Annamese voyager had just witnessed the historical Viet expansion southwards in reverse. Reunited at home, the father solemnly convened his sons to collect the five petals they had brought him. The family business was saved – and Indochina forged.

The Five Flowers was the Indochinese version of the popular French children's tale: *Le Tour de France par deux enfants (devoir et patrie)*, published in 1887 by G. Bruno. To make it work in the colonial world, Marquet took the model of the Annamese family and its children as an effective means to explaining the existence of the Indochinese 'patrie'. There were no Lao, Khmer or Rhadé travellers. It was a Franco-Annamese trip, a subtle spatial reorientation of a traditional 'Annam' away from its

Figure 4: Towards an Indochinese form of the nation – roads, rivers and work (map probably from the early 1940s).

Chinese roots and eastern geographical tilt towards its French Indochinese future. By the mid-1920s, Annamese youngsters had reason to believe in an Indochinese space. For perhaps the first time, in 1932 an Annamese geographer could write in a textbook that together with the Lao and Cambodians, the Annamese formed 'one country: the Indochinese Union.'[22]

Marquet's choice of a fictive voyage throughout Indochina in 1928 was not farfetched. A growing number of compatriots were catching trains, hitching rides in cars or embarking on steamships to discover for themselves the Indochina that French technology and Annamese labour were opening up around them. The appearance of *The Five Flowers* in Indochinese school libraries was linked to a simultaneous explosion in the publication of Annamese travelogues, a fascinating source for exploring Annamese views of their landscape.[23]

Pham Quynh provides the best example of how travel was expanding traditional Annamese horizons westwards. As the editor of *Nam Phong* and a regular contributor to the daily *France-Indochine,* Quynh was aware of the expansion of the road system into Laos and the increasing Annamese immigration to Laos and Cambodia. Inspired by travelogues, Quynh set out with a map of the new colonial roads to make his way to Laos. He travelled first down Colonial Route 1 to Dong Ha to take Route 9 to Savannakhet, carefully noting the distance that separated each major urban centre from the other. He observed how French technology had subdued the mountains which historically had prevented the Annamese from crossing westwards. It was a new world for this Confucian intellectual. As he reflected later: 'The further we drove from Hue, the further we stepped into the Indianized world, leaving the Sinic realm vanishing behind us in the distance.' This reflection on the two sides of Indochina is important. Writing in Annamese, he marvelled: 'One side is "Chi-na", while the other is "An-Do" [India], and thus we have this land of "Dong Duong", which is quite rightly given the name of "An-Do-Chi-na".' Quynh could not help himself from imagining what his country would have looked like had the mountain range protecting Laos not blocked Annamese expansion before French conquest. And in several articles written after his return to Hanoi,

---

22. Nguyen Van Que, *Histoire de l'Union Française,* Saigon, Impr. Nguyen Khac, 1932, p. 220.

23. Christopher E. Goscha, 'Quelques regards viêtnamiens sur la péninsule indochinoise pendant l'époque coloniale', *Bulletin de l'École Française d'Extrême-Orient,* forthcoming.

Quynh called on the French to accelerate Annamese immigration to Laos immediately.[24]

By 1930, thinking in Indochinese terms for an Annamese was not as hard as it once seemed. Pre-colonial notions of time and space had been eschewed by the necessity of *creating* and *running* a modern, Indochinese entity. Writing from *within* the system in 1930, an Annamese civil servant in Laos or Cambodia never thought twice when sending a letter in *quoc ngu* to a compatriot in the east, even on official colonial stationery marked *Gouvernement Général de l'Indochine, Protectorat du Cambodge (Battambang)*.[25]

This irony did not escape Cambodian elites. Their colonization had been double-edged – first French, then Annamese. After World War II, the Khmer Court would make every effort to reverse this process by demanding control of immigration as a major precondition to renewing their co-operation with the French. They insisted to their bewildered French interlocutors that controlling Annamese immigration was a 'matter of life or death.'[26] In the eyes of many Lao and Khmer, the Annamese were not always on the losing end during the colonial period.

Annamese Conservatives between Annam and Indochina

The spatial and racial reworking of Indochina was at the heart of a series of tense debates which broke out in communist and non-communist circles in 1930–31 over how to conceive the geographical patterns of Annamese nationalism. Nationalists asked if federalism or outright Annamese immigration could bridge the gap between a pre-colonial conception of an Annamese space and the new one circumscribed by the boundaries of French Indochina. The idea of an Indochinese federation had first been floated by Albert Sarraut in his 1919 speech designed to give more of a say to Annamese. He went so far as to call for an Indochinese Charter, 'a sort of Constitution.'[27] But if he was thinking of Indochinese autonomy in

---

24. Pham Quynh, 'Du-lich xu Lao', *Nam Phong*, January 1931, no. 158, pp. 5–7 and part II, *Nam Phong*, no. 159, February 1931, p. 105. On Quynh's trip to Laos, see: Christopher E. Goscha, 'L'Indochine repensée par les "Indochinois": Pham Quynh et les deux débats de 1931 sur l'immigration, le fédéralisme et la réalité de l'Indochine', *Revue française d'histoire d'outre mer*, forthcoming.

25. Letter published as an advertisement in *Tan-Thoi*, no. 31, 29 August 1935, p. 23.

26. Commission d'Études franco-khmère, 'Procès-verbal partiel de la séance du 29 mars 1946' et 'Compte Rendu de la séance du 29 mars 1946', in Papiers Alessandri, 1K306, SHAT.

27. Sarraut, 'Discours prononcé', p. 1, 11.

administrative terms, Annamese editors were imagining an Indochinese entity along political lines.

The formation of the Indochinese Constitutionalist Party under Bui Quang Chieu was one of the first clues that Annamese nationalism was running in an Indochinese direction. As editor of the Party's official mouthpiece, *La Tribune Indigène* (renamed in 1926 *La Tribune Indochinoise)*, Chieu took the prospect of an Indochinese federation seriously. The Constitutionalists applauded the idea of giving greater 'autonomy, decentralization and freedom of action' to Indochina. They called on the French to allow them to form 'a constitutional charter' with 'all the structures needed for a modern State.' This transformation, they argued a week after Sarraut's speech, was necessary if the colony were to become a *pays autonome* and if 'its Annamese personnel [were to] become Indochinese citizens'.[28]

Chieu was not alone in making these associations between Annamese and Indochinese. In his famous *Revendications du Peuple Annamite*, Nguyen Ai Quoc (the later Ho Chi Minh) unintentionally set off an intense debate in 1919 when he opened his petition: 'the People of the former Annamese Empire, today French Indochina, submit to the honourable governments...'[29] Hostile editors at the *Courrier Saigonnais* took Annamese nationalists to task for this linkage. Indeed, the future Ho Chi Minh had provoked what may be the first open exchange on the 'Indochinese' and 'Annamese' lines. As the *Courrier* retorted:

> They say: 'former Empire of Annam, today French Indochina.' There you have it. What are the Cambodians, the Laotians and the countless other nations occupying the summits of the Annamese Range going to say? They are annexed by a stroke of a pen by our so-called Annamese patriots.

The *Courrier* was walking a fine line by forgetting that there were no nations in French Indochina, only five 'pays'. Quoc's association of Annam and Indochina was, after all, what the French Governor Generals had called for. The famous patriot Phan Chu Trinh had made the same association a decade earlier.[30] But whatever their intentions, the *Courrier*'s editors posed Annamese nationalists a major problem: 'Yet by speaking of an Annamese people and by attaching these words to the expression of French Indochina,

---

28. Editorial, 'La peur des mots,' *Tribune Indigène*, 23 March 1919, p. 1 and 'Ce que nous voulons: Le Parti Constitutionaliste Indochinois', *La Tribune Indigène*, 8 May 1919, p. 1.

29. 'Notes d'un Saigonnais: Cri d'alarme', *Le Courrier Saigonnais*, no. 5260, 23 July 1919, p. 1 and *La Tribune Indigène*, 5 August 1919, p. 1 and also Nguyen Ai Quac, 'Le Droit des peuples', *L'Humanité*, 18 June 1919.

you seem to want to establish a concordance between [Annam and Indochina] which does not exist.'[31]

The debate over this 'concordance' remained at the fore of nationalist debates for the next three decades. Much (not everything) was in flux. Annamese were tapping into a new vision of Indochina, taking what the French had offered them for a road-map and moulding it into something altogether new, often linking up with a pre-colonial Annamese vision of the peninsula. In 1921, the Indochinese Constitutionalist Party in Cochinchina published an article to this effect, entitled *L'État indochinois*, in which they stressed that an Indochinese state could be realised through further Annamese-French collaboration.[32] One week later, *La Tribune Indigène* published a three-part series, entitled: 'La prépondérance politique des Annamites en Indochine est-elle justifiée?' in which the Indochinese Constitutionalist Party explained the 'concordance' between Annam and Indochina on the grounds that it was in keeping with historical Annamese expansion westwards.

> The Annamese ... are thus first in line for historic, ethnographic and geographic reasons which would be childish to deny and against which it would be futile to argue. In Indochina ... , it's the law of the majority that rules ... , within the French Indochinese Union our supremacy is the logical consequence, the very nature of things.[33]

Borrowed from French colonial discourse and given a special cultural twist by a historic sense of a Confucian civilizing mission, Annamese conservatives used references to Charles Darwin in many arguments calling for a leading position in France's policy of association.[34] On another level, Indochinese Constitutionalists were reworking traditional Annamese geo-history by trying to resurrect and link pre-colonial Dai Nam to French Indochina in an attempt to 'justify' their 'preponderance'. It was a sort of 'Manifest Destiny'

---

30. 'Union Intercoloniale', p. 1 and Phan Chu Trinh, 'Des manifestations annamites en 1908, demande d'amnistie,' p. 1, c. 372, Service de Protection du Corps Expéditionnaire [hereafter, SPCE], CAOM. Trinh wrote: 'L'ancien Empire de l'Annam qui porte aujourd'hui le nom d'Indo-Chine ...'

31. Quoted by *La Tribune Indigène*, 'Notes d'un Saigonnais : Bas les Masques', 12 August 1919, p. 1.

32. Editorial, 'L'État indochinois', *La Tribune Indigène*, 19 April 1921, p. 1.

33. 'La prépondérance politique des Annamites en Indochine est-elle justifiée?' *La Tribune Indigène*, 26 April 1921, Part I, p. 1.

34. 'La politique indigène en Indochine doit être avant tout une politique Annamite', *La Tribune Indigène*, 7 August 1919, p.1 and above all Pham Quynh, 'Du-Lich Xu Lao', no. 158, pp. 5–6.

vision of Indochina which many conservative Annamese nationalists were fond of evoking. To them, a glorious imperial past distinguished the Annamese race from the 'less' civilized Lao and Khmer, who threatened to slow down the evolution of Indochina.[35] Tieu Vien, an outspoken supporter of French industrialization of Indochina, took this projection of the Dai Nam past into the Indochinese future a step further in 1939. With Tonkin's demographic problems firmly in mind, he argued that:

> Annamese emigration is not only an economic or a nutritional problem. It is a tradition, the historical mission of our race. ... The peaceful expansion towards the south and the west remains one of our national goals. What is considered to be the Annamese nation is only a beginning. The Indochinese Nation will be the logical outcome, the last word in our evolution. In other words, one must recognize the right of the Annamese people to make use of their 'vital space' within the limits of the Indochinese territory.[36]

It would be naive to deny the imperialistic impulses driving these arguments. What makes this passage so interesting here, though, is that if Tieu Vien conceded that Indochina was not exactly Dai Nam, he reveals nonetheless that a new Indochinese Nation was coming into being: a nation-of-intent (to borrow Shamsul A.B.'s expression). In this sense, the Javanese were clearly not the only ones rethinking national identity along the geographical lines of the colonial state. Tieu Vien had already captured this idea in unequivocal terms: 'The day will come when Indochina will no longer be an amalgam of distinct and isolated countries, but rather a single country which Annamese blood will have fertilized by breathing into this creation his dynamism, strength of action and desire to react. That day, the Indochinese Nation will be a beautiful and living reality.' As the future anterior tense gave away, this nation was still to be born. However, it was clearly being 'imagined' (to borrow Anderson's term) and being projected both forwards and backwards into time and space. It is notable, however, that these conservatives rarely thought to consult Lao, Khmer or ethnic groups on this 'Indochinese form.' Moreover, as long as the French were there, they seemed to have completely forgotten that the Thais and Chinese looking in from the outside might one day have different ideas about 'the coming into being' of an Annamese-dominated Indochinese 'vital space' on their respective eastern and southern flanks.

---

35. 'Annamite colonisateur', *L'Echo Annamite,* 4 March 1927, p. 1 and Hung Giang, 'La formation du pays d'Annam', *Nam Phong,* no. 131, juillet 1928. I am grateful to Agathe Larcher for help on this point.

36. Tieu Vien, 'L'espace vital, le nôtre', *La Patrie Annamite,* no. 307, 1 July 1939, p. 1.

Ho Chi Minh would be more careful to avoid this expansionist character of Annamese history, when he went back to the past in the early 1940s in search of national symbols. He preferred to evoke historic Annamese resistance against Chinese expansionism. Indeed, these conservative Indochinese ambitions were not monolithic; and one would be committing a serious error to throw Ho, or even Pham Quynh, into the same basket with Tieu Vien or the Constitutionalists. This is particularly true for the new generation graduating from colonial schools during the 1920s, many of whom would go on to become important revolutionaries. They were having Indochinese visions of another kind. The fiery young radical from the south, Nguyen An Ninh, is a case in point. Educated entirely in French Indochinese classrooms and then in France, Ninh had little in common with the Confucian education of his father or Quynh or Ho, other than their patriotism. In 1924, he wrote a famous essay on Annamese nationalism in which he limited his discussion to the need to unify into one nation what French colonialism had divided into Cochinchina, Annam and Tonkin. Ninh did not mention Laos or Cambodia, he used the word 'Annam' throughout his text, and denounced 'the arbitrary division' of Annam into three parts which, he insisted, 'the Annamese still consider to constitute *the same body.*' However, Ninh revealed the pervasive power of his Indochinese formation when he chose to entitle his essay – 'Towards the Indochinese Nation', calling it 'the greatest of [his] dreams, the dream of [his] race.'[37] Unlike Tieu Vien's Indochinese nation, what Ninh's 'dream' symbolizes is a remarkable confusion of two very different geo-political entities, the first a traditional remembrance of a unified Annamese empire, the loss of which his father had long lamented to him, and the new one being a French Indochinese space that geography teachers had drilled into his head in the colonial classrooms he had entered as a child. In 1924, Ninh (and many of the revolutionary elite of his generation) were lost somewhere in the grey area between the extremes of Marquet's imaginary vision of the Indochinese future and Tieu Vien's interpretation of Dai Nam's imperial past. Having read most of Ninh's works, I have found no evidence that he harboured

---

37. Nguyen An Ninh, 'Vers la nation indochinoise', p. 1. My emphasis. In his intellectual history of Vietnam published in 1975, the well-known historian, Tran Van Giau, took the time to scale-back Ninh's 1924 Indochinese leap to 'Annam', before converting it to 'Vietnam'. Forgetting his own Indochinese education and former Comintern accent, Giau explained 'Indochina' away in one curt sentence: 'Here, [Ninh's] expression an "Indochinese Nation" means a Vietnamese nation unified from north to south'. Tran Van Giau, *Su Phat Trien cua Tu Tuong o Viet-Nam*, Hanoi: Committee of Social Sciences, 1975, vol. II, p. 483. Giau's Indochinese accent is in Tønnesson, *Vietnamese Revolution*, p. 392.

territorial designs on Laos or Cambodia, leading me to postulate that it was a combination of Harmand and Sarraut's policy of association and his Indochinese schooling that made him jump. On 19 May 1924, Ninh repeated this when he spoke of revolution in exclusively Annamese terms but posed the question in Indochinese-speak: 'Is a revolution possible in Indochina?'[38]

A few weeks later, in a thoughtful response to this question, a certain Trung Ky (Annam) awakened *La Cloche Fêlée*'s readers to the dangers manifest in going beyond the traditional boundaries of Annam, reminding all of the historical Khmer and Lao hostility for the Annamese and of the ethnic contradictions inherent in Ninh's confusion of 'Annam' with 'Indochina'.

> Indochina is not just Annam. Indochina consists of Laos where the people have their own habitat and are absolutely different from us. In Cambodia, where the people have always been our age-old enemies, as well as in the Mois regions, we can count on few friends. It is a fact that must be recognized.[39]

The contradiction between Indochina and Annam came to a head in 1930–31. Faced with violent nationalist and communist revolts in Tonkin and Annam, the French resurrected the idea of an Indochinese federation. Like Sarraut, Governor General Pierre Pasquier insisted that only the maintenance of French sovereignty could hold Indochina together and form 'the federal Indochinese citizen' (*le citoyen fédéral indochinois*). Always concerned by the need to preserve local identities, languages and traditions, Pasquier had little confidence in the reality of an Indochinese 'national entity' given the diversity of the colony.[40] As Pasquier defined Indochina's still ambiguous status in 1928: 'Indochina is not a colony, nor a protectorate nor even a possession. Indochina is all of this, and even more; She is a federation of states (*une fédération d'Etats*).[41] Governor General Alexandre Varenne argued in similar terms. One day he said, 'I can see the emergence of a kind of Asian [Indochinese] state linked politically and economically through ever looser links to the metropole, an [Indochinese] state which would find its place next to us just as the Dutch Indies stand next to

---

38. Nguyen An Ninh, 'Une révolution est-elle possible?', *La Cloche Fêlée*, no. 15, 19 May 1924, p. 1.

39. Trung Ky, 'La révolution est-elle possible?', *La Cloche Fêlée*, no. 18, 16 June 1924, p. 1.

40. Le discours du Gouverneur général de l'Indochine au Grand Conseil', *L'Asie Française*, no. 285, December 1930, p. 395 and 'La politique indochinoise du gouvernement', *L'Asie Française*, no. 283, October 1930, p. 306.

41. Cited by Paul Isoart, 'Rêver l'Indochine: A propos d'un film!', *Approches Asie*, no. 12, March 1994, p. 232, note 43.

Holland.'[42] Pasquier conceded in 1930 that the day 'that each federated Indochinese will be proud to feel like a son of France as an Indochinese citizen, that day our work will have acquired a solidity that nothing will be able to break.'[43]

Although the French created no federation at this juncture, Annamese elites of all political colours were closely following these French debates. In fact, the federal ideas advanced by Pasquier and Varenne set off a parallel series of debates in communist and non-communist circles over how to reconcile the geographical limits of Annamese nationalism with the Indochinese model required by the French. In 1930 Pham Quynh resumed the debate a few weeks before his Lao trip in the article 'Fédéralisme indochinois et nationalisme annamite'. He conceded that Annam was not alone in an envisioned federation, but made it clear that the Annamese remained the most important partner in French Indochina. To Quynh, it was clear that 'Annam' came first, with federalism being the only way to 'conciliate' the Annamese nation with the French Indochinese concept. A constitutional monarchy had to take form within the confines of Indochinese federalism, not the other way around.[44]

Yet, if Pham Quynh sought a preponderant place for the Annamese nation within the French-led Indochinese federation in early 1931, his cultural counterpart, Nguyen Van Vinh, came down in favour of an *État indochinois de fait*. This concept formed the central idea of his 1931 political programme. Vinh demanded that eventually the French would have to recognize the reality of the 'Indochinese state' and its 'Indochinese citizen.'[45] Vinh had gone a step further than Quynh and the Constitutionalists to join Tieu Vien by calling for the grafting of Annamese nationalism on to the Indochinese model. Vinh justified this on the grounds that there was nothing wrong with the historic, westward expansion of the Annamese. They worked productively in Lao mines, on Cambodian plantations, throughout the bureaucracy. He was deeply interested in developing Laos

42. 'M. Varenne prononce à la Chambre un important discours au sujet de l'Indochine', *La Revue Franco-Annamite*, no. 19, 1 April 1930, p. 13.

43. 'Le Discours du Gouverneur Général de l'Indochine', pp. 395, 399 and 'Un important discours de M. le Gouverneur Général', *La Revue Franco-Annamite*, no. 30, 16 September 1930, p. 15.

44. Pham Quynh, 'Fédéralisme indochinois et nationalisme annamite', *France-Indochine*, no. 3325, 28 November 1930, p. 1. On the monarchy, see: Pham Quynh, 'Vers une constitution', *Nam Phong*, no. 151, June 1930, pp. 39–46.

45. Nguyen Van Vinh, 'Le citoyen indochinois,' *L'Annam Nouveau*, 15 mars 1931, p. 1 and Nguyen Van Vinh, 'ENFIN un programme,' *L'Annam Nouveau*, 5 avril 1931, p. 1.

and Cambodia. He had travelled to Laos and Cambodia and had written prolifically in support of immigration westwards, concessions to Annamese immigrants, and he himself had left his editorship and family to search for gold in the rugged Indochinese west. He died there in 1936, while engaged in telegraphing back 'live' reports to the *Annam Nouveau*'s readers on indigenous cultures in Laos and gold prospecting.[46]

Quynh broke with Vinh on the idea of an 'Indochinese state', taking him to task for 'speaking Indochinese' when he should be 'speaking Annamese.' To him, Annamese nationalism could not be grafted on to an Indochinese model, for the geo-historical abstraction of French Indochina was incompatible with a notion of 'Annam' which continued to exist despite French policies designed to build an Indochinese structure on top of it.

> But ethnically and linguistically, Indochina has never existed and will never exist. Politically, it could take form within the context of a Federal Assembly; but there will never be a citizen in flesh and blood. No doubt, Mr Vinh will answer us by saying that he wanted above all to say Annamese when saying Indochinese, and that this dispute over words is silly. But on the contrary I find it very important, for, depending on the point of view you take, Annamese or Indochinese, the problem changes entirely. Seen from the Indochinese angle, it is basically a federal question ... But seen from the Annamese angle, the problem is uniquely national. And the Annamese nation is a reality that dances before the eyes ...[47]

Unlike Quynh, Vinh was ready to go with the French model of Indochina:

> All right, Indochina is a French creation, but does not this creation have for a base our country of Annam? ... I distinguish perfectly, like Mr Pham Quynh, between the Indochinese point of view and the Annamese one. But I intend to conciliate the two points of view between which I see no incompatibility ... While repeating that our country is not called Indochina but Annam, I submit nonetheless that French Indochina is the fulfilment of an Annamese destiny with French power. Whatever you call it, this fact remains.[48]

But Quynh held the line for the 'real' Annam:

> Annam has always had and will always have its own national existence ... Like us, Mr Vinh calls for a Constitution, but with the key difference that he

---

46. Nguyen Van Vinh, 'Chercheurs d'or au Laos', *L'Annam Nouveau*, 5 and 9 April and 7 May 1936, p. 1.

47. Pham-Quynh, 'Les conceptions politiques de M. Vinh', *France-Indochine*, no. 3432, 10 April 1931, p. 1.

48. Nguyen Van Vinh, 'Mes conceptions politiques jugées par M. Pham Quynh,' *L'Annam Nouveau*, Part I, 12 April 1931, p. 1.

proclaims an Indochina that remains nothing but a simple geographical and political entity, for which we have little need, whereas we seek a Constitution for Annam, which is truly a national reality to which we are tied by the most profound sentiments of our soul.[49]

If Quynh did not like the Indochinese pattern of Vinh's nationalist ideas, he seems to have carefully downplayed his own penchant for 'speaking Indochinese.' This no doubt stems from angry reactions he had provoked in Lao circles in earlier articles calling for increased Annamese immigration to Laos. Days before Quynh and Vinh began their exchange of views, Quynh had been caught off-guard when a Lao elite took him to task in *France-Indochine* for belittling Lao culture and pointed out that Annamese immigration to Laos was considered as a danger by the Lao. Even Prince Phetsarath entered the debate during a brief stop-over in Hanoi. Interviewed by the same paper, he embarrassed Quynh publicly for his articles on Laos, saying that 'the Annamese are already too prone to think only of Annam when they speak of Indochina.' The prince was not against Annamese immigration, but it had to be regulated to avoid creating in Laos 'a state within the state.' More importantly, the prince insisted that 'Laos existed.'[50]

The concept of Indochina was imagined quite differently – or was not imagined – by those living in Laos and Cambodia. As Phetsarath explained: 'First of all, all confidence in French promises fades away and the Indochinese federation appears, to the weakest nations making it up, like an eye wash designed to allow the Annamese to rule over the others, under the protection of the French flag.' In short, national identity in a time of colonialism was complicated. It depended on who you were and where you were standing: Vinh wanted to become 'Indochinese'; Pham Quynh to remain 'Annamese'; Ninh to be both; and Prince Phetsarath to unify 'Laos'.

Annamese Revolutionaries between 'Indochina' and 'Vietnam'

Meanwhile, a similar debate was dividing the revolutionary camp. For the communists, the question was: Could they graft communism on to the Indochinese structure? The concept was less alien to young militants than to their parents. The young were armed with an Indochinese education, fresh from courses on its history and geography, and avid readers of editorials and travelogues covering Laos and Cambodia. Like Nguyen An Ninh, many of

---

49. Pham Quynh, 'Les conceptions politiques de M. Vinh', p. 1.
50. Goscha, 'L'Indochine repensée par les "Indochinois"'.

them were speaking of an Indochinese revolution in enthusiastic terms by the late 1920s. And in their eyes, there was nothing contradictory about his 1924 vision of 'the Indochinese nation.' After all, French colonialism had been promoting the pattern for decades and the Comintern started marketing it, when its leaders issued directives in the late 1920s calling for the formation of an Indochinese Party based on the French Indochinese model.[51] The Soviet Union was also a multi-ethnic union dominated by one 'historical nation' (Russia), which had sacrificed its historical identity to the modernizing idea of a union based on Soviets. In 1929, young Annamese revolutionaries put the Comintern's orders into practice by forming the Communist Party of Indochina (Dong Duong Cong San Dang) and the League of Indochinese Communists. They approved the geographical limits of their revolutionary actions by the slogan: 'Complete Indochinese Independence!'[52]

However, not everyone was ready to make this leap. Ho Chi Minh himself balked, when it came time to create a new and unified Communist Party in early 1930. Like Pham Quynh, Ho still had one foot firmly planted in the traditional world of the Annamese empire and the other in this new Indochinese realm. As in 1919, Ho was again struggling with the 'concordance' between concepts of space. During one conversation, Ho not only rejected 'Annamese' (referring to the short-lived Annamese Communist Party) because of connotations of Chinese domination, but he allegedly found 'Indochina' (*Dong Duong*) 'too wide' a framework for Annamese-run revolutionary activities. He argued that people could confuse this term with a larger space running as far as Burma. And the idea of a 'French Indochinese Communist Party' would do little to dissipate the confusion. Ho pushed 'Vietnam', and it appears that such reasoning won out a few weeks later, when he presided over the formation in Hong Kong of a unified Vietnamese Communist Party (VCP; Dang Cong San Viet Nam). The guiding revolutionary slogan became: 'Complete Vietnamese Independence' (*Viet Nam hoan toan doc lap!*)[53]

The use of 'Vietnam' at this juncture deserves a special detour in our discussion of competing concepts of space, for an increasing number of

51. 'Ve Van De Lap Dang Cong San Dong Duong', in Ban Nghien Cuu Lich Su Trung Uong Xuat Ban, *Van Kien Dang, 1930–1945, Tap I,* Hanoi: Nha Xuat Ban Su That [hereafter, NXBST], 1977, pp. 9–17.

52. Ban Nghien Cuu Lich Su Trung Uong, *Nhung Su Kien Lich Su Dang, Tap I, 1920–1945,* Hanoi: NXBST, 1976, pp. 148, 163, 180.

53. Tran Cung and Trinh Dinh Cuu, in *Ngon Duoc,* Hanoi: NXBST, 1980, pp. 112 and 114 and *Cac van kien co ban cua Hoi Nghi thanh lap Dang,* Hanoi: NXBST, 1983, p. 29, note 2.

nationalists were using it to capture the idea of the eternal national identity that would eventually triumph over its 'Indochinese' and 'Annamese' competitors. To many, the idea of 'Annam' was increasingly problematic, since it implied humiliating submission to foreign rule, both Chinese and French. By resurrecting 'Vietnam', nationalists expressed a strong counter identity that evoked the unification of the northern and southern parts of the country in the late 18th century, and an association with a long tradition of struggle against foreign domination. In fact, Ho Chi Minh was not alone in his preference for 'Vietnam', but rather a part of a larger reorientation. The militant scholar-patriot, Phan Boi Chau (a friend of Ho's father), had given this term a clear nationalist hue, when he formed the Vietnamese Restoration Association (Viet-Nam Quang Phuc Hoi) and wrote his 'History of the Loss of the Country of Viet Nam' (*Viet-Nam Quoc Vong Su*). Pham Quynh had used 'Vietnam' as early as 1917 to evoke a timeless tradition, and three years later, Tran Trong Kim opened his *Outline History of Viet-Nam* (*Su luoc Viet-Nam*) in 1920 by *asking* his readers to give up 'An-Nam' in favour of 'Viet-Nam'. Ho followed suit in 1923 when he set up a nationalist paper, *Soul of Nam-Viet* (*Hon Nam Viet*), but initially reversed the words in the same way as Gia Long had done: 'Nam Viet'. He had turned to the more familiar order in 1925, when he established his blended communist-nationalist organization, the Vietnamese Revolutionary Youth League (Viet Nam Thanh Nien Cach Mang Dong Chi Hoi).[54]

However, much stronger competition for appropriation of the term Vietnam came from the non-communist Vietnamese Nationalist Party (Viet Nam Quoc Dan Dang; VNQDD), truly set in motion by Nguyen Thai Hoc and Nguyen Khac Nhu in early 1928. The VNQDD is particularly important at this juncture. It had direct links to Phan Boi Chau and strong roots in a militant, ethnocultural patriotism, which the Nationalist Party kept alive during the 1928–35 journey by the Indochinese Communist Party (ICP) into the desert of anti-nationalist internationalism and a proletarian Indochinese identity.[55] More than any other group at the time, the

54. Pham Quynh, 'Luan thuyet: van quoc ngu', *Nam Phong*, 1917, p. 80; Tran Trong Kim, *Su-Luoc Viet-Nam*, Hanoi: Trung Bac Tan Van, 1920, p. 1; and Nguyen Ai Quoc, 'Hon Nam Viet', 15 May 1923, p. 1, in c. 3, SLOTFOM, série III, CAOM.

55. 'Qu'est-ce qu'un Annamite?', *La Lutte*, no. 31, 29 April 1935, pp. 2–3; Daniel Hémery, *Révolutionnaires vietnamiens et pouvoir colonial en Indochine*, Paris: Maspero, 1975, pp. 105–106, 113–147; and Christopher E. Goscha, 'Tradition militante et rénovation culturelle au Vietnam: Réflexions sur le VNQDD et le TLVD, 1907–1946', Paris: DEA, Paris VII, 1994, pp. 23–48. During the life of *La Lutte*, the word 'Vietnam' appeared only once, on 8 May 1935. Hémery, *Révolutionnaires vietnamiens*, p. 105.

Nationalist Party made a conscious effort to put the word Vietnam in the patriotic vocabulary – writing it in 'iron and blood' (*bang mau va sat*) if need be. Going a step further than Phan Boi Chau, the VNQDD took traditional symbols of ethnic identity, such as 'Rivers and Mountains', 'Children of the Lac Hong' and 'people of the same family' and started linking them to a modern concept of the nation that they called 'Vietnam'. In the call-to-arms days before the unforgettable suicide attack of Yen Bay (and at the precise moment that Ho was arguing in favour of a Vietnamese Communist Party in Hong Kong), Hoc and Nhu went so far as to *demand* that the people shout 'Long Live Vietnam!' (Viet Nam van tue!) before shedding their blood for the 'nation' (Quoc gia). The power of the word 'Vietnam' became legendary on 17 June 1930 with the execution of Nguyen Thai Hoc. Stepping last on to the scaffold at daybreak, Hoc bowed to the Vietnamese crowd and then screamed with a chilling northern accent – 'Viet Nam van tue!' – seconds before being decapitated. [56]

Yet despite this dramatic semantic reorientation, the word 'Vietnam' remained largely unknown to the common folk between 1930 and 1945.[57] That Hoc, Nhu and Tran Trong Kim had actually to *ask* the people to pronounce this term instead of 'Annam' is in itself revealing. And less than a month after the execution of Hoc, the famous poet Tan Da defended the place of 'Annam' in his literary review, *An-Nam Tap Chi,* insisting that neither scholars nor peasants used the word 'Vietnam' in their daily language. In short, 'Vietnam' was taking form in the minds of revolutionary leaders. When it comes to planning a nationalist revolution, it is the elite who searches out new symbols and names. The French Sûreté understood what was going on, and continued to translate 'Vietnam' into French as 'Annam'. But a French journalist who had witnessed the execution of Hoc published a sympathetic account of the events of 1930, entitled *Viet-Nam: la tragédie indochinoise.* The title is important. Not only was it the first time that the word 'Vietnam' appeared publicly in French, but it brings us back to this on-going contradiction between 'Indochina' and what was now

56. 'Police de l'Indochine, secret, no. 7880/sg, Hanoi, 18 June 1930, 'Compte rendu de P[aul] Arnoux', pp. 1–2, in d. 2525, c. 323, NF, CAOM and 'Arnoux à Monsieur le Résident Supérieur au Tonkin', Hanoi: Déclaration faite par Nguyen Van Nho', no. 3791-S, Hanoi, 20 March 1930, in d. no. 2 – Phan Boi Chau, c. 353, SPCE, CAOM.

57. See Huong Giang, 'Faut-il appeler autrement l'Annam et les Annamites', *Echo Annamite,* 30 April 1927, p. 1; Linh Chieu, 'Annam, Viet-Nam, hay la Dai-Nam', *Trung Lap,* no. 6356, 26 January 1931, p. 1; and Phan Khoi, 'Nen Xung Viet Nam la Phai', *Trung Lap,* no. 6367, 7 February 1931, p. 1.

replacing 'Annam' to become 'Vietnam' in the nationalist discourse, a term which I will now take up in my text.[58]

Ho Chi Minh shared, at this point in time at least, the VNQDD's preference for 'Vietnam'. However, if the Nationalist Party limited its revolutionary purview to the eastern part of the peninsula, the communists did not escape the pull of the Indochinese model. It was during a Central Committee meeting in October 1930 that the VCP became the Indochinese Communist Party (ICP; Dang Cong San Dong Duong) on instructions from the Comintern that Cambodia and Laos be officially included as part of the Party's domain in view of the Indochina-wide nature of French colonialism. There was strong support from young Viet militants. Ho Chi Minh's narrow-minded nationalism and failure to fuse the communist organizations of Indochina from top to bottom were severely criticized by pro-Indochinese proponents pushing a proletarian line. Whatever the case, the rewritten October Political Platform addressed this matter by incorporating Vietnam, Cambodia (Cao-mien) and Laos (Ai-Lao) into a new political unit referred to as the 'land of Indochina' (xu Dong Duong). Besides continuing the call for the overthrow of feudalism, the implementation of land reform, and the expulsion of French imperialism, the ICP picked up the earlier slogan calling for 'Complete Indochinese Independence!'[59] As a communist journal explained,

> Although three countries are made up of three different races, with different languages, different traditions, different behaviour patterns, in reality they form only one country. … Although the Party's name is only a form, since the form is important for the revolution, the change has to be made.[60]

If Nguyen Van Vinh and Tieu Vien saw an Indochina in capitalist terms by 1930, communists saw a budding Indochinese proletariat in the form of the growing Vietnamese communities working in Laotian mines and Cambodian rubber plantations. Since the early 1920s roads built by the French between Laos and the Vietnamese coast, especially Colonial Route 9, had increased Vietnamese migration. By the mid-1930s there were around 6,000 Vietnamese coolies working in Laotian mines, among whom novice communists had

---

58. Tan Da, 'Kinh ngo … ', p. 1 and Louis Roubaud, *Viet-nam, la tragédie indo-chinoise*, Paris: Librairie Valois, 1931.

59. 'Goi cho nhung nguoi cong san o Dong Duong', in *Van Kien Dang*, vol. I, pp. 31–49; Huynh Kim Khanh, *Vietnamese Communism*, Ithaca: Cornell Press, 1982, p. 185; and Tran Phu, 'Luan Cuong Chinh tri Nam 1930 cua Dang', Hanoi: NXBST, 1983, pp. 11, 16–17.

60. As cited by Khanh, *Vietnamese Communism*, p. 128.

been militating since 1930.[61] A few years later, these populations were such that Vietnamese communists started forming their own Workers Associations in Vientiane and Thakhek alongside the bureaucrats' Amicales. Moreover, technology and political relaxation were such that in 1938 Vietnamese communists could send administrative instructions by telegraph to their Laotian and Cambodian-based cells, in much the same way that Vinh had wired his reports on gold prospecting in Laos back to editors in Hanoi.[62] In Cambodia, Vietnamese communists concentrated their activities on the thousands of coolies working on eastern Cambodian plantations. Things continued in this direction during the laxer Popular Front period, when Vietnamese communists organized the famous 'Indochinese Congress' (Dai Hoi Dong Duong), whose Lao and Cambodian branches centred, unsurprisingly, on Vietnamese urban communities. ICP activists attracted hardly any Khmer or Lao ethnic support.[63] Ethnically, Indochinese communism remained a Viet affair.

In brief, from 1930 many communist and non-communist nationalists were borrowing the French Indochinese model. And even Ho Chi Minh could go Indochinese if need be. He was one of the Comintern's most important delegates in Asia. While Ho probably had doubts about the viability of the Indochinese model, he seems to have accepted the new line. In a letter dated 20 April 1931, he even scolded dissenting colleagues who balked at accepting the Indochinese name on the grounds that 'Cambodia and Laos would first have to be [properly] organized.'[64] Four years later, in a Resolution approved at the ICP's Macao Congress of 1935 (which Ho did not attend), communists promised the Lao, Khmer and other ethnic minorities the right to 'self-determination', but they also aimed to place them within the 'Soviet Union of the Indochinese Republic' (Lien bang cong hoa xo-viet Dong-duong). Even the Central Committee of the

61. Charles Robequain, *L'Évolution économique de l'Indochine française*, Paris: Centre d'Études de Politique Étrangère, 1939, p. 292.

62. 'Thai do cac nha cam quyen o Thakhek doi voi viec xin lap Ai Huu Tho Thuyen', *Tin Tuc*, no. 23, 3–8 August 1938, p. 4 and 'Cung ong Ha Van Thoat o Vientiane', *Tin Tuc*, no. 37, 24–28 September 1938, p. 2.

63. 'Tim Hieu ve Dang CPC', Hanoi: Military Library, undated but clearly post-1979, pp. 7–9 and Georges Freysey, 'Le peuple cambodgien et la commission d'enquête parlementaire', *Le Travail*, no.1, 16 September 1936, p. 4.

64. Gouvernement Général de l'Indochine, *Contribution à l'histoire des mouvements politiques de l'Indochine Française, Documents* – vol. IV., Hanoi, 1933, 'Traduction de la lettre autographe de Nguyen Ai Quoc, Envoyée de Hong Kong, le 20 Avril 1931, au comité central du Parti Communiste Indochinois,' p. 114.

Communist Party of China supported the idea of a future political structure to be known as 'Soviet Indo-China.' Vietnamese communists conceded at the Sixth Plenum of November 1939 that 'the alliance of Indochina need not form a single nation, for the peoples of Vietnam, Cambodia, and Laos have been independent.' However, the idea of an Indochinese Union was transformed in 1939 into plans for two Vietnamese-led political forums, the National United Anti-Imperialist Front of Indochina and – after the expected revolution – the Federal Government of the Democratic Republic of Indochina (Chinh Phu Lien Bang Cong Hoa Dan Chu Dong Duong).[65]

Ho's return to the Vietnamese revolutionary scene in 1940–41 would bring young internationalists back to the nationalist fold, when he breathed new life into the word 'Vietnam' through the Vietnamese Independence League (Viet Nam Doc Lap Dong Minh; Viet Minh for short). Yet this does not necessarily mean that Ho or his followers had abandoned the Indochinese model. In what may be a compromise to the internationalist Indochinese line, Vietnamese communists attempted simultaneously to form both a Cambodian Independence League (Cao-Mien Doc Lap Dong Minh) and a Laotian Independence League (Ai-Lao Doc Lap Dong Minh). Working together, the three national leagues were part of a Vietnamese vision of a larger politico-strategic body that was to be known as the Indochinese Independence League (Dong Duong Doc Lap Dong Minh). The Indochinese body would be directed by a Central Executive Committee (Tong Bo) under which three national committees (*chap uy*) would represent 'each country of the Union.' Even in his famous letter to his countrymen (written in Chinese) in 1941, Ho gave away a 1930s Comintern accent when he criticized the French for having ceded parts of 'our land' (*dat dai cua ta*) to Thailand. Ho was referring to western Cambodia and Laos.[66]

The slogan of a 'Union of Socialist Indochinese Soviet Republics' was allegedly dropped during the Eighth Plenum of the ICP's Central Committee

65. 'Nghi Quyet ve Cong tac trong cac Dan toc thieu so', in *Van Kien Dang*, vol. I, pp. 528–535; 'Open Letter to the Communist Party of Indo-China from the Central Committee of the Communist Party of China', August 1934, *Straits Settlements Police, Political Intelligence Journal*, (39 September 1934), pp. 77–80; Hollis C. Hebbel, 'The Special Relationship in Indochina', in Joseph J. Zasloff, (ed.), *Postwar Indochina*, Washington: Foreign Service Institute, 1988, p. 110; and *Nhung Su Kien*, p. 484.

66. Tønnesson, *Vietnamese Revolution*, pp. 124, 150, note 46, citing a French intelligence translation of the Viet Minh's 1941 Political Programme; 'Thu cua cu Nguyen Ai Quoc Gui ve Nuoc Nam 1941 (6 June 1941)', in Minh Tranh and Hoang Luong, *Nghien Cuu Lich Su*, no. 249, (February 1990), p. 49; and Trinh Van Thao, *Vietnam du confucianisme au communisme*, Paris: L'Harmattan, 1990, p. 220.

on 20 May 1941, but it did not rule out the possibility of a future '[Indochinese] Union of Democratic Republics'.[67] Vietnamese communists were envisioning three nations taking form within an Indochinese Union or Federation.

Trying to Have It Both Ways, 1940–45

So why, if the Indochinese idea was acquiring such a palpable consistency by the outbreak of the Pacific War, did an Indochinese nation not come into being when the war ended, whereas the Javanese adopted the geo-patterns of the Dutch colonial model to form an independent Indonesia? Up to this point, I have tried to show that the idea of an 'Indochinese nation' was quite 'real'. The problem, however, is that from 1930 this 'Indochinese nation' started hitting up against an equally real ethnocultural identity that had links in a pre-colonial patriotic culture and was firmly anchored in the eastern part of the peninsula, mainly Annam and Tonkin. When French colonialism crumbled following the March 1945 Japanese coup, Vietnamese nationalists found themselves caught between the two – tempted to take over the Indochinese model pushed by French colonialism and international communism, but pulled back by a strong ethnic and historical attachment to Vietnam.

Time was certainly part of the problem. A few more decades of French colonialism, as Hoang Xuan Han put it (or large-scale industrialization as I would argue), and the mechanisms of French colonialism might well have transformed the Indochinese idea into a concrete bureaucratic, economic and military reality, turning the Vietnamese into Indochinese nationals like the Javanese in the plural nation of Indonesia. Indeed, had the Trans-Indochinese railway penetrated into Laos and Cambodia as Sarraut had originally envisioned, one can ask whether this would have provided stronger material momentum to the Indochinese idea. But the Dutch had a considerable head start on the French. The latter first laid tracks for southern China before heading southwards to Saigon. The Dutch had largely completed their rail system and maritime services in Indonesia by 1920, whereas the French did not finish the Trans-Indochinese until 1936. The lines between Saigon and Phnom Penh and Vinh and Thakhek remain unachieved. As a French expert wrote in 1936: 'The Trans-Indochinese line will constitute firstly a material and tangible link in the union of the different *pays* of the Indochinese federation. But it will take years before "a

---

67. Hebbel, 'The Special Relationship in Indochina', p. 110.

sense of nation", to borrow Mr Albert Sarraut's term, can emerge from this amorphous mass of races.'[68]

But there is more to it than time. Benedict Anderson is correct to emphasize differences between the Dutch and French education policies, the latter implementing language policies that worked against a common bureaucratic language, while the former facilitated an Indonesian person, with a language that was not Javanese, but Malay (Bahasa Indonesia).[69] Also, in French Indochina, the Lao and Khmer were 'not imagining' Indochina in the same way that many intellectuals of Sumatra, Kalimantan and Sulawesi imagined Indonesia. Khmer and Lao participation in the French Indochinese administration was limited. Travel lists in the *Bulletins administratifs* make it clear that they were certainly not going east to work in Vinh as often as the Vietnamese were going west to work in Phnom Penh or Vientiane.[70] Furthermore, for cultural reasons far too complex to explore here, the Lao and Khmer did not share the Confucian penchant for linking education to bureaucratic careers. The French reinforced these cultural divergences by promoting Reformed Pagoda Schools that were never designed to form Lao or Khmer civil servants. The number of students formed in these Pagodas in Cambodia increased from 53 in 1924 to 3,000 in 1930, reaching 51,991 in 1946, whereas in Laos 7,549 youngsters filled 387 Pagoda Schools by 1935. There, they learned Khmer or Lao, studied a little Buddhism and history, and even absorbed some French-programmed stereotypes of the Chinese and Vietnamese before returning to their villages.[71] Of those who undertook advanced studies in eastern Indochina or France, most were of royal blood. Unlike the 'Indonesians', the Viet, Lao and Khmer students did not often mix in upper-school, Indochinese classrooms, scouting organizations or even in the 'Indochinese' army. And the division of the Laotian and Cambodian bureaucracies into two separate halves did little to create shared work experiences.

---

68. André Maignan, *L'achèvement du transindochinois La ligne Tourane-Nha-Trang*, Paris: Larose Editeurs, 1936, pp. 14–23.

69. Anderson, *Imagined Communities*, pp. 124–130.

70. One might note that Prince Souphanouvong was schooled in Vietnam and France. He was as much at ease in French as in Vietnamese. His *voyage* east and marriage to a Vietnamese gave perhaps more substance to his ability to go Indochinese in a Vietnamese way. See: 'Le Prince Souphanouvong répond au Commissaire de la République française', *La République*, no. 8, 25 novembre 1945, pp. 1, 4.

71. 'L'Enseignement au Laos: Les écoles de pagode', pp. 11–12 and Pascale Bezançon, 'La Rénovation des écoles de pagode au Cambodge', *Les Cahiers de l'Asie du Sud-Est*, forthcoming, pp. 10, 11, 14.

Significantly, during the Vichy period in Indochina between 1940 and 1945, Admiral Decoux tried earnestly to change this, to create a stronger Indochinese identity, and to promote the standing of the Khmer and Lao. To do this, he aimed to stimulate and then canalize Lao, Khmer and Vietnamese nationalisms into the Indochinese federation in order to defuse counter-nationalisms fanned by Japanese occupants, Thai competitors and Vietnamese revolutionaries. Adhering to cultural and educational policies already underway in Vichy France, Decoux put the accent on tradition and the idea of 'discovering' and resurrecting the 'true' Cambodian, Vietnamese and Laotian patrimonies as part of a larger Indochinese one to be led by *la Mère Patrie* herself. Decoux's highly erudite cultural team (arguably better than Ho Chi Minh's in 1941) consciously fanned particular nationalisms through subtle propaganda drives, the formation of youth groups, as well as expanding sports and scouting organizations. Textbooks were rewritten; articles evoked the glorious nationalist histories of the three *patries* of Indochina; Buddhist tradition and Confucian values were emphasized. Vichy designed and diffused national anthems, flags and symbols for all three countries.[72] Decoux even marched Sihanouk around the Cambodian countryside and into Vietnam in a sort of counter-travelogue, an informal 'getting finally to know your Indochinese neighbourhoods', while Lao elites were asking: *Qui sommes nous?*[73] In December 1942, an important article appeared in Vichy's mouthpiece *Indochine*, entitled 'Fédéralisme indochinois', in which it was explained why the three *pays* could not stand alone as 'nations', but rather had to be associated within the tripartite framework of the 'federation of the Indochinese nation' (nation fédérale indochinoise), because 'only Indochina as a whole' could serve as the model of 'a viable nation.' Each would maintain its unique cultural and linguistic character-istics, just as the Bretons, Basques and Corsicans had done in becoming French, but they would all function within a newly created *Conseil Fédéral Indochinois*, consisting of 23 French and 30 Indochinese – 24 'Annamese', four 'Cambodians' and two 'Laotians.' [74]

---

72. On 'discovering', see: Saumont, 'Notre programme' and Duong Quang Ham, 'Cul-ture française et culture annamite', both in *Indochine*, no. 1, 12 September 1940, pp. 1–3.

73. Thao Poui, 'Une voix laotienne: Qui sommes nous?' *Indochine*, no. 56, 25 September 1941, p. 5 and Nhek Suong, 'Opinion Cambodgienne', *Indochine*, no. 62, 6 November 1941.

74. 'Indochine: Création d'un Conseil Fédéral Mixte, décret no. 1525 du 31 mai 1943' and 'Note à Vichy de Decoux sur la création d'un Conseil Fédéral Indochinois', both in d. 2762, c. 344, NF, CAOM.

If Indochina was not quite yet 'real', this triangular entity, Vichy argued in late 1942, constituted at least 'a national virtuality' (une virtualité nationale).[75] In a fascinating essay, Bui Quang Chieu chimed in, agreeing that the 'Indochinese federation' was becoming 'a nation' and that French had 'become the common tongue of the Indochinese elite.'[76] Even the editorial board of the *Annam Nouveau* had to forget the chauvinistic arguments of its founder, Nguyen Van Vinh, to join with Decoux and Chieu to proclaim that the 'interpenetration' and 'interdependence' of Indochina was giving rise to 'a living reality' (*une réalité vivante*).

> The large-scale youth movement that has been unleashed in Indochina ... and the common education that is being dispensed to all the children of Indochina will soon have fused Cambodians, Laotians and Annamites into one unique personality.[77]

Yet this was still fiction, as the reliance on the future anterior tense belied. The appearance of Lao and Khmer children in what was in effect an updated version of Marquet's 1928 vision of *Five [Indochinese] Flowers*, now turning *three*, was too late. In fact, Vichy actually worked against an Indochinese man by stressing inner cultural, linguistic and racial particularities.[78] Decoux did not have enough time to create a Cambodian and Lao elite capable of joining their Vietnamese counterparts in the bureaucracy. Despite Vichy's optimism, this would not occur overnight. Of the 4,200 members of the Indochinese Youth Movement in 1941, 91 per cent were Viet, the rest were Khmer and there were few, if any, Lao or Moï.[79] Even a photo published in Vichy's Indochinese mouthpiece gave away the fiction. The title hails a patriotic demonstration in Laos rallying in support of France, but the vast majority of the 'indigènes' portrayed are easily identifiable as Viet.[80] In terms reminiscent of Pham Quynh's debate with Prince Phetsarath in 1931, a member of the Lao elite put it best when he wrote in 1946 to Charles Rochet, the French father of Laotian nationalism under Vichy:

75. 'En marge du voyage des souverains d'Annam en Cochinchine et au Cambodge: Fédéralisme indochinois', *Indochine*, no. 119, 10 December 1942, p. 2.

76. Bui Quang Chieu, 'Fédération indochinoise', *La Tribune Indochinoise*, 19 December 1941, p. 1.

77. Editorial, 'L'Union indochinoise', *L'Annam Nouveau*, no. 1064, 28 December 1941, p. 1.

78. *Hymnes et Pavillons d'Indochine*, Hanoi: IDEO, 1941. The word 'Campuchéa' was officially used for perhaps the first time here to get at the timeless Cambodia.

79. J. Lebas, 'Les mouvements de jeunesse en Indochine', *Indochine*, no. 37, 15 May 1941, p. 9.

80. *Indochine*, no. 121, 28 November 1940.

> Neither our heart nor our blood pulls us towards the east. The children of Annam are of a different race than us and we have seen what forced marriages produce. However difficult it may be for *geographers*, we will never be 'Indochinese'. Indochina may be a necessity for us, but she will never be a *patrie*.[81]

In short, the Lao and Khmer never experienced Marquet's, Sarraut's or Decoux's Indochina, nor that of the ICP. And it is here that the 'myth of the lazy' Lao and Khmer may have transformed itself into a certain sense of cultural resistance that kept them outside of the Indochina house being built by the French and Vietnamese.[82]

As for the Viet, Vichy accentuated things by trying to coopt the 'true' Vietnam that had resurged in nationalist circles since 1925–30 and by promoting an Indochinese 'reality'. Neither of these was fiction. Pham Quynh and Ho Chi Minh would find themselves pursuing remarkably similar nationalist policies between 1941 and 1945, when they tried to take hold of the 'real' Vietnam, while striving at the same time to keep it in step with the French and Comintern's Indochinese orders. Decoux gave a loose rein to Pham Quynh's cultural nationalism by making him minister of education in Vichy's Révolution Nationale. Ridiculed by the highly Westernized Self Autonomy Group (Tu Luc Van Doan) since 1932, Quynh took his revenge under Vichy to give the nation back its 'tradition': a heritage that, in his eyes, had been blurred by years of Westernization and competition from anti-colonial parties. He paid lip-service to Decoux's Indochinese model, but what mattered to him was the return to Confucian values, the resurrection of national symbols, culture and the realization and unification of the Annamese entity he had defended so passionately in 1931.[83] In October 1942, Decoux thrilled conservative spirits, when he became the first French official to pronounce the word 'Vietnam' in public.[84] He thus tried to deprive the anti-colonialists of their most powerful nationalist symbol since the executions at Yen Bay in 1930.

---

81. Cited by Charles Rochet, *Pays lao. Le Laos dans la tourmente, 1939–1945,* Paris: Jean Vingeau, Editeur, 1946, p. 205. My emphasis.

82. J. Parisot, 'Situation politique générale de la circonscription', 3ème trimestre 1938, p. 3, in Résident Supérieur du Laos, F4, CAOM.

83. Agathe Larcher, 'D'un réformisme colonial à l'autre. La redécouverte de l'identité culturelle vietnamienne, 1900–1930', Aix-en-Provence, Journée indochinoise, March 1994.

84. Amiral J. Decoux, 'Allocution prononcée à l'Université Indochinoise', *Indochine,* no. 112, 22 October 1942, p. 11.

Meanwhile, Ho Chi Minh was preparing his own nationalist revolution. He evoked many of the same heroes and symbols of 'Vietnam' as Decoux and Quynh; and he was as careful as Decoux to avoid resurrecting certain chapters of Vietnamese history that could irritate Lao and Khmer sensibilities. Through the Viet Minh, Ho fostered a strong counter-nationalism. Unlike Quynh, he could draw upon a full blown cultural militantism running from Phan Dinh Phung and Phan Boi Chau to the VNQDD, elements of which were to be found within his own communist ranks (General Nguyen Binh is a good example). In brief, Ho had every intention in mid-1945 not to fail like the VNQDD had done in early 1930. The Japanese provided the favourable conditions for the Viet Minh to take power. The irony, however, was that once Ho returned to Vietnam from China he had to hold this re-surging, militant nationalism within the Indochinese framework demanded by the ICP, the Comintern and the New France under General de Gaulle.

When French Indochina collapsed on 9 March 1945 this contradiction had still not been resolved by either the conservative or revolutionary Vietnamese. But with the French finally gone, they had to choose. Even the name was still undecided. On 12 March, *Dan Bao* (People's News) heralded formation of Imperial Viet Nam (*Viet-Nam De Quoc*).[85] It was the first time the word 'Vietnam' had appeared publicly as the name of the country since Emperor Gia Long. On 16 March, though, another daily published a proclamation referring to a 'Dai Viet' nation and people.[86] 'Annam' had been the most widely used term since the arrival of the French but, as writers argued in mid-1945, it was to be rejected for it implied 'submission' to foreign powers. After considerable debate, on 12 June 1945, Bao Dai announced finally that the word 'Vietnam' would be the official name of the country, thereby ending the Nguyen dynasty's century-old use of 'Dai Nam'.[87]

Yet, if nationalists had agreed on the name 'Vietnam', they had also to choose a space – was it Indochinese, Vietnamese or something else? Unfortunately, we do not know how Pham Quynh felt on this question in his

---

85. *Dan Bao*, no. 644, 12 March 1945, p.1.

86. 'Bao Cao Nhan Dan Dai Viet', *Dong Phat*, no. 5966, 16 March 1945, p. 1 and Interview with Hoang Xuan Han, 1 August 1993, Paris.

87. 'Y Chung Toi doi voi Thoi Cuc: Quoc Hieu cua ta la gi?' *Dong Phat*, no. 6000, 20 April 1945, p. 1; 'Noi Cac Viet-nam da hop ky dau tien', *Dong Phat*, no. 6008, 7 May 1945, p. 1; 'A propos du drapeau national de l'Empire du Viet-Nam', no. 50, 12 May 1945, *L'Opinion-Impartial*, p. 1; 'An-Dinh Quoc-Hieu, Quoc-Ky va Quoc-Ca', *Dong Phat*, no. 6052, 28 June 1945, p. 1; and Linh-Nam, 'Notre appellation nationale: Dai-Viet? Dai-Nam? Annam? Viet-Nam?', *Sud-Est*, no. 6, November 1949, p. 32.

role as advisor to Bao Dai. We do know, however, that many tried to have it both ways; and like the French they saw the Federal idea as the best way out. On 25 April, an editorial appeared in the daily *Binh Minh* arguing for an Indochinese federation (Lien Bang Dong Duong). Though vaguely defined, it envisioned a union of the states of Vietnam, Laos, and Cambodia, which together would constitute a Central Committee to govern the Indochinese federation. Particular attention was paid to guaranteeing minority rights.[88] Nguyen Van Luyen, an important politician, developed the idea in greater detail in the widely read *Trung Bac Chu Nhat* in early August. Aware of rising anti-Viet feelings, Luyen guaranteed that, as a part of a United Indochinese federation (Dong Duong Lien Hiep Quoc), Laos and Cambodia would share power as part of a tripartite federal government in charge of foreign affairs, defence and finances. By combining their economic potential, communications systems, and defence, Luyen argued, they could not only create a 'great nation', an Indochinese federation, but they could also become 'Indochinese citizens' (*cong dan Dong Duong*).[89]

Communists of the same generation were having similar trouble concealing their Indochinese accents. In June the ICP's general secretary himself, Truong Chinh, wrote in the party's journal that resistance forces would defeat the Japanese and then 'establish an Indochinese Democratic Republic.' Even in the famous Directive No. 1 calling for the general insurrection, Truong Chinh was preparing an 'Indochinese uprising', and not just a Vietnamese one. All of this changed suddenly when the Viet Minh came to power in late August 1945. Vietnamese communists could easily have announced the formation of Truong Chinh's envisioned 'Republic of Indochina' at this time. They balked. Also quietly changed was the term 'Indochinese' in the 1929 revolutionary slogan, 'Complete Indochinese Independence!' It reverted to Ho's 1930 preference for 'Vietnamese': 'Complete Vietnamese Independence!'[90] There must have been high-level inner-Party debate on this change of line, most probably during the ICP All-Country Congress at Tran Trao on 15 August or shortly thereafter.

The Vietnamese line became government policy on 31 August 1945, when the acting minister of the Interior signed legislation ordering the word 'Indochine' in the *Journal Officiel de l'Indochine* to be deleted and

---

88. Do Tu, 'Lien Bang Dong Duong', *Binh Minh*, no. 31, 25 April 1945, pp. 1–2.

89. Nguyen Van Luyen, 'Giao thiep … ', no. 256, pp. 2–4, 27 and no. 257, pp. 7, 24.

90. *Co Giai Phong*, no. 14, 28 June 1945 and no. 15, 17 July 1945, as cited by Stein Tønnesson, *Vietnamese Revolution*, pp. 336–37 and p. 377 for Directive no. 1 and *Nhung Su Kien*, p. 643.

replaced, as of 1 September, by the word 'Viet-Nam' in the Official Record of Viet Nam, *Viet-Nam Dan Quoc Cong Bao*.[91] The next day, Ho announced the formation of the 'Democratic Republic of Vietnam' (Viet Nam Dan Chu Cong Hoa) before thousands of cheering Vietnamese citizens who were proud to be part of an entirely independent *Vietnamese* nation. On 20 October 1945, Ho Chi Minh signed Decree No. 53, in which Article 2 defined a 'Vietnamese national' as an individual born to a father or mother of Vietnamese citizenship or any individual 'born in Vietnamese territory of unknown parents or nationality.' Article 3 turned 'ethnic minorities' residing in the *pays* of the 'Tho, Man, Muong, Nung, Kha, Lolo, etc.' and with 'fixed residence in Vietnamese territory' into 'Vietnamese citizens.'[92] On 16 September 1945, an interesting communist essay on the 'national question' appeared in Hanoi, citing Soviet Russia (Nga-so-viet) as the model to follow in dealing with the 'minority' question and in creating a new 'nation.'[93]

Meanwhile, even after the August Revolution, the tension between the 'Vietnamese' and the 'Indochinese' lines continued in communist political thinking. This was best symbolized by the fact that the Viet Minh's official mouthpiece, *National Salvation* (Cuu Quoc), used the slogan 'Complete Vietnamese Independence!', while the ICP's *Liberation Flag* (Co Giai Phong), edited by Truong Chinh, continued to call for 'Complete Indochinese Independence!' (Dong Duong hoan toan doc lap!). Even after the latter's closure following the public dissolution of the ICP in November 1945, the 'Indochinese' call was renewed in the Party's new mouthpiece, *The Truth (Su That)*. This led to a double line: the communist-run nationalist front, the Viet Minh, advocated 'Vietnam', while the Communist Party, now operating under the cover of a Marxist Study Group, stuck unequivocally to 'Indochina'. Indochina was not dead. In a fitting confusion, a communist faction in the South had even explained at the height of the

---

91. Democratic Republic of Viet-Nam, *Viet-Nam Dan-Quoc Cong-Bao*, no. 1, 29 August 1945, p. 13.

92. French translation of 'Décret no. 53, Article 2, réglementant la nationalité vietnamienne, tel qu'il [*sic*] a été modifié par le décret no. 25 du 25 février 1946' and 'Article 3', in Commissariat de la République pour le Tonkin et le Nord Annam, Haut-Commissariat pour l'Indochine, 'Note à l'attention de Monsieur le Commissaire Fédéral aux Affaires Politiques [Léon Pignon], Saigon, d. Relations avec le GRA [Gouvernement révolutionnaire annamite], c. 157, Conseiller Politique, CAOM. Missing is any mention of the Khmer and Cham ethnic communities.

93. Quoc Thuy, *Van de Dan Toc*, Hanoi: Dai Chung, 1946 but signed 16 September 1945, pp. 28–32.

Revolution that the five points of the star in the Viet Minh's flag represented 'the five lands of the Indochinese federation that had been liberated under the leadership of the Vietnamese nation.' [94]

If one lists Vietnamese communist debates on 'Indochina', it is striking how closely they mirror the debates of the French and those conservative Vietnamese aligned with them in 1919–20, 1930–31, 1935–39, 1941–42, 1945–46, and later in 1950–51 (the Conference of Pau/Replacement of the ICP by the Vietnamese Workers' Party). Archimedes Patti, the first OSS officer to arrive in Hanoi after the August 1945 Revolution, noted this spatial contradiction between 'Vietnam' and 'Indochina':

> I asked Truong Chinh and Hoang Minh Giam to clarify the apparent contradiction in terms between Viet Nam as a nation and Indochina as used in the name of the Indochinese Communist Party. They both held that the terms were compatible since the three nation-states, under French rule, had developed commonalty of geographical, political and economic interests. Hence Viet-Nam, the name of the three *kys* (regions of Tonkin, Annam and Cochinchina) was also applicable to the French 'federation' of Indochinese states. [95]

Conclusion

Though the Vietnamese did not follow Indonesia's lead in 1945 to declare an 'Indochinese nation' as Nguyen An Ninh had dreamed in 1924, they did not abandon the Indochinese pattern overnight. Communists did not revamp the geographical limits of their revolutionary thinking along Cambodian, Laotian and Vietnamese lines until 1951 – after the French had abandoned their last Indochinese federation project in favour of Bao Dai's Vietnam and the DRV had been officially recognized by China and the Soviet Union. In a November 1951 circular, Vietnamese communists conceded that one reason they made this decision was that the 'word Indochina' risked offending 'nationalist Lao and Cambodian elements who [were] distrustful' of Vietnamese intentions in Indochina. But as the French found, strategic, historic and economic reasons would make discarding the Indochinese model easier said than done. As this 1951 circular concluded: '[L]ater, conditions permitting, the three revolutionary parties of Vietnam,

94. 'Lich su Mot Cay Co', *Giai Phong*, no. 1, 25 August 1945, p. 1, Fonds Julien, 47, c. 1, Entrée par voie extraordinaire d'outre-mer, CAOM.

95. Archimedes L.A. Patti, *Why Viet Nam? Prelude to America's Albatross*, Berkeley: University of California Press, 1980, pp. 567–568, note 2.

Cambodia and Laos could associate to form the Party of a Vietnamese, Cambodian, and Laotian Federation.'[96]

As the fiftieth anniversary of the August Revolution was celebrated last year, no one would deny the power of the word 'Vietnam'. But we might also remember that behind that name and its space lurk others, now long forgotten, but against which 'Vietnam' had to define its present national form. This 'working out process' was never simple and the idea of 'Vietnam' was not so sure at the time as it is today. It was the determination of so many to put it on the map – be it at Yen Bay or during the August Revolution or in war – that makes it so powerful. At the same time, however, we might also look to last year's celebrations commemorating the fiftieth Anniversary of the Indonesian Revolution to remind ourselves that the pull of the French model of Indochina was also strong. Indochina is certainly no longer a reality, but older nationalists of the generation of Hoang Xuan Han would probably agree that the idea of an Indochinese nation was not quite as 'unreal' in their youth as we may think today.

---

96. Haut Commissaire de France en Indochine, Service Diplomatique, Saigon, 17 January 1953, no. 261/Cab/CD, Captured Vietnamese communist document dated 1 November 1951 and entitled: 'Considération sur l'apparition officielle du Parti ouvrier vietnamien', p. 3, in v. 398, Asie-Océanie, Indochine, MAE.

CHAPTER FIVE

Gender and Nation in Hindu Nationalism

Peter van der Veer

In 1990 Lal Kishan Advani, leader of the Indian People's Party (BJP), decided to start a ritual procession that would pass through ten states (from Somnath in Gujarat to Ayodhya in Uttar Pradesh)[1] with the ultimate goal of demolishing a mosque in Ayodhya that had been built in 1528 by a general of Babar, founder of the Mughal dynasty. The BJP and its close religious ally, the Vishva Hindu Parishad (VHP), argued that this mosque had been built in the sixteenth century to replace an ancient Hindu temple which had commemorated the place where Rama, the god-hero of the *Ramayana* had been born. In their view it was about time that in independent India the Hindu majority should set right the wrongs done throughout history to them. Mr Advani had chosen the starting-point of his ritual procession deliberately, since the temple of Somnath had also been destroyed by Muslim rulers. After independence it had been rebuilt by the Union Government of India. Hindu nationalists now sought to implement a similar plan of destruction and rebuilding in Ayodhya.

These events have been described and interpreted at some length in my recent book *Religious Nationalism*.[2] On the cover of that book one can see a photograph of Mr Advani, featuring him during that ritual procession as the god Rama with the iconographically correct bow and arrows. That

---

1. See Map 3 on page 150.
2. Peter van der Veer, *Religious Nationalism. Hindus and Muslims in India*, Berkeley: University of California Press, 1994.

procession was called a *rath yatra*, 'a chariot procession', a term used for
processions in which the divine icon (*murti*) of a temple is taken around on a
temple chariot. Mr Advani was carried as an embodied icon of the god
Rama. His *rath*, 'temple chariot', was an extended DCM-Toyota, designed
after the chariot of Arjuna in the televized *Mahabharata*, a 'reli-soap' of
great success at that moment on Indian television. Thereafter his brand of
Hindu nationalism was called 'Toyota-Hinduism' by his opponents. Before
Mr Advani could reach Ayodhya he was stopped by police in Bihar, a state
under the control of a rival political party. Nevertheless, Hindu nationalists
attacked the mosque in Ayodhya on 30 October 1990 and widespread
rioting and arrests followed. The Union Government fell over this issue a
week later. Two years after these events, on 6 December 1992, Mr Advani's
campaign claimed success and the mosque was destroyed with communal
killings and riots breaking out in various parts of the country.

In this chapter I want to address the use of the story of Rama by Hindu
nationalists. In the Ayodhya campaign Rama is the obvious icon, since it is
the 'liberation of his birthplace' which is at stake. However, Rama is more
than an accidental choice from the Hindu pantheon. In the *Ramayana* he is
portrayed as the just king who rules according to religious prescriptions
(*dharma-raja*) and his rule (*rama-rajya*) is presented by Hindu nationalists
as their model. While he is the killer of demons (Muslims, in the Hindu
nationalists' imagination), his restrained conduct (especially in sexual
matters) is a model of behaviour. The choice of Rama as the icon for Hindu
nationalism today is thus anything but accidental.

A powerful analysis of the meaning of Rama for current Hindu
nationalism has been given in a recent, thoughtful and challenging article
by the Sanskritist Sheldon Pollock. In his view there is a longstanding
relationship between the *Ramayana* and political symbology: 'From an
early period the story supplied, continuously and readily, if in a highly
differentiated way, a repertory of imaginative instruments for articulating a
range of political discourses.'[3] Pollock has a specific historical thesis: he
wants to demonstrate that a royal cult of the worship of Rama in temples
arose in the mid-twelfth century and became in some instances central by
the middle of the fourteenth century. According to Pollock, this
development was in reaction to the encounter of Hindu polities with
Central Asian (Muslim) political power. In his reading, the Ramayana is

---

3. Sheldon Pollock, 'Ramayana and Political Imagination in India', *Journal of Asian Studies*, vol. 52, no. 2, 1993, p. 262.

about divine kings and about demonic Others who threaten the divine Order of the World. Its symbology was appropriated in the embellishment of royal cults in embattled Hindu kingdoms.

The proposed relation between a symbology of the cult of Rama and actual historical events between the twelfth and fourteenth centuries is very suggestive. Pollock goes on to also suggest that this symbology is again applied in the 'mythopolitics' of the BJP and VHP today:

> If the Ramayana has served for 1,000 years as a code in which proto-communalists relations could be activated and theocratic legitimation could be rendered... it makes sense that it would be through this mytheme par excellence that reactionary politics in India today would find expression in the interests of a theocratization of the state and the creation of an internal enemy as necessary antithesis.[4]

It seems likely that at least at one level the Rama cult is about the divinization of the Hindu king (*raja*); in other words, that it is a royal cult. This level has been important in Indian history, certainly until the twentieth century and probably in some parts of the country even till independence. Nevertheless, rajas lost their political importance gradually during the nineteenth century and their rituals of legitimation have lost potency.[5] Surely, it is not kings in which politicians of today are interested, but rather a Hindu public of voters. The emergence of the modern political idea of *ramarajya*, 'the rule of Rama', does not show a continuity, but a significant rupture. While Hindu ideologies indeed make use of the symbology of kingly power in their invention of tradition, they do not aim at the establishment of a Hindu kingdom, but of a modern Hindu nation-state. The link between the Rama cult and the modern nation-state can therefore only be partly understood by demonstrating that, historically, the Rama symbology has been used in the legitimation of Hindu kingship. That link has to be inserted in a larger field of religious transformation which has the gradual nationalization of religion, particularly in the middle class, as its main feature. It should therefore be understood as a modern, ideological move. Therefore an understanding of religious symbols of power, as used

---

4. *Ibid.*, p. 288.

5. From the 1877 Imperial Assemblage, at which Queen Victoria was proclaimed Empress of India, imperial ceremonies, such as the Durbars, became the occasions for the establishment of status and authority of the 'native rulers'. See Bernard S. Cohn, 'Representing Authority in Victorian India', in Eric Hobsbawm and Terence Ranger (eds), *The Invention of Tradition*, Cambridge: Cambridge University Press, 1983, pp. 165–209.

by the BJP, has to be based on an analysis of their relation to contemporary devotional practice and to the formation of a national Hindu public.

Another point to be made here is that the term 'politics' should not be restricted to the activities of kings or politicians. It is important to look also at the micro-politics in the household, in religious institutions, in schools. If one wants to interpret what the worship of Rama *does* (perhaps more than *means*) one has to look at these micro-practices and historicize them, at least as far as one can. In this way one moves from meaning to practice, from symbol to discipline, and that move enables one to get at the power to construct meaning and its contestation. The worship of Rama is embedded in various practices which do differ strongly from one another. This implies that it is impossible to get at a master meaning of Rama and it is precisely the politics of constructing a master meaning which has to be understood. Moreover, it is not only modern politicians who are in this game, but, primarily, it is elites of religious specialists. This is precisely why in current Hindu nationalism the Vishva Hindu Parishad (VHP), led by an assembly of monks, is so important. Considering the role militant Buddhist monks play in Sinhala nationalism in Sri Lanka and Shi'ite clerics play in Iran, the case of the Hindu activist monk might in fact not be that exceptional.[6]

Rama is worshipped today in temples throughout northern India. One often finds his image (with the bow) together with those of his brother Lakshman and his wife Sita. This ensemble refers to the period of exile in which Rama fought the demons in the jungle, as narrated in the many versions of the Ramayana. Not only temple worship is significant in the Rama cult, but also the miracle plays of Rama, which take place every year over several weeks in many parts of northern India and in an especially grandiose manner in Benares. Also, there are the frequent sacred retellings of the Ramayana in Hindi by story-tellers who are invited at special family occasions or on religious festivals to narrate the story of Rama and to explain it to audiences. Finally, there are the pilgrimage centres connected to the Rama story, most of which are in the north (Ayodhya, Chitrakut, Janakpur), but some in the south (Rameshwaram). Pilgrims who visit these places are taken to the temples that are connected to sacred sites, where episodes of the Rama story are said to have taken place.

---

6.   Stanley J. Tambiah, *Buddhism Betrayed? Religion, Politics and Violence in Sri Lanka*; Chicago: University of Chicago Press, 1992; Michael Fischer, *From Religious Dispute to Revolution*, Cambridge: Harvard University Press, 1980.

Since the sixteenth century an important force behind the propagation of the worship of Rama in north India has been the ascetic order of the Ramanandis. They are by far the most important monastic order among the so-called 'four traditions' of the north Indian Vaishnavas. Although Vaishnavas commonly regard Rama as an incarnation of Vishnu, the Ramanandis see him as the Supreme Lord in his own right. Tulsidas was probably not a Ramanandi himself, but his sixteenth-century Hindi rendition of the Ramayana, the *Ramcaritmanas* was promoted by the Ramanandis who spread from Rajasthan to other parts of north India during the sixteenth century. In the seventeenth and eighteenth centuries the Rama-nandis had established themselves in holy places connected with episodes in the Rama story, such as Janakpur in the Nepalese Terai, and Ayodhya and Chitrakut in what is now called Uttar Pradesh. Ramanandi ascetics roam the countryside and the cities spreading the devotion of Rama and Hanuman. Their contribution to the modern cult of Rama has been immense. Their disciplines are among the data that one might turn to in an analysis of the devotional worship of Rama in modern north India.

The Gender Politics of the Rama Cult

Ramanandi monks (*vairagis*, lit. men without desire) are celibate men. There are almost no nuns in the order, since women are regarded to be too weak for a religious calling; moreover, they should be mothers, not renouncers. As I have explained elsewhere, there are three suborders in the Ramanandi order: *tyagis* (renouncers), *nagas* (militant ascetics) and *rasiks* (devotional-ists).[7] The *tyagis* accumulate heat (*tapas*) and ascetic power (*shakti*) through their ascetic disciplines. With them image worship and sedentary life in temples is marginal. They worship fire and ashes. They live in huts or roam around in travelling groups. The *nagas* specialize in physical strength. They live in fortified temples and train themselves in wrestling. Their worship is often focused on the monkey-god Hanuman. The *rasiks*, finally, specialize in devotional theatre in temples. In their discipline they try to perform a role in the imaginary life of Rama and his wife Sita, often as the maid-servants/female companions of Sita. What do these three groups have in common? They all see themselves as 'slaves' (*das*) of Rama and they are all initiated in the Ramanandi order through the Rama mantra (meditation formula).

7. Peter van der Veer, *Gods on Earth. The Management of Religious Experience and Identity in a North Indian Pilgrimage Centre*, London: Athlone Press, 1988.

Much could be said about the historical development of the Ramanandis over the last few centuries and I have tried to contribute to that discussion in my earlier work. One of my historical arguments has been that the *rasiks* with their 'sweet devotion' have gained in importance as compared to the other two groups because of a long-term process of settling in temples and pilgrimage places.[8] What I want to stress here, however, is that I found all these three groups to be still very much present and viable in my fieldwork of the late 1970s and early 1980s. If we want to get at the micro-politics of the Rama cult of the Ramanandis, we shall have to take all of these groups into account with some more attention perhaps to the *rasiks*.

A central element in the disciplines of the Ramanandis is the trans-formation of (sexual) energy into power. As I have said before, Ramanandis are men without passion. Detachment is also a striking aspect of Rama in the Ramayana.[9] This is evident from his reaction to his exile but, even more importantly, from his detached love for his wife Sita. The relationship between Rama and Sita is often taken to be the paradigm of married love. Rama is the ideal, detached husband who puts the socioreligious order (*dharma*) even above his love for his wife. He is the Lord of Propriety. Sita, on the other hand, is the ideal submissive wife who shows unquestioning loyalty to her husband (*pativrata*). The concept of *pativrata* implies a special form of holiness for women that lies in selfless surrender to the husband-god. There is a Hindu belief that the wife is responsible for the well-being of the husband. If he dies before her, she 'has eaten her husband', as the Hindi expression goes. However, the husband can only survive when he resists the attractions of the female body through detachment. It is his duty to love his wife with detachment and to preserve order in the family by his male authority.

I would suggest that, while at one level the political symbology of the Rama story and the Rama cult centres on kingship, at another level it centres on patriarchy. It is this level which is paramount in the Rama devotion, propagated by the Ramanandis. It is not an unambiguous message by any means, since the ideal of the detached, married man is propagated by a detached, celibate man. My Ramanandi informants argued that detachment could perhaps be attained by a married man, but that it was

---

8. Peter van der Veer, 'Taming the Ascetic: Devotionalism in a Hindu Ascetic Order', *Man* (NS), vol. 22, 1987, pp. 680–695.

9. Robert Goldman, 'Ramah Sahalaksmanah: Psychological and Literary Aspects of the Composite Hero of Valmiki's Ramayana', *Journal of Indian Philosophy*, vol. 6, 1980, pp. 149–189.

extremely difficult. They have a notion that, in principle, passionless pro-creation is possible through ascetic discipline. A connected aspect of this issue is that the blessing of especially radical ascetics, the *tyagi*s, is much sought after by barren women. The Rama-mantra is, interestingly, called a *bija-mantra* (seed-mantra). Nevertheless, celibacy is absolutely crucial in the ascetic discipline of the Ramanandis. The ideal image of masculinity conveyed by tyagis is that of the independent, self-sufficient male who stores his 'heat' and acquires power. However, an interesting element in this is that power (*shakti*) is seen as feminine in Hinduism. Thus, in a way, a *tyagi* realizes a feminine power within himself by refraining from sexual inter-course with women. In a similar vein, a *rasik* needs celibacy to be able to be transformed in a female attendant at the love play of the gods. Finally, Hanuman, the patron-deity of the *naga*s, is both the paragon of masculine, physical strength (*bal*) and of selfless devotion which is also seen as feminine.

The patriarchal message of the Rama story then is ambiguous. It is caught in a dialectic of femininity and masculinity which plays itself out in a variety of religious forms. This dialectic unsettles a straightforward Rama-yana narrative of 'the Hindu family' by offering an alternative in the possibility of renunciation. On the other hand, it has to be realized that these ascetic groups, while ideologically resisting domesticity, are to an important extent themselves domesticated by their total dependence on the charity of a lay population. It would therefore be incorrect to interpret their beliefs and practices as outright 'resistance' to married life. On the contrary, they continue to stress the sacredness of married life, if it is well disciplined. This discipline depends on the detachment of the husband and the devotion of the wife. Since the Ramanandis want to combine detachment and devotion, they have to link femininity and masculinity.

The Nationalization of Devotion

If my argument that the Ramanandi version of Rama devotion is concerned with gender and patriarchy is correct, how is this concern incorporated and interpreted in Hindu nationalism? To answer this question I want to turn our attention to the nineteenth-century Hindu reform movements which are the main ideological sources for Hindu nationalism today. One of the early instances of a 'Hindu public' responding to colonial rule deals precisely with the issue of gender and patriarchy. I am referring here to the debate on the abolition of sati (widow immolation) by the British in 1829. Rammohan Roy (1772–1833), sometimes called 'the father of the Bengal

Renaissance', wrote between 1818 and 1832 a great deal on the subject. In January 1830 Roy, together with 300 residents of Calcutta, presented a petition to Governor-General William Bentinck in support of the regulation prohibiting sati.

Rammohan rejected the practice on the basis of his reading of Hindu scripture. He distinguished authoritative sources (such as the Vedas) from other sources. It is interesting to note that he did not refer to any authoritative interpretation of these sources by learned gurus, but entirely relied on his private, rational judgement. This is certainly an important step in the laicization of Hinduism. What we also see here is the importance of scriptural authority which can be referred to by a lay person without mediation of a sacred interpreter. One of Rammohan's most important objectives was to abolish the rules of the caste-based, hereditary qualification to study the Veda.[10] Following Lata Mani, I would suggest that the colonialist insistence on the unmediated authority of written evidence for Indian traditions, enabled by the orientalist study of these texts, made a gradual shift in emphasis from the spoken to the written possible in Hinduism.[11] This shift enables the rise not only of a public, but also of a public debate in Habermas's sense.[12]

The main issue in the debates about sati in the nineteenth century is that of the free choice of the widow. One of the central colonial criticisms of Indian civilization, as for example in James Mill's *The History of India* (1817), was its treatment of women, of which widow-immolation was perhaps the most abhorrent example. According to Gayatri Spivak, the Sanskrit tradition defines the woman as object of a *one and only* husband who is her god and locates her free will in the act of self-immolation as a means to free herself from her female (lower) body.[13] The question of freedom receives an interesting twist in the context of Hindu discourse on spiritual liberation. The freedom of the Hindu woman, as debated by

---

10. Wilhelm Halbfass, *India and Europe*, Albany: State University of New York Press, 1991, pp. 205–206.

11. Lata Mani, 'Contentious traditions: The Debate on *Sati* in Colonial India', in Kumkum Sangari and Sudesh Vaid (eds), *Recasting Women: Essays in Indian Colonial History*, New Brunswick: Rutgers University Press, 1990, pp. 88–127. See also Peter van der Veer, 'Sati and Sanskrit: the Move from Orientalism to Hinduism', in Mieke Bal and Inge Boer (eds), *The Point of Theory. Practices of Cultural Analysis*, Amsterdam: Amsterdam University Press, 1994, pp. 251–260.

12. Jurgen Habermas, *The Structural Transformation of the Public Sphere: An Inquiry into a Category of Bourgeois Society*, translated by Thomas Burger. Cambridge: MIT Press, 1991.

13. Gayatri C. Spivak, 'Can the Subaltern Speak?', in Cary Nelson and Lawrence Grossberg (eds), *Marxism and the Interpretation of Culture*, Urbana: University of Illinois Press, 1988, pp. 271–313.

colonial officials and Hindu reformists on the one hand and Hindu defenders of the practice on the other, has therefore to be related with questions of inauspiciousness and auspiciousness. As we have argued earlier, the auspicious woman has to protect her husband from death. If she fails to do so, she can only regain her auspiciousness by following him into death. Otherwise she will become an inauspicious widow.

While the sati debate ends with the prohibition by the British, the 'women's question' continues to be one of the main issues in Hindu reform movements. Later in the nineteenth century the arguments are more influenced by Victorian ideas about 'domesticity', 'companiate marriage' and female education, but, as Dipesh Chakrabarty has recently argued, 'the ideal of the 'modern', educated housewife was almost always tied to another ideal, the older patriarchal imagination of the mythical divine figure of Lakshmi'.[14] A woman had to be educated to be civilized, but she should not become free in the same way as the modern Western woman (the *memsahib*, the wife of the colonial official, being the negative stereotype), but as a true Hindu, that is a modest and auspicious woman entirely devoted to her husband.

Both the sati debate and the later debates on the 'Hindu housewife' took place in elite and middle-class circles. One of these circles was the Brahmo Samaj, founded in 1828 by Rammohan Roy. This was a small movement, propagating a deist and universalist kind of religion, based, however, on Hindu sources and especially the Upanishads and the philosophical commentaries on the Upanishads (together known as the Vedanta). The intellectual Vedantic and Unitarian views of the Brahmos left them to an important extent isolated from the larger Hindu society. On the other hand, the Brahmo Samaj was perhaps no smaller than the circles of Deists in England or Freemasons in France and Holland, which are the subject of European writing on the history of the Enlightenment. Obviously, the question of the structural transformation of European or Indian societies cannot be addressed from a history of ideas only. The ideas of Rammohan did not cause the emergence of a Hindu public which came to be represented in anti-colonial, nationalist politics. The colonial politics of representation (in census operations and legal practices, for instance) as

---

14. Dipesh Chakrabarty, 'The Difference-Deferral of (A) Colonial Modernity: Public Debates on Domesticity in British Bengal', *History Workshop*, no. 36, (1993), p. 7. Lakshmi is the wife of Vishnu and, just as Rama is an incarnation of Vishnu, Sita is an incarnation of Lakshmi, the goddess of wealth and happiness.

well as the improvements in communication, and a host of other things, have played a crucial role in this. Given the colonial transformation of Indian society, however, the question remains how modern reformist thought reached a broader Hindu audience and could thus serve as a basis for Hindu nationalism.

In the 1860s Keshabchandra Sen (1838–84), one of the most influential Brahmo leaders, introduced devotional singing in the Brahmo congregational meetings.[15] He also no longer spoke English, but only Bengali. He moved to the rural outskirts of Calcutta and introduced an ascetic lifestyle among his followers. The next step seems to have been his encounter with the contemporary guru, Ramakrishna (1836–86), a priest in a temple for the Mother Goddess Kali in Calcutta. In his two newspapers (one in English, one in Bengali) he introduced Ramakrishna to the wider reading public as a true saint in the authentic Hindu tradition. In that way he authorized this illiterate Hindu ascetic as an acceptable guru for the Hindu middle classes. In a recent book on Indian nationalism, Partha Chatterjee portrays the meeting of these two personalities as constituting the 'middle ground' occupied by the emergent middle classes, between European rational philosophy and Hindu religious discourse.[16] In his view this 'middle ground' enables the anticolonial nationalists to divide the world into two domains: the material, outer world which is dominated by Western science and the spiritual, inner world which is dominated by Hindu values. Again, it is in the spiritual 'inner' world of the home that the question of gender is of paramount importance.

In an analysis of the *Ramkrsna Kathamrta* (the 'sayings' of Rama-krishna), Chatterjee shows that the female body is represented as 'the prison of worldly interests, in which the family man is trapped'.[17] The theme of the necessity of the detachment of men which we have encountered earlier in our discussion of the Ramanandis comes up again. While the language of this kind of asceticism is often misogynous, Ramakrishna actually propagates an androgynous state, in which man realizes the feminine in himself, in a manner similar to that of the Ramanandi ascetics. His discourse stresses the dialectic of femininity and

---

15. David Kopf, *The Brahmo Samaj and the Shaping of the Modern Indian Mind*, Prince-ton: Princeton University Press, 1979.

16. Partha Chatterjee, *The Nation and Its Fragments; Colonial and Postcolonial Histories*, Princeton: Princeton University Press, 1993.

17. *Ibid.*, p. 63.

masculinity in the detachment of men. This detachment is necessary not only for spiritual perfection, but also for recovering the masculine strength which has been sapped by colonial domination. The British colonial stereotype of the effeminate nature of Hindus is thus countered and transformed in the Hindu theme of the dialectics of femininity and masculinity.

The theme of Hindu spirituality as against Western materialism definitely becomes the principal theme in Hindu nationalist discourse from this period onwards. A major step in the popularization of Hindu reformist ideas was made by linking it to emergent nationalism. 'Hindu spirituality' had to be defended against the onslaught of colonial modernity. Perhaps the most important expounder of the doctrine of 'Hindu spirituality' has been the founder of the Ramakrishna Mission, Vivekananda (1863–1902). Vivekananda was an extremely talented student who had been thoroughly educated in contemporary Western thought. He joined the Brahmo Samaj briefly before he met Ramakrishna. The encounter with Ramakrishna had a transformative impact on the young Narendranath Datta who adopted the name Vivekananda when he took his ascetic vows. As Tapan Raychaudhuri emphasizes, Vivekananda was 'more than anything else a mystic in quest of the Ultimate Reality within a specific Indian tradition'.[18] It is this tradition which was vividly presented to Vivekananda not by learned discourse in which he himself was a master, but by the charismatic presence of a guru, Ramakrishna, whose trances had first been treated as 'insanity', but later became regarded as possession by the goddess. What I want to argue is that the articulation of Brahmo 'rational religion' with the religious discourse of Ramakrishna produced the specific brand of 'Hindu spirituality' which Vivekananda came to propagate.

The typical strategy of Vivekananda was to systematize a disparate set of traditions; make it intellectually available for a Westernized audience and defensible against Western critique; and incorporate it in the notion of 'Hindu spirituality', carried by the Hindu nation which was superior to 'Western materialism', brought to India by an aggressive and arrogant 'British nation'. His major achievement was to transform the project to ground 'Hindu spirituality' in a systematic interpretation of the Vedanta (the Upanishads and the tradition of their interpretation). This project which started with Rammohan Roy and had produced Rational Hinduism was now combined with disciplines to attain perfection from the ascetic

18. Tapan Raychaudhuri, *Europe Reconsidered*, Delhi: Oxford University Press, 1988, p. 230.

traditions in what Vivekananda called 'Practical Vedanta'. The practical side also included participation in social reform. This kind of 'spiritual Hinduism' has later been carried forward by Mahatma Gandhi and Sarvepalli Radhakrishnan, but it has also become a main inspiration for the current brand of Hindu nationalism today.

A good example of the construction of Hindu spirituality is Vivekananda's efforts to systematize disparate notions of ascetic practice in an 'ancient system of yoga', which is now India's main export-article on the 'spirituality market'. Yoga is a Sanskrit word that one can translate with 'discipline'. The classical text is Patanjali's *Yoga-Sutras*, dated from probably not later than the fifth century AD. Vivekananda systematized this tradition in a doctrine of salvation, in which rational thought, Patanjali's ideas on meditation, social action and religious devotion were combined. This is a new doctrine, although Vivekananda emphasized that it was 'ancient wisdom'. It is a remarkable step in systematizing 'Hindu spirituality' as healthy for body and spirit. It is also noteworthy that Vivekananda's project got a major impetus when he was enthusiastically received in Europe and the USA. His visit to the World Parliament of Religions in Chicago in 1893 made him a celebrity in the USA and consequently also in India. His new status as international guru strengthened his view of India's contribution to world civilization.

A major element of Vivekananda's message was nationalist. He saw his project very much in terms of a revitalization of the Hindu nation. In 1897 he founded an ascetic order, the Ramakrishna Mission, to make ascetics available for the nationalist task. National self-determination, social reform and spiritual awakening were all linked in his perception. The Ramakrishna Mission established itself throughout India and also outside of India. It did not become a mass-movement, but Vivekananda's rhetoric of spiritualism exerted an immense influence on the way Hindu gurus in the twentieth century came to communicate their message. One can readily see how different such reformist ascetics are from the Ramanandis whom we discussed earlier. Although these differences are real and considerable, it would be wrong to conclude that there is a watertight division between the Ramakrishna Mission and the Ramanandis. It is fair to say that Vivekananda's ideas have permeated beyond Hindu Reformism into the beliefs and practices of many ascetic groups in India. This is obvious for ascetics whose lay following consists of partly Westernized sections of the middle class, ranging from Aurobindo to Swami Shivananda and Swami

Chinmayananda, the founder-president of the Vishva Hindu Parishad, the major Hindu nationalist movement today. But it is also true for ascetics who have a more 'traditional' middle-class following, such as the Shankaracharya of Kanchi or the lone Dashanami Dandi ascetic 'Swamiji', described by Kirin Narayan.[19] Finally, Vivekananda's ideas have also influenced both those older Ramanandi monks who during my fieldwork claimed that they had been active in the independence movement and the current supporters of the Vishva Hindu Parishad among the Ramanandis.

Vivekananda transformed Hindu discourse on asceticism, devotion and worship into the nationalist idiom of 'service to the nation' for both men and women. Vivekananda does not oppose female education, but the ideal of the 'modest, self-effacing, devout' Hindu woman, modelled after Sita, remains the same. Female modesty becomes now a sign of national Hindu pride. This is not an unambiguous, uncontested narrative of bourgeois patriarchy, but the sign of modernity with a difference, inscribed on gendered bodies. Interestingly, it is in India's foremost nationalist leader Mohandas ('Mahatma') Gandhi that we can see both an elaboration of Vivekananda's ideology and an incorporation of the devotional theme of masculinity and femininity which we found both among the Ramanandis and in Ramakrishna. Gandhi's programme of satyagraha exemplified the devotional theme that true selfless devotion is feminine and that women are therefore better qualified for 'non-violence' or 'passive resistance' than are men. Indeed, to realize feminine power and devotion within himself he took a vow of celibacy. Gandhi also demanded from his group of followers that they take the vow of celibacy, which, like Vivekananda, he saw as a prerequisite for a total devotion to the national cause. Non-violence, a feminine attitude which could only be attained by celibacy, was the answer to colonial violence which had emasculated the Indian nation.

Gandhi's view, informed by Hindu devotionalism, was perceived as an enormous threat to another vision of Hindu masculinity by Gandhi's assassin Nathuram Godse, a Maharashtrian Brahman, who declared in his trial that:

> I firmly believed that the teachings of absolute ahimsa as advocated by Gandhiji would ultimately result in the emasculation of the Hindu Community and thus

19. Mattison Mines and Vijayalakshmi Gourishankar, 'Leadership and Individuality in South Asia: The Case of the South Indian Big Man', *Journal of Asian Studies*, vol. 49, no. 4, 1991, pp. 761 784. Kirin Narayan, *Storytellers, Saints and Scoundrels. Folk Narrative in Hindu Religious Teaching*, Philadelphia: University of Pennsylvania Press, 1989.

make the community incapable of resisting the aggression or inroads of other communities, especially the Muslims.[20]

Godse refers in his argument directly to the physical weakness of Hindu men, but indirectly to a larger process of emasculation of the Hindu community. This is a constant theme in Hindu nationalist writings since the British census started to enumerate the numerical strength of Hindus and Muslims.[21] It is one of the main fears of Hindu nationalism that Hindus are dying out and that Muslims with their greater population growth will take over. This fear had been eloquently put into words in U.N. Mukherji's influential book *Hindus: A Dying Race* which was published in 1909.[22] More than anything else, differences in population growth have become a crucial sign of the difference in masculine prowess between Hindu and Muslim men.

Godse had been a member of the Rashtriya Swayamsevak Sangh (RSS), a militant Hindu organization, founded in 1925 by a Maharashtrian Brahman, K.B. Hedgewar. The organization was banned after the murder of Gandhi, but later allowed to function again. Currently it has some two million member-activists all over India. The Maharashtrian connection is significant, since Hedgewar took his inspiration less from religious traditions than from that of the Maratha war bands of the pre-colonial period, led by Shivaji and his successors, who were the main rivals of the Mughals and later of the ascending power of the British. It is this militant tradition of the Maratha Hindu state that was developed by the RSS. In the RSS we find a tradition harping on martial masculinity, in which the dialectic relation with femininity as stressed by Gandhi and most north Indian devotional traditions is much less evident. This is perhaps even more true for the Shiv Sena (the army of Shivaji), another organization in Maharashtra, but of much more recent origin. In the 1960s it started as a nativist movement 'Maharashta for the Marathas' especially against Tamil migrant labourers in Bombay, but it has gradually become the most aggressive anti-Muslim force in West India. As its name already makes clear, it emphasizes even more the martial and anti-Muslim tradition of Maharashtra, and while its appeal was

20. Quotation from Ved Mehta, *Mahatma Gandhi and His Apostles*, Harmondsworth: Penguin, 1977, pp. 175–176.

21. Arjun Appadurai, 'Number in the Colonial Imagination', in Carol A. Breckenridge and Peter van der Veer (eds) *Orientalism and the Postcolonial Predicament*, Philadelphia: University of Pennsylvania Press, 1994, pp. 314–341.

22. P.K. Datta, '"Dying Hindus"; Production of Hindu Communal Common Sense in Early 20th Century Bengal', *Economic and Political Weekly*, 19 June 1993, 1305–1319.

first limited to the slum areas of the big cities, it has now spread to the middle class. Its leader, Bal Thackeray, constantly brings up the theme of the weakness and impotence of the present-day Hindus which has to be countered by Maratha masculinity. In his wild speeches he sometimes goes so far as to celebrate Godse, the murderer of Gandhi, as a hero.[23]

The gender identity of Hindus is clearly the ground of contestation in Hindu nationalism. The practical role of educated, middle-class women in the independence struggle remains an unresolved issue when devotion is nationalized. Women are the supporters of their men, who are actively involved in nationalist debate and struggle. The modest and submissive woman as an ideological construct is the site on which the honour of the Hindu nation is inscribed. This seems to have changed, however, in the last decade, in which low-caste female *sadhus*, like Sadhvi Ritambara, have come to play an important role as orators in the campaigns of the BJP and VHP.

Gandhi sometimes referred to the concept of Ramraj, the rule of Rama, as it is used in Tulsidas's *Ramcaritmanas*. He used it interchangeably with the term for 'self-rule' or independence (*svaraj*). In his view, 'Ramraj was not only the political Home Rule but also dharmaraj ... which was something higher than ordinary political emancipation' and, distancing himself from notions of Hindu kingship, 'Ramraj means rule of the people. A person like Ram would never wish to rule.' [24] Gandhi emancipated in a democratic move the notion of 'the rule of Rama' from its 'royal' aspects and, further, related it to a 'higher' utopian goal, namely the transformation of society by religious reform. This kind of laicization and ethicization of devotional notions is fairly typical for Gandhi. His interpretation easily links up with Vivekananda's reformist notions of Hindu spirituality. It is thus not surprising that this has become an important reading of the notion of 'the rule of Rama'. At the same time another reading, propagated by a short-lived Hindu chauvinist party, Rama Rajya Parishad, in north India in the 1950s, came to co-exist with the Gandhian one. This reading emphasized a programme of exclusivist Hindu nationalism, relating 'the rule of Rama' to a number of conservative points, such as the upholding of caste and communal distinctions. The current radical brand of Hindu nationalism

---

23. See the excellent paper by Thomas Blom Hansen, 'Recuperating Masculinity: Hindu Nationalism, Violence and the Exorcism of the Muslim "Other"', delivered at the Workshop 'Comparative Approaches to National Identities' in Copenhagen, May 1994.

24. Cited in Philip Lutgendorf, *The Life of a Text; Performing the Ramcaritmanas of Tulsidas*, Berkeley: University of California Press, 1991, pp. 380–381.

takes the modern nationalist interpretation of the Ramarajya notion over in its propaganda and is, appearances to the contrary, more indebted to Gandhi and Vivekananda than to Swami Karpatriji, the founder of the Rama Rajya Parishad.

Conclusion

The political use of the Rama cult by Hindu nationalists today is the result of a series of particular, historical processes over the last century. Nationalism is also in Europe a thoroughly modern phenomenon, although it often feeds on earlier formations of identity. One of the developments in at least part of Europe has been the gradual secularization of society. This development has not taken place in India nor, for that matter, in many other parts of the colonized world. What we find here is that religion is conceived of as the main sign of difference in relation to the Western colonizing powers. In that way religion becomes in the second part of the nineteenth century a site of nationalist thought and action. Although there are straight secularists in the nationalist leadership, such as Jawaharlal Nehru, nationalism in India cannot be understood without giving people like Vivekananda and Mahatma Gandhi an important place in the analysis. This is obviously not to argue that Hindu nationalism is of one cloth. There are very important differences among the nationalists who are inspired by Hindu discourse. Gandhi did refer at various occasions to the Ramayana and the Rama cult, but he would not have thought of using it in any way against India's Muslims, although people may have interpreted his idiom in a different way to what he intended.[25] Whatever interpretation we give of Gandhi's political oratory, he was killed for his ideas by a man who belonged to one of the Hindu nationalist groups who are prominent in the current use of the Rama cult for political purposes.

At one level the Rama cult conveys a message about 'the legitimate state'. The post-colonial state has inherited the divisions in civil society which had been created by the British. Politicians depend on votes and the electoral process almost forces them to exploit the religious divisions in society. This is enhanced by the fact that the Indian state has increasingly turned to reservation policies for so-called backward classes in order to

---

25. Shahid Amin, 'Gandhi as Mahatma: Gorakhpur District, Eastern UP, 1921–1922', in Ranajit Guha and Gayatri Spivak (eds), *Selected Subaltern Studies*, New York: Oxford University Press, 1988, pp. 288–351.

change access to education and government employment. This is part of what one might call the penetration of the modernizing state in civil society and many see this as a disruption of the social fabric of society and thus the cause of violence. Hindu nationalists argue vehemently that the Muslims are pampered by the state bureaucracy, because they are a vote-bank for the politicians. It is the perception of the state as thoroughly corrupt and in the hands of the other community, which leads to the utopian idea of a *Ramraj*, a divine rule according to Hindu principles which would solve all the problems of modern society. The BJP has been extremely successful as opposition party in stressing that the illegitimate state is in the hands of the Congress Party and that the 'clean' BJP offers an alternative in *Ramraj*.

At another level the Rama story conveys an ideal patriarchy which legitimizes the political authority of men in the household and in the state. One has to understand, however, that patriarchy acquired new meanings in the nineteenth century when Hindu reformers tried to nationalize devotion and new forms of domesticity. Moreover, a straight, one-dimensional narrative of patriarchy is unsettled by Ramanandi ascetic disciplines, which deal with the transformation of the self by the conquest of desire. The male body is shown to be not the 'natural' source of power, but has to be 'feminized' to become powerful. It is this dialectics of masculinity and femininity in devotional cults which is adopted in Gandhi's brand of nationalism and is contested by his opponents.

Ramanandi ascetics, historically, have played an important role in the spread of Rama devotion over northern India. They continue to do so up to the present day. They are, however, not isolated from the nationalization of Hinduism by reformist movements. Especially, Vivekananda's ideas about the relation between 'Hindu spirituality' and national revival have had an enormous impact, which explains the participation of many monks – but by no means all – in the activities of the Vishva Hindu Parishad. The disciplines concerned with the transformation of the self are now related to reformist notions about the transformation of society. In this new configuration the notion of 'the rule of Rama' gets a salience which it never had for Rama-nandis, and still does not have for a number of them. It has come to stand for 'the rule of the Hindu majority', a totally modern notion that is of little use to those engaged in the worship of fire, Hanuman or Sita's love-play with Rama. It is the Hindu middle-class laity which is primarily the audience for this political reading of the Ramayana, divorced from established devotional practice, but open for devotional enthusiasm. To the extent that the Ramanandis depend on lay patronage, it is a reading that they have to take into account.

A good example of the current nature of middle-class devotionalism is offered by the worship of Hanuman. Interestingly, although Rama is undoubtedly the main character in the Ramayana, his worship has always been less important for Hindus than that of Hanuman, the monkey-god who is Rama's main ally in the Ramayana. Obviously when one wants to understand the worship of Rama, Hanuman worship has to be considered also. Philip Lutgendorf has recently drawn our attention to the ever-expanding worship of Hanuman – the monkey companion of Ram and hero of the *Ramayana* – in the Indian middle classes.[26] In 1989 a 45–foot monolithic granite image weighing some 1,300 tons, hewn by artisans near Mangalore in south India, was brought to Vasant Gaon, a Delhi suburb near Gandhi International Airport. The statue was erected in the ashram of Prabhudutt Brahmachari who had, according to a priest interviewed by Lutgendorf, envisioned the image as a gatekeeper for India's capital, 'so that the Pakistanis and so on cannot attack'. The 'defence of the nation' against Muslim Pakistan is a stock phrase in the propaganda of BJP and VHP. This statue is not exceptional by any means. Very large ones are also erected in middle-class areas elsewhere in the country. Until 1989 the largest was in Himachal Pradesh and erected by the founding president of the VHP, Swami Chinmayananda, a guru with an international, middle-class following. On November 1990, an estimated 500,000 devotees of Satya Sai Baba, the South Indian guru, watched him sitting under a 70–foot image of Hanuman.

Striking in this new middle-class religiosity is its ostentatiousness in going for 'the really big', but also its militant assertiveness. It is very interesting that Hanuman is chosen from the Rama cult as the main symbol. Hanuman combines as no other god the dialectics of feminine devotion and masculine strength. He is the patron-god of the wrestlers and the militant ascetics because of his incredible strength. These ascetics and wrestlers train in special gymnasiums. In my view the immensely popular wrestling sport has developed out of militant asceticism, but contemporary wrestlers are no longer aware of that historical link.[27] In Joseph Alter's terms, wrestlers

---

26. This paragraph is based on Philip Lutgendorf, 'My Hanuman is Bigger than Yours'; Paper delivered at the Symposium on 'Hinduism Today' at the University of Pennsylvania, 30 March 1992.

27. Joseph Alter, *The Wrestler's Body; Identity and Ideology in North India*, Berkeley: University of California Press, 1992, pp. 225–226.

engage in a 'utopian somatics' which resist consumer items and fashion styles that are deemed 'modern'. Wrestlers see physical health and fitness as directly related to one's civic duty.[28] In their vision, modern society is corrupt and this corruption directly affects the body. As so often in this kind of discourse, a relation is laid between the body of the individual and the societal body. Society should be reformed and the reform should start with the individual's body. Much of this abounds with Hindu nationalist rhetoric which can also be found among organizations like the Rashtriya Swayamsevak Sangh (RSS). The latter organization also advocates physical exercise and self-discipline, while Hanuman is duly revered. Unlike the rather unorganized wrestlers, however, the RSS is directly geared at street fighting and direct anti-Muslim warfare. The RSS is, to an important extent, an organization of adolescent boys – the same age cohort which is also interested in wrestling – and it is precisely the energies of these boys which are channelled through a mixture of ascetic celibacy, physical exercise and the worship of Hanuman into communal fighting. It is highly significant that the youth movement of the VHP is called Bajrang Dal, 'the army of Hanuman'. This is the movement which was primarily responsible for the demolition of the Ayodhya mosque in 1992.

Hanuman is a protector (amongst other things against spirits) and a wish-fulfiller. Clearly a useful god for a middle class that is, like its counterparts elsewhere, in need of growing consumption and in fear of falling down the societal scale. But there is one thing that is crucial in the context of my argument. Although he is the patron of wrestlers and a martial figure, Hanuman is at the same time seen as a paramount devotional and sentimental figure as the leading female companion of Sita, Rama's wife in the mystery play which is a central feature of the Rama cult. Hanuman's popularity among the middle classes epitomizes the relation between nation and gender which I have tried to explore in this chapter.

---

28. *Ibid.*, p. 243.

Asian Forms of the Nation

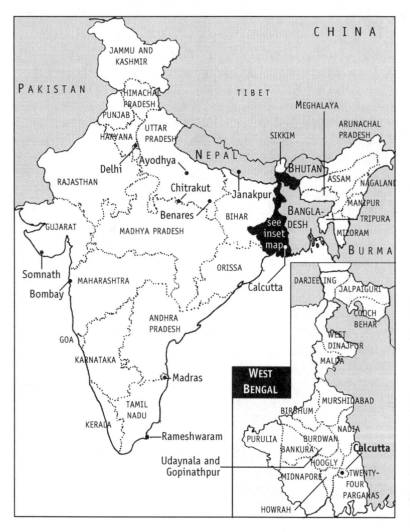

Map 3: Modern India, showing details of West Bengal and pilgrimage centres associated with the worship of Rama

CHAPTER SIX

Contradictions and Ambivalence in the Hindu Nationalist Discourse in West Bengal

Arild Engelsen Ruud

In January 1989 the Rashtriya Swayamsevak Sangh (RSS) – a Hindu nationalist organization – held an opening ceremony for its newly constructed branch office at Maniktala, a poor area of northeast central Calcutta. The ceremony was well designed and carried out, and also well attended with more than a hundred guests – most of them local activists. There were several speeches in Bengali by Calcutta-level RSS leaders. And on the wall facing the audience were displayed large posters of Hedgewar (founder of the RSS) and the Bengali 'hero' Swami Vivekananda, a major religious reformer of the late nineteenth century.

Together, Vivekananda, Nobel Laureate Rabindranath Tagore and Subhaschandra Bose are Bengal's three main 'heroes'.[1] They are commonly depicted on poster-calendars distributed free to customers by shops and enterprises all over the state. Both Tagore and Vivekananda were important figures in the so-called 'Bengali Renaissance'. Important in Vivekananda's continued hero status was his advocacy for Hinduism at the 1893 Chicago World Parliament of Religions, where he gained acceptance for the view that Hinduism is as philosophical and rich as any other world religion. In

---

1. Subhaschandra Bose led the Indian National Army which fought the British in India during World War II. The fourth 'hero', somewhat less commonly depicted, is the Muslim 'revolutionary poet' Kazi Nazrul Islam.

popular perception Vivekananda is considered to have emphasized masculinity and physical prowess as integral to strength of mind and consequently also to national strength. At the same time, though an advocate of Hinduism, he is known to have favoured co-existence among believers of different religions.

At a village meeting I attended several years later, in 1993, in Burdwan district of West Bengal, another huge poster of Vivekananda was displayed, and pamphlets with quotes from him were distributed. The meeting was organized by the Communist Party of India (Marxist) (CPM for short) – the dominant political party in West Bengal – in a drive to refute the message of the Hindu nationalists. This dispute over who is the legitimate interpreter of Vivekananda's thought, the CPM or the Hindu nationalists, is not a dispute over religious doctrine (to which the CPM hardly qualifies); rather it is a dispute over the appropriation of an important period in Bengal's cultural history, over legitimacy derived from Bengali history and identity.

This chapter seeks to investigate the strength of regional identities, or nationhood(s), in India, and the influence of these on what aims to be an all-Indian ideology, Hindu nationalism.[2] Hindu nationalism as it exists today grew largely out of the historical experience and social conditions of northern and western India. Nonetheless it aims to represent Hindus all over India. This aim has not been achieved, but the Hindu nationalist organization, the Bharatiya Janata Party (BJP), has to a considerable degree been successful in terms of election results also in regions outside the Hindu nationalist heartland. What is interesting is that, as the displays of respect towards Vivekananda indicate, even Hindu nationalist ideology bows to the imperatives of a specifically Bengali identity.

India and Hindu Nationalism

The republic of India is a federation of 22 states and 9 centrally administered 'territories'. Most of the larger states are linguistically based. India has 15 official languages, but altogether more than 1,600 languages were listed in the 1961 census. India is also divided along religious lines, with a majority belonging to that complex social phenomenon we call Hinduism, and a large minority constituting the world's third largest Muslim population. Lastly, sizeable populations are Christians or 'animists' (or 'tribals'). In addition to denominational variations, the many regions of India have very

---

2. The field material for this chapter derives from my many trips to West Bengal over the last eight years. Most of the trips and the writing have been made possible by scholarships from the Norwegian Research Council.

different historical experiences. Bengal was under British rule from 1757, while Awadh, as the last major region to be subjugated, was annexed only in 1857. About one-quarter of the population experienced only indirect colonial rule as subjects of the 'princes', and were only integrated into the Indian state structure in 1947. This social and historical fragmentation has given rise to complex and varied regional identities, each with its own specific characteristics, moulded in a relationship to the formation of a national (Indian) identity.

Hindu nationalism is not new in India. Its modern form can be traced to the Cow Protection Movement of the 1880 to 1920 period. It was most popular in northern India, and evolved alongside – although often in the shadow of – the formation of a (quasi-)secular Indian nationality from the late nineteenth century, under the leadership of the Indian National Congress. Today a major Hindu nationalist organization is the Rashtriya Swayamsevak Sangh (RSS), formed in 1925 by K.B. Hedgewar.[3] According to Peter van der Veer, 'Religious ritual and doctrine are kept to an absolute minimum in the RSS'.[4] It is above all a youth organization which emphasizes drill, physical exercise, and a militant form of love for the nation.[5] A member of this organization shot Gandhi and it was subsequently banned for a few years. However, from the 1980s onwards it has come to function as the backbone of the cadre that populates modern-day Hindu nationalism. Prominent among the Hindu nationalist organizations is the Bharatiya Janata Party (BJP), a party that can trace its origin to pre-independence parties such as the Hindu Mahasabha and the Jana Sangh. The BJP enjoys wide electoral support and has governed the states of Uttar Pradesh (north India), Madhya Pradesh (central), Himachal Pradesh (northwest), and Rajastan (west), and governs (at the time of writing) Maharashtra and Gujarat (both in western India). Its present-day government in Maharashtra is in coalition with the Shiv Sena, another Hindu nationalist organization strong among the Marathas, the dominant group in that state. A last, very important organization is the Vishva Hindu Parishad (VHP) which was established in 1964 by a congregation of Hindu holy men. The VHP's

3. See Basu, Tapan, Pradip Datta, Sumit Sarkar, Tanika Sarkar, Sambuddha Sen, *Khaki Shorts and Saffron Flags, a Critique of the Hindu Right, Tracts for the Times 1*, New Delhi: Orient Longman, 1993.

4. Peter van der Veer, *Religious Nationalism: Hindus and Muslims in India*, Berkeley: University of California Press, 1994, p. 131.

5. Joseph S. Alter, 'Somatic Nationalism: Indian Wrestling and Militant Hinduism', *Modern Asian Studies*, vol. 28, no. 3, 1994, pp. 557–588.

objective is to forward a 'spiritual' Hinduism among all Hindus, but many of its leaders have also more specific cultural and political objectives and work closely with the BJP.

Over the last few years the Hindu nationalist 'family' of the BJP, RSS and VHP (also known as 'the Saffron brigade') has come to be primarily identified with the dispute over whether or not the Babri Masjid (Babur's mosque) in Ayodhya had been built on the site of an ancient Ramjanma-bhumi (the land of lord Ram's birth) temple. It is from this dispute that Hindu nationalism has made the deity Ram a primary symbol. The mosque was torn down on 6 December 1992, after which the four BJP state governments were dismissed and widespread unrest and Hindu–Muslim clashes took place. Especially Bombay witnessed a carnage of Muslims in January 1993. Hindu nationalists are also promoters of Hindi as national language and the wish to rename north Indian towns that now have Muslim-sounding names. Both by the media and through its cadre's involvement in the Hindu–Muslim clashes and the Ayodhya incident, the Hindu nationalist organizations have become associated with strong anti-Muslim sentiments. Although the organizations officially deny being anti-Muslim, that view of these organizations is nevertheless very strong in popular perception.

Hindu Nationalism in West Bengal

However, by looking closer at one region, West Bengal, we shall find several qualifications to the above picture of main issues in Hindu nationalism. First of all, the Hindu organizations do not enjoy support in West Bengal on any scale similar to the states mentioned above. Although the West Bengal BJP and RSS did send delegates to Ayodhya, the level of animosity between Hindus and Muslims does not come close to what it is in certain other places. This in spite of the fact that West Bengal has the highest proportion of Muslims after Uttar Pradesh, plus a long and porous border with Bangladesh. Although clashes did take place in Calcutta after Ayodhya, these were limited to the city itself. The Bengali countryside saw practically no disturbances.

Second, the issue of the Hindi language is very difficult for the Hindu nationalists in Bengal. Both Hindi and Bengali belong to the Indo-European group of languages and share a wide number of features. However, vocabulary, grammar and script are all different, and Bengalis have to make a conscious effort if they wish to learn Hindi. Moreover, Bengali is not only considered superior to Hindi in many respects (by Bengalis) but also forms an integral part of the identity of Bengalis. Besides the obvious problems of learning a new language, the BJP's insistence on the pre-eminence of Hindi as the national language of India runs contrary to many Bengalis' pride in their own language.

Third, the position of the god Ram in BJP's north Indian derived ideology is equally difficult. In Bengal, Ram is a marginal god. For urban Bengalis the most important goddesses are Kali and Durga, followed by Saraswati, Lakshmi and Ganesh; while in the villages the most prominent deities are Olaichandi, Manasa, Shiva, Krishna and Dharmaraj – and, increasingly, Kali and Durga. Rather than revering it, the name of Ram is often used in sarcasm. Lastly, the Ayodhya dispute was considered 'not our business', and when the structure was finally torn down, even BJP activists in West Bengal talked about it only with embarrassment and distanced themselves from the perpetrators.

Rather than wholeheartedly following the policies of their fellow partisans of northern India, Bengali Hindu nationalists represent the Hindu nationalist discourse with an ambiguity and evasion that reflect the awkward relationship between Bengal's self-consciously 'modernist' cultural identity and the dominant political heartland of both Indian and Hindu nationalism, northern India. This will be shown here through a discussion of views and perceptions of Bengali Hindu nationalist activists in Calcutta and in two villages in Burdwan district. The material concerns two analytically different although closely related issues: the appropriation of Hindu nationalism as an extension of socio-cultural concerns or aspirations, and second, the (re-)interpretation of Hindu nationalist discourse within a regional culture that sees itself as distinct in crucial respects from where present-day Hindu nationalism has been articulated.

This chapter will mainly focus on Bengal as a separate space within India.[6] Since the arrival of nationalist discourse in India, Bengal has understood itself as different from north India – specifically as more 'modern'. In many respects, north India has played a crucial role in the

---

6. It may also be noted that there are several 'spaces' within West Bengal. Above all, the two localities that will be encountered here constitute two different worlds. Calcutta is a congested, overpopulated metropolis inhabited by people speaking many different languages, while the villages are underdeveloped, wholly agricultural, and inhabited by people who all know one another. The Calcuttans long for the tranquil village, the villagers for the excitement of city life.

formation of a separate and distinct Bengali identity by constituting an inverted mirror image.

It is important to consider the historicity of the process of formation of this specific Bengali identity, and to relate that process to the evolvement of a new and differing ideology – that of Hindu nationalism – in this region which is not the homeland of Hindu nationalism. It is also important that we relate the continued relevance and constant reformulation of Bengali identity in face of a differing ideology to a totality of experiences of would-be nationalists.

Gyan Pandey has most clearly shown the relevance of people's experienced life-world in understanding the growth of 'communalism' in colonial north India.[7] In one case Pandey argues that 'communalism' (in the form of alliances between socio-economically very different groups belonging to the same religious denomination) could arise at a particular historical juncture due to economic decline and a subsequent sense of lost 'honour'.[8] His study poignantly shows how relevant it is to locate political movements (in the sense of 'changes') in the proper cultural context. This 'cultural context', I wish to argue, may also be regional in nature. In investigating how Hindu nationalism can emerge in the periphery of the Hindi heartland, where it was originally formed, we need to understand its local expressions, interpretations and wider implications. The present investigation seeks to recover the processes by which Hindu nationalism in West Bengal has been reformulated to the point of becoming almost transformed. Even prominent aspects of that discourse are ignored or admitted only with embarrassment, while other aspects are promoted in what seems to be an attempt to accommodate Hindu nationalist discourse to the basic tenets of the regionally dominant discourse. We may say that at one level, Hindu nationalist discourse exists in Bengal in an uneasy truce with 'Bengali culture'. At another level, however, Hindu nationalism is appropriated as an answer to aspirations and concerns that are largely internal to Bengal.

---

7. Gyanendra Pandey, *The Construction of Communalism in Colonial North India*, Delhi: Oxford University Press, 1990. 'Communalism' is a term derived from Orientalist discourse, as shown by Pandey. He argues convincingly that the colonial power's perception of a 'communal' problem was part of the problem. I do not raise these issues here, and since I deal with a post-independence situation I have instead chosen to follow van der Veer *Religious Nationalism* in terming the phenomenon not 'communalism' but 'nationalism'. 'Nationalism' is a concept used in two different contexts in the case of India. In this chapter 'Indian nationalism' refers to the pre-independence, anti-colonial movement, while 'Hindu nationalism' is taken to denote the more recent political developments involving parties such as the BJP.

8. Pandey, *The Construction of Communalism*, chs 3 and 4.

Bengal in India: an Ambiguous Identity

Bengal constitutes an interesting case of nation-building. Although there exists a strong and self-conscious sense of Bengali identity, Bengal is rarely if ever represented as a nation in itself but always as part of India. The main feature is that Bengalis tend to see themselves as more cultured and advanced than other Indians. At the same time they remain staunch advocates of Indian unity. In the words of a Bengali friend, '*Vis-à-vis* other Indians we consider ourselves more Western, but *vis-à-vis* Westerners we are Indians'. This ambiguity, which has strong implications for how Hindu nationalism can be represented in West Bengal, is based in the historical development of Bengali identity and Indian nationalism. Although present-day Hindu nationalism in West Bengal in some respects seems to represent a break with past history, it is nonetheless conditioned and constrained by the Bengali's sense of being 'the more advanced Indian'.

Bengal's modern-day identity was created with the development of a sophisticated discourse in the nineteenth century, the so-called Bengali Renaissance. Bengal was the first province of India to be colonized by the British, and the one province most strongly influenced by Western-style education and ideas. The first critics of the British presence in India were Bengalis. A large number of philosophers, writers and politicians influenced by or reacting to Western education and ideas sought an Indian riposte to the influence of Western teaching, norms and culture, and against British imperialism and racism. Some of them sought material for identity creation in an image of an idyllic past which had been lost, while others advocated the re-creation of Indian society in the image of the West.[9] Whatever their immediate programme, these writers mostly saw Bengal within the larger entity of India. One reason may be that Bengal's immediate and distant past did not constitute the material in vogue at that time for nation-building. As Sudipto Kaviraj points out, 'As a nation, the Bengalis turn out to be a great disappointment' since they appeared to their contemporaries as 'woefully inadequate for a task as daunting as taking on the British empire'.[10] Instead

---

9. For studies of these developments, see Tapan Raychaudhuri, *Europe Reconsidered: Perceptions of the West in Nineteenth Century Bengal*, Delhi: Oxford University Press, 1988; Sudipto Kaviraj, 'The Imaginary Institution of India', in Partha Chatterjee and Gyanendra Pandey (eds), *Subaltern Studies VII: Writings on South Asian History and Society*, Delhi: Oxford University Press, 1992, pp. 1–39; and Partha Chatterjee, *The Nation and Its Fragments: Colonial and Postcolonial Histories*, Princeton: Princeton University Press, 1993.

10. Kaviraj, 'The Imaginary Institution', p. 15.

links were created to other 'peoples' in India, and the 'daunting task' was bestowed on communities such as the Marathas, the Sikhs, the Rajputs and others with whom the people of Bengal had previously had little in common. This Kaviraj calls a 'widening of the collective self', the early beginning of the creation of an Indian nationhood. However much the leading writers were aware of their own Bengaliness, they regarded Bengalis merely as the first politically aware group of people of the larger nationality of India.

Within this larger identity, however, Bengal retained and developed its own identity. Much of this development hinges on the historical development of the Bengali language. During the nineteenth century, Bengali emerged as the dominant language of the region and replaced other languages (Persian, Urdu, Arabic, Sanskrit). Originally developed from a Hugli dialect (near Calcutta), it became the prominent mode of spoken and written interaction among the growing (and increasingly self-assured) indigenous Calcutta elite. Bengali became (together with English) the main medium of public debate, scholarship and, increasingly, politics. In this period, Bengal was the richest province of the Indian empire, with her main city Calcutta second only to London. Moreover it was from the school and colleges of Bengal that the leading political critics and opponents of the British emerged. In Congress-leader Tilak's famous phrase, 'What Bengal thinks today, India thinks tomorrow'.

But Bengali was more than a politicized medium, it was an increasingly versatile language that in all respects begged comparison with major European languages, particularly in literary achievement. The Bengali Renaissance, which spanned most of the nineteenth century and lasted well into the twentieth, saw a huge literary production with the development of a 'modern' but distinctly Indian literature. It culminated with the awarding of the 1913 Nobel prize in literature to Rabindranath Tagore as the first non-Western writer.

In Kaviraj's study it is the spread of a standardized written and spoken language which created a Bengali identity from a mass of minor dialects that had blended into neighbouring languages-to-be (such as Bihari and Oriya).[11] Though one may well argue that there must have been 'something' there, some 'proto-nationalist' idea common to most inhabitants of the province of Bengal, the point to drive home is that the arrival of a standardized language focused the formation of a 'modern' identity primarily upon a literary and political reaction to colonial rule among the growing population of a Western-educated elite.

---

11. *Ibid.*, p. 15.

The spread of this identity, or the standardized language, is interesting and crucial. Here I shall limit myself to the case of West Bengal. The audience of the Bengali Renaissance was the so-called *bhadralok*, the mainly but not exclusively Calcutta-based elite literate in both English and Bengali.[12] The *bhadralok* is a specifically Bengali social group, consisting of the educated professionals or the leisured classes. The *bhadralok* drew mainly from among the high Hindu castes (in particular the Brahmin, Vaidya and Kayastha castes). Although individuals and families from other castes or denominations were also included, these were exceptions more than the rule. Conversely, however, large numbers of Brahmins, Vaidyas and Kayasthas in Bengal remained uneducated villagers, some shading off into rustic or 'petty *bhadralok*', such as primary-school teachers, doctors, etc.

The hallmark of the Bengali *bhadralok* was his education, his non-manual labour, and his refined mannerisms and dress – derived from service positions or from landed property.[13] It is important that they thought of themselves as the original 'Bengalis' and did not include the majority of illiterate villagers with rustic tongues into this identity. Still today, 'Bengali' is an epithet largely reserved for those educated; the rest tend to be known by their respective geographical or caste-derived denomination (Sekh Musalman, Namasudra, Sadgop, etc.). Bengali identity is thus still not entirely bestowed upon all residents within Bengal's borders. The identification of a certain well-mannered and cultured lifestyle – derived from education, non-manual labour, interest in literature, poetry and songs – is a strong and dominant theme in how 'true' Bengalis tend to present themselves *vis-à-vis* other Indians.

Bengal retained its hold on Indian nationalist politics well into this century. First there was the establishment of the Indian National Congress in 1887, a movement dominated by Bengalis at its outset. An increasingly open defiance of the British (although still not to the extent of demanding independence) soured relations between the colonial power and Bengalis – who were more educated than other Indian groups and who manned a majority of bureaucratic positions, even outside Bengal proper. The British for their part increasingly regarded Bengalis as both effeminate and quarrelsome, unreliable and 'out of touch' with the masses.

---

12. For a study of the *bhadralok* and their politics, see John H. Broomfield, *Elite Conflict in a Plural Society: Twentieth Century Bengal*, Berkeley: University of California Press, 1968.
13. *Ibid.*, ch. 1.

The 1905 partition of Bengal into one Hindu and one Muslim majority part was interpreted by most *bhadralok* as an effort to diminish the power of the Bengalis.[14] It threatened not only the employment basis for most educated Bengalis but also thwarted potential political ambitions of the Hindu *bhadralok*. The ensuing widespread unrest, known as the Swadeshi movement, recruited mainly from among the *bhadralok*. In 1911 the partition was retracted, but the capital was moved from Calcutta to Delhi. Bengal was thus reduced to being just one among other provinces, and the prominence of Bengalis in the imperial administration was ended.

For a while Bengalis retained their prominence in Indian anti-colonial politics but their grip gradually loosened. An end came with Gandhi, whose prominence symbolized a shift towards a different type of nationalist movement, but also a shift of focus and leadership from Bengal to northern and western India. The following generation of Congress leaders were all drawn from these regions (Gandhi, the Nehrus, Patel, Azad). The last important Bengali Congress politician was Subhaschandra Bose. Bose's political views, however, differed substantially from those of Gandhi. He was primarily a secularist (although a Hindu one) with leftist leanings and a dislike for Gandhi's 'obscurantism'. Bose was elected president of the Congress in 1935, but Gandhi refused to cooperate and Bose had to resign.

Bose's opposition to Gandhi's 'obscurantism' seems to have been quite representative of more general sentiments among the Hindu Bengali *bhadralok*. Symptomatic of the same ideological currents was how a small but growing number of young *bhadralok* joined the Indian Communist Party from the 1930s onwards. It is important to keep in mind that the *bhadralok* were primarily raised within the English educational system and attuned to 'Western' values (as opposed to those represented by Gandhi). They were also much informed about international developments, such as the unification of Italy, the independence struggle in Ireland, and the Russian revolution. Against these developments, Gandhi's emphasis on *ahimsa* ('non-violence') and the spinning wheel offered no plausible alternative, either to Subhaschandra Bose or to the *bhadralok* in general. On the contrary, the shift of emphasis in the Congress seems to have strengthened a Bengali sense of difference.

---

14. See for instance Sumit Sarkar, *The Swadeshi Movement in Bengal, 1903–1908*, New Delhi: People's Publishing House, 1973.

Post-Independence: Opposition and Regionalism

After independence the West Bengal political scene was characterized (but not dominated) by a large number of leftist political parties. Prominent historian Marcus Franda has drawn links between them and the *bhadralok*.[15] He finds the origins of the radicalized elite in a sense of political frustration among the *bhadralok* in the 1930s. Although the *bhadralok* origins of Bengali radicalism have been largely accepted, the 'frustrated *bhadralok*' theory has been criticized by pointing out that most *bhadralok* did not turn into radical leftists.[16] It seems more plausible to understand the radicalization of the Bengali *bhadralok* on the background of international ideological currents and political events, and of a general self-identification of the Bengali *bhadralok* as 'modern' and attuned to these currents.

With leftism and the sense of being more 'modern', it was not possible to define Bengal (or the small state of West Bengal) as a nation in itself, one that should be independent. The 'nation' was India, and although immense pride continued to be attached to Bengali identity, there has never been any question of a Bengali nation-state (except for some minor groups). All the major and most of the minor political parties are All-India in name and theory[17] – although not necessarily in practice.

Historically, Bengali identity developed with a large degree of ambiguity; at the same time part of and different from 'India'. This sense of a separate Bengali identity has translated into a sense of distance to the central government in the post-independence period, without leading to secessionist movements. We find this primarily in two distinct areas of life: in literary (or cultural) pretention, which is a continuation of the concerns outlined above; and in the emphasis on centre-state relations. Although the CPM, the dominant political party in West Bengal since 1977, aspires to an All-India position, its base is found in three states only: Kerala, the minuscule Tripura, and West Bengal. Its position is by far the strongest in the latter. Opposition to the mainly Congress-dominated central government has been a prevalent theme in the CPM's history, since the instalment of India's first communist state government in Kerala in 1957, to the present

---

15. Marcus F. Franda, *Radical Politics in West Bengal*, Cambridge: MIT Press, 1971.

16. Leonard A. Gordon, 'Radical Bengalis: Alliances and Antagonisms' (review article), *South Asian Review*, vol. 5, no. 4, 1972, pp. 341–344.

17. For instance, the Indian National Congress-I, the Communist Party of India-Marxist, the Socialist Unity Centre of India.

West Bengal government's drive to make people donate blood when the promised central government funds for the Farraka dam were not forthcoming.[18]

The division between the CPM and the central government runs parallel to the common Bengali feeling of being culturally distinct, an identity that the CPM indirectly represents. The CPM never openly advocates purely Bengali sentiments but presents itself as representing interests that are somewhat more Bengali than anything else. In an odd but evocative case, CPM Chief Minister Jyoti Basu advocated in early 1993 the replacement of the state's English name (West Bengal) with a Bengali name, Banga. The initiative was taken in connection with the Bengali New Year 1400 (in April 1993). The plan was eventually dropped, but the state government remains a main patron of 'Bengali culture', envisaged for instance in the state-sponsored construction of 'Nandan', a beautiful arts and film centre in Calcutta where the annual Calcutta Film Festival is held and 'art films' are shown throughout the year.

This somewhat lengthy outline of elements in the historically constituted Bengali identity has been necessary for two reasons. First, it places Bengali identity as distinct within but still part of the larger Indian identity. This ambiguity has given rise to a rather difficult relationship between the two entities (as seen from West Bengal). On the one hand Bengalis regard themselves as superior and more advanced than other Indians, but they are also aware of how they are stereotypically regarded as effeminate, ineffective day-dreamers incapable of coping in a fast-moving modern world. Bengali identity is profoundly ambivalent, with a sense of having fallen short of required physical and entrepreneurial standards but of being culturally superior.

The second important point here has been to underline the linkage of Bengali identity to the *bhadralok* social status group and to literary pursuits. With the spread of education, this particular and, in a rural context, attractive status has come within reach for an increasingly large number of

---

18. The claim that West Bengal does not receive a fair share of central funds is supported by several scholars. See Atul Kohli, *The State and Poverty in India: the Politics of Reform*, Cambridge: Cambridge University Press, 1987; Atul Kohli, 'From Elite Activism to Democratic Consolidation: the Rise of Reform Communism in West Bengal' in Francine R. Frankel and M.S.A. Rao (eds), *Dominance and State Power in Modern India: Decline of a Social Order* (Volume II), Delhi: Oxford University Press, 1990, pp. 367–415; and T.J. Nossiter, *Marxist State Governments in India: Politics, Economics and Society*, London: Pinter Publishers, 1988.

people, including villagers. This has caused a diffusion to villages of a paradigmatic model for status advancement. This modernization model, based on Western education, is a new version of the old process of cultural reform for social advancement (variously known as Sanskritization, Brahminization, etc.).[19] In rural West Bengal the role model is the *bhadralok*. The *bhadralok*'s lifestyle, professions, manners, language and literary pursuits have come to form the main model for social advancement. Naturally not everyone can aspire to the full package, but the tendency is for even moderately well-off and upwardly mobile households to adopt aspects of this model, such as education and literary pursuits rather than business or perhaps intensified agriculture; simplicity in taste rather than conspicuous consumption; composed and restrained manners and speech rather than the brawling outward style of *kshatriyas* popular elsewhere.[20]

It is with these two elements in mind – the ambivalence of Bengali identity *vis-à-vis* north India in particular, and the paradigmatic role model of the *bhadralok* – that we proceed to investigate how Hindu nationalism is constrained and perceived in West Bengal. Here, Hindu nationalism is presented as distinctly separate from how it appears in north India. Many of the tenets of Hindu nationalism in north India are denied any relevance to the West Bengal situation, while certain other programmatic elements with negative consequences for Bengal identity are only grudgingly admitted. Rather, Hindu nationalism in West Bengal is legitimized as a continuation of historical developments that are both Bengali and Indian. A strong and self-conscious Bengali identity, profoundly associated with the *bhadralok* model, does not deny the relevance of its own history. Rather, it interprets a new ideology within its own tenets. Hindu nationalist ideology and its

---

19. For 'Sanskritization', see M.N. Srinivas, 'The Dominant Caste in Rampura', *American Anthropologist*, vol. 61, 1959, pp. 1–16. For a sensible critique, see C.J. Fuller, *The Camphor Flame: Popular Hinduism and Society in India*, Princeton: Princeton University Press, 1992, esp. pp. 24–28; the notion of 'modernization' was first introduced in this context by Bernard S. Cohn, *An Anthropologist Among the Historians and Other Essays*, Delhi: Oxford University Press, 1990 [1987].

20. For the *kshatriya* ('warrior') model, see for instance Adrian C. Mayer, *Caste and Kinship in Central India: a Village and Its Region*, London: Routledge, 1960. This picture of the *bhadralok* role model may be changing. Particularly among the village generation now in school or college, the interest in literary pursuits seems extremely low. These 'Yuppies of rural Bengal', as we may term them, sport sun-glasses and fashion-wear, ride scooters (if they can afford it), and will visit cinemas or video-halls more frequently than poetry recitals. Their role model, I suggest, is the All-Indian 'hero' (*nayak*), inspired by the 'Bollywood' Hindi films. However, this is a recent phenomenon and does not affect the general argument here since it does not legitimize political behaviour among adults.

political programme (as locally interpreted) are made use of in a specific local context, to strengthen the image of the would-be *bhadralok* (or high-status aspirant) as distinct from other groups. We shall find, from the village material, a close association of Hindu nationalism with the *bhadralok* as historically formed and locally understood. Here it will be seen that Hindu nationalism, as a politically potent and religion-based movement, lends credibility and legitimacy to purely local processes of social advancement and difference.

Hindu Nationalism in Calcutta

The first case I take up is one of Hindu nationalism among lower-middle-class residents of a poor area of Calcutta. In this metropolis Hindu national-ism has had a certain measure of success over the last few years. The BJP has won several by-elections, and in collaboration with the RSS cadre, the party occasionally organizes fairly large-scale meetings and demonstrations. This has seemingly not threatened the stronger position of the Congress Party and the CPM – both of whom still organize meetings with an attendance that by far outstrips anything the Hindu nationalists can muster. Nonetheless, Hindu nationalism is increasingly present in the city, particularly in lower-middle-class areas of central Calcutta and in the milieux of north Indian immigrants.

The six individuals involved are all young Bengalis in their twenties or early thirties.[21] All of them have attended college, and two have university degrees. They were either underemployed or felt underpaid. One was an assistant shopkeeper, two were salesmen, one was a regular schoolteacher, and two were slum schoolteachers for a voluntary organization. Among the latter was the only female interviewed. A few years later she became leader of the Durga Bahini, an RSS women's organization. Most of the inter-viewees were RSS activists, and the main part of their RSS-related activities consisted of physical training every morning at a particular field. There they line up in uniforms (in standard RSS fashion) and perform exercizes in unison. They also learn to fight with the *lathi*, a large stick historically used as a weapon.[22] In Bengal, *lathi*s have in general been associated with the

---

21. The informants have not been 'interviewed' in the traditional sense. The opinions expressed and presented here arise from a long series of 'gossiping' (*adda dewa*) over a few years.

22. For a study of the RSS and physical training, see Alter, 'Somatic Nationalism'.

lower castes. Among the *bhadralok*, however, *lathi*-fight (or 'play', *khela*) was part of the efforts to strengthen the Bengali 'nation' through physical training during the 1905–11 Swadeshi movement and thus has a place in the history of the *bhadralok*.[23]

The views expressed by these six informants varied a little from one another. In the main their opinions reflected the official RSS line although much seems inspired from the political campaigns of the BJP. Their doubts and the ambiguities of their appropriation of the RSS line emerged only in intimate conversations with one or two at a time. Below I have put together some of their views on a few important topics.

LANGUAGE

Most of the activists expressed the view that Hindi as the official language of the Republic should be taught all over the country and should finally replace local languages, including Bengali. This seemed to me an odd point given Bengali's integral position to Bengali identity and its close association with refinement and education. Also, the activists themselves know only rudimentary Hindi, can follow a Hindi-language movie but not news programmes, and are not able to read Hindi newspapers with any ease. Their argument ran mainly as follows: India is one nation and as a nation should have a national language that will integrate it. They view this, however, as a long process which will take generations and can only start when Hindu nationalism has become the official line of the state. In this manner the language issue was not considered an immediate goal and not directly of concern to themselves. The teacher taught English, not Hindi. The slum schools in which the female schoolteacher taught do not teach Hindi to the pupils, only English and Bengali. In different contexts, they expressed much pride in the literary achievements of Bengali authors. They all know poems by Tagore by heart, and two of them proudly showed me their collection of Bengali prose and poetry. They also knew of Hindi authors such as Premchand, whom they had read in translation, but tended to dismiss Hindi literature, in particular Hindi poetry, as insignificant in comparison with Bengali literature.

---

23. See, for instance, Nirad C. Chaudhuri, *Autobiography of an Unknown Indian*, London: The Hogarth Press, 1987; for an academic investigation, see Sarkar, *The Swadeshi Movement*.

'ENEMIES' OF THE NATION

In their perception the Hindu *jati* (the Hindu nation or the Hindu people) has two main enemies, and by extension aims. The first to crop up in conversations was the CPM. The CPM was regarded as having ruined society, in particular 'confidence' and 'reciprocality' between people. The contrast they used was occasionally pre-CPM Calcutta but mainly the village society from where their parents came (most of them were second- or third-generation Calcuttans). The CPM was criticized for being 'ungodly' and for adhering to a foreign ideology. The ruling party was also blamed for the economic decline of West Bengal and the diminishing importance of Calcutta (but so were the Hindu Marwari businessmen). The CPM, they argued, based its position on corruption and *goondas* (touts) and never did anything for 'the people'. The CPM in their opinion thus fell short of its own standards – an argument also encountered among other middle-class Calcuttans. One main concern for these Hindu nationalists was therefore to 'rebuild' society, to create mutual trust and reciprocation among people, and to recreate the proper order of society (*dharma*). What was meant by the latter seems to be on the one hand religious observances, and on the other respect for the elders and for authorities.

Another 'enemy' of the 'Hindu nation' was foreign culture, in particular what was perceived of as American consumerism. Among the problems associated with the intrusion of this culture were alcoholism, divorce (seen as an effect of 'love marriages'), and the dissolution of society into individuals. This has particularly affected and threatened to ruin the ideal Hindu joint family. American culture, like communism, was also known as atheistic and fermenting a disregard for the gods. To counteract these 'degenerate' influences, the main long-term aim was to create a strong Hindu polity with a cultural identity comparable to 'Europe, America, China and Arabia'.

MUSLIMS

Interestingly, Muslims did not figure as major enemies of the 'Hindu nation' in these Calcuttans' views, only as a minor social irritant. The question of Hindu nationalism's relation to the Muslim minority was one they were reluctant to talk about. Particularly the Ayodhya issue and the Shiv Sena's role in the ensuing Bombay riots seem to have been somewhat embarrassing for them. The many riots between Hindus and Muslims in Calcutta or elsewhere were squarely blamed on the Muslims, whereas the Hindus were merely 'defending' themselves. Some of my informants said that the Muslims should 'go home' (to Pakistan, or preferably the Middle East), only to laugh it away immediately as a joke. Whether this reflects an uneasiness in my presence or an ambivalence to Muslims in general, I cannot tell. They asserted that they have some Muslim friends, although not close. However, even the Hindu side was differentiated; most of the Hindus that participated in riots in Calcutta, they asserted, were 'up-country' Hindus, i.e. migrants from Bihar and Uttar Pradesh. They were not Bengalis, the proof being that most riots took place around Park Circus, an area of Calcutta inhabited by immigrants (mainly Muslims). A similar division between groups of Hindu nationalists was introduced for the Ayodhya issue and the destruction of the Babri Masjid. The Ayodhya issue was necessary, they assert, as a rallying point for the north Indians, because people in north India were 'uneducated villagers' who could not grasp complex arguments and therefore needed simple issues.

On an encompassing level, the Ayodhya issue was interpreted by these Bengali Hindu nationalists as a struggle, not against Muslims, not aimed at reappropriating a temple from the Muslims, but as a fight against the 'secularists' (or 'pseudo-secularists') and politicians who manipulate the system by keeping Muslims as vote-blocks against a divided Hindu majority. The aim was not to defeat the Muslims, because the Muslims are not strong. They are only pampered by ambitious politicians. The tearing down of the Babri Masjid was seen as a part of a long struggle to make the Hindus aware of their own potential and to create a sense of unity.

Interestingly, this interpretation served a double purpose. First, it differentiated between Bengalis and north Indians, so that it became possible for my informants to distance themselves from distasteful elements within the movement they supported. Second, by interpreting the issue within a larger struggle – as is the BJP's official line – my informants had assured themselves of an excuse for what they seemed to consider a rather unnecessary and silly affair.

In this manner they were able to retain their identity both as nationalist Hindus and as Bengalis. The distinction between Bengalis and north Indians within the movement, as having different perspectives and concerns, opened up the discussion to a way of linking their political outlook to a perception of India as a modern civilization: one where India compares (its internal problems and backward sections notwithstanding) favourably with other contemporary civilizations. The distinction also permitted justification of unsavoury aims and practices and instead put them on a par with the CPM in terms of being 'modern'. This distinction made it possible for my informants to retain their specifically Bengali identity, self-consciously 'modern' and 'educated', while at the same time adhere to an all-Indian movement that in many respects appeared as backward, distinctly unmodern, and centring on what they argued were patently 'obscurantist' issues such as the Babri Masjid.

The BJP in Rural Bengal

In West Bengal, the BJP and the RSS as organizations lead a very limited existence outside the urban areas. Nonetheless, during the last Panchayat elections in June 1993, the BJP did receive 12 per cent of the votes at the Gram Panchayat level.[24] In the two villages in which I lived for some time, Gopinathpur and Udaynala[25] in Burdwan district, the BJP has become quite prominent in local affairs. During the June 1993 Panchayat elections, the BJP received a fair 14 per cent of votes in Udaynala and a substantial 34 per cent in Gopinathpur where the local Congress chose not to run. In the main it was upper-caste Hindus who voted for the BJP, although a number of low-caste Hindus were also known as supporters and activists.[26]

A short introduction to the two villages may be in order. Udaynala has a population of approximately 2,200, with 51 per cent Muslims and the rest Hindus. Of these, one-quarter are high-caste, one-tenth tribal (Santal), and the rest low-caste (Scheduled Caste). The Muslims constitute the 'dominant caste' of Udaynala in the sense that they have historically owned most of the land and have held most of the political power. For the Muslims the situation did not change much after the coming of the CPM raj. They still own the same proportion of land as they did thirty years ago, and most of the village's political leaders are Muslims. Over the last two decades the

---

24. The Panchayat system consists of three tiers: the lowest being the Gram Panchayat which is an elected body representing 10 to 15 villages; the middle tier, the Panchayat Samiti, covers the 'Block', the lowest administrative unit; and the top tier is the Jela (or Zilla) Parishad, which covers the district.

25. Fictitious names.

26. It should be emphasized that far from all high- or clean-caste Hindus voted for the BJP. Voting is of course secret, but BJP voters were easily identified within these small-scale transparent communities from a variety of concurrent 'evidence'. It is some of this 'evidence' we shall address here, in particular the 'statement' of the Durga-*puja* with its wider implications.

higher Hindu castes have become quite affluent from engagement in business, although they have lost land. And with the emergence of the CPM as the dominant political party at all levels from state to village, a certain low caste, the Bagdis (about 10 per cent of the village population), has gained new land, subsidized loans and other material and political benefits. Other low-caste groups have not been equally lucky.

The situation in all-Hindu Gopinathpur (with a population of about 1,200) is somewhat different. The formerly dominant castes – Aguris, Kayasthas and Brahmins – have lost some land under the CPM but more importantly political positions and power. This is now in the hands of the village Bagdis, who constitute about one-third of the total population. Other low-caste groups, such as the Muchis and the Dule, have not been able to reap the riches of the new political order and gain political positions or land.

In these two villages few individuals openly support the BJP, possibly from fear of inflicting the anger of the dominant CPM. Among those who openly advocated Hindu nationalism there was a great deal of embarrassment connected with a number of core elements of the BJP's programme. During my last stay (autumn of 1993) I was able to interview three local BJP activists (two in Gopinathpur, one in Udaynala). Interestingly, none was of high ritual status, although most supporters were upper caste. Much of what I say below on attitudes on Hindu nationalism in rural Bengal is based on less formal interviews or even entirely private gossiping with local upper-caste BJP supporters.

It may also be in order to introduce the three BJP activists of Gopinathpur and Udaynala. The first and most important leader was of the Barber caste – of intermediary position in the caste hierarchy. He was only 32 years old but quite successful as a businessman, representing a medical firm. His family was large, relatively land-rich, and increasingly successful in business (with two barber shops and one goldsmith shop). The other two BJP activists were of lower caste, one Bagdi and one Namasudra (both Scheduled Caste). One was a schoolteacher from a previously land-rich family whose wealth had been spent on educating nine sons and paying dowry for five daughters. This decline in the family's landholding reflects a common pattern for 'Sanskritizing' families; unless their income is such as to allow relatively large expenses, the education of one or more sons can deplete the family wealth. The other Bagdi BJP leader was not the usual activist or politician. He was very poor, owner of some marginal lands and wholly dependent on employment as agricultural labourer. His family was poor too. Both his parents died while he was young and he grew up with an uncle. He was the first in the family to be literate.

Let me mention that Hindu nationalism, however understood, was represented in altogether milder forms and terms in these villages than in Calcutta. There have been no clashes or riots, and the general commensality between Hindus and Muslims did not change with Ayodhya. The main argument in support for the BJP was disgust with the CPM. Each interview was introduced with a harangue against the CPM. The arguments fell into two groups; the first being complaints of general corruption of both the party itself and of the administration. In this respect, the CPM, it was argued, had fallen short of its own standards. The second group of laments concerned lack of proper development of village society. They saw a need for higher road standards, a post-office, electricity and drinking-water supplies, and schools.

However, the three villagers also vented a more general critique of society and what they saw as its decline. They complained of people watching football games on television instead of playing themselves; of how people 'nowadays' watch TV movies with song and dance, being more interested in entertainment than in building the community. Furthermore, the BJP activists complained of how the traditional (as they saw it) Hindu joint family was fast eroding, how people quarrel more than previously, and how the elders are not respected. In particular, one of them argued that 'modern education' has a disruptive effect because children are not taught 'tradition and ideology' (*riti o niti*). In elaborating on the latter point, he pointed out that the general decline of the social order was due to lack of knowledge of the ways of old, in particular of religion, of *dharma*, but also of what we may term 'high culture' (*sanskriti*), by which he referred to the masters of the Bengali Renaissance. These were subjects that should be emphasized alongside disciplines such as mathematics and Bengali.

These points of view had a familiar ring. The lack of a proper road was lamented by everyone, political activist or not, as was the decline of the social order. Moreover, these same views had also been expressed in countless interviews by CPM activists critical of their own party (of whom there were many), and by party officials outlining the future of the party's work. Even the phrasing and the 'Sanskritized' vocabulary were in many cases the same.[27]

---

27. Literary Bengali sports two distinct varieties, the *calit bhasa* and the *sadhu bhasa*. The latter contains a wide Sanskrit derived vocabulary. It is a common sign of education and status to be able to use such words.

Most political activists complained about a general decline in social values, increase in 'individualism', and a relaxation of morality, but also emphasized the positive material growth and more equitable sharing of wealth in rural Bengal – a point acknowledged by BJP activists as well. What both groups saw as profoundly lacking is summed up in the terms 'development' and 'progress', both material and cultural. The general complaint that people spend too much time watching television was swiftly followed by the suggestion that people should read more of the great literature, which for both groups meant the Bengali masters (the BJP activists also included the epics). The choice of 'heroes' from the Bengali Renaissance varied some- what: the communists favoured Vidyasagar while the BJP activists tended towards Bankimchandra, while both groups wished to appropriate Swami Vivekananda. However, very few activists have read these masters in the original; they know them only from extracts or from school textbooks. The point does not seem to have been a desire to implement the thoughts of Vivekananda, Bankimchandra or others into the reality of today's society, but to legitimize political stances with their social and cultural ramifications within the tradition that has become the main legitimizing force in Bengal, namely the Bengali Renaissance.

The reason for this oddity is that all educated people, schoolteachers and political activists of all hues, share the same cultural heritage, the Bengali Renaissance. This heritage should not be seen as a mere smoke- screen legitimizer of any political ideology. As elaborated above, it forms a main constitutive element in normative thinking about Bengal and Bengali society. It defines Bengal. Bengal (and its language) is hardly ever considered without reference to Tagore. Without Tagore and the Renaissance, there are only localities, dispersed villages and a giant city. The supra-local identity of Bengal is defined by the language (the Standard Colloquial Bengali, not the dialects), the formulation of which is attributed to Tagore. This remains to this day an identity of the supra-local, of those social groups who are familiar with the supra-local language, i.e. the educated, the *bhadralok*.

In villages such as Udaynala and Gopinathpur the social status of the *bhadralok* represents a strong and clearly understood attraction because the social norms and values and the mannerisms of the *bhadralok* were only recently introduced to village society to any measurable extent and have come within reach for most people only in the last generation. Aspirations towards *bhadralok* status have become possible with the increase in literacy and schooling. At the time of independence, when none of these two villages had schools, some 11 per cent of Udaynala's male population and some 7 per cent of the men in Gopinathpur were literate.[28] We may also note that in general they had not read 'the great Bengali masters', only the epics or other religious writings. In 1993, both villages had schools teaching up to class 8, and only some 20 per cent of the population in both villages remained illiterate. Of these, practically all were elderly.

The recency of this situation makes aspiration towards *bhadralok* status insecure. This is particularly the case for individuals from formerly poor or only moderately well-off families, such as the school-teaching BJP activists and many of the CPM activists in these villages who have only recently shaken off the image of the unrefined rustic peasant. As poorly paid school-teachers with only a little more than a rudimentary education themselves, more often than not from peasant background, and still living more off their inherited lands than from their salaries, they were barely petty *bhadralok*. If seen from outside, from the vantage point of an urban well-educated *bhadralok*, these schoolteachers were hardly distinguishable from ordinary villagers. Only a close adherence to the norms and values of the *bhadralok* role model (as popularly perceived) could enhance their status. Furthermore, the Bengali Renaissance also defines the *bhadralok*'s place in society as the secular, modern sage, and at the same time it legitimizes his role as the dominant reservoir of knowledge and thus his status. Engagement in politics is one important way of expressing this role.[29]

Low-Caste Hindus and Village Hindu Festivals

Over the last two decades the caste division in the Hindu population of Udaynala has been confirmed and enlarged in two significant disputes. A site in the middle of the village of Udaynala had for decades been used for the annual Olaichandi celebrations – Udaynala's main festival. The Olaichandi-*puja* is celebrated by all villagers together, but as a rustic goddess, Olaichandi is above all associated with lower castes. The few upper-caste Hindu families have tended to keep a studied distance to it, particularly to its more un-puranic aspects. The site where the celebrations took place was owned by one of the village Baniya-families (traders by caste occupation,

28. Field data.

29. Atul Kohli, 'Parliamentary Communism and Agrarian Reform', *Asian Survey*, vol. XXIII, no. 7, 1983, pp. 783–809, also notes the large proportion of schoolteachers in rural politics.

businessmen by profession) who lived next to it. Around the early 1970s, the owner expressed the wish that the celebrations be restricted to only one night instead of three. This caused much resentment among the low-caste Hindus in the village (Bagdis, Muchis and Namasudras) who organized themselves under the leadership of Umakanta, a Brahmin ostracized among his own. After a few months of simmering conflict the protesters established a fund and bought the site. It is now owned by a public committee charged with arranging the *puja*.

The committee is not wealthy but enjoys a prestigious position because it arranges the village's main festival, and for a long time it was the only stable religious committee in the village (such committees had normally been set up on an *ad hoc* basis). Previous committees had always been manned by the clean castes, never by the low castes. The Brahmin Umakanta continued to head the new committee, with two or three other representatives, all of whom have been low caste. Apart from Umakanta, other upper-caste persons have taken no interest in it.

Umakanta was also involved in another conflict, in the late 1970s, over some land that had several decades back been bestowed by the *zamindar* for the village *gajan*-celebrations for Shiva and Dharmaraj – an even more clearly low-caste celebration. That land had been given on a share-cropping basis to three families who were to pay half of the surplus to cover festival expenses. This they had ceased to do, and instead regarded the land as their own. Another committee was established under the leadership of Umakanta, and its quest was supported by the *zamindar*'s heirs – legal owners of the disputed land – who decided the committee should be put in charge of the land and the proceeds. A quarter of the annual proceeds was put aside for development of a fund, to be managed by the committee. This religious fund was the first ever in the village, and the land the committee came to control was quite substantial.

From the late 1970s onwards, Udaynala's Hindu religious life has been dominated by these two committees, both mainly manned by lower castes. Three individuals were found in both: Umakanta the ostracized Brahmin; the BJP activist Namasudra schoolteacher; and one Bagdi schoolteacher (the latter two from 'Sanskritizing' families).

In neighbouring Gopinathpur the situation was very different. The Bagdis constituted a much larger percentage of the village population, and the village was dominated by clean-caste Hindus, not Muslims. In addition, Gopinathpur had a permanent and wealthy public (*baroari*) celebrations committee, the owner of twice as much land as the committee in Udaynala came to possess. In spite of poor shares received over many years, the committee constituted the village's dominant forum for public activities, and represented its most prestigious positions. For nearly thirty years it was led by an Aguri, who maintained his position as village leader over all these years through an alliance with two Bagdi leaders. From the early 1960s onwards, these two were introduced into the increasing number of new institutions in the village: the cooperative society board, the school board and the Panchayats. The various committees and boards of Gopinathpur thus had a multi-caste character very early due to the alliance building efforts of the village leader. Only the *baroari* committee was excluded from these integration moves and continued to be dominated by the clean castes until the late 1970s, when the CPM took over both in the state and in Gopinathpur. The former village leader withdrew and his CPM-affiliated nephew took over and introduced low-caste representation to the *baroari* committee. Presently all castes are represented in the village *baroari* committee, while all other institutions have been taken over completely by Bagdis supported by the CPM. The nephew has left the village and the upper castes have lost all prominence.

Since the late 1970s in both Udaynala and Gopinathpur – and the pattern was probably the same for most villages in the region – the lower castes have become increasingly prominent in village public affairs:[30] they have gained substantial clout through involvement with the CPM, and they have in many cases side-lined the formerly dominant clean castes even from their privileged position in religious rites. To dominate local religious life represented a significant change in the position of the lower castes, a very tangible symbol of a levelling of ritual status.

Bengali Regionalism and the Durga-puja

This new situation never caused any public protest from the upper castes. However, it was in the same period that the Durga-*puja* celebrations were reintroduced in a manner that restated social divisions. From the late 1970s onwards Durga and her *puja* were reintroduced to villages of Burdwan in a style reminiscent of the modern-day Durga-*puja* in urban Bengal. The

---

30. The increase in lower-caste representation in the Panchayats of an area close by is documented by G.K. Lieten, 'For a New Debate on West Bengal', *Economic and Political Weekly*, vol. XXIX, no. 29, 1994, pp. 1835–1838.

celebrations were introduced to Udaynala in 1978, and apart from a gap between 1981 and 1984, they have since been organized annually. In Gopinathpur they were introduced only in 1992, but the reintroduction of the Durga-*puja* is more general and seems common to most of village society. In the ten Hindu villages immediately surrounding Gopinathpur and Udaynala there were only three Durga-*puja* celebrations fifteeen years ago (in two villages), all of them private. In 1992, the Durga-*puja* was cele-brated in all except one village, and all the new celebrations were funded by public collection (the three older celebrations still continued, privately funded).

Interestingly, the new Durga-*puja* was initiated by upper-caste Hindus. Moreover, the lower castes were not invited to contribute towards the expenses, nor did they participate in the arrangements. The celebrations were not arranged by the existing committees, such as Gopinathpur's well-off and prestigious *baroari* committee (in which the lower castes were also represented). Instead, in both villages, a separate (annual) committee was convened and manned by upper-caste individuals; contributions were collected from among upper-caste households only, and they alone performed the rituals and brought offerings.

Durga is not another rustic goddess, she is the unofficial patron goddess of Bengal. Her reintroduction is part of a process we may term 'regional culturization' of village society. In this process, villages of Burdwan have been brought closer to an urban-derived culture. This, however, was not a national culture, but the culture of a region: that of Bengal. The varied and fragmented culture of village India is being replaced by regional cultures, identities that have developed not in India's centre but in one of its several regions.

The Durga-*puja* period – or merely 'the *puja*s' (it includes several other *puja*s, such as those of Kali, Lakshmi and Karmakar) – is the longest continuous celebration of all in Bengal, the highlight of the year. Schools are closed for a month, television covers the event in special programmes, and the newspapers have special '*puja*' sections. It is therefore remarkable that until fifteen or twenty years ago the Durga-*puja* was not celebrated in a grand manner or at all in most villages in this area. There were no images, no pandals, no troupes of musicians or any theatre performances, merely the private observance of certain rituals. However, the Durga-*puja* does have a history in village society. Until the early years of independent India, the Durga-*puja* was celebrated in a number of villages in a relatively grand style (image and pandal, occasionally theatre performances) by landlord families. It was the celebration of splendour, with huge and costly displays of wealth. Ordinary villagers participated, gazed on the image, received *prasad* and sweets, and were entertained, but it was typically a private celebration, entirely arranged by and paid for by landlords, and held within the compound of their households.

Until the 1970s village society did not belong to the suave and urbane world of the Calcutta-based *bhadralok*, of which the Durga-*puja* was a central celebration. Calcutta society had evolved on its own path from an interaction with and reaction to British and European culture.[31] Urban Bengali society developed its own distinct culture, centring on the *bhadralok* and his literate culture. After the *zamindar* abolition of the mid-1950s, however, the *zamindar*-sponsored grand Durga-*puja* celebration lapsed many places. It had been a landlords' festival, destined to die out when these could no longer afford even these occasions of lavish patriarchal bene-volence. The *zamindar* abolition cut off a relatively secure source of income and abolished any remaining paternalistic incentives for a family to bear such expenses.

While it lapsed in many villages, the Durga-*puja* became increasingly significant in Bengal's urban society. 'The *puja*s' became the grand occasion of the year, increasingly costly, and increasingly more integral to a version of 'the Bengali way of life'. But the celebrations that were quickly becoming the unofficial Bengali national holiday remained largely uncelebrated in the countryside. Crucially, the focus on Durga as 'the Mother goddess' is part of the *sakti*-cult to which most high-caste Bengalis – and by consequence most *bhadralok* – belong. Village Bengalis on the other hand have historically tended toward *bhakti*-cults, which do not give any place of pride to Durga.

The reintroduction of the Durga-*puja* to village society followed the same ritual pattern. Although the village clean castes in the main belonged to the same *sakti*-cult as the high caste landlords, they had not celebrated the Durga-*puja* on the same scale as their urban counterparts. When it was reintroduced, it was done by those of the village clean-caste Hindus most familiar with the world of the urban *bhadralok* and most like them by profession. In Udaynala the initiative was taken by a Kayastha household

---

31. Although not without romantic ideas about the sophistication of simple, rustic cul-ture, as shown by Partha Chatterjee, 'A Religion of Urban Domesticity: Sri Ramakrishna and the Calcutta Middle Class', in Chatterjee and Pandey (eds), *Subaltern Studies VII*, pp. 40–68.

(an archetypal *bhadralok* caste), originally inhabitants of Udaynala but for three generations engaged in the medicine business in Calcutta. He was followed by the village Baniya and Brahmin families. The five Baniya households were by that time doing well in business (printing presses), and among the Brahmins one counted three schoolteachers and one household married into a successful business-family. In Gopinathpur the initiative was taken on a broader basis, although the pattern was the same. Representatives from the three highest castes were behind the initiative, and a committee was established that comprised several small businessmen, two school-teachers, and one clerk – all from among the higher castes. By their occupations, their education and social status, these no longer regarded themselves as mere cultivators. They had become professionals and were closer to the world of the *bhadralok* than the world of their co-villagers. As businessmen, schoolteachers or clerks, they were in touch with and spent most of their time in the social world outside the village – in towns, at an office or business.

It was at the initiative of formerly poor but ritually clean cultivators turned businessmen, schoolteachers or clerks that the urban *bhadralok* celebration was reintroduced to village society. It was reintroduced as a semi-public *puja*, paid for by collections among a limited stratum of society. Rather than estranged urbanites coming to celebrate idealized and idyllic village roots, the Durga-*puja* now became the festival in which estranged villagers could celebrate their belonging to a larger community, the com-munity to which they aspired as would-be or petty *bhadralok*. Business or teaching connected locals to a social environment where one did not celebrate Olaichandi but Durga, not the rustic *gajan* but 'the *puja*s'. For these villagers – because they were still villagers, living in villages – to celebrate 'the *puja*s' was to celebrate their links to the urban part of Bengali society, connecting them to a segment of West Bengal's society that was urban, educated, and earning a livelihood in business or in the administration. Above all, the Durga-*puja* connected them to a high-status section of society, a section where the literate *bhadralok* was the dominant role model. To celebrate the Durga-*puja* symbolized one's belonging to that social group. It underscored an aspiration to move on to a higher status, a desire to be seen as belonging to a different and more prestigious social group. By aspiring to a higher status on the modernized Bengal level, the upper-caste Hindus of Gopinathpur and Udaynala villages were distancing themselves from the village low castes who were catching up on the village level.

Conclusion

The upper-caste Hindus who reintroduced the Durga-*puja* to the villages have in the 1990s associated themselves with the BJP and Hindu nationalism. The very same people (not just the same 'kind' of people) who reintroduced the Durga-*puja* as a village variety of an urban celebration with an actively retained exclusive upper-caste character, openly supported the BJP in the 1993 panchayat election. This concurrent 'evidence', which for villagers identified the BJP supporters and which for me by the same token has identified broader concerns into which Hindu nationalist discourse has been imported, suggests that voting for the BJP was to a large extent motivated by local concerns, by resentment over lost status in local village society.

The 'evidence' suggests that we cannot talk of a Hindu nationalism in rural Bengal of the kind encountered in certain areas of northern and western India. Rather, what we have encountered is a village middle class seeking to re-establish or re-confirm a superior social standing by publicly stating – through the medium of a festival – their closeness to the urban middle classes. The urban middle-class lifestyle represents a model, that of the *bhadralok*, which was and is formed by the history of Bengal. The increasing adoption of this model by the rural middle classes was evident from well before members of these same classes turned to Hindu nationalism. Because the role model of the *bhadralok* has grown out of Bengali society and its historical experiences, it constitutes a model which has a very strong and immediate appeal, its high status is easily recognized, and it is part and parcel of a larger packet of social values and cultural patterns and of Bengal's historically formulated concerns.

In urban society the situation is somewhat different in that most of those who have turned to Hindu nationalism were not first-generation *bhadralok* with the same precarious hold on their social status as the village Hindu nationalists encountered here. Rather they were relatively secure in their status, although as lower middle-class *bhadralok*. But the security of this status has not prevented the pervasiveness of Bengali identity in their political ideas. The distinctive character of their self-conscious Bengali identity tends to permeate divergent political views. The dominant themes of any formulated political ideology in Bengal are about modernity, progress and rationality, whether the ideology is of a Hindu nationalist tinge or communist. The nature of this identity, its orientation towards what is perceived of as 'modern', grows out of Bengali history: the specific place and role the Bengali *bhadralok* cut for themselves in Indian history, in the independence movement and in the cultural development from resistance to the state of colonial subjugation towards (still imperfect) maturity and modernity. The *bhadralok*, as they see themselves, had and still have the special obligation of defending the rational against the obscurantist, and the modern and progressive against backwardness. With many of India's foremost social reformers and *littérateurs* coming from Bengal, the *bhadralok* also see themselves as heirs to and upholders of a tradition of reflected social and political critique and of a cultured alternative to a materialistic lifestyle.

Against this, Hindu nationalism – as an ideology 'imported' from the region of northern India which most Bengalis do not consider culturally equal to Bengal – represents but a minor challenge to the basic tenets of the existing Bengali model. In many respects, Hindu nationalism as formulated by political action in northern India contradicts basic tenets of the dominant socio-cultural model of Bengal. This is why, in their voicing of Hindu nationalist policies, the two groups of Bengali Hindu nationalists encountered in this chapter tended to reformulate and condition the aims and concerns of their chosen party. In fact, in their practical conception, they seem to go further, beyond a mere reformulation or conditioning. Both in the Calcutta and the village interviews, adaptation of elements from Hindu nationalist discourse – rather than the whole – to a homely model is much pronounced. This was particularly evident in the villages, where support for the BJP constituted but a late element in a drawn-out effort to retain social distance. But it was also evident among the urban interviewees, who tended to dismiss incidents such as Ayodhya as unfortunate although politically necessary.

This adaptation suggests that a Hindu nationalist ideology formulated in north India is experienced in Bengal as largely alien compared to the concerns that centre around the model of the *bhadralok* – with which they are familiar and which has been formulated in the historical experience of the region. Rather than denying the relevant tenets of Bengal's cultural heritage, the selective argumentation seems to confirm it. The striking difference between Bengalis and north Indians in Hindu nationalist discourse represents only in part an identity conflict. Rather it re-establishes Bengalis' sense of superiority.

In conclusion we may make the following observation. In a society as large and complex as India, even a 'nationalist' ideology tends to emerge from and find its practical expression in the concerns and socio-political realities of one particular region. A strong regional tinge and flavour prevent a smooth export into other regions. Bengal's nineteenth-century modernist variety of cultured nationalism could not be exported to other regions but had to be reformulated in Gandhi's tradition-inspired vocabulary to gain a mass following (there were other factors too, but this was an important one). And modern-day Hindu nationalism is strongly modified by the historically formed concerns of the Bengali *bhadralok* in its meeting with Bengali Hindus.

In Bengal the self-consciously modernist and cultured *bhadralok* still reigns supreme because he grew out of her soil. Ideologies formulated in regions outside one's own will remain partly alien because they do not relate to the experiences and realities of one's home region. In India, 'nationalist' ideologies coloured by region of origin will in other regions tend to become ideologies only in the strict sense of a conscious and formulated (and often adopted) world view, not in the more extended sense of signs and symbols with an immediate appeal to profound and unconscious emotions.

CHAPTER SEVEN

'This God-Forsaken Country': Filipino Images of the Nation

Niels Mulder

This chapter is part of a wider-ranging investigation into the cultural construction of the public sphere in the Philippines, or what and how people think about it.[1] We shall examine why contemporary thinking about this sphere is so negative and why Filipinos indulge in 'self-flagellation' and 'Philippines-bashing' (as it is popularly referred to in the Philippines). While some may hold that people the world over tend to be critical about their government and the political process, and others maintain that an inner discourse of self-debasement may function as a pleasant assertion of we-feelings, the sheer frequency and quantity of negative evaluations of self and country in the Philippines are so baffling that they strike both foreign observers and Filipinos themselves as extraordinary. While this may be a characteristic that has especially come to the fore since the Aquino assassination of 21 August 1983, it does warrant a search for deeper reasons while tracing the evolution of the public sphere in the Philippines.

The existence of a public sphere should not be taken for granted. In non-complex, communally organized societies – such as the Philippine

---

1. For some early results, see Niels Mulder, *Filipino Images. The Cultural Construction of the Public World*, Quezon City: Ateneo de Manila University Press, forthcoming; 'Philippine Public Space and Public Sphere', Working Paper No. 210, University of Bielefeld: Sociology of Development Research Centre, Southeast Asia Programme, 1994; 'The Public Sphere and Its Legitimacy in the Culture of the New Urban Middle Classes in the Philippines', in Johannes Dragsbæk Schmidt, Niels Fold and Jacques Hersh (eds), *Emerging Classes and Growing Inequalities in Southeast Asia*, Aalborg: Aalborg University Press, forthcoming.

baranggáy upon Spanish contact – people distinguish between insiders (that is, those who are known and belong) versus outsiders (that is, irrelevant others with whom one does not share common space or good). The world outside is a field of opportunity at best, the place where one may hunt for a prize but where one does not carry responsibility. In other words, socially there is the 'private', common sphere of familial and communal bonds that is felt to be 'ours' alongside similar spheres that are 'theirs' (and none of our business); territorially there is the space surrounding the communal domain that is nobody's and everybody's land.

A public world, though, is different. One could think of it as the overarching sphere of a *Gesellschaft*, of a society-in-the-abstract that comes into being in a process of differentiation and growing complexity. In the Philippines, the first subsystem to differentiate was constituted by the colonial state and its institutions of government, politics and church; subsequently, we see the differentiation of the economy; later still the developing independence of civil society and the media. This world is animated by a certain culture and filled with the discourse that is called 'public opinion', especially the opinions of the members of the educated, urban middle classes of professionals, civil servants, teachers, priests, writers, artists, labour leaders, business people and, sometimes, military men. It is these who compose the media, who write novels and plays, who teach in schools, and so spread myth, history and other common knowledge; who propagate ideologies, nationalism, self-images and religious ideas. In brief, they create public opinion and national identity, at one time preoccupied with religion, at another with independence, and at another still with the rape and decline of the economy, and sometimes with the evocation of the nation and the mythicization of People Power.[2] How these, and the public sphere in general, are currently represented becomes apparent in school texts and the press. To understand this representation, we should first briefly reflect on the relationship between the public sphere and middle classes.

It may be argued that these middle-classers are essential to the creation of a modern public world; that it does not exist in a two-class situation of rulers and ruled, of a monarch or an oligarchy that dominates a little

---

2. The mainly middle-class masses who stopped Marcos's armed might with their physical presence on EDSA ringroad in February 1986 became known as People Power. It has often been observed that this is different from people's power; so far ordinary people have had very little political power, unless they start shooting back, such as in the New People's Army (NPA), that is, the armed branch of the National Democratic Front (NDF).

differentiated populace.[3] Be this as it may, in the process of societal evolution, the state, economy and civil society assume a kind of independence both *vis-à-vis* the rulers and from individual and communal experience, at the same time that society also differentiates in classes, including those of the middle stratum. Henceforward, it is the institutions of state, economy and civil society that are the subject matter of the public world. This world is in the main debated and given cultural shape by educated members of the middle classes whose discourse is essential to bring about and form the idea of the nation, of national identity, and less lofty self-images.

One of the curious features of the Philippine polity is that the political elite dominating the state hardly interferes in these debates, with the recent exception of Marcos. This relaxed attitude of a self-confident oligarchy can perhaps be best understood by their disinterest in and persistent avoidance of all forms of social mobilization (whether in the name of nation-building or national development) and the relative harmlessness of the 'free' intellectuals. It was only under Marcos's legal terms in office that this appeared to change, yet his attempts at development and control of the discourse while imposing an image of his own liking were such a dismal failure as to stimulate the currently endemic self-flagellation. This negativism, though, only makes sense when we understand the public sphere historically, with an emphasis on the happenings of the current century.

Evolution of the Public Sphere and Its Current Representation

By establishing their dominion, the Spaniards gradually brought in place an overarching 'public' sphere of government and religion that was at a considerable remove from the mass of the population; it definitely did not belong to the latter. Yet, in order to be effective, the colonizers depended on

---

3. The two-class model – that is, elite or oligarchy versus the common people or mass – has a great deal of appeal in the Philippines, not only to the ideologues of the NDF, but also to the rabid nationalists of the University of the Philippines (UP). Whereas the former propagate and practise class struggle, the latter propose the fusion of elite and masses in a deep-seated feeling of nationalism. Both these ideologues and nationalists are firmly members of the middle classes, yet they have to struggle very hard to influence public opinion, and so far they have difficulty in creating something like a national discourse in which the opinions of the leading intellectuals are discussed rationally. A simple bipartition is also attractive to all those who reason in the popular oppositions of colonizer (to be blamed) versus colonized (to be exploited), and similarly, foreigners versus natives, or the United States of America versus the Philippines.

the cooperation of the native chieftains to whom they extended privilege in exchange for the taxes they should deliver. As an intermediate class of principales (*principalía*), they found themselves in an ambiguous position, dependent as they were on Spanish favour and native compliance. This balancing act and the care for their own interests led to a certain understanding of the public sphere and to what Corpuz sees as the beginnings of a persistent political culture of artfulness, shrewdness, self-interestedness and indifference to the common good.[4]

It is only much later that, next to the sphere of the colonial state, a new realm of life differentiates from indigenous existence, yet, in the nineteenth century, a separate sphere of 'the economy' came into existence upon which the class of the principales and the Christianized Chinese-Filipino mestizos acquired a firm purchase. It is these people, with an admixture of Spaniards, who are the traceable ancestors of an important part of the contemporary oligarchy. Because of their fortune they could invest in the advanced education of their offspring, which gave rise to the so-called *ilustrados*, the hispanicized professionals and intellectuals who began to ask uncomfortable questions about their colonial predicament. The least they desired was equality and representation within the Spanish empire. Castilian intransigence and discrimination paved the way for their discovery of a Filipino identity, the formulation of nationalism, and then for revolution, the First Republic and the first Constitution.

In their violent undoing of Philippine independence, the American opponent initially stimulated the nationalism and desire for freedom that filled the public sphere during the last decade of the nineteenth century. However, by coopting the more pliable exponents of the Philippine elite, public discourse began to focus on politics. Because of American dependence on the cooperation of the local elites, the latter acquired a good measure of political power with which they could strengthen their hold on the political economy; soon they came to see the country as their private preserve. Culturally, things changed even more. By their massive injection of public education, the Americans succeeded in implanting the ideas of American superiority, of the United States as the fountainhead of modernity, while replacing the relevance of the past for a future orientation and the idea of progress.

---

4. O.D. Corpuz, *The Roots of the Filipino Nation* (2 vols.), Quezon City: Aklahi Foundation, Inc., 1989, pp. xii–xiii.

By engineering this break in cultural history, the significance of hispanicization, of Catholicism, of the self-confident claim for equality, and of nationalism were relegated to the wings while centre-stage became occupied by politics and American-made modernity – from jazz, movies and consumer goods to literary writing in English; from public health and rapid transportation to massive schooling and an effective civil service. While appropriating American ideas and standards, the Filipinos became alienated from their past and historically grown identity while beginning to view themselves as inferior. It is this complexity that constitutes the so-called 'colonial mentality' which is, in its simple form, thought to be expressed by a persistent preference for 'stateside' consumer products.

The History of the Philippines in School Texts

The contemporary texts for the last three grades of primary school and the first of high school offer a good illustration of the above interpretation and are quite explicit in their positive and uncritical depiction of the American period. As soon as the Filipinos take over, beginning with the Commonwealth, progress is apparently frustrated and an atmosphere of pessimism and decline begins to colour the narrative. The official text for the fifth grade is both representative of and explicit about all this.[5] Summarizing, we are informed that:

> The impact of Spanish culture is remoulded by the Americans whose introduction of public education and health, democracy, elections, and modern communications are relevant to the present [the Filipino-American war is underexposed]. In their preparation for [self]government, the Americans introduced new and progressive technical devices; government began to

5. For the purposes of my research, I made a thorough analysis of the following officially and privately authored textbooks: Kagawaran ng Edukasyon, Kultura at Isports, *Pilipinas: Heograpiya at Kasaysayan* (1986; reprinted 1990) [The Philippines: Geography and History]; *Ang Pilipinas sa Iba't Ibang Panahon* (1987; reprinted 1992) [The Philippines in Various Periods]; *Ang Pilipino sa Pagbuo ng Bansa* (1988) [The Filipino in the Formation of the Nation], Quezon City: Instructional Materials Corporation. E.D. Antonio, L.L. Oriondo, A.S. Flora, R.R. Belarde, E.L. Banlaygas, *Pilipinas: Ang Bansa Natin IV, V, VI* [The Philippines: Our Country], Manila: Rex Book Store, 1989–91. Kagawaran ng Edukasyon, Kultura at Isports, *Araling Panlipunan I (Pagtatag ng Bansang Pilipino). Batayang Aklat para sa Unang Taon ng Mataas na Paaralan* [Social Studies I (The Establishment of the Philippine Nation). Basic Book for the First Year of High School], Quezon City: Instructional Materials Corporation, 1989. Bro. Andrew Gonzalez, FSC, L. Sta. Ana-Rankin, A.N. Hukom, *Kasaysayan at Pamahalaang Pilipino. Unang Antas, Araling Panlipunan para sa Mataas na Paaralan* [Philippine History and Government. First Level, Social Studies for High School], n.p.: Phoenix Publishing House, 1989.

penetrate everywhere; education became secular, health accessible; the country began to urbanize; worship was free [mentioned are the Iglesia Filipina Independiente (IFI) and the Protestants].

Progress gets into higher gear still when the text ingenuously states that:

the purposes of American education were (1) to teach everybody to become a good citizen of a democratic country; (2) to provide elementary education for everybody; (3) to spread American culture and English; (4) to develop livelihood; (5) to develop the feeling of nationalism in everybody; (6) to enable every poor peasant to get his own land.

In view of the colonial situation, points 1, 2, 5 and 6 are quite amazing already, yet the text goes bravely on to mention the effects of colonial education:

So, everybody could go to school, irrespective of social place. However, education was available in English only, and emphasized things American. This resulted in the spread of a colonial mentality and a preference for white-collar occupations. Thanks to general and health education, along with sports, the people gained a better physical condition. Also because of this education, the consciousness of the Filipinos became democratic and strengthened their nationalistic feelings.

The inherent contradictions between colonial tutelage along with its hand-maiden, America-oriented formal education, on the one hand, and democracy, nationalism and citizenship, on the other, escape from the authors' awareness. America equates with progress, technology, industry and democracy, and while some criticism is allowed to surface, especially in relation to colonial land policy, the Americans are credited with introducing modern methods of agriculture and irrigation. The American period is a golden age.

When the book reaches the Commonwealth period, the representation of the country's history begins to contrast with the reporting about the American era:

The economic plans of the Commonwealth administration are doomed to failure because the economy is dominated by Americans, Chinese and Japanese. The Japanese occupation does away with democratic rights, and leads to disorder, material decay and theft. So, the Third Republic is inaugurated in a time of poverty and devastation, yet it is inspired by the lofty purposes of modernization, development, and the return of peace and order.

As in all such books, republican times are chopped up and presented by way of presidential dispensations, which shifts the focus away from cultural evolution and political continuity.

In order to achieve rehabilitation, Roxas had to amend the Constitution to allow for the parity rights that were protested by J.P. Laurel and C.M. Recto. Quirino wanted to restore peace, order and trust in government while bringing welfare to the troubled countryside; yet, his government was corrupt and distrusted in a period of armed rebellion, low productivity and unemployment. Magsaysay chose for the common man and concentrated on the problems of the rural population but he could not solve the basic problems of livelihood. President Garcia tried to free the economy of American and Chinese control and did not want to rely too much on the United States. Macapagal thought that land reform was essential to remedy livelihood and peace; he needed to solve the problem of corruption in government while striving after national self-sufficiency in the provision of primary necessities. Yet, when Marcos took over, the country was in disorder and its problems persisted. Inflation, social unrest, and more and more rebellion led to the declaration of martial law at the time when the government was broke and the morality of the citizens low.

The deep roots of this situation are specified as (1) slow development; (2) slowness in establishing peaceful conditions; and (3) the lack of identity as a free nation. Be that as it may:

> people were hoping for a new society; for many, however, martial law became a frightful experience comparable to Japanese times. Moreover, after some initial successes, in the late 1970s, the country was back at corruption, private armies, political feuding, killings, the absence of justice, a weak administration, absence of government service, with the people no longer respecting officials. There is rebellion, a communist party, the NPA (New People's Army), the MNLF (Moro National Liberation Front), and with an expanding AFP (Armed Forces of the Philippines) a lot of fighting is going on. It is a time of scarcity and shortage of funds. The collapse is in 1983; the peso devalues, inflation reigns, repression increases, and women are discriminated against in law, work and opportunity.

All the books for the higher grades that I consulted evoke this same dismal picture. The public world appears as an area rife with problems, in which politics dominate while government is perennially unable to ameliorate the situation. This image is different from that projected in the lower grades. In the latter, wider society is imagined along the lines of the family, the government becoming a super-parent showering beneficence on its nationals; the general view is hierarchical and ethically obliging. In progressing through the grades, though, the picture becomes less orderly. Whereas the scant examination that is given to the family, its hierarchical order and obliging relationships conforms to the earlier teachings, subsequently citizens and government are projected as mutually dependent partners. Of course, government is still projected as awfully important, but it can only succeed if people and officials hold the positive values that create a good society.

A structural approach is avoided. While moving into the present, from the Commonwealth period on, perennial problems crop up; yet how they are rooted, and from where they originate, remains vague, and the few reasons given are unclear, such as 'slow development', 'absence of peaceful conditions', 'lack of identity as a free nation', and 'foreign dominance of the economy'; the last condition also 'weakens freedom'. Cause and effect remain shrouded in mystery. The government seems to be incapable and impotent. People lose confidence. Apparently, the government does not express the aspirations of the people, and the slogans about democracy and being a republic do not result in development, the self-proclaimed first task of the government. Perhaps that is why ideas such as state, citizenship, constitution and law can only be explained in a technical-legal sense while not connecting with the moral, consensual experience of everyday life.

The picture projected of the American period is one of order, progress and modernization. From 1935 onwards that order is gradually breaking down, and especially Japanese times subvert morality. The presidents and the republic are faced with corruption, rebellion, irregularities and failure. In spite of good intentions – and knowledge of the right values – the outer public world appears untameable, unconstructable and, in moving towards the present, the picture gets increasingly confused. Continuity is lost sight of; disorder and frustration become normal; they are exacerbated by growing numbers of poor people who tend to antisocial behaviour. Interestingly, the question is not seen as the structural problem of poverty, but as having many individually poor persons.

This non-institutional approach which fails to reason in terms of systematic relationships, naturally results in an excessive emphasis on individual morality; if individuals are good, so shall society be. For that reason people should be taught values. They learn that Filipinos have good values, but also that they should have more of them to progress, to develop, and to achieve a peaceful and orderly society. Because they are reified, becoming causes in their own right, values become of paramount importance yet appear to be unconnected to the social process; free of context they are as loose ends dangling in the air. Because of all this, the resulting 'image' of society does not cohere; there are painfully many trees that fail to compose a forest. As a result, wider society remains vague and identification with the public sphere encompassing private life becomes difficult and ambiguous.

Recent Evolution of Self-Image

Such vagueness and difficulty of identification have not always been the case. In this respect, it is relevant to trace the evolution of the self-images that school-books present. Before doing so, we should note that postwar, and post-grant-of-independence history is one of accommodation with the Americans, at the same time that people really wanted to believe in the 'special relationship' that tied the two countries.[6] Accordingly, the first three presidencies were low in nationalism, and textbooks were still illustrated by Filipino and American flags flying at par;[7] the national anthem was sung in English.

In those days, and into the 1970s, the colonial part of Filipino identity was not yet felt to be problematic in the textbooks then in use. On the contrary, people apparently prided themselves on their association with Western culture, a relatively highly educated population, a school system that attracted students from Thailand and Indonesia, and a 'democratic' system of government. In brief, there existed a certain smugness *vis-à-vis* other Asian nations and a pride in the colonial past, such as is readily apparent in the following school text of 1974:

> As long as we Filipinos remain Christians we shall always remain indebted to Spain. Christianity is Spain's most lasting heritage to our people. Christian virtues have elevated our way of life and our ideals. The Spaniards enriched our culture. By absorbing the best and the beautiful of Spanish culture, we have become the most socially advanced of the Asiatic peoples who have shaken off Western rule. We have learned much of the sciences, arts and letters from the Spaniards. The Spaniards also taught us an advanced system of government and laws.[8]

Yet, the greatest blessing was to have been conquered and colonized by the Americans.

---

6. Trust in and dependence on the United States was successfully instilled. In 1943, Quezon wrote to President Roosevelt, 'that the Filipinos, "spiritually" speaking, had an "Occidental way of life" that could be preserved only through continued association with America and the Western world.' In his biography we find, 'I swore to myself and to the God of my ancestors that as long as I lived I would stand by America regardless of the consequences to my people or to myself.' (Corpuz, 1989 II: 566, 568). Also his protégé and later president, Roxas, can be quoted again and again for his absolute reliance on America and identification with its culture.

7. Alfred W. McCoy, 'The Philippines: Independence without Decolonization', in R. Jeffrey (ed.), *Asia: the Winning of Independence*, London: Macmillan, 1981.

8. F.T. Leogardo and J.R. Navarro, *Challenges in Philippine Community Life*, Manila: Philippine Book Company, 1974, p.127.

Asian Forms of the Nation

We shall always associate America with democracy. We are forever indebted to her for our democratic system of government and laws. Because America trained us in self-government, the Philippines has become the outpost of democracy in the Orient ... The American occupation brought about material prosperity never before enjoyed by our people. The standard of living was improved. The Filipinos took to the American way of life as ducks took to water. The Filipinos became Americanized and were proud of it.[9]

Under the Marcos dictatorship (after 1972), self-images began to change drastically. With the suppression of the demands for nationalism and democratic citizenship, school education became geared to the development of human resources, to technocracy and progress rather than to the development of the human being, resulting in a vast generation of politically naive and socially unattentive martial-law babies indifferent to history, nation and citizenship. Materially motivated, they could not get excited about the American flag on the new (1986) 100-Peso bill; 'As long as I can pay with it, it is fine by me.'[10]

The later Marcos period did more than demobilize and demotivate people in relation to questions of national identity and the common weal. The steady decline in real income and the continuous erosion of the economy reinforced a pervasive survival orientation in which attending to one's own interests came first. Add to this the degeneration of the institutions of the state, such as parliament, the judiciary, the military, the Constitution and the law in general, plus the abuses against ordinary and privileged citizens; it all resulted in disaffection and vague hopes – often for emigration. So, when Doronila in the mid-1980s researched the national identity orientations of school children, she found that 'if these young students had their way, they would rather be citizens of another country'.[11]

This depressing picture is reflected in the school texts of those days. According to a social studies book for economics used in the third form of high school, Filipino working habits are characterized as follows:

9. *Ibid.*, pp. 130–132.

10. The bill depicts the ceremony inaugurating Philippine independence; the flag of the Republic of the Philippines goes up while the conspicuous Stars and Stripes is hauled down. Such a picture on the banknotes of a former colony strikes one as weird, because normally colonizers are seen as illegitimate oppressors. The picture here may be interpreted as a recognition of the legitimacy of the American occupation while symbolizing the blessing of the Americans to the perennial ruling class that was their steady collaborator.

11. M.L.C. Doronila, 'The Nature, Organization and Sources of Students' National Identity Orientations', in Education Forum (ed.), *Towards Relevant Education*, Quezon City: Association of Major Religious Superiors in the Philippines, 1986.

> [They] do not work hard; *ningas kugon* [never finishing a project]; *mañana* habit [postponing]; sacrifice work just to meet social obligations; absenteeism; lack pride in work; work just to please the boss; the quality of work is inferior; spend money recklessly, then borrow.[12]

When the students advance to college, the knowledge is imparted – the book is still in use – that Filipinos are:

> [i]rresponsible, imitative, improvident and indolent; they dislike manual labor; their government is corrupt and serves foreigners; they are not self-respecting, not self-reliant, and have an inferiority complex. Moreover, they are the laughing stock among their fellow Asians.[13]

To understand this evolution from a self-confident to a self-abasing picture of the collectivity and its public sphere, we should remind ourselves that the granting of independence to the Philippines in 1946 had little to do with the war and its aftermath; it was on schedule, at a time that the Americans were hailed as liberators. Rather than the culmination of a fight for freedom, it inaugurated a period of profound dependence on the United States, culturally, economically and even politically. In terms of a culture of the public sphere, it signalled a malaise from which the country has yet to recover. Only a few diagnosed this cultural crisis. In the late 1950s, Claro M. Recto reminded his countrymen that continuing dependence on the USA was a betrayal of their nationhood, and that the attitude of mendicancy was an insult to independence. In his newspaper columns, Soliongco also tried to contribute to awareness and spiritual independence, while it was Constantino who dug to the roots of the problem with his famous comments upon the (neo)colonial miseducation of the Filipino.[14] While all of them stimulated the subsequent discussions about social, cultural and nationalist reconstruction, their criticism largely fell on deaf ears because, in spite of the havoc wrought by war, rebellion and confrontational 'traditional' politics, they were up against a self-congratulatory mood which considered the Philippines as the most advanced of Asian nations.

---

12. J.B. Bilasano and T. Abellera, *Socio-economic Development and Progress*, Quezon City: Educational Resources Corporation, 1987, pp. 62–63.

13. M.B. Garcia and L.O. Militante, *Social Problems*, Metro Manila: National Book Store Publishers, 1986, pp. 193–199.

14. About Recto, see Renato Constantino, *The Making of a Filipino*, Quezon City: Malaya Books, 1971; about Soliongco, Renato Constantino (ed.), *Soliongco Today*, Quezon City: Foundation for Nationalist Studies, 1981; about (neo)colonial education, Renato Constantino, 'The Miseducation of the Filipino', in Renato Constantino, *The Filipinos in the Philippines and Other Essays*, Quezon City: Malaya Books, 1966.

Into the 1960s, the Philippine economy appeared as one of the most robust in Asia and boasted by far the highest per capita income in the Southeast Asian region, with an entrepreneurial class exposed to American methods and privileged access to the United States market. Culturally, people saw themselves to be part of Western civilization; the third largest English-speaking country in the world; the only Christian nation in Asia; the showcase of democracy in a region ruled by strongmen; the bridge between East and West. This orientation to the Occident, the emulation of the American model, and their unreflected position in Asia by its own logic became the fountainhead of bedevilling dilemmas that, at the time, were seldom recognized. And then, where to begin? How to create consciousness of nationhood, of history, of identity? In its aimless quest for progress and future, and glorification of the American period, society at large had drifted far from any historical moral moorings.

The sham of it all, the perfidity of politics, the depth of social cleavages, and the question of identity all burst into the open during Marcos's expedient exercise of power. In 1969, the New People's Army (NPA) was established; the disillusionment caused by Marcos's fraudulence and mendacity took violent shape during the protracted protests of 1970, which became known as the First Quarter Storm. In view of the president's personality, it logically led to the declaration of martial law in 1972. One by one the 'achievements of civilization' were destroyed; civilian control of the army gave way to the nightmare of militarization; dictatorship replaced democracy; censorship killed the free press; propaganda substituted for information; the 'independent' judiciary became a travesty of justice; the superficiality of the Christian tradition was exposed; the introduction of bilingualism in school eroded the understanding both of English and of Filipino (Tagalog). At the same time education was made instrumental to propaganda and history-less progress, resulting in that amazingly meek and blank generation of martial-law babies. Economically, the country became the 'sickman of Asia'; and more than ever violence thrived.

The euphoria of having expelled Marcos, of People Power, of a new beginning, resulted in the widespread visibility of the 'I am a Proud Filipino'-sticker. They had shown the world – much like the Iranians in 1978 – that they were capable of driving out the dictator in a non-violent manner. But soon the hopes for resurrection and redemption waned. Early in 1987, the talks about national reconciliation broke down and the sword of total war against the 'rebels' was unsheathed, unleashing the military and vigilantes again, just as under Marcos. Peacefully demonstrating peasants were first ignored, then massacred; all the progressive elements of the early Aquino administration were eliminated while labour leaders were simply killed, or imprisoned on the most tenuous charges. When late in the year an American-written journalistic impression appeared that characterized the Philippines as 'A Damaged Culture',[15] it made a deep impact among people who had begun to lose hope again. By the end of the Aquino period, there were no Proud Filipinos left and the inner discourse was one of pessimism with hopes dashed, such as the following newspaper excerpts demonstrate.

'We Filipinos' according to the Newspaper

Throughout December 1993 and January 1994, I set myself the task of collecting the 'we'-statements I found in the editorial and opinion pages of the *Manila Standard*, the *Philippine Daily Inquirer*, *The Philippine Star* and the weekly *Philippines Free Press*. These 'we'-statements do not project a rounded self-image. Most of them say something about the perceived state of affairs in the outer public world that people experience as beyond their grasp and with which they identify to a limited degree only; identification is, however, indicated by the use of 'we', 'our', 'us', 'this nation', 'the Filipino', and so forth. During the period of amassing data, the economy had begun to show signs of recovery and a moderate sense of optimism pervaded. In spite of this, the inexorable self-bashing continued juxtaposed with moralistic advice about how to do better.

Generally the perception of the national character, or the Filipino in the public world, is negative, and so is the perception of the public world itself: 'Our society has really gone to the dogs' or 'What do we Filipinos have today? You answer that question and you cry' compete with 'This God-forsaken country', 'This vice-ridden land', 'This chaotic republic', 'The country's unending crisis', 'Our floundering ship of state', 'As a nation of underdogs, we ... ', 'This country is truly one of the most murderous in the world', and 'Our culture of violence/corruption/political idiocy/etc.' Of course, not everybody wants to see it this way, yet the comment of a letter-

---

15. James Fallows, 'A Damaged Culture', *The Atlantic*, November 1987. The author's thesis was 'that culture can make a naturally rich country poor', and that the damaged culture roots in 'a failure of nationalism'. While the left could easily dismiss such thinking, and others denounced it as 'blaming the victim', many people who hold centre stage in the cultural scene took it seriously and began to discuss about 'Undamaging Filipino Culture' (*Philippine Daily Inquirer*, 18 March 1988, p. 16).

writer about newspaper columnists 'having ... the unnatural wish to see us all fail' is very rare indeed.

To explain the dominant perception, or 'The present crisis in our national life', the authors either blame it on the way society and state are governed, or on the negative values and traits that, if changed to their positive counterparts (say, corruption versus honesty) would augur the good life, bringing order and prosperity. Let's concentrate on the political aspects first. Positively stated, 'It is our singular blessing that being such a disorganized people, we have no method in our madness; so we are still quite a distance from self-destruction.' This concurs with the comment about a very confused situation: 'They are running this place like our country is being run by its government.' Why is this so? 'Our politicians try to tear the country apart'; 'Our lousy system of justice'; 'It is a good thing that Justice is blind. In the Philippines she wouldn't like to see what's really going on'; 'A government that stakes our lives to the dictates of foreign creditors'; 'Our businessmen bribe'; 'Corruption has seeped to the top of our law enforcement system'; 'Years of corruption and tunnel vision have kept our economy in an infant state'; 'Here, in this lousy, graft-ridden, incompetently governed country'; 'The country's image as lawless, anti-American, anti-business'; 'The eminent corruptibility of our officialdom'; 'We have a crisis in leadership'; 'Our beloved president, who does best when he does nothing'; 'What we've got is a nation over whom nobody presides'; 'Our insensitive leaders'; and finally, 'Can we trust our officials to keep our [cultural] heritage intact? Of course not.'

It seems that the negative perception of politics and government has a deeper cause, namely, that the people are failing in their democratic duties. 'We're in a bad fix ... But in theory, at least, we are not helpless. In a so-called democracy like ours, the ultimate power rests in us – the people.' However, 'The Filipinos have developed a somewhat confused concept of this thing called democracy ... most Filipinos believe that when you have freedom of speech and of the press, freedom of worship and periodic elections, the requirements of democracy are substantially complied with.' Therefore: 'Our problem is that we regard politics and government as a spectator sport. We simply cheer and condemn, while the politicians and officials provide the entertainment'; 'What we have is a fiesta democracy', or, more to the point, 'Do we have democracy? What we have is skull and bones dressed up to look like Glorietta'; 'We ... spending money on fraudulent elections and referendums, outright stealing and expensive junkets'. 'We Filipinos have never had the knack for organization' while

'Our professed ideology is that we need to be free in order to prosper', which very much leads to giving free rein to 'The Filipinos' undisciplined nature' and 'The Filipino daredevil attitude'.

From all this logically follows 'This God-forsaken country's near-terminal case of poverty, population boom, environmental decay, agricultural and business failures, and vanishing social values'; 'In our country where justice is selective and where law-enforcers are involved in crimes'; 'Most Filipinos cater to mediocrity and sensationalism and succumb to their baser instincts.' This balances with 'We seem unable to attain class' and 'We aren't taken seriously by foreign investors', also because of 'Our national notoriety for being always dependent on foreign aid'. Yes, 'As a nation of underdogs', 'we are outclassed' by 'others, who take their politics and religion seriously, and who have a certain degree of commitment beyond our nature to make', while 'we unknowingly show a "poverty" consciousness by our excusing, blaming, begging'.

Looking at this picture from the lighter side is Raffy Recto. He 'slams those critics who keep describing the Philippines as the sickman of Asia.' On the contrary, he says, 'we have developed a land vehicle which has six wheels and flies ... a garbage truck without a canvas cover.' Or, 'The Philippines will rise ... but we will rise into becoming Asia's biggest Smokey Mountain [a notorious garbage dump]. A Mt. Everest of discarded speeches and minimum wage laws.' Are such 'jokes' told 'Because we have become such hidebound cynics in self-defense against all the lies we know we're being told'? Probably, if the questioning of the Ramos slogan 'The Philippines can' is 'jokingly' answered with 'Garbage can'.

Naturally, not everything is bad, and I also found a few positive statements, such as 'Our police authorities have shown competence'; 'We complacently conclude that certain of our officials do exercise a measure of vigilance'; 'After all, isn't it time we regained some trust in our country's judiciary?'; 'There is still hope for the Filipino [upon observing that not all public utility vehicle drivers are traffic rule violators].' Also, 'Filipinos are known to be intuitive problem-solvers'; 'We are all one and the same race of peaceful Filipinos'; and 'No one beats the Pinoy in adapting to anything. Try to stop him from coming up with his own version of any popular song.' More deeply insightful is the observation, 'There is a part of our nature that draws us powerfully to examples of self-denial that may be beyond us; the part that finds nobility where weakness and solitariness have combined with courage', which agrees with 'Filipinos are great hero-worshippers.' Then, in spite of 'our hospitality' (often abused by foreigners), a trip to Hong

Kong, 'Inveterate shoppers that we Filipinos are', 'brings us into contact with a place where "Filipina" is the equivalent of maid ... it does not mean that we have to perpetuate the lowly jobs. We have self-worth'. Moreover, 'The Philippines has much to offer the global community; the world takes much inspiration from [there follow the names of artists thought to be at par with other internationally known names]', and so, Ruffa Gutierrez, 'a Filipina [second runner up in the Miss World contest], was proving once and for all, that we are not a country of domestics.'

The opinion of foreigners, or the image of the country abroad, inspires many writers. 'Many Filipinos abroad have given their countrymen a bad name', and many of them are supposedly domestics. Not everybody agrees; in protesting 'The "negative image" that domestic helpers, mail-order brides and entertainers are supposed to have given the Philippines abroad', the writer asserts that 'It is these incarnations of cartoon characters that we have for public officials ... that give us a bad name abroad.' This jibes with the observation that 'When members of Congress show unabashed contempt for our President, to the point of insulting the office he holds, we should not be surprised if foreigners look down on him and the people he represents.'

According to many, culture seems to be the culprit. 'The Filipino is talented but wanting in many other virtues', which can be illustrated at 'Our *waláng pakí* [do not involve yourself where you have no business], *maka sarili* [care for yourself only] populace'; 'Honesty, it seems, is lacking in the Filipino character'; 'Filipinos are indeed stubborn ... They only think of what feels good at the moment. They only think about the present ... Their unconcern makes them even more stubborn'; 'We do not have the right values' yet, 'we are too frightened to change'. So, is it that 'The Filipino needs to shake him out of his lethargy, his complacency, his smugness'? Max Solliven seems to agree: 'Our problem is not to restructure or even "re-invent" our government. It is to re-invent our approach to life and politics. What I see all about me is disunity, name-calling, pomposity, selfishness, greed and overweening ambition. Truly, *kaya natin itó*. We can do it. But we won't progress until we overcome ourselves.'

According to a columnist, it would be beautiful if we could 'turn back the hands of time to those years when values ruled the roost in Philippine society', but alas, they do not seem to rule now because of 'the weakness in our culture' and 'the malaise of Philippine society'. Ours is 'a culture more concerned with how we look to Washington than to ourselves', 'an impotent culture' where 'our idea of originality is to follow the ways of a stranger' so making us 'the mental colony that we are'. 'How advanced is the decay of our culture' from which 'social values have vanished'? Even 'Intelligence is undervalued in our society. The measure of smart is what you get away with.' And so, 'Do we have a damaged culture? Yes, we have.' 'We're a country in which there is too much mischief and malice, and too little discipline and consideration for others.'

The last quoted observation implies a remedy: there should be less of the first and more of the latter; people should look at themselves critically, and turn negative traits into positive ones. Easier said than done. In one column, the historian Agoncillo was quoted as having said that 'Self-deception is the worst tragedy of the Filipino as a people.' This agrees with other opinions, 'Why is the plain truth so difficult to establish in this country? Is it because we Filipinos are such gulls to believe every rumor we hear?', and 'The Filipino is afraid. We stay away from the religion issue. We are victimized because we soft-pedal, because we do not dare unsettle hurt feelings.' This type of beating around the bush was also shown by 'The Filipino lawmakers, unaccustomed to tough and fearless talk from national leaders [Mahathir] on such sensitive issues (domination by and relations with Western countries), who were stunned.' Dodging the real questions and problems seems to be endemic, 'Ah, we Filipinos! How easily are we duped!', which is corroborated by 'many Filipinos believe or want to believe we are a land of miracles (expelling Marcos in 1986; Marian apparitions; faith healing).' Well, hope for miracles combined with 'the deterioration of our moral values' may lead to 'the Filipinos' propensity to put down each other' which may be the result of 'the Filipino male's psyche of machismo and self-centeredness' from which naturally follows 'our lack of unity as a people' and the 'sense of community service that is also so rare in Filipinos today'. Indifference to one another and recklessness created 'What folly this is that we have now made New Year's Eve too dangerous even to go to Mass.' Apparently there is more than a problem of firecrackers in keeping the outer public world in order, 'How can people respect our policemen when we have such misfits in the service?' It is almost as if wider society reflects 'Our prisons [that] are run as vice dens.'

Discussion

I found the stringing together of the above 120 'we'-statements a depressing exercise; besides, I would not like to subscribe to a single one of them. Yet, what are the possible reasons for this 'Philippines-bashing' and 'self-flagellation'? Why this exasperating image of the collectivity?

The statements about being Filipino were taken from that segment of the English language press that excludes the largest newspaper by far, namely, the *Manila Bulletin*. This daily that had no difficulty in appearing throughout the Marcos period, is pro-business, gives the best financial and market analyses, and carries a very sizeable quantity of advertizing. It does not, like virtually all the other periodicals, attempt to attract readers by way of saucy columns; on the contrary, its rightist commentary is conventional and dull.

The discourse in the segment of the press from which I quoted goes on among a more socially attentive membership of the middle classes in the capital region. If we go by the frequency of their commentary, they do have a concern for the image of the nation, the question of national identity and desirable values; yet what they express most of the time is a sense of desperation. Both in the press and in interviews many are given to see the Chinese as superior 'because they have Confucianism', or show envy of the Thais 'who have a king' and the Indonesians 'who have the Pancasila', all apparently thought to inspire right values and national direction.

Such pointed references to (South)east Asian neighbours are revealing of many things and partly explain why self-flagellation and Philippines-bashing can be so freely expressed. When the neo-colonial successor elite took over from the Americans, they had long forgotten their fathers' ideas about nationalism, and there has never been any attempt at nation-building. This agrees with their non-emancipatory way of coming to power and with their hold on the political economy which both discourage all forms of popular mobilization. Indeed, the Philippines is a country without a national or nationalistic doctrine and so, whereas in Thailand the accusation of *lèse-majesté* is to be avoided, and whereas in Indonesia the Pancasila is beyond discussion, the Philippines is without such personifications of statist nation-hood, and questions of identity and the state of the nation are free to be discussed.[16]

What came in place of nationalism or a doctrine was a set of rootless assumptions about Filipino superiority in Asia and 'optimistic inferiority' *vis-à-vis* the United States. After all, the Americans had been astonishingly successful in weaning the Filipinos away from their history while imposing

---

16. American-style, democratic freedom of expression is a longstanding feature of the Philippine press that often considers itself as a controlling 'fourth estate'. This may be conferring too much honour; very often its licentiousness has more to do with political confrontations among factions of the oligarchy who own and control most newspapers, and who use them as political weapons.

themselves as essentially superior, modern and future-directed. So, while the establishing of 'colonial democracy'[17] resulted in devaluing the spirit of the nationalism that had fired the imagination of those who first fought the revolution, then fought the United States of America, to mere political sloganeering, a new generation of Filipinos was effectively indoctrinated with the exemplariness of American civilization. Gradually, they started to measure themselves against its – idealized – standards.

To clarify the consequences of appreciating oneself with alien norms, it may be useful to reflect briefly on the Filipino culture that had come into being towards the later part of the nineteenth century. After more than 300 years of Spanish domination, a distinct lowland Christian civilization had evolved around the central institution of Catholicism which had, in the process of establishing itself, been unselfconsciously filipinized.[18] Accepted and understood in local terms, it had become an unquestionable part of the culture. At the same time a Europe-oriented intellectual tradition was developing among the *ilustrados*. Among these intellectuals one finds a few who had begun to search for the Philippine roots of their being, such as Pedro Paterno, Isabelo de los Reyes and, of course, José Rizal.[19] This quest for a meaningful past – and the critique of colonialism it entailed – came to an abrupt end when Filipino history was invalidated, not just by the advent of the Americans, but especially by their massive effort at education and indoctrination.

Apart from imposing their language while closing the door to the past, the Americans were able to inspire pride in being associated with that well-spring of modernity and progress, and Filipinos took to things American as ducks to water. The avalanche of modern gadgets introduced – movies,

17. For elaboration of the contradictions between being a colony, native ideas about leadership, and democracy, see Ruby R. Paredes (ed.), *Philippine Colonial Democracy*, New Haven: Yale University Southeast Asia Studies, 1988.

18. See Niels Mulder, 'Localization and Philippine Catholicism', in *Philippine Studies* vol. 40, no. 2, 1992, pp. 240–254.

19. Pedro Paterno's essayistic fantasizing about original Filipino religion and culture may be considered as an extreme demonstration of *ang pangkaming pananáw*, that is, explaining oneself to foreigners (see *ang pantayong pananáw* below), and the earliest manifestation of the 'we-had-a-civilization-of-our-own' syndrome, of which the Gonzalez textbook is a good contemporary example (note 5; for a discussion, see Niels Mulder 'The Image of History and Society (in Philippine High School Texts)', in *Philippine Studies*, vol. 42, no. 4, 1994, pp. 475–508). Because of his pioneering publications on popular culture, Isabelo de los Reyes, Sr., is now remembered as the father of Philippine folklore studies. The same motive of uncovering the original past drove the scholar José Rizal to study and annotate one of the old Spanish sources, namely, Antonio de Morga, *Sucesos de las islas Filipinas*, Mexico, 1607.

automobiles, railroads, jazz music, radio – made it appear as if the process of modernization had no history either, and so even the ideas about ordering the public world were seen as unprecedented and new.

Although it must be granted that the latter ideas and their institutions were the greatest real contribution of the Americans, yet the introduction of democratic representation, constitutionalism, rule of law, separate branches of government, a disciplined civil service, and so forth, may not have been as original as they appeared.[20] Besides, and more importantly, these ideas and institutions were imposed; they had (and continue to have) great difficulty in finding a matrix in the local culture. As normative ideas and institutions, they were dissonant with local practice, and are at the root of the cultural confusion caused by seeing the nation as a representative of Western civilization in the East.

Such a self-imposed half-truth that is in permanent contradiction with how life is lived, understood and experienced, bewilders identity and pride.[21] Especially the American ideas about good government and the majesty of the law have grown to become irritating measuring rods that can only serve to demonstrate the shortcomings of the country, the system, 'the Filipino', and so on. Thus it is thought by some that Filipinos should measure themselves against standards of their own, or at least, develop such norms. Already in 1960, Corpuz argued that in Filipino politics nepotism is ethically normal and that party loyalty is subject to family-based interests. That is why 'We do [should] not judge ourselves by the irrelevant idiosyncrasies, eccentricities, and even wishes, of alien nations.'[22] Similarly, this time in the field of literary criticism, Lumbera argued that Filipino literature should be judged by Filipino standards and measured by its relevance to life in the Philippines.[23] Since the early 1980s the search for such standards is vigorously pursued in the College of Arts and Sciences of

20. According to Veneracion, many of these ideas and institutions were introduced by the Spaniards during the last three decades of their dominion. Jaime B. Veneracion, *Merit or Patronage: a History of the Philippine Civil Service*, Quezon City: Great Books, 1988, Chs. 4 and 5.

21. Such colonially imposed confusion in facing the wide world is nicely demonstrated in the quip about national identity, 'A Filipino is an English-speaking, Roman Catholic Malay with a Spanish name eating Chinese food.'

22. O.D. Corpuz, 'The Cultural Foundations of Filipino Politics', in J.V. Abueva and R.P. de Guzman (eds), *Foundations and Dynamics of Filipino Government and Politics*, Manila: Bookmark, 1969, pp. 6–18.

23. Bienvenido Lumbera, 'Breaking Through and Away', in Bienvenido Lumbera (ed.), *Revaluation. Essays on Philippine Literature, Cinema and Popular Culture*. Metro Manila, pp. 91–101.

the University of the Philippines (UP) where the various branches of *pilipino-lohiya* try to bring a we-centred view (*ang pantayong pananáw*) to life that does not need explaining to outsiders; logically, they prefer to express themselves in Filipino.

However this may be, the outer, wider world of shared space offers little with which Filipinos can identify wholeheartedly, and governments have done little to change this. Of course, in the early days of martial law 'the problem of nationhood' was recognized, and school-books were supposed to be designed to do something about it. Yet the government that aspired to represent a nation-state and stimulate identification with it, did almost everything it could do to devalue itself in the eyes of its repressed subjects by making a sham of the 'achievements of civilization'. And although the expulsion of Marcos in 1986 led to brief expectations of nation and solidarity, soon the public space was again filled with cynicism, hopeless-ness, hypocrisy, injustice, confrontation, violence, and traditional politicians. 'I do not deserve this country' is what a disappointed UP professor told me. Another described the country as a cruel place, devouring the sincerity and dedication of its people, while another observed that there was no longer honour to be gained from having opposed Marcos.

With so much standing in the way of positive identification, people may develop a kind of a hate-love relationship with what is, after all, their native country.[24] At the time of the international recognition of a beauty queen or a boxing champ, they are overjoyed. The non-violent toppling of the durable dictator in 1986 attracted the admiring attention of the world, and that still sparks some pride. But then, there have been so many bad things happening in this country apparently forsaken by God in spite of its prayerful population – the killer typhoons of 1987, 1990, and 1993; the sinking of the *Doña Paz*, the greatest civilian maritime disaster ever, in 1987; the devastating earthquake of 1989 and the Pinatubo eruption of 1991 that laid waste to most of Central Luzon; the flash floods that killed thousands at Ormoc in 1991; the brownouts; the traffic jams; the civil wars; the coups d'état; the confrontational political process; the crushing national debt – that it all seems to be too vast and too catastrophe-prone to master. It seems beyond redemption. Willy-nilly, one is part of it; yet ambivalent about one's identification with it.

---

24. The weakness of nationalism as identification with a transcendent community of fel-low Filipinos is compensated by the more tangible feelings attached to the motherland, or rather, Mother Land (*Inang Bayan*) representing the native soil. People identify with *Hei-mat* rather than with nation.

In their quest for a positive identification with the collectivity, many people believe that they can travel up the course of history, to times before colonialism inflicted insult and injury, to the paradise of pristine nobility, such as certain *ilustrados* were already doing a little over a century ago. That is where they believe the real Filipino values are located; they should be traced, dug up, and brought to life again. This naive trust in values as a *deus ex machina* – at the expense of structural, systemic forces – is endemic.[25] It surfaces in all the social studies school texts, in the official Moral Recovery Program,[26] and in newspaper columns and letters to the editor. It is the individual – or rather his or her morality – who appears to be responsible for the good order of society.

Since the individual is the product of his family of origin, the family should be built and strengthened, because it is believed that if the family is whole, so will society be. Yet this promotion of values that essentially belong to family and community life cannot be expected to develop national pride in oneself as a Filipino citizen because the image of the public sphere remains one of moral decay if measured against those very values. In the absence of localized positive ethics of a wider society, there merely remain the dull rules (pay your taxes, respect the flag, honour the Constitution, obey the law, vote) which are taught in school. It takes little observation or newspaper-reading to come to the conclusion that taxes, flags, constitutions, laws and polls are not precisely awe-inspiring.

Wider society is a disorderly, unsatisfactory place going by the rules of political and economic expediency with which it is difficult to identify. Because of the negative self-image propagated in school and because of overly critical commentaries in the newspapers, it appears even more disorderly than it really is. All this can be related to the colonialism-imposed syndrome that makes many Filipinos see themselves as the eternal

---

25. See Niels Mulder, 'Filipino Culture and Social Analysis', in *Philippine Studies*, vol. 42, no. 1, 1994, pp. 80–90.

26. Creating morally aware individuals as the mainstay of a good society is the purpose of the compulsory study of the Constitution in school; it emphasizes the noble intentions of the Filipinos as a people, plus the rights and duties of the citizen. Next to this, values education is an integral and important part of social studies in school. Aiming at the populace in general is the Moral Recovery Program proposed by Senator Leticia Ramos-Shahani in 1988; it was officially inaugurated by her brother, the incumbent president, in 1993. See, *Building a People, Building a Nation. A Moral Recovery Program*, Quezon City: Instructional Materials Corporation, 1988. This document, mainly composed by well-known social scientists from UP and the Ateneo de Manila, lists seven strengths and seven weaknesses, or values, of the Filipino character, or way of life; it proposes cultural measures, that is, values propagation, to remedy the negative traits.

underdog, who feels the need to explain himself, to apologize *vis-à-vis* outsiders. These days this is aggravated by a representation as the 'sickman of Asia' against the burgeoning economic success of Southeast and East Asian neighbours.

Conclusion

The peculiar image of the nation we find among contemporary educated Filipinos derives from a unique historical experience and a social perspective of the public world that is grounded in the moral, private sphere of the family. By tracing the evolution of the public sphere, we noted its colonial origin and thus its low degree of legitimacy; the surrender of that sphere to a mercenary oligarchy; and the imposition of American ideas and standards which denigrated the Hispanic heritage to a kind of proto-civilization while depicting the period of independence as one of perennial failure. It is remarkable that this is blatantly propagated in the schools while simultaneously the students are given neither the tools nor the ideology to come to grips with the public world. Positively they are being taught values that properly belong to the moral, private sphere and are being imbued with the message that the desirable order of society follows from individual good conduct. The idea behind this values education is that such reified values have regulatory power all by themselves.

The current negative image of the nation is the outcome of de-colonization and the cultural destruction inflicted by Marcos. Although the periods of the Pacific War and early independence offered little to be proud of, and are depicted as periods of moral decay in the textbooks currently in use, a positive image persisted into the Marcos dictatorship, then to be destroyed and exposed as baseless pretence. From that time on Philippines-bashing and self-flagellation have become an inveterate feature of the discourse among those who aspire to a more positive image. Interestingly, they feel addressed by values education and the Moral Recovery Program, and their social imagination sets on moral rather than structural melioration. Within the academic community we noted the *pilipinolohistas* who want to construct an image that is at the same time positive and indigenously based. The population at large is not part of all this, except for being exposed to school and media negativism. They may be indifferent to discussions about 'the Filipino'; feel secure in their regional and local identity; simply aspire to emigration; or they may be plainly survival-oriented in an impoverished environment, leaving the luxury of seeking for and debating national images to the few who care about such things.

Those concerned with constructing a positive image of the nation have to start from scratch because of the weakness and distortions of the collective memory; the absence of a positive imagination of the public world; the cultural destruction of the Marcos period; the disinterest of the central government in nation-building; and the clumsiness of the social studies curriculum. Besides, most people feel secure in their particularistic bonds of family, community, friendships, ethnicity and religion, a type of bonding that seems to be strengthening in an increasingly open, globalizing world. Multi-ethnic nationalism, call it nation-statism, is on its way out; in the Philippines it had its heyday a hundred years ago.

CHAPTER EIGHT

Blood, Territory and National Identity in Himalayan States

Graham E. Clarke

This chapter provides a historical account of the formation of modern ethnic and national identities in the Himalaya from the colonial encounter of the nineteenth century onwards. The mountain topography was a critical feature in the formation of these new identities.

The history concerns the expansion of the British Raj north-westwards through the periphery of India in its relations with peoples and civilizations in the sub-continent. This is of significance both locally in the Himalaya, and more widely in relations with China and Russia. Though at first this expansion was little more than nominal, these processes resulted in the inclusion of local polities within the ambit of British India. Subsequently, the fixing of borders and mapping were to result in a change of socio-political form from a traditional religious hierarchy to a more Western model of territorial statehood. The geographical region considered briefly here stretches in the west from modern Afghanistan to the north of Upper Burma; though Nepal is the main case taken, the argument can be extended to Afghanistan, Baltistan, Bhutan, and Ladakh.

There is an irony to this historical progression: the power of the British Empire to control an area was a precondition for the transfer of the model of the nation-state; yet the availability of this model destroyed that very power by giving rise to Western-style nationalist movements within these colonially-secured and bounded territories. The eventual result was a political segmentation, and the creation of new nations. This sequence is contained in a key insight of Benedict Anderson, namely that the colonial imposition of states behind newly-formed borders was to create a wider 'imagined community'of nation, one projected not only outwards in space but also backwards in time in the guise of a presumed 'natural' nation-state.[1]

There are two classic principles of local association in anthropology, kinship and co-residence, which can be paraphrased as 'blood' and 'territory'. The idea that these two principles were the basis of small-scale communities that make up villages, was first put forward by the nineteenth century English writer on comparative institutions and jurisprudence, Henry Maine, in his work on India and Ireland.[2] This chapter brings together the ideas of Maine and Anderson to give a more general account of state and identity formation, which can be introduced as follows. In terms of historical sequence, the colonial encounter set in force a progression that elevated the ideas of 'blood' and 'territory' into wider idioms of civil association. In terms of model, at one extreme is the hierarchy of Empire, with the focus on the central metropolis and an integration of all groups under its territorial control at their appropriate level and place. At the other extreme is an exclusive nationalism, in which all people within a territory have to be seen as in essence the same in kind: those deemed to be of different blood are, one way or another, removed. In between these two polar extremes is to be found the particular compromise of the modern nation-state. Historical change in identity reflects the swing of a pendulum between these two forms of civil association, played out successively at different political levels, such as the local village group, local area, and the state. The European historians of the so-termed French and German schools also arrived at the mid-point of the 'nation-state' from two such opposed directions, the one from the idea of the primacy of nation or common blood and the other from the idea of primacy of the state or territorial control.[3]

There also may be a third feature to Himalayan development, namely the extreme mountain topography itself. Mountains help give rise to at least two particular social and cultural features, namely a tendency to socio-cultural enclaving, and a progressive variation between areas. It would be as well to introduce these ideas here.

---

1. Benedict Anderson, *Imagined Communities*, London/ New York: Verso, 1983; also the extended and revised edition (1991).

2. Henry Maine, *Ancient Law,* London: Murray, 1863 (10th edn 1912), pp. 137, 225.

3. On the difference between these views of the primacy of 'nation' or 'state', and their respective association with German and French historians, see the resumé of Meinecke given in Louis Snyder, *The New Nationalism*, Ithaca: Cornell University Press, 1968, p. 58.

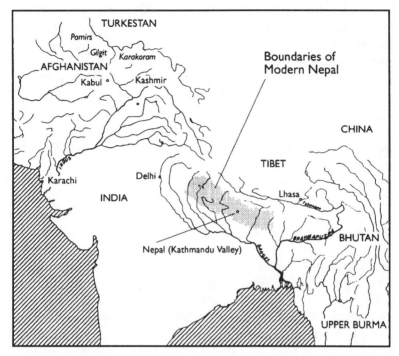

Map 4: Himalayan region with boundaries of Modern Nepal

Overall, the Himalaya is important as a natural laboratory of human social and historical variation. Compared to many other mountain areas it is densely populated, but this is not a uniformly distributed or homogeneous population. A contorted maze of ridges and rivers has laid out separate, terraced enclaves along the convoluted slopes and side-valleys of the High Himalaya, which overall has resulted in a territorial and social mosaic. Mountain villages cluster together along valley systems like so many buds on the branch of a tree, often with their own, separate and tortuous access. Despite the high profile of development programmes, the topography still acts centripetally, and restricts communication to maintain as separate entities valley systems which may be no more than small, spatial clusters of enclaves.

Many of the Himalayan states have little other than mountain territory and their population is still predominantly rural. For example, in the case of Nepal some 90 per cent of the territory is mountainous: in 1985 some 70 per cent of the population of Nepal was still more than one day's round-trip by foot from a road, and of the 71 districts 21 had no motorized roads; only some 8 per cent of the population inhabited urban areas but the narrow strip of the southern plains has had an increasingly large percentage of the population.[4] Historically, local clusters have linkages and relations with others beyond their local territory; but the degree of routine separation is such that many have developed apart, giving rise to varied histories.

At the current time there still is a large degree of heterogeneity. This appears as a variegated social and ecological 'patchwork'. Each local group can be characterized along a range of possible natural, socio-cultural and economic dimensions; each occupies one possible set of positions across various dimensions, along which they are related to others, with cross-cutting clusters of larger groups forming as sets of variations on related groups of themes. In such a configuration, local ethnic groups do not exist as sub-types of an absolute, higher-order, ethnic identity, but rather represent a particular set of positions within this wider multidimensional framework. For example, there is no real 'Sherpa' cultural prototype, but only a cluster of related Sherpa ideals and social forms. Some people may be born Sherpa, others consciously become Sherpa, and yet others find themselves considered as Sherpa. Hence, with the exception of a total separation, the question is not whether or not a group 'really' is or is not Sherpa, but in what ways it is similar or linked to other groups who are also termed Sherpa. Analytically, such a category is just one possible cluster in terms of which local groups may be considered together.

The contact of the pre-modern with the modern, of different ages co-existing at one point together, can be seen today at virtually any road or terminus in Nepal, where buses seem to collect people from different times as much as places. People, clothed in homespun carrying wickerwork baskets, not in one detail different from an early nineteenth century illustration of the same, can be seen walking along the road within eyeshot of the capital, Kathmandu. They can state that they 'are going to Nepal', using the pre-modern term for the Kathmandu Valley as a sacred space of the three Royal Cities, and not for the entire territory of the modern state.

Common territory is one important aspect of identity in the Himalaya. To the outsider a collection of village enclaves and their local river-valley system may appear as a single unit. Yet within the local territory other factors of status and identity, as defined by kinship, caste and economic position, cross-cut these divisions. Locally, such markers serve to differentiate one

---

4. WB-7498-NEP, *Nepal, Social Sector Strategy Review*, vol. 1, Table 2.5, Washington DC: World Bank, 1989; WB-8635-NEP, *Nepal: Relieving Poverty in a Resource Scarce Economy*, Washington DC: World Bank, 1990, vols I & II.

group from another; and also provide lines of incorporation beyond the local. It is along these lines that other, wider social activities, such as traditional pilgrimage, the visit of a high religious dignitary, military conquest, and now modern electoral campaigns and migration, can be mobilized. At times, *any* such factor may extend outwards in a unifying manner and become important to a consideration of national identity. Historically, what formerly were only *local* features may progress to stand for wider wholes, such as ethnic and national identity. At the same time, the problems of communication and transport across mountainous terrain imply a tendency for routine relations to drop back into the local space.

One may come from a certain place, say 'Gorkha' which on the map of today is a district of Nepal to the north-west of Kathmandu. Therefore, in that territorial sense of identity one *is* a Gorkha. Yet within that local territory, any such common place is likely to be of little importance. A feeling of commonality between people who come from the same place may be more important away from the home area than in the original area itself. In the capital city, in the national army, trading in India, in the civil service, and in metropolitan areas a common local origin may indicate a presumed historical and cultural 'sameness'.

New interactions in urban contexts are one of the main factors in the creation of country-wide identities, whether for sub-groups such as 'the Sherpa' or for overall 'national' identity. In Kathmandu, people from the same local areas but of differing Hindu and Tibetan cultural backgrounds live in close quarters. When people from a local area are brought together with others from wider afield in novel institutions located in urban areas, it may be socially functional to co-operate and forget what were locally salient differences.

That modern ethnic identities tend to appear at the time of the creation of the state was first established for Nilotic Africa.[5] Here, adjacent territory, that is occupying sequential positions in the same two-dimensional space, is one way of ascribing a wider common identity in relation to the state as a whole. In mountain areas there is a further common way of sorting local groups together, in terms of 'upland' and 'lowland'. In the Himalaya there is a widely recognized correlation between being Tibetan Buddhist, upland

5. On Nilotic ethnicities see Aidan Southall, 'The Illusion of Tribe', *Journal of African and Asian Studies*, vol V, 1/2, 1970, pp. 28–50. More recently, in accounts of state-local relations in Southeast Asia, this process has been termed 'ethnicization', on which see Oscar Salemink, 'Primitive Partisans: French Strategy and the Construction of a Montagnard Ethnic Identity in Indochina', in Hans Antlöv and Stein Tønnesson (eds), *Imperial Policy and Southeast Asian Nationalism, 1930–1957*, London: Curzon Press, 1995.

and pastoral, and being Hindu, lowland and agricultural, with so-termed 'tribals' in various kinds of dependent relations. To a degree this is an accurate description; at the same time it is a statement on the status of peoples relative to each other, of a hierarchy of 'above' and 'below', a stereotype that reinforces a social order.[6] For example, the 'tribals' as a residual category are ranked in a subordinate place in the social order.[7] Such a hierarchic conception is an aspect of the local order and is also important in determining how regional groups become incorporated into nations within the fixed, territorial borders of a dominant state, and more widely into empires.

Overall, the traditional picture evoked is that of a territorial area made up of small village enclaves, each integrated with others in the locality by relations of kinship, economic exchange and political authority. The patterns of these territories were variously elaborated according to wider historical and natural circumstances, with a progressive change along these dimensions from one area to another across the Himalaya.

In anthropology, grouping by kinship especially in the assumption of a common descent, and grouping by contiguity within a local area, have long been seen as two main ways of forming a local political community; this distinction has been paraphrased here as that between the two principles of 'Blood' and 'Territory'. Though Henry Maine saw kinship or 'blood' as the earlier institution, he also referred to the historical process by which the basis of a community which originally might have been formed through territorial association subsequently was likely to become recast or re-interpreted in terms of blood relations. He did not develop this point into an explicit theory of nationalism, but he did think of this distinction as applying at a higher political level, that is for national identity at the level of the overall state.[8] He illustrated this idea as the difference between 'Britain' as the area occupied by the British people, and 'the British people' as constituting those who variously occupy the territory of Britain. A penetrating illustration of the widespread significance of these two differing types of formulation is

6. For an account of the application of hierarchy in highland Nepal, see Graham E. Clarke 'Hierarchy, Status and Social History in Nepal' in Robert H. Barnes, Daniel de Coppet and Robert J. Parkin (eds), *Context and Levels: Anthropological Essays on Hierarchy*, Oxford: JASO, 1985, pp. 193–209.

7. Tessa Morris-Suzuki, in her account of the frontiers of Japanese identity (see Chapter 2), makes the significant point that literate civilizations tend to recode the difference of subordinate peoples on their peripheries as 'backwardness' or 'underdevelopment'.

8. For the use of a similar expression in National Socialism, that is the Nazi ideology and the 'back to the land' *Volk* agricultural movement of Germany of the 1930s, see Anna Bramwell, *Blood and Soil: Walther Dárre & Hitler's 'Green Party'*, Buckinghamshire UK: The Kensal Press, 1985.

articulated in modern British politics, between nationalist and loyalist politicians in Northern Ireland: the one party holds that all born within the territory of Ireland are 'Irish'; the other party holds that the territory of Britain extends to wheresoever the 'English' live.

In subsequent theoretical writing in political anthropology, Fortes and Evans-Pritchard made the well-known and parallel distinction between states as acephalous kin groups, and states as centralized polities.[9] Political historians follow a similar argument in the debate on the historical primacy of nation or state, that is whether modern states reflect the model of the 'state-nation' or that of the 'nation-state'. Whether considered at a national or local level, the logic here is the same. The area occupied by people originally considered 'the same' in blood may define the territory; or control of the territory may prescribe who will be thought of as 'the same' in blood.

In the case of the Himalaya, the general salience of these two principles of blood (kin) and territory (place), for the processes specifying social identity, is suggested by two ethnographic facts. First, that the names of local lineages often are taken from the name of the place of origin of an earlier ancestor. Second, that settlement and intermarriage in a village commonly come to be regarded in subsequent generations as descent through the collateral line, that is as a 'blood' relation of kinship.

In earlier traditional Himalayan states, local definitions of status, both kin and territorial, were predominant; prior to Western contact local politics were played out against a more-or-less common and static cultural back-drop of the 'Great Religions' of the region. The socio-cultural ideal was the 'sacred-centre'; borders and territories were fluctuating, empirical entities. At first, the exchange with the British Empire was built on the traditional pattern, and was necessarily hierarchical and integrative, in the manner of contact with oriental empires such as that of Manchu China.

Yet the colonial encounter with the West, in particular the British Raj in India, and to a lesser degree with the Russian empire, eventually resulted in the imposition of a Western spatial model with larger state units defined by fixed territorial borders. Through the colonial imposition of these nascent 'state-nations', there arose 'imagined communities', projected not only out-wards in space but also backwards in time in the guise of nation-states.

The Himalayan topography , however, continued to give economic if not technological limits to the formation of wider, homogeneous identities,

---

9. Meyer Fortes and Edward Evans-Pritchard (eds), *African Political Systems*, Oxford: Oxford University Press, 1940.

both national and regional, and so has helped to maintain the more traditional local, hierarchical integration of difference. The larger national identities that exist at the present in the Himalaya, such as 'Nepalese', are not homogeneous and exclusive. One is not Nepalese in the sense that one is French. Nations have been only half-formed out of local community and empire, and the modern Himalayan citizen often can appear more as an individual than as the representative of a nation. It is also ironic that in this sense of part-identity, of *anomie*, a Nepalese may appear as truly modern, and that in having avoided the European nation-state phase, a Nepalese at the same time may be both traditional and post-modern.

Much of this chapter concerns how these mountain features of encapsulation and variation, as lived out in local civil association, came to be transformed and elevated into idioms of state, nation and ethnicity by the colonial encounter. The particular argument is that extremes of integrative device of the nation-state, that is the full swing from blood, through territory and back to blood again, do not manage to pass as freely or as fully through the Himalaya as they have in the plains societies to the south. The mountains act as moderators, physical baffles to the full and lasting incursion of fundamental social changes, whether these are the forces of religion, the economic market, or of nationalism.

The Traditional State

Up until the late eighteenth century a myriad of small polities in flux covered the land of present-day Nepal; grouped together they could be referred to in various ways, such as the 'twenty-four kingdoms' (*Chaubīsī Rāja*) or the 'eighteen princedoms' *(Aṭhāra Thakuri)*. Each such small principality covered a territory approximately twice the size of the present-day districts of Nepal; further to the west the small kingdoms of the north-west Himalaya such as Ladakh, Balte (or Baltistan), Hunza and Kabul were essentially similar in kind, as were those to the east of Sikkim and the ones that made up modern Bhutan. The overall political system was constituted by the interacting set of such parallel, local, political units.

Typically, these would have their centres at northern ridge or southern valley locations, points critical for control of north-south trade across the Himalaya. Their authority was associated with these urban foci, which prototypically were also cultural centres, with vertical linkages at once political, economic and religious: as blessing and legitimacy radiated out and downwards, so goods and statements of fealty flowed inwards and upwards. Materially, they were supported by their control over the local agrarian surplus and inter-regional trade.

Wider political alliances could be expressed in common descent, marriage, war, and in common dedication and offering to the same religious shrines; but at a popular level there was an absence of any general, wider, solidary political sentiment, and instead of the modern notion of a homogeneous nation there was the idea of a multitude of different 'kinds', 'types' or 'species' (*jāt*), ranked by degrees of sameness and difference. In practice, inter-marriage between similar peoples across the Himalayan chain was one form of wider integration, and such groups would occupy analogous positions in local political structures and possess gross cultural similarities.

Conceptually, being of the same kind requires a recognition of a shared or basic unity of substance. This comes in part from the idea of a shared blood or kinship, representing an elemental quality complemented by a shared 'earth' or territory. 'Air' and 'water' are similarly elemental substances, and the term *hāvāpāni* which is glossed as 'climate' (or now even 'environment'), literally conveys this sense of 'air and water'. Of course, 'earth', 'fire', 'air' and 'water' together is an ayurvedic specification of elements, and such local forms often were subsumed within values expressed in the Great Religions of Hinduism and Buddhism. Traditionally, adaptation to a local climate would be through the offices of a priest and a religious ceremony, a purification, with offering and rededication to local territorial and lineage deities. This would take place on return from pilgrimage abroad, or on taking up new residence on marriage.

The place we know today as the Kathmandu Valley of Nepal contains three minor polities or royal cities; occasionally and most recently under Kathmandu, these were united into one kingdom. In these royal cities the body of the king symbolically acted itself to purify and integrate the kingdom, and so acted quite literally as the 'kingpin' to the state. This was illustrated in public ceremonies, such as the annual ceremonies at temples in each of the four quadrants of what was more traditionally known as the 'Nepal Valley' by the King. The symbolic bounds were also restated in the annual pattern of encampments of the nomadic Court of Mongolia, which followed a similar model of the sacred centre.[10] In Nepal, a ceremonial

---

10. On the architectural and iconographic representation of the symbolism of the four quadrants in the Nepal Valley see Mary Slussor, *Nepal Mandala*, Princeton: Princeton University Press, 1982; also see Francis Hamilton, *An Account of the Kingdom of Nepal*, Edinburgh: Constable, 1819, p. 192; also see Gérard Toffin, 'Dieux souverains et rois dévots dans l'ancienne royauté de la vallée du Nepal', *l'Homme 99*, vol. xxvi, no. 3, 1986, pp. 71–95.

integration in which the King is identified with the State and the Cosmos was illustrated as recently as the Coronation in Kathmandu of 1974, in which the King was anointed with basic organic substances representing the different types of people of his realm: in this the person of the 'God-King' and the city were identified with such politico-religious authority, and the land and the people.[11] The sacred centre was a hierarchy. The closer one was to the person of the 'God-King', the greater the religious purity and material position, the higher up one was. Empirically, some such centres were more important than others, but even the Islamic west of the region was not without this regal, courtly manipulation of space, in which time spent in the proximity of the ruler was viewed as a blessing.

This account has many cultural similarities with pre-industrial Europe. In ideal form the sacred centre appears like an Apollonian Olympia, and the model of the four quadrants and the central 'quintessence' is well known in medieval Christian art. In its empirical political expression, the fluctuating fortunes of a myriad of states focused on city centres, within a wider encompassing religious order, has a direct parallel with Europe before the rise of nationalism, especially with the Holy Roman Empire. These states too, were isolated urban foci of civilization and order set at key locations in a more rustic, agrarian fabric, and their political authority, too, sometimes extended more in principle than in practice. One difference between Europe and Asia may have been the relative lack of separation between state and church in the Asian as contrasted to the European model.[12] The more recent Western notion of the state as an exclusive sovereign and dominion body, with control of a fixed, absolute territory, as powerful in the periphery as the centre, indicates a radical conceptual break from this model.

North of the Nepal Valley there were few political spaces demarcated unambiguously as spatial units, and many areas were without land-titles. It has been argued that in 'Nepal' there were various, differentiated, indigenous

---

11. The *axis mundi* model also corresponds to other cultural complexes, including the model of the *devarāja* propounded by Coedès for the 'Hindu-Buddhist' kingpins of Southeast Asia (Georges Coedès, *Pour mieux comprendre Angkor*, Paris: Musée Guimet, 1947). Clearly it is a suitable cultural vehicle for any high culture with 'tantric' or 'shamanic' linkages, associated with this Himalayan area which would equate self, divinity and kingdom in ceremony. This notion of the 'god-king' as *axis mundi* has subsequently become referred to as the 'Theatre State' or the 'exemplary centre' in Southeast Asian literature. See Clifford Geertz, *Negara: The Theatre State in Nineteenth Century Bali*, Princeton: Princeton University Press, 1980.

12. See Louis Dumont, 'On Value', in *Proceedings of the British Academy*, vol. LXVI, 1980, p. 225.

notions of territory and political form such as 'polity', 'realm' and 'country'.[13] However, since all are translations of the same single term *deś*, a traditional fluctuating, ambiguous ideal order is far more likely than an elaborated code based on a single cultural term. In the highland Himalayan region of Tibetan culture known as *Yolmo* due north of the Nepal Valley, the early land-titles which date from the eighteenth century onwards are from that Nepal Valley.[14] They imply that this location, well within the current southern border of Nepal, is immediately 'south of the Lama's land'. The reverse was also true, and kingdoms, lords and priests at various political levels in Nepal had authority over various shrines and their associated fiefs further abroad, such as north of the Himalaya in Tibet, as they did over Nepalese shrines and temples at Benares in India. Sacred locations within the Kathmandu Valley, such as shrines at Swayambhunāth and Bodnāth, could be under the authority of people of Tibetan culture who, whatever their authority from the courts in Nepal, were also dependants of monasteries in central Tibet and who enjoyed that wider religious authority and material protection.

Pilgrimage gives a good example of the operation of this broad political order, which was based on culture rather than exclusive secular rights. As one travelled north from Kathmandu and the Nepal Valley there never was any particular point at which one left a wider country named 'Nepal' to enter another country named 'Tibet'.[15] One crossed the boundaries of the Central Court, the Royal City and the topographical threshold of the Nepal Valley; each would be treated as a conceptually related ritual boundary at which there would be an offering in the same ceremonial form. These same ceremonies would be carried out crossing any such threshold, the top of a mountain pass, a river, and when entering the next, smaller, centre of Nuwakōt, where one would also make offerings at the local temple to the local gods. And so pilgrimage and more generally travel would move onwards from one temple and resting place to another, each of which if only a cairn or water-spring by a tree, was imbued with the same type of sacredness.

13. See Richard Burghart, 'The Concept of Nation-State in Nepal', *Journal of Asian Studies*, vol. 44, no. 1, 1984, pp. 101–124.

14. For a consideration of the history of political authority in the Tibetan-Nepal borderlands based on indigenous orthography, see Graham E. Clarke, 'The Great and Little Traditions in the Study of Yolmo, Nepal', in Ernst Steinkellner and Helmet Tauscher (eds), *The Proceedings of the Csoma de Kőrös Symposium held at Velm-Vienna, Austria, 1981, Wiener Studien zur Tibetologie und Buddhismuskunde*, Heft 10, Vienna: Vienna University, 1983, pp. 21–37; also Graham E. Clarke and Thakurlal Manandhar, 'A Malla Copper-Plate from Sindhu-Palchok', *Journal of the Nepal Research Centre*, vol. VIII, Wiesbaden: Franz Steiner, 1988, pp. 105–139.

15. Thongchai Winichakul makes the same point for Siam in Chapter 3.

As one cut across local areas with allegiances variously to Kathmandu, Bhaktapur, and Lalitpur (Patan), or even to Shigatse in Tibet, there was none of the *angst* that modern man would associate with rapid border crossings or a 'no man's land'. At the present day this idea of a religious and cultural unity that holds above secular politics and nation continues, in the presumed moral right of Hindus to cross state boundaries between Nepal and India for ceremonies without any passport or visa; in some ways this is similar to the status of being on pilgrimage to Mecca for Muslims. Traditionally, in travelling a path northwards across the Himalaya from India to Tibet safety relied on a common cultural vision of order, one that included respect for the sacred, not immediately on secular authority. One made offerings to local gods and paid respect to local authority, these being local manifestations of the greater, cultural order, idealized in religious form. Ceremonial precedence and rank as perceived through shared cultural conventions, rather than a particular political chain of command, tended to define authority.[16]

From a traditional world-view, the notion of a national or state-wide, territorial exclusivity that covered all aspects of legitimate authority would appear as profoundly odd and 'other'. Even today in Nepal these older, varying conceptions persist. The term 'impression management' has been introduced to characterize the activities of trans-Himalayan traders of border regions of the west of Nepal. These peoples, from a modern viewpoint, appear to change national identity as they move south and north, from one area to another, presenting themselves as Tibetan to Tibetans and as Nepalese to Nepalese.[17] The analysis is from the viewpoint of the modern, and suggests that they 'really are' in an absolute sense, either Tibetan (Chinese?) or Nepalese nationals, and that they know that they are, and manipulate. And while in some cases at the individual level this is undoubtedly true, it is not true socially; this dual allegiance conveys a more basic truth for the people as a whole, namely that a historical assimilation as modern nationals of Nepal simply has not occurred. In the case of these poor traders in salt, wool and grain, this dualism is not so much a modern entrepreneurial development in which

16. The ideas summarily presented here are from Durkheimian sociology as developed by Louis Dumont, 'The Anthropological Community and Ideology', in Louis Dumont, *Essays on Individualism: Modern Ideology in Anthropological Perspective*, Chicago: University of Chicago Press, 1986, p. 227; also see Clarke, 'Hierarchy, Status and Social History in Nepal', p. 202.

17. James F. Fisher, *Trans-Himalayan Traders: Economy, Society and Culture in North-West Nepal*, Berkeley: University of California Press, 1986; also Andrew Manzardo, 'To be Kings of the North: Community Adaptation and Impression Management in the Thakalis of Western Nepal', Unpublished PhD. thesis, University of Wisconsin, 1983.

they consciously manipulate cultural tools to present themselves to advantage, as it is a cultural residue of a pre-modern world-view in the Himalaya.

In a traditional Asian state, the focus was not on peripheral borders but on the pomp, ceremony and the sacred architecture of the symbolic centre. Remoter places, which for some implied the entire Himalaya and the 'north-west frontier' or 'tribal' areas, were naturally associated with disorder, wildness, and powers of nature and tribes.[18] Even around urban locations, state power did not imply an exclusivity of authority; there was rather a loose interpenetration of control over territories, held by princedoms or churches in various states of alliances, a secular and hence imperfect order that fluctuated according to political fortune. Especially in these peripheries, authority changed and overlapped, and to come under the authority of more than one lord was a normal fact of political life. Whereas in the remoteness of the Himalayan highlands, peripheral areas could be taxed by no-one, on the Gangetic plain and the plateau of Tibet the result could be *double* taxation.

Traditionally, local groups could have double or no secular status in wider political systems; at times could play one lord off against the other and *de facto* would act independently. Such freedom mirrors the attempted actions of the Himalayan states themselves, squeezed between the imperial might of Britain and China. Frontier disturbance over presumed 'borders' was to provide the immediate justification for the Raj's occupation of territories held by the Court of Nepal as it was for taking over those held by the Court of Pagan in lowland Burma.[19]

The Colonial Encounter: Territorial Definition

In the traditional state described above, local attributions of kin and locality were key features to social identity; a wider sense of belonging came from a shared hierarchical culture and a common conception of the 'order of things'. The colonial encounter was to alter the basis of this commonality, shifting it towards a notion of identity based on state membership. In the nineteenth century Himalaya the relations of empire to empire, presaged by traders and explorers, continued by armies and political envoys at royal courts, and

18. See Mary Douglas, *Purity and Danger*, London: Routledge & Kegan Paul, 1966, for a general analysis of this theme of symbolic power and boundary areas.

19. On these results of overlapping authority in the northern Gangetic plain, see Ludwig F. Stiller J. S., *The Silent Cry: The People of Nepal, 1816–1839*, Kathmandu: Sahayogi Prakashan, 1976.

finishing with missions of boundary commissions, fixed exclusive borders
for the political space.

Though like other states in the Himalayan region, Nepal was never
directly colonized, from the eighteenth century onwards its political transformation is a product of the colonial encounter. From the royal courts of
the Nepal Valley, no fundamental change in kind of relation was at first
perceived. Imperial contact, whether to British India or to China, was viewed
as a continuation of factional intrigue: that is, it was presumed to be with a
protagonist of roughly similar ways. For example, the British monarchy like
the Nepalese was presumed to symbolize divinity: Queen Victoria could be
regarded as a 'White Tara', a Buddhist Himalayan tantric aspect of Shiva.[20]
There were enquiries from Nepal (as there were at this period from elsewhere in princely India) whether the monarch of England would give, or
take, a daughter in marriage as a sign of alliance. War and conflict were seen
as a temporary stage of a cyclic process, a passing point that would be
accommodated to and recast through the dynastic welter of Himalayan
court politics: this was a mistaken assessment of the nature of the British
state and presence in India.

From the turn of the nineteenth century onwards, the history of
contact by the empires of Manchu China and British India was itself to lead
to a change in conception of the state within the region. From the late
seventeenth century onwards the Manchu Empire had been expanding its
authority westwards, and by 1720 had reached Tibet and Lhasa; the British
Raj had been expanding westwards from Bengal across the Gangetic plain
of India at the same time. These imperial movements began to lay out the
map of India and the borders of the Himalayan states. As the power of Manchu
China began to wane later in the nineteenth century, the idea of the 'Great
Game' between Britain and Russia on the north-west frontier and in Tibet
became a further stimulus for a definition of authority in this area.

Two main British concerns thread their way through the history of the
north-west frontier. One was to secure India's borders against French and
Russian expansion; the other was not to be dragged into a global confrontation with another empire by chance contact. Britain's actions also had regional
political effects. First, they halted processes of expansion from within the
region which might have turned a local state into a competing empire.
Second, they tended to fix territorially smaller states within the region as

---

20. *Tārā* is in some ways parallel to *Durgā* of the Bengal plains, on which see Ruud's
account of current socio-political significance in Chapter 6.

lesser-order constructs, the 'Princely states' and 'Himalayan kingdoms'. The Sikh court of the Punjab was one such expanding and competing state that was destroyed; the so-termed 'House of Gorkha' was similarly involved in expansion out from the Nepal Valley, but was constrained.

The earlier conquest of the three Royal Cities of the Nepal Valley around 1769 by the Gorkha Kingdom is often regarded as a key feature of the establishment of modern Nepal. Some accounts stress from that date onwards a process of 'unification', as if a modern territorial Nepal had always existed as such in some natural state awaiting discovery. Though there were some innovations in the Gorkha manner of rule, it is mainly the timing of their presence in relation to Britain in India that gave permanence to their state. More correctly, the period that follows on from 1769 is one of a wider process of territorial expansion, a local empire in the making outwards east and west along the Himalayan from the new-found centre of the Nepal Valley. The colonial encounter both brought this expansion to a halt, and held static what it contained.

The 'House of Gorkha' had expanded in the eighteenth century, reaching from present-day Garwahl in India east along the Himalayan chain to Sikkim; at one point it took an area on the high plains of the Tibetan plateau, well to the *north* of Everest and the main Himalayan chain. The possibility of further expansion north on the Tibet plateau was stopped by China: in 1791, a Chinese army passed south from Tibet through the Himalaya towards the seat of the Kingdom of Gorkha at Kathmandu, and for a number of months in 1792 they were within half a day's march of the Nepal Valley. But this victory produced only a bi-annual tribute mission from the Gorkha Court of Kathmandu to the Manchu Court of Beijing and had no permanent territorial implications.

The traditional implications of such changes in political fortune were few. Local lords could have their rights to land confirmed or removed after such events: it is only during this period of colonial redefinition that landholdings began to be considered as potential enclaves of a differing nationality. By 1792, nationality was still not a salient dimension: there was no general sense of 'Nepalese' versus 'Tibetan' or 'Chinese', only of kinship and a more contingent political allegiance within a wider, common, cultural milieu.

The British Raj was closer to hand than China and increasingly powerful. The Raj had cut back the expansion of the House of Gorkha to the west and east along the Himalayan chain, and to the Gangetic plain in the south, through the Nepal-Britain War of 1814–16. At its end some two-thirds of the territory remained from the peak of the House of Gorkha, now bounded and isolated east, west and south by directly controlled British territory. In the subsequent Nepal-Tibet (China) war of 1855–56 much of the Nepal Valley kingdoms' authority north to the Himalaya was re-established; this was in part effected with British complicity. In the south, Britain later gave back the Western plains area, which was a grain-basket for the Court of Nepal, in return for the military assistance of the House of Gorkha following the outbreak of the Indian Mutiny in 1857. The border finally established between China (through Tibet) and Nepal was only fixed on the ground and ratified by a Nepal-China Boundary Commission in the 1950s, and still follows roughly the areas of influence established militarily in 1856.

Britain's policy of control and support for their Gorkha ally fixed the territorial integrity of Nepal and so promoted the power of the existing local rulers now firmly within the power orbit of the British Raj, with a resident at the Court of Kathmandu. The cycle of dynastic growth, fission, and conquest from the outside, which in the normal course of events could have been expected to split the House and Kingdom of Gorkha within a few generations, was halted. Hence political units, the integrity of which formerly had been based on the coherence and continuity of elite families, now became maintained behind fixed borders, and the basis of the political structure of the state began to shift from 'blood' to 'territory'. In the case of Nepal this transition is said to have occurred during the rule of Bhimsen Thapa, who spent a number of years living in the Raj at Benares and is credited as being the first ruler of Nepal with an understanding of the British territorial model.[21]

There are other examples of such colonially driven change in the Himalaya on the northern and north-west frontier of British India from the nineteenth century onwards, for Afghanistan, Kashmir, Ladakh and Baltistan, Bhutan, and others. In the north-western Himalaya the varied names of lands and peoples used by writers in the last century well illustrates the contingent historical nature of the political formations of the time, and map-making and boundary commissions of the nineteenth century have been politically significant to the present day. For example, Johnson's expedition north from Ladakh along the route to central Asia to Chinese-controlled Turkestan produced a map with political borders that still is significant in the Sino-Indian boundary dispute.[22] Yet prior to map-making and boundaries, the very fact of naming and the choice of local name to elevate to statehood

21. Stiller, *The Silent Cry*, pp. 220ff.

22. On the Johnson map that resulted from the expedition of 1865 see Alistair Lamb, *The Sino-Indian Border in Ladakh*, Canberra: Australian National University Press, 1973, p. 113.

was a significant act. Elphinstone stayed mainly in the area between the Khyber Pass and Kabul, and focused on the viewpoint of the Kabul Court. The result was his well-known *Account of the Kingdom of Caubul* of 1815, which used the term Afghanistan, *prescriptively*, to cover the land between the Oxus and the Indus.[23] Yet there was no such wider territorial state for some seventy years, it being the Durand Convention of 1893 (also known as the Kabul Convention), and the 1895 Anglo-Russian Pamirs Agreement, which established the northern frontiers (also known as the Durand Line) of the land to be known as Afghanistan.[24] In the north, areas if referred to generally at all were called Russian or Chinese Turkestan; further to the west there was a 'Zabulistan' which focused on Herat; the principality that lay between the Hindu Kush and the Indus centred on the city and valley of Kabul, and was usually referred to as 'Kabulistan'. Up until the turn of the twentieth century the name Afghanistan was not much used internally for any part of this area: normal reference to the area (that is the local Kabul Valley) was the Kingdom of Kabul. Up until 1880, the term Afghan was used mainly as a collective name for the various kin-based groups in that Kabul area.[25] Afghanistan as a kingdom controlled from Kabul was historically successful not because all the people were initially 'Afghani', or because there was some other underlying natural unity, but because it was a useful buffer state. Afghanistan, quite literally, was the mountain territory that occupied the space between the end of the Russian and the British railways!

Further telling examples come from the 'kingdoms' and states that do not exist today and have been incorporated in the colonially-supported formations. Few people know of the supposed 'Zabulistan' centred on Herat, or of 'Dardistan', a model of presumed people that never was, extended to a state that never was. The term Dardistan was coined by one inspired Western 'observer' to cover much of the north-western area between Kabul and Kashmir, including Gilgit and Yasin, an area without a political centre.[26]

---

23. Mountstuart Elphinstone, *An account of the Kingdom of Caubul, and its dependencies in Persia, Tartary and India; comprising a view of the Afghaun Nation, and history of the Dooraunee Monarchy*, London: Longman/ Murray, 1815.

24. On imperial interest and the political history, see Alistair Lamb, *Kashmir: A Disputed Legacy, 1846–1990*, Hertfordshire: Roxford, 1991.

25. See Louis Dupree, *Afghanistan*, Princeton: Princeton University Press, 1973; Schuyler Jones, *Men of Influence in Nuristan*, London: Seminar Press, 1974.

26. See Graham E. Clarke, 'Who Were the Dards? An Introduction to the Ethnography of the North-West Himalaya', *Kailash, Journal of Himalayan Studies*, vol. 5, no. 4, Kathmandu: Ratna Pustakh, 1977, pp. 323–356; that account has been summarized by John Keay in *The Gilgit Game*, London: Murray, 1979.

The term 'Dard' itself appears to derive from a Persian root for the word 'fierce', that is a generic type rather than proper name; the would-be creator of that Himalayan state, Gottlieb Wilhelm Leitner, *himself* stated that no such local people recognized it as applying to themselves, and that he used it specifically to connect them to classical antiquity. 'Dardistan' was an unsuitable vehicle for the policy of the British Raj and did not become a political formation. Yet writings on 'the Dards' still haunt modern ethnological and linguistic accounts of that region, and the term continues to be used in some scientific circles to refer to the 'tribal' and the supposed linguistic types of the area. Historically, the use of the term Dardic to refer to a linguistic type was based on the assumption that the people of the area were, in some anthropological sense, 'Dards'. It is ironic that the logic of subsequent writing of the 1950s on peoples of this region turned full-circle, grouping people together ethnologically as 'Dards', and positing an underlying 'Dardic Ethnos', based on these very self-same linguistic distinctions.[27]

The Colonial Encounter: Cultural Models

In the classification of peoples, the administrative map and the territory which themselves were results of historical circumstances, prescribed the scientific form, and elevated essentially local identities to a higher order as terms of kind. Peoples were grouped into fine spatial taxonomies of type, hierarchies for which there was little scientific basis other than the most gross mapping of languages and presumptions on common origin. For example, until the third decade of this century, 'Nepal' was a name used solely for the central valley of the Kingdom of that name today. It is only within this century that these identities have become more than local labels. They have extended outwards from the former politico-religious centres, filling in the spaces between the outlines on the map like a child's colouring book, so extending a pattern of nation over the local peoples of the Himalaya.

One important question is why Western knowledge of these territories and peoples was presented in that form. Up until that time knowledge had come mainly from classical Greek sources, elaborated by myth and travellers' tales. These now could be interpreted by the discoveries of Western science and scholarship, based on the direct contact of explorers and envoys with the peoples and locality. In practice there were flaws in this logic which

---

27. See for example, Karl Jettmar, 'Ethnological Research in Dardistan 1958, Preliminary Report' in *Proceedings of the American Philosophical Society*, vol. 105, no. 1, 1961, pp. 79–87.

derived not so much from discovery as from scientific revelation. Theory was tied to historical speculation, and common form was to be explained by common origin, with all projected back to ancient Greece and Egypt, the fount of all civilization. Links tended to be forced from local peoples back to those mentioned in the texts of classical antiquity, and anthropological speculation on the region to the north of the Gangetic plain moved in endless circular speculation of who a people *really were* in origin and race.

Common items and parallels were noted; but though this literature contains excellent accounts of particular ceremonies and events, these are not accounts of people in the round. In the age of discovery, reference to variety fitted well. Yet, despite the evolutionary dressing of the language of race, this literature was not based on knowledge of the region; systematic analyses of Himalayan social and cultural variation comparable to those made for natural species were simply not available at that time. The empirical complexity of society and culture in the Himalaya is such that much basic linguistic and textual work needed first to be carried out, before abstractions could sensibly be pursued. The typologies of peoples and frameworks of social change and evolution applied at the time were monolithic, classic-bound, and forced in application, and did not result in any systematic gains in knowledge.

The accounts of natural resources and economic products continued, as they had in the earlier period of contact through the East India Company which then had been justified by advantage in trade. The writings of the late nineteenth century gave a shift in perspective away from commercial inventories, to pseudo-scientific accounts of peoples from the viewpoint of a civilizing mission, to the needs of government, and the correctness of imperial order. These accounts had a direct effect as the work was carried out not solely by and for academics, but largely by scholars who were also political agents of Empire. Hence these accounts of peoples and lands were fed back into the government of these newly-created territorial states. They acted as 'self-fulfilling prophecies' and in some cases came to prescribe the very definition and naming of the peoples of the area.[28]

The copious late-nineteenth-century Gazetteers of the northern regions of India, such as Sikkim and Kashmir, illustrate this typologizing tendency: that is they try to place peoples as 'tribes' and 'castes' with an absolute and fixed position in various regionally defined territorial segments, a spatial

---

28. This term 'self-fulfilling prophecy' derives from the work of Daniel Joseph Boorstin, *The Image, or What Happened to the American Dream*, London: Weidenfeld & Nicholson, 1961.

expression of an ideal hierarchy.[29] Such accounts helped redirect and legitimate the political future of the region and its peoples, as a people's status no longer depended on local factors of fortune, interpretation and power, but on a more static and centrally prescribed ascription by an imperial expertise.

In the Victorian era the true discoveries were not thought of as the people in-and-of themselves, but as the 'ideal types' that stood behind the empirical order observed there and then. What was recorded on the ground was not so much a naturally occurring variation as a 'mixture' of sub-types, imperfect exemplars of supposed underlying ideal racial types and evolutionary stages. There were various devices and patterns by which such labels were acquired and extended as nations, but generally the progression was for the name of the main people or town of a local area to become applied to the local state, then to the language, and then to become a 'national' name. Variety, under this over-arching national name, was constituted by a taxonomy of various local 'caste' and 'tribal' divisions. In this way Afghanistan and Nepal became superordinate categories, containing within them as spatially-fixed entities all the local variation of which they formally were an integral part.

As mentioned above, in the case of Afghanistan, the progression begins with the tribes known as Afghani who lived in the Kabul Valley and who also controlled the Court of Kabul. As the local state extended from Kabul outwards (in part with British patronage), there came the early use by British commentators of the term 'Afghanistan' to cover all territories considered by the Raj to be under the authority of the Court of Kabul. It was only later that Afghanistan became on the ground not just the land where the Afghani tribes lived, but this wider territory. By the turn of the twentieth century no longer were the people within that territory just seen as subject to the Court of Kabul, but as 'Afghani' – the term being used not only for the Afghani tribes but also as the name for all within the territory, quite independent of their tribal origin. Those who previously had been known by a particular local name, or more generally in their contact with the imperial Raj as 'the north-west frontier tribes', now increasingly became considered by outsiders as 'Afghani'. Yet within the territory itself, well into the twentieth century, the ruler at the Court of Kabul simply referred to his people collectively as 'Yaghi', and his land as 'Yaghistan' (literally, the 'Land of the Unruly'). Within the state itself, it was only later that the term Afghani

---

29. See Edwin Felix Atkinson, *The Himalayan Districts of the North-Western Provinces of India*, Allahabad, 1882–1886, Vols. I, II, & II; also Charles Ellison Bates, *A Gazetteer of Kashmir and the Adjacent Districts ...* , Calcutta, 1873. A number of these Gazetteers have begun to be reprinted today in India.

was successfully projected as a higher-order, national classification of local peoples or tribes; this use is still resisted by some today.

The case of Nepal is a variation on this theme, and illustrates how the Western encounter could penetrate the cultural processes defining nationalism. The two names, 'Gorkha' and 'Nepal', were both territorial loci, and both came to be used as wider national labels. The term 'Gorkha' has been used in two ways: first, as the name for the ruling House of Gorkha, which is now situated at Kathmandu rather than Gorkha and contains high-caste Hindus; second (now often spelt as 'Gurkha'), as the generic name for martial castes or 'tribes' recruited from within the Kingdom of that ruling House of Gorkha. Books referred to the language spoken by these 'martial castes' as 'Gorkhali'.[30] This double-specification helped cement the British image of 'Gorkha' both as the proper name of the wider Hindu state, and of the warlike tribes of Nepal.

The idea of the natural military genius of Gorkha tribes was British, and came through experience on the field of combat during the British-Nepal war of 1814–16. The recruitment of some individuals from the Himalaya into the army of the East India Company dates from before that time; specific, local, 'martial castes' from within the territory of the Kingdom of Gorkha already had been named as such, in the eighteenth century. Lists of these peoples were made by the official visitors to the area, who were scholars as well as political representatives; these were elaborated by those who followed after the war, both for science and as a practical measure to assist in selection in recruitment.[31] After the support of the Gorkha State for Britain in the India 'Mutiny' of 1857 and subsequent understandings established by exchanges of letters towards the close of the nineteenth century, soldiers were more openly recruited by Britain from within the Gorkha state itself, and the people came to be referred to widely as 'Gorkhas'.

In written classification there were four such main groups of names. In the west of Nepal, the labels Gurung and Magyr (later spelled Magar), and in east Nepal the labels Rai and Limbu, were elevated as names of presumed martial tribes, with further subdivisions. These two sets of two were singled out from the myriad of varying local names in the middle hills of the region

---

30. Also 'Gurkhali'. See M. Meeradonk, *Basic Gurkhali Grammar*, Malaya, 1949, which in Lesson Two has such value-laden phrases for translation as 'A Gurkha eats rice' and 'The rifle is dirty'.

31. Francis Buchanan Hamilton, *An Account of the Kingdom of Nepal*, Edinburgh: Archibald Constable & Co, 1819; various articles of Brian Hodgson including 'Origin and Classification of the Military Tribes of Nepal', *Journal of the Asiatic Society of Bengal*, no. 17, May 1833, pp. 217–224.

of Nepal as the 'tribes' with the supposed military qualities of 'Gorkhas'. In these cases, as with the colonial experience of East Africa, the higher-order named units of local 'tribes' and the corresponding 'peoples' and 'nations' that were so listed or created within these territories, in scientific terms usually were abstractions at the wrong analytical level.[32] They were to be distinguished from the higher Hindu priestly and lower untouchable groups, identified mainly with lower-living valley populations, who were seen as physically weaker and less suitable for military recruitment. In general terms, a gross distinction between a tougher 'hill' and more soft-living 'plains' population is a useful first criterion for the selection of soldiers, as is the avoidance of those whose 'twice-born' Hindu caste position would make for prohibitions in social contact. The analytical error is in elevating a useful tool as a fixed absolute classification, and in taking such a set of ethno-nyms as a 'once and for all' indicator of those needed qualities. From that time onwards, these terms take on the nature of a 'self-fulfilling prophecy' as those who wished to be recruited learned to present themselves in suitable ethnic terms. Combined with the normal tendency for sons and co-villagers to take on the same profession, this helped give territorial expression to these 'tribes' as collections of local groups.

Such points and the progression have been reported of Magar and other peoples who wished to be recruited to the British army. For example, the Magars of Tichurong are known collectively as Magar mainly because the term is convenient, both for them and for the ethnographer.[33] Of the eastern set of ethnonyms, Limbu appears to be a local corruption of another Tibeto-Burman word;[34] the Nepalese term '*rāi*' is related to the Sanskrit term for king (*rāja*), as an adjective *rais* or *rahis* means noble, and was a term used among non-Hindus in the eastern hills for a headman, lord, or chiefly, and so was a prime candidate as an ethnonym for upwardly mobile people of that region.[35] The disparity between the peoples classified together under labels such as Rai, and today Sherpa, Lama or Tamang, outside of a local area,

32. This point was first made in 1970 in the seminal article by Southall, 'The Illusion of Tribe'.

33. James F. Fisher, 'Homo Hierarchicus Nepalensis: A Cultural Subspecies', in James F. Fisher (ed.), *Himalayan Anthropology: The Indo-Tibetan Interface*, The Hague: Mouton, 1978. John Hitchcock, *The Magars of Banyan Hill*, New York: Holt, Rinehart & Winston, 1966.

34. On the eastern hills of Nepal see A. Campbell, 'Note on the Limboos and Other Hill Tribes hitherto Undescribed', *Journal of the Asiatic Society of Bengal*, vol. 9, 1825, pp. 595–615; also Nancy Levine, 'Caste, State and Ethnic Boundaries in Nepal', *Journal of Asian Studies*, vol. 46, no. 1, 1987, p. 74.

35. Ralph L. Turner, *A Comparative and Etymological Dictionary of the Nepali Language*, London: Routledge, 1931.

is such that a serious ethnography of the Nepal Himalaya always is prefixed with a highly localized area, e.g. *The Sherpa of Kumbu, The Thulung Rai*.

State-wide lists with fixed ascriptions of the 'martial castes' and other 'castes' and 'tribals' as used by the British Raj were both a prototype for, and a legitimation of, this nascent Himalayan state. This extension of central authority and symbols value was occurring in other areas: for example, early land-grants in outlying areas for the upkeep of temples were now reconfirmed in written certificates sealed by the Gorkha state, some of which listed festivals for Buddhist and local deities re-interpreted as Hindu and specifically Gorkha lineage deities.

The visit of the ruler of Nepal, Jung Bahadur, to England and France in 1850 is credited as a voyage across the sea to impure lands, a voyage that questioned the absoluteness of the religious ideals of Nepal. This second half of the nineteenth century was also a period of change in elite conception of state and nation, and was illustrated in new national cultural symbols. On his return there was the adoption of European military apparel, aristocratic dress and recreations, and architecture at Court. The stucco palaces of Kathmandu were built as conscious echoes of Versailles and the Paris Opera, followed a neo-classical style, and communicated a new model. Images derived from European secular power stood alongside the ceremonies of the Great Religions to define a new image of state, with now ambiguous representations of royalty and power. Their existence gave rise to a questioning of world view by elites. The symbols were copied by those intent on upward mobility, and so in turn Western symbols extended outwards.

A state-wide caste hierarchy was formulated by the House of Gorkha which brought together various local caste hierarchies, including the Tibetans and other 'tribals' of the Tibeto-Burman culture, and hence was given currency as an overall model by the state. This *Legal Code of Nepal* of 1854 was a fixed, prescriptive taxonomy of the peoples of the territory, and from the viewpoint of the dominant centre then established in Kathmandu, it laid out in principled form who should eat with whom, who should marry whom, who should carry out what occupation, and how groups were to be differently punished. This taxonomy, imposed on top of the pre-existing local definitions of relative political status, and the segmented political hierarchies across the country, helped to create the current ethnic map of Nepal.[36] As an ideal, the hierarchy was seen as a codification of custom, something in itself fixed, timeless and to be projected back into antiquity.

---

36. Andreas Höfer, *The Caste Hierarchy and the State in Nepal: A Study of the Muluki Ain of 1854*, Innsbruck: Universitätsverlag Wagner, 1989.

The purpose of creating such a seemingly fixed hierarchy within the kingdom was not an account of history or social process. In practice, as before, social relations were fluid: social climbing was well-understood, taken for granted, and commonly used for redefinition, with the upwardly mobile seeking to differentiate themselves in name from their equals and those below, and take on the identity of those above them. It had two purposes. On the one hand, it was the restatement of an ideal or divine order beyond empirical fluctuation, expressed through the institution of the kingship, but now extended beyond the Valley of Kathmandu; on the other hand, it was a recognition of a new external model through which the Gorkha Kingdom had come to acquire a fixed, exclusive and bounded territory.

The incorporation of a new model was to set the stage for a wider integration, that is the extension of a national identity communicated outwards throughout the territory from the old centre. If we apply Maine's distinctions between 'Britain' and the 'British' to Gorkha and Nepal, we will see the change in perspective. In this case, the idea that the local territories listed as the possessions of the House of Gorkha should be recognized as a single entity, that is Nepal (or perhaps more correctly at that point as a 'Gorkhalistan'), started to shift to the idea that those encapsulated within the territory of Nepal, including its rulers the House of Gorkha itself, should be considered as Nepalese (or at that time as Gorkha).

The use of the terms Nepal and Nepalese also begins to change from being just one way that people who came from the Royal Cities of the 'Nepal Valley' could be identified, to becoming a superordinate national label for the various 'peoples of Nepal', including those from what was now increasingly known as 'The Kathmandu Valley'. Within Nepal, it was only in the 1930s that the Court at Kathmandu itself began to refer to the country as the 'Kingdom of Nepal', rather than as 'the entire possessions of the King of Gorkha'.[37]

The above cases indicate a general shift from a political identity based on fluctuating local and kinship allegiance, through a wider imperial dynasty, to political identity as fixed, exclusive and based on residence within a wider bounded territory. This shift was brought about in a colonial encounter in which the primacy of territory and political linkage of peoples within such a space was assumed to be the norm, and imposed by the imperial power. In the terms used here, this represents a shift from 'blood' to 'territory' and part of the way back again. This was not a modern national integration of the ideal-typical kind, that is a mythical social

---

37. Burghart, 'The Concept of Nation-State in Nepal ', p. 119.

contract with equal rights of citizenship for all individuals within a state. Instead it had much in common with the traditional hierarchy, still a divine order but given fixed form as combined lists of peoples within the new territorial borders of the state. The intention in creating a 'nation' was to promulgate unity and order within the Kingdom of Gorkha.

Such taxonomic tendencies and the propensity to erect fixed absolute typologies centring on the symbolism of sacred kingship, may be a general ideological feature of many Asian empires. It may be no coincidence that current Chinese scientific writing has this same, taxonomic tendency. Many publications on natural habitat on the Tibetan Plateau focus on typologies using territorial and sinicized names, rather than descriptions and accounts of process. In classifications of ethnic groups within the People's Republic of China today, the 'minorities' or 'minority nationalities' (*min-ʒu*) are included as national elements within a higher order state-wide 'family of nations' (*min-ʒu da-jia-ting*) in which the Han are the senior and Beijing is the paternal focus.[38] One sees the same 'Orientalizing' tendency in the British Empire itself, with its own ceremonial surviving well beyond the time its own political control and power had passed its height. The capital architecture of Empire (as much in New Delhi designed by Lutyens as in the centre of London), and events such as Great Durbar of the Jubilee of 1937 (in which tribal rulers from as far afield as Hunza had their allotted positions, variously distant from the representative of the British throne), indicate just such a symbolic understanding of the integrative use of sacred space and ceremony.

In this wider conception, the extreme Himalayan diversity was encapsulated within a fixed, taxonomic hierarchy. These were not scholarly abstractions at a distance, but features of elite ideology imposed on local peoples as administrative facts. In this process people's own names became logical sub-types to the new, national identity imposed from above. Names and lists are political instruments that direct the ethnic and national future of a region in the manner of a 'self-fulfilling prophecy'.

A Post-Colonial State, and Modernity

I have suggested a further aspect to the progression from state to nation in the Himalaya, namely the extension of the name of the dominant kin group or of the main urban centre outwards to the newly-fixed boundaries, at first as a name for the entire territory, and then subsequently as a national

---

38. On Chinese notions of nation see Lodén, Chapter 10 in this volume.

identity for all peoples within it. Their own names are taken as logical sub-types to the new, superordinate identity. The pendulum having swung full towards inclusion of peoples within the borders of the territory under Empire, in the modern nation-state (or rather state-nation), it then may move back again to specify a greater homogeneity of nation, of one people, within the state. This is a move from 'territory' back to 'blood'. Such a movement also sets the stage for a modern nationalism, and for extreme forms of fundamentalism.

There is more than one irony in this progression. Western ideas of the nation-state were used by regional elites to extend nationalism outwards from their courts to their colonially-defined boundaries. These ideas also introduced the notion of 'foreigners' or 'others', with two consequences. First, this legitimated political segmentation, and led to the disintegration of the overall chain of Empire. Second, the very idea of different descent that in the traditional, small-scale society had helped integrate local groups, when taken to an extreme in a modern, egalitarian nation-state could be used as a justification for exclusion, and bloodshed.

As one would expect, given the difficulties of communication and transport in the Himalaya, change applies only in part and then unevenly. States and nations in this boundary area are not completely formed, and the overall processes of separation and consolidation continue at the present time. As well as the mountains, some of the direct reasons are external and socio-political. The nineteenth century created half-formed Himalayan states between empires, and the circumstances of partition of the sub-continent in 1947 have maintained some of these formations. The stand-off between Pakistan and India between the 'northern territories' and Kashmir, has helped preserve older, local names and identities and hindered the penetration of these two competing nationalisms. Locally, populist forces have clustered around Hindu and Islamic religious markers, but these have not been subsumed within wider, national identities. In the north-west of the Himalaya one still refers directly to the people of the separate valleys of Chilas, Yassin, Hunza, Nagyr, Baltistan and Ladakh, without considering these to be 'Kashmiri', in the way that those to their east along the Himalaya are thought to be 'Nepalese'.

Modern national unity can develop in various ways. First, as depicted in the major part of this chapter, it can come from the imposition of a classi-fication of peoples and languages to be considered as local sub-divisions of a newly-discovered nation. Second, following on from this equation, longer-term processes of physical assimilation or integration may be set in place.

There may be a change from an economic or social plurality to a single national order. This is especially the case given wider state and market exchanges, and there is likely to be an attendant solidification of such changed status through more open intermarriage. Third, there is also a more fundamentalist approach to the creation of nation, one that uses physical threats, violence and massacre to enforce migration or physically exterminate those deemed as different by blood. Before 1947 and the end of the British Raj, the third extreme of populist ethnic violence was little known. Though now it appears in Kashmir and Bhutan, mass ethnic violence is relatively unusual in the mountains compared to the plains; in these cases it appears to be at least as much state-directed, as it is an expression of local popular sentiment. To summarize, from reclassification, through intermarriage, to pogrom, all is directed towards producing 'one people', seen as a nation.

One institution that can help create a uniform national identity is the state apparatus itself. A modern state requires a range of technical specializations, and an administrative infrastructure for the management of its territory. The routine activity that results is a powerful reinforcement for uniformity. Daily interaction, greater geographic mobility along roads, the communication of norms through the radio and press, state programmes active in local centres, and country-wide political events such as elections, all extend and superimpose national over local identities.[39] In the case of modern Nepal, cultural uniformities of language also were consciously communicated in primary education programmes from the 1950s onwards.

The cultural content of these processes is important as a marker of national identity, and here for Nepal there have been two cultural aspects. One is the image of Nepal emphasizing international independence and relations to the West (above all to Britain). There is also an image of Nepal as a place where a timeless, religious Asia survives, locally a sign of permanence and, in occidental terms, of exoticism. Here, the persistence and extension of the notion of 'being Nepalese' is projected not just forwards into the future, but also back into an imagined community of the past.

For example, in the 1960s in Kathmandu the sole national newspaper carried articles, no doubt read tongue in cheek by some educated Nepalese, arguing that since Lumbini, the birthplace of the historical Buddha (Gautama),

---

39. Popularly, the disbursal outwards of these state benefits is regarded as a gift from above in return for political allegiance: though this is integrating, in its extension this model of integration tends to the traditional model of hierarchy, rather than one creating national sameness. See Graham E. Clarke, 'Development in Nepal: Mana from Heaven', in Samten G. Karmay and Philippe Sagant (eds), *Festschrift pour Alexander W. MacDonald*, Nanterre: Université de Paris-X (in press).

was located some few miles north of the current southern border, that Buddha was *therefore* Nepalese and not Indian.[40] Nepal is the land where the Nepalese live and have always lived in this nationalist conception, an idea which gives a 'natural' legitimation for Nepal's separateness rather than leaving it as a contingent state in relation to India. This reversal of sequence and causality between state and nation moves beyond the fictions of the founding of a modern Nepal in the eighteenth century. The backward projection through time of the Nepalese nation prior to the formation of the Nepalese state frees it from what is now seen as ignoble, a nation whose unity depends on colonial historical circumstance.

In the 1960s, Nepal presented itself to the West as the *only* Hindu Kingdom, a timeless, peaceful land to be contrasted to a secularizing, industrializing India. Within Nepal, since the 1950s, there has been a thin political line between representing oneself as pro-Nepalese and hence separate from India, and being depicted by others as anti-Hindu and hence anti-Nepalese. Given the current resurgence of Hindu fundamentalism as a cultural feature of Indian national identity, such a symbolic separation is now even more difficult than before.

The presence of the world's highest mountain is a major contrasting feature for Nepal with regard to India, especially when it is referred to by the internationally known name (Mt Everest after the then English Head of the Imperial Map Service), rather than by existing Sanskritic or Tibetan linguistic ascriptions. It is symbolic of the distinction between the mountains or 'hills' of Nepal and the plains of India.

Mountains remain crucial to Nepal's international image. The conquest of Everest by a New Zealander and a Nepalese Sherpa as members of a *British* expedition, news of which was publicized in Britain alongside that of the coronation of a new Queen of Britain and the British Empire, was an imperial feature in 1951. Global linkages have helped shift the external image of Nepal away from war. The term 'Sherpa' in the Western world has acquired a generic sense of loyal, high-altitude porter; Mt Everest itself acts more as a symbolic world-centre, a place for international co-operation, a 'battlefield' against pollution for nature and the environment, than a national arena.[41]

---

40. See Winichakul in Chapter 3 of this volume for a similar point on Thailand.

41. It is curious that the conflict between India and Pakistan in northern Kashmir has made for a move in the other direction with regard to mountains: rather than Everest as a symbolic area of global co-operation and peace, in Kashmir the equally high Sziachen Glacier has become the main military theatre for the dispute.

A distinct language is one important feature of national identity. Linguistically, Nepali is on a 'cline ' with other Indo-Aryan languages of the northern Gangetic plain, such as Hindi and Bengali, and within the borders of Nepal there has been as much dialectical difference of 'Nepali' as externally. The northern languages are from an entirely different language family, Tibeto-Burman. Technically, this argues against a clear linguistic base for a Nepalese identity. However, as indicated above, there has been an institutional standardization of Nepalese, and in the 1950s, there was the exclusion of Hindi, and the promotion of 'the Nepalese Language'. Moreover, within the bounds of the state other languages are popularly viewed as 'dialects', and hence subordinate to Nepalese. For example, at a conference in the capital of Nepal in the 1970s, 'Sherpa' was referred to as a 'dialect of Nepalese', and reference was made to the need to study rare documents in 'Sherpa script' of Nepal, rather than as the need to study the Tibetan texts of the Sherpas. Clearly, such taxonomies have nationalist rather than scientific agendas, and are directed towards maintenance and extension of Nepalese national identity.

A separate identity can also be maintained through the manner of use of other languages. The English language, as in India, is the technical and intellectual working language of the higher elite, much as was French in Russia in the nineteenth century. The English normally spoken in Nepal is not the Indian English of the sub-continent, which is almost its own idiolect, but is closer to modern English. It is here, in the somewhat different parallels of experience with India, that some of the long-term contradictions for modern Nepalese national identity are found.

More locally, arguments on the underlying difference of Nepal are rarely taken into Indian conceptions. As one retired civil servant from south of the border informally commented, Indians see the State of Nepal as a junior family member: 'for India Nepal is like a child, a younger-brother: you indulge him, and enjoy seeing him grow and become strong; but if he steps out of line too far and becomes a nuisance, then you administer a sharp smack.' The idiom he used was one of kinship, of common blood.

Against this familiarity, the penetration of more recent Western cultural features is an important constituent of Nepalese identity. Whereas in India the image of cultural 'Englishness' has tended to carry over a solid echo from the 1940s into modern times, that presented in Nepal is more modern and fragmentary, a combination of a residue of Empire combined with the western individualism of the 1960s. The pilgrimage of Western youth in the 1960s to Kathmandu, and more generally of tourism, has raised a new image of Nepal in the West as peaceful and spiritual, as well as exotic, mountainous and warlike. The positive reception for Western culture was in part a result of the desire for international recognition, in part a 'cargo-cult' type raised expectation of material affluence. There was no necessity of such an open cultural embrace of the west by an Asian country, and the doorway opened does not enhance popular identification with the Nepalese state. One illustration of the weakness of identification with the state comes from a development project that was carried out with assistance from a foreign state in a rural mountainous area of Nepal in the mid-1970s. When asked about the project, villagers volunteered the information that they preferred being under the authority of that foreign government to Nepal; they had no feeling of any contradiction in terms of sovereignty, of a *necessary* loyalty to Nepal or a Nepalese identity.[42] There are many other examples of the absence of a highly developed idea of state allegiance from the ready ease with which Nepalese enter into long-term contract and loyal service with people from beyond their state borders: there is the 'Gorkha' soldier in the service of Britain, Brunei, India, or Singapore; the 'Sherpa' mountain guide as a member of a foreign expedition; the administrator or expert in the service of international organizations in the capital (or in large numbers elsewhere in the world).

In the above examples there is little to signal that one party is 'Nepalese' and that the other is 'foreign', or that links of nationality and the state provide a proper superordinate context for consideration of allegiance and loyalty. In a sense, this lack of national allegiance also is a modern characteristic, akin to the internationalism of some elite circles globally, as well as being a traditional, pre-modern trait.

In the case of Afghanistan, control over Kabul is now only in part emblematic of control of the national territory. The tendency is for fission, that is to split into the older statelets, one around Kabul and the south-east, one to the north, one to the west. It is only to the degree that rival groups from within the whole territory compete for control of the centre of Kabul, rather than accept the smaller, traditional centres over which they have actual control, that the notion of Afghanistan survives.

To the south, on the plains of India, the pendulum may have swung more extremely up to territory in the nineteenth and early twentieth centuries, and then more recently fully back the other way with the rise of extreme fundamentalist movements, towards a 'blood-based' integration. In the

---

42. Graham E. Clarke, 'Nepal, IHDP Evaluation – Summary; Commentary; Problems & Recommendations; Field Data for Babre, Barabise, Bigu, Chagu, Karthali *et al*', Report for *HMG Nepal/ Swiss Directorate of Development Co-operation*, Oxford, 1983.

northern Gangetic plain, in the Indian states of Uttar Pradesh and Bihar which are each as large as Nepal, there has been a rise of populist imagery in the terminology of 'blood' rather than 'territory'. Ideas of 'nation' and 'one people' are now used to express a countervailing, disintegrative tendency. The expressions of intercommunal violence, such as have been experienced in north India or in Sri Lanka, appear as the imperial residue of hierarchy dissolves and the model of 'one nation' extends more fully within their entire territory. In extreme developments, ethnic and national affiliations no longer serve to integrate into a hierarchy of ranked and complementary difference, but become identified with political conflict between groups which compete for control of economic resources. They are visible in fundamentalist expressions of separation and independence, and used in wider competitive interaction to lay exclusive claims to the entire territory of the new state, leading to what has now been termed 'ethnic cleansing'. This is carried out in the name of the nation defined by common descent, and not alliance by marriage, economic integration, or common citizenship. Such national movements project their claims as 'one people', the original people of the land, and so are underpinned by ideologies of purity of 'blood'.

There are pressures for the adoption of the more exclusive model of national identity in the Himalaya. In Nepal, 'pan-Hindu' or 'pan-Aryan' political movements of the Gangetic plain have local branches in main urban centres. There are nascent 'pan-Mongol' fundamentalist movements, with links beyond Nepal and to a degree across the highland areas. To the east of Nepal, extending into Sikkim and Bhutan, there are also pressures from those who speak Nepalese for the establishment of a 'Greater Land of Gorkha', using political imagery that plays on the historical empire of Nepal.

Groups that existed in rural areas largely in balanced, complementary, relations, or in relative isolation from each other, now may compete in Himalayan cities. However, overall in the Himalaya these divisions have not yet been acted out in terms of the underlying populist conflict, whether urban or rural, ethnic or national. In the Himalaya, fundamentalism tends to be constrained by the mountain topography itself. In Indian Kashmir, the protest has been of the people against the national order of the state, a division which largely correlates with religion. In Nepal, these forces have been expressed in civil protest against a traditional political order, one which in cities was seen as unfair. In neither case has there been large-scale fundamentalist violence. Bhutan is the exception; but even here violence has been very much the prerogative of the state. Political protest here seems to rely on the state rather than represent an unassisted populism, and to a degree seems to be catered for by political moves towards fission and traditional mountain independence, rather than the broad sweep of integrative movements across the plains.

The traditional model of change in the Himalaya, whether through warfare or economics, is of highland people descending and taking over the towns of the plains, rather than any permanent change in the highland regions themselves. The twentieth century has seen qualitative changes from markets, roads and new technology in some areas; but these have not yet made a systemic penetration into the mountain valley enclaves of the Himalaya. Rather, economic and demographic growth has resulted in emigration from these highland regions, with growth and change crystallizing out in the burgeoning towns of the main valleys, and the narrow plains of the south. These are the arenas for future competition, and in part the idiom of such competition is liable to be ethnic.

In the mountains, the topographical separation of parallel valley systems, together with the different economic bases at different altitudes of the mountainsides, have acted quite literally as a baffle against the internal territorial spread of any such conflict. The lack of spread of plains fundamentalism into the Himalaya depends on the lack of regional integration, that is, on the topographical constraint on interaction that raises the political strength of the *local* territory – which traditionally has had a variegated productive base and ethnicity – over and above wider notions of unity through blood as the basis for identity. Mountains hinder communication, and promote enclaves with their own local identities that cut across the wider divisions of kin that appear to fuel fundamentalist conflict. The only wider form of integration is a hierarchy that itself follows the form of the territory, from enclave up through local regional centres to the capital.

Hence within its own highland territory, the Himalayan chain still continues to act as a barrier to integration by such overall, nationalist movements as have been seen in the northern Gangetic plain. Ultimately, this topographically-induced separation in the Himalaya is a constraint that modern technology has not transcended. While migration from the Himalaya may well fuel fundamentalist conflict in the plains, and though they themselves may experience the effects of such local disturbance from both south and north, overall the Himalaya itself may still be a traditional refuge, a half-way house between the extreme swings of 'Blood' and 'Territory'.

CHAPTER NINE

The Karen Making of a Nation

Mikael Gravers

Since independence in 1948 Burma (Myanmar) has been entangled in ethnic rebellions. Ethnic opposition escalated during the colonial rule and became an integrated part of the nationalist struggle against the British. And it has had an enormous impact upon the political processes ever since. Nobel Peace Prize Laureate, Daw Aung San Suu Kyi, made this clear in the following statement during a tour in Kachin State in 1989:

> At this time there is a very great need for all our ethnic groups to be joined together. We cannot have the attitude of 'I'm Kachin', 'I'm Burman', 'I'm Shan'. We must have the attitude that we are all comrades in the struggle for democratic rights ... like brothers and sisters. We won the independence through the unity of the various nationalities.[1]

This 'unity of the nationalities' in 1946–48 can be questioned and it ended in 1949 when widespread insurgency commenced. On the other hand, the ethnic oppositions of the present day are not an expression of pure pristine animosities. They have been in the making since the eighteenth century.[2] However, it is the ethnic oppositions of 1946–49 and the system of ethnic classification of the British colonial rule which haunt present-day Myanmar.

Burma's ethnic conflicts have their roots in the colonial model of society, the *Plural Society* as J.S. Furnivall named it. In the plural society

---

1. Aung San Suu Kyi, *Freedom from Fear*, London: Penguin Books 1991, p. 231. 'Ethnic groups' and 'nationalities' are used synonymously.
2. On ethnicity in the history of Burma see Victor B. Lieberman, 'Ethnic Politics in Eighteenth-Century Burma', *Modern Asian Studies*, vol. 12, no. 3, 1978, pp. 455–482; Robert H. Taylor, 'Perceptions of Ethnicity in the Politics of Burma', *Southeast Asian Journal of Social Science*, vol. 10, no. 1, 1982.

there was a division of labour by 'racial lines' and the different ethnic groups 'mix but they never combine'. The British empire claimed it had 'pacified' ethnic conflicts, created a common political unit of these differences, and thus prevented anarchy. In order to prevent this anarchy erupting in post-colonial Burma, Furnivall argued that nationalism was the best remedy against the collapse of the state. Nationalism would modernize Burma and make it possible 'to capture the imagination of the people and to create a new environment and a new common society.'[3] His view had a great impact upon the postwar nationalism in Burma.

Aung San Suu Kyi's emphasis of a union of nationalities is based upon her father's (Aung San's) vision from 1946: '*A Nation is a collective term applied to a people, irrespective of their ethnic origin.*'[4] Aung San imagined a unity of all ethnic groups based on their common historical experience. The national minorities would have special rights within a union state. With the assassination of Aung San in 1947 his vision receded, and when the military and General Ne Win came to power in 1962 a unitary, corporate state developed and 'Burmanization' of society increased. The Karen – in particular the Christian led Karen National Union (KNU) responded with a contradictory model of a nation: '*It is a dream that Karen and Burman can ever evolve a common nationality*'. The KNU emphasized differences in race, civilization and history.[5] All of these visions of a nation can be seen as reactions against the colonial model. Nationalism became the rationality and substance of the anti-colonial and modern society (cf. Furnivall's proscription). Unfortunately, nationalism has also reinforced ethnic opposition, blocked cooperation across ethnic boundaries, and inhibited development of a *civic pluralism* to replace the colonial plural society, as Aung San Suu Kyi urged in her speech.

The aim of this chapter is to discuss the consequences of ethnic opposition by counterpoising two contradictory models of nation and society:

3. John S. Furnivall, *Colonial Policy and Practice*, New York: University Press 1956, p. 158; John S. Furnivall, *An Introduction to the Political Economy of Burma*, Rangoon: Peoples' Literature Committee & House, 1957, pp. vii–viii. See Robert H. Taylor, 'Disaster or Release. J.S. Furnivall and the Bankruptcy of Burma', *Modern Asian Studies*, vol. 29, no. 1, 1995, pp. 45–63 on the relevance of Furnivall in understanding contemporary Burma and the influence he had on postwar politics.
4. Cited in 'Burma Socialist Program Party', *The System of Correlation of Man and His Environment*, The Burma Socialist Programme Party Rangoon, 1963, p. 49. See further Josef Silverstein (ed.), *The Political Legacy of Aung San*, Ithaca: Cornell University, 1992 (revised edition).
5. Saw Po Chit, 'Karens and the Karen State', Rangoon 1946, in 'The Karen's Political Future', M/4/3023, Oriental & India Office Collections (OIOC), p. 167.

the Karen separatism based on ideas of ethnic and cultural particularism irreconcilable with everything Burman, and the Burmese model of a unitary and corporate state represented by the military.[6] I suggest that ethnic categorization, which originated during colonial rule and its cultural differentialism, has had wide implications for the present identification of peoples and nations, in political practice as well as in public and scientific debates. The Karen participated in the process and contributed to the making of their own concept of a nation and national identity.

Thus, looking to the colonial past in the subjective formation of an ethnic identity is not a mere construction which we can dismiss as un-authentic in a theoretical nihilism of deconstruction. On the other hand, authenticity of ethnic and national identity does not automatically confer legitimacy on any political claim made by ethno-nationalistic organizations. This discussion is crucial in modern anthropology and has often landed its practitioners in a serious predicament. In his article titled 'Do the Karen Really Exist?', Peter Hinton implies a distinction between real ethnic categories and those invented by colonial power.[7] Now, if we are left with the colonial classification as the only authentic categorization of identity, it would indeed be tragic. But if we deny its authenticity as a mere colonial invention, we simultaneously deny these people any active role in history. I shall return to this complicated and urgent issue in the last section of this chapter.

Before analysing the model of the Karen nation as it has been com-municated during the decisive negotiations for independence of Burma in 1946–48 and their insurrection since 1949, I shall briefly outline the role of ethnicity in Burma since the present military regime came to power in 1988.

Ethnicity in Burma/Myanmar 1995

The emphasis on ethnic opposition is mirrored in recent statements by the military regime, the State Law and Order Restoration Council (SLORC). Since 1989 SLORC has used the name *Myanmar* to emphasize the unity of state and nation. Myanmar signifies the citizenry of the country and includes all indigenous ethnic groups (Burmans, Karens, Kachin, etc.):

6. I am grateful for many valuable comments and suggestions by Christopher Goscha, Benedict Anderson and Anders Baltzer Jørgensen, among others. In London in 1993, on a one-month European scholarship granted by NIAS, Curator Patricia Herbert and Profes-sor Robert H. Taylor kindly helped me in the search for documents and literature. This research is financed by the Research Fund of the University of Aarhus, Denmark.

7. Peter Hinton, 'Do the Karen Really Exist?', in John McKinnon and Wanat Bhruksari (eds), *Highlanders of Thailand*, Singapore: Oxford University Press, 1986, pp. 155–168.

The nation should be one in which only Myanmars reside and which Myanmars own. We will have to be vigilant against Myanmar Ngaing-Ngan (the Union of Myanmar), the home of Myanmar nationals, being influenced by anyone. And it is important that Myanmar Ngaing-Ngan does not become the home of mixed blood influenced by alien cultures though it is called Myanmar Ngaing-Ngan.[8]

SLORC has warned against foreign culture and tried to mobilize people for the preservation of 'cultural identity and national personality'. Among the foreign agents which SLORC warns against we may find a mixture of ethnic rebel organizations, Aung San Suu Kyi, the BBC and Amnesty International. They represent the alien forces which are disintegrating the nation and the state while the army and SLORC fight for 'non-disintegration of the Union, non-disintegration of national solidarity, and perpetuity of sovereignty'.[9]

The military model of Burmese society can be characterized as *cultural corporatism*, that is, the nation of their imagined Myanmar has one singular cultural essence which is embodied in all individual citizens. This one-dimensional identity is defined in the citizenship law of 1982. An individual has to prove that his/her ancestors were members of an ethnic group living in Burma before 1824 when colonization began. Thus, Karen, Kachin or Chin are indigenous ethnic groups, while ancestors of Indian and Chinese immigrants are probably not qualified for a genuine Myanmar national identity. This model is obviously based on a historicist imagination of a pure genealogical relationship. Thus, culture, ethnicity, nationality and race are ingrained *in corpore*.[10] And SLORC warns against people who may represent foreign influence, have less patriotic spirit, and lack any idea of preserving national dignity. Such persons must be excluded.[11] Race has reappeared as an important concept in the rhetoric of SLORC.

When SLORC in 1992 announced that 'the eight major races' (Burman, Mon, Shan, Karen, etc.) could never constitute the basis for a

8. Former SLORC Chairman Saw Maung in David I. Steinberg, 'Myanmar in 1991: Military Intransigence', *Southeast Asia Affairs 1992*, Singapore: Institute of Southeast Asian Studies, 1992, p. 229. Myanmar (Mranma) is an old form of the colloquial term *Bama*, i.e. Burma. It has been a part of the official name of the country since 1948.

9. Steinberg, 'Myanmar in 1991', p. 225.

10. On the corporative ideology of the military since 1962, see Tin Maung Maung Than, 'Neither Inheritance nor Legacy. Leading the Myanmar State since Independence,' *Contemporary Southeast Asia*, vol. 15, no. 1, 1993, pp. 24–63.

11. Steinberg, 'Myanmar in 1991', p. 230. The history of xenophobic nationalism is analysed in Mikael Gravers, *Nationalism as Political Paranoia in Burma. An Essay on the Historical Practice of Power*, NIAS Report no. 11, Copenhagen: The Nordic Institute of Asian Studies, 1993, where further references are available.

relative autonomy within the Union and that 'the theory of the big races were fading', the corporative model became even more blurred: SLORC now claims that there are 135 ethnic (or racial) groups and that a new Constitution must provide local autonomy for these where they are the majority of the population. These district councils will be controlled by a strong centralized government but they will exercise the power formerly held by the state councils and in this way undermine a possible control by the major ethnic groups.

This may in fact be a clever move against the ethnic rebels and their idea of a federate state – a union of autonomous ethnic states with their own parliament and army. While SLORC is making a sly riposte to the colonial classification of ethnic groups, the regime unintentionally retains the cultural differentialism of the colonial era. For example, the category 'Karen' (from Burman: *Kayin*) include several groups: Sgaw, Pwo, Kayah, Bwe, Kayan, Bre, Pa-o, but also some minor groups and subgroups. These groups both share general similarities and express significant local differences in language, culture, religion, social and political organization. The new Constitution being prepared by SLORC intends to give local autonomy to the smaller ethnic groups living in areas dominated by the larger groups. Thus, to divide by a new ethnic classification and to rule by retaining state corporatism seems to be the strategy of SLORC.

Cultural differences and ethnic opposition appear as if they were a determining force in post-colonial Burma. This process began in the colonial 'plural society' when ethnic categories were made into fundamental, primordial and bounded social entities. Thus, any support to the minorities is considered by SLORC to be a foreign intervention and a plot to destroy Burmese/Burman cultural identity. Therefore, the European foreigner must be kept out. Further, all discussion of democracy, economic development, nation, state and minorities tends to be entangled by the questions of national and ethnic identity.

This process can be characterized as *ethnicism*. By ethnicism I mean the political process in which a continuous accentuation of ethnic identity and groups appear as the most genuine cultural and natural fulcrum for political autonomy. It may implicate the right to a homeland and a state, and the right to a legitimate position as a nation in the world system of United Nations and other global forums. At the same time, ethnicity becomes inseparable from a definitive social organization and division of labour; a destiny which is so fundamental and essential that it is synonymous with 'freedom'. To paraphrase Furnivall: neither mix nor combination is possible. Ethnic autonomy seems often to be equal to the universal human rights in Western political conceptions of the present world order. Ethnicism has also become a deadly *-ism* of the same world order.[12] Ethnic differentialism may legitimate ethnic cleansing, killing and looting in the name of a "clean" ethnic core of a nation. Or the political conflict may be rationalized as a 'crisis of ethnicity'.

A decisive issue in the analysis of former colonial societies, such as Burma, is thus the way in which culture, ethnicity, nation and state are imagined. In a riposte to Benedict Anderson's 'Imagined Community', Partha Chatterjee has posed the question 'whose imagined community?' Are they forever trapped within the imaginations of state and nation inculcated by their former colonial masters, or are they able to create models based on their own cultural imaginations and their own genuine practices? Can a nation exist outside the bounds of a territorial state?[13]

The Karen ethnic model of a national identity is precisely an attempt to combine the scattered fragments of the past into one common cultural identity, and to place it in a territorial space and historical time. By this effort they create a particularistic imagination in opposition to the Burman corporative model of nation and state briefly outlined above. Both models contain the fiction of a common ethnic core of a nation. The present Myanmar version of a nation is a unification of all ethnic categories under a kind of supra-patriotism. Although the two models are incompatible, they are based on the same logic of ethnicism. The Karen model of their political organization, Karen National Union, is a cultural unification of local groups and of religious denominations: Christian, Buddhist and Animist Karens. Buddhists and Animists are more closely connected and represent a majority of all Karen groups.[14] Alone, the Christians never constituted more than 15 per cent of all Karens and were estimated at about 6.5 per cent in 1989.

---

12. Or 'world disorder' as Benedict Anderson has described it, including 'nationalism and its much less respectable younger relation "ethnicity"'. 'The New World Disorder', *New Left Review*, no. 193, 1992, p. 7.

13. Partha Chatterjee, *The Nation and Its Fragments. Colonial and Postcolonial Histories*, Princeton: Princeton University Press, 1993, p. 5.

14. The term 'Animist' is not adequate to signify one religious system. However, it has been used in Burma's first Constitution and in the literature. On the relation between Buddhism and spirit cults among the Pwo Karen, see Mikael Gravers, 'The Pwo Karen Ethnic Minority in the Thai Nation: Destructive "Hill Tribe" or Utopian Conservationists?' *Copenhagen Discussion Papers*, no. 23, pp. 21–46, The Center for East & Southeast Asian Studies, University of Copenhagen, 1994.

In order to examine the KNU model of a nation, I shall refer to a selection of important official documents and statements from 1946–48 (when the independence of Burma was negotiated) and to recent publications. The Karen definitions of ethnicity and nationality are then related to the more recent discourse in an attempt to estimate the consequences of ethnicism. The documents have had a significant impact on the ensuing events and on the semantics of the discourse even today.[15] Owing to constraints of space, I can merely present a brief outline of the extremely complex ethnic and historical details of Burma here.[16] Moreover, it must be emphasized that I selected the documents and quotations that I found most representative.

'The Case for the Karens' of 1946: the Making of an Authentic Nation

The negotiations leading to Burma's independence in January 1948 were complicated by the heritage from colonial plural society, that is, ethnicism. The British Frontier Areas Administration worked to establish autonomous states for the ethnic minorities along the borders with China and Thailand. Simultaneously, Aung San strived to maintain a union state comprising all ethnic groups. The Karen, in particular the Christian, had enjoyed a favoured position in the colony: in the army, in the police, and in education, Karen nurses and nannies were preferred by the British. The majority of Karens had remained loyal to the British during the Japanese occupation. In all, the Karen had reason to believe that they qualified for a particular attention from their retiring masters. And they looked to London to collect the rewards.

In 1946 a delegation of four Christian Karen leaders went to London as the Karen Goodwill Mission in an attempt to persuade the British government and public that the Karen had a legitimate claim to an autonomous state within the Commonwealth. Officially no negotiations took place. In order not to offend Aung San and his delegation, who were expected in London in January 1947, the Goodwill Mission was accepted by the British

15. On the use of documents in analysing colonial rule and ethno-history, see Frederick Cooper and Ann L. Stoler, 'Tension of Empire: Colonial Control and Vision of Rule', *American Ethnologist*, vol. 16, no. 4, 1989, p. 619.

16. On the role of the Karen in Burma's history, see J.F. Cady, *'A History of Modern Burma*, Ithaca: Cornell University Press, 1969; for a detailed study of ethnic insurgency in Burma since 1949, see Martin Smith, *Burma Insurgency and the Politics of Ethnicity*, London: Zed Books Ltd, 1991.

government only as a delegation to thank HM Government for the liberation from the Japanese. A delegation of two plus one secretary was accepted by the British. However, four names appear in the documents: Sidney Loo-nee, chairman of the delegation, Barrister-at-law, veteran politician; Saw Po Chit, Barrister-at-law; Saw Tha Din, president of the Karen National Association, chairman of the Karen Central Organization (nominal leader of the delegation), timber trader and headmaster of a high school; Saw Ba U Gyi, Barrister-at-law, leader of the young and militant Christian Karens and future president of the KNU. The delegation obtained wide publicity in the Parliament and in the media. They were received by ministers, as well as by Lord Mountbatten and General Slim.

The Karen delegation published a pamphlet and a memorandum during their visit. This publication has been referred to as the 'Case for the Karens'. One of the participants in the Karen Goodwill Mission, Saw Tha Din, mentioned this publication to me in 1970 as the one representing the true narrative of the Karen Case and their legitimate political claims in terms of ethnic and national identity. In 1993 I was able to locate the document among personal correspondence of former colonial officers registered at the Oriental & India Office Collections (OIOC) in London.[17] It was probably never registered as an official document since it was a public relations effort by the delegation.[18]

The title of the four-page pamphlet is 'After India ... Burma?' Attached to the pamphlet is a memorandum entitled 'Historical Background'. However, I shall refer to the pamphlet together with the attached memorandum (pp. 1–11) as the 'Case for the Karens' (CK), the words of an important headline on page 2 of the pamphlet. It is possible from this publication to index some of the most significant arguments of the KNU for a particular ethnic and national identity. To make the presentation as clear as possible, I have chosen to summarize the Karen discourse under the following subjects:

---

17.   Printed by Higgs & Co, Henley-on-Thames and signed by three members of the delegation, November 11, 1946, in Sir John Clague Collection, Mss. Eur. E. 252/22, OIOC. Sir John visited the Salween Karens in 1938 and called them 'marvellous – this gallant, pro-British race', a view shared by many British officials who worked with the Karen; see the Rance Papers, Mss. Eup. YF. 169/20e, OIOC.

18.   Cady, *History of Modern Burma*, p. 553; Frank N. Trager, *Burma. From Kingdom to Republic*, London: Pall Mall Press, 1966, p. 104. Note no. 19 refers to the 'Case for the Karens'. Other important official documents have been published in Hugh Tinker, *Burma. The Struggle for Independence 1944–48*, 2 vols, London: Her Majesty's Stationery Office, 1983–1984.

1. History, origin and relations with the Burmans;
2. Census;
3. Religion, myth and culture;
4. Modernization of tradition;
5. National identity;
6. Territorial claims.

All these subjects are part of establishing the definitive proof of *nationhood as a common identity* uniting local differences. First I shall cite the document(s); then the background will be explained, followed by my own interpretation, comments and additional quotations.

History

In the KNU interpretation of history, opposition to the Burmans is inseparable from the loyalty to the British.

> The Karens successfully resisted further encroachment and developed through the centuries their own nationality and way of life – a hard way of life hammered out on the anvil of Burmese aggression. Is it any wonder that almost alone of all the peoples of Asia the hill peoples of Burma remained so constant and so loyal to the British cause.[19]

The historical position of the Karen in 1946 can be outlined as follows: During the Japanese occupation many Karens fought the Japanese as part of Force 136 (Special Operation Executive, SOE) in guerrilla actions. Especially Christian Karen were active. They have a historical record of supporting the British in the wars against Burma in 1852 and 1885. Approximately 2,000 Karens, including Sandhurst-trained officers, were recruited to the British army in Burma together with Chin and Kachin, while only 200 Burmans were included. The Christian Karens also had a favourable position in education in colonial times. During colonial rule the Christian minority of about 15 per cent came to represent the whole Karen category *vis-à-vis* the British, and the Karen were often presented as if they constituted a relatively homogeneous ethnic/national unit.

The position of Karen in history as anti-Burman, mainly Christian and loyal to the British, does not take into consideration that the Buddhist Karen, in particular Pwo and Pa-o, did not accept the Baptist and Catholic missionary offer of salvation. In Salween and in the Irrawaddy Delta

---

19. 'Case for the Karens', p. 3.

thousands of Buddhist Karens joined in an extensive and protracted rebellion between 1856 and 1860 against missionaries and colonizers. The leaders were *mìn làung* , 'Embryo Kings', preparing the arrival of the next Buddha (*Ariya Mettaya*).[20]

Already in 1881 the Christian Karens formed the Karen National Association (forerunner of the KNU) open to all groups and religious denominations. After the active Christian participation in suppressing the Burman resistance in 1885, the KNA gained support from some British officials. The most notable and often cited by the KNU is the book by financial commissioner Donald M. Smeaton, *The Loyal Karens of Burma*: 'Recognize once for all the fact that the Karen is a separate nation distinct from the Burmese in origin, manners, religion and tradition.'[21] Smeaton argued that cooperation between the colonial administration and the Karens organized as a nation was important to the development of the colony and that the loyal Karens deserved this alliance. The book stimulated further interest in the Karens and enhanced sympathy for their claims.

In the 1930s the Karens made a plea for a distinct administrative entity within a new constitution. They referred to their continued loyalty to the British Raj as being 'law-abiding and tolerant citizen'.[22] The Karen often expressed fear of future Burman domination and of being assimilated into an independent Burmese state.

The outstanding Karen leader before World War II, Sir San Crombie Po, published a book in 1928 and proposed an autonomous Karen area comprising the Tenasserim division. He quoted extensively from Smeaton in arguing for this reward to the 'passionately loyal Karen'. Sir San C. Po warned that a new generation of Karen extremists would arise if loyalty was not rewarded.[23] In 1931–32 the Karen, and especially the Christians, had been active in suppressing the widespread Burman rebellion lead by Hsaya San. In the 1937 Constitution the Karen gained a special representation.

---

20. Gravers, *Nationalism as Political Paranoia*, p. 28. The rebellion came as a surprise to the British. They believed that the Burman king was behind it and did not realise the religious background. The Karen, Shan and Pa-o, and some Burmans from the mountains who participated, did not want to change their Buddhist identity or surrender their tributary position as frontier peoples between the major political powers in Burma and Siam.

21. Donald M. Smeaton, *The Loyal Karens of Burma*, London: Kegan Paul, Trech & Co., 1887.

22. See speech by Karen representative, Thra Shwe Ba, before the Round Table Conference in London 1931–32, in Benda and Larkin, *The World of Southeast Asia*, p. 202; and CMD4004, vi 233 (House of Commons) p. 86, OIOC.

23. San C. Po, *Burma and the Karens*, London: Elliot Stock, 1928, pp. 78–80.

Significantly, the British made a distinction between British Burma and 'Burma' by excluding 40 per cent of the territory from 'Ministerial Burma' under the Constitution. The excluded areas came under direct control of the British governor. The excluded and scheduled areas were considered outside the pre-colonial state or only marginally controlled by the king. Among the excluded areas were Kayah state and Salween district, that is, areas with a sizeable Karen population. Naturally, Burman nationalists reacted with anger and saw these arrangements as divide-and-rule tactics. They vehemently opposed the Karen claim to be a separate race and nation. The Karen National Association on their part demanded an extension of the excluded areas, referring to the Toungoo area as 'the cradle of their traditions and the centre of Karen population – never under Burman rule'.[24]

During the 1930s, colonialism and nationalism deepened the ethnic opposition and with the British routed by the Japanese army, open conflict between Burmans and Karens came to the fore. The Burma Independent Army, the nationalist army supported by the Japanese, killed 2,000 Karens in Myaungmya and Papun in 1942. The Karen were punished for their loyalty and support to British officers hiding behind the Japanese lines.[25] Christian, Buddhist and Animist Sgaw as well as Pwo Karens were killed, and this ethnic violence became deeply ingrained in the historic memories of future Karen generations. To the majority of the Karen the atrocities confirmed the reasoning behind Karen autonomy as a nation as opposed to the Burman nation. The Christian Karen leaders gave their explanation in the 'Case for the Karens': 'Why? Because the Karen people feel that their national consciousness, their religion – 33 per cents [*sic*] are Christian – and their way of life will not at present permit them a happy or close collaboration with the Burmese people'. The Karen cultural particularism is thus presented as the ultimate argument. But the unfortunate events during the occupation had another effect. Despite the above denial, Karen leaders and Aung San began to cooperate and prepare for the last fight against the Japanese, for the return of the British and for inevitable independence.

In 1946, when the KNU decided to send its delegation to London and formulate its historical argumentation, it had good reason to believe that their loyalty would be rewarded at last. The delegation believed it represented

24. Memorials and other documents, M/1/33; M/1/94, OIOC.

25. Dorothy Guyot, 'Communal Conflict in the Burma Delta' in Ruth T. McVey (ed.), *Southeast Asian Transitions Approaches through Social History*, New Haven: Yale University Press, 1978; Gravers, *Nationalism as Political Paranoia*, pp. 46–47.

all Karens. However, many of the Buddhist Karens and their organization were against the Goodwill Mission and did not want a separation from Burma. They wanted continued cooperation with Aung San. The Buddhist Karens may have lacked the effective leadership and organizational power of the Christian Karen.[26] In the KNU historicism, differences and dissent were ignored. For example, in the 'Case for the Karens', history begins like this: 'The Karens, or *Pghar Ka-Nyauw* (*P'ga Nyauw*), are the Ancient Britons of South-East Asia, a pastoral people of Mongolian descent who were the first inhabitants of what we now know as Burma and Siam'. The Karens are being elevated to the 'first human race (aborigines) to inhabit Burma and Thailand'[27] and the term *P'ga Nyauw* used here is actually the term used by one of the groups: the Sgaw Karen. This we-came-first is then connected with Burman aggression which forced the Karens to live in the mountains. The KNU claims that the Karen were discriminated against more intensively by the Burmans than other groups and regarded as an inferior race by the Burmans. The definitive proof of Burman aggression was, naturally, the atrocities committed by the BIA during the war.[28]

By 1946 the ethnic fragments had become one single Karen category aiming to be a nation and this was confirmed by the experience of many Karens as well as by books and traditions: 'The Case for the Karens' transformed this ambiguous historical narrative into political practice.

Census

The census made by the British became an important justification for elevating the Karen from ethnic minority to a nation. The 'Case for the Karens' emphasizes 'the haphazard way of taking census' by the British. The unreliable figures were caused by 'the Karen nomadic way of life and the habit of Burmese officers to classify Karens as Burmese if they were Buddhist'.[29] The British census of 1941 gave the same figure for the Karen

---

26. According to U Maung Maung, 'Burmese Nationalist Movements 1940–48', Edinburgh: Kiscadale, 1989, p. 346, the Buddhist oriented All Burma Karen National Association was equally as strong as KNV.

27. 'Case for the Karens', p. 5.

28. See KNU, *The Karens and Their Struggle for Freedom*, Kawthoolei 1992, p. 4ff., on the role of the atrocities in arguing for a separate state: 'The bitter experiences... taught us one lesson... unless we control a state of our own we will never experience a life of peace and decency, free from persecution and oppression', p. 6.

29. 'Case for the Karens', p. 8.

as the census of 1931: 1,367,000. However, the Japanese counted 4.5 million Karens and this figure has often been quoted by KNU representatives during and after negotiations for an independent Karen state.[30] Today the KNU uses figures of 7 to 8 million – a figure which is difficult to assess, but which is probably too high.

The first census of British Burma was taken in 1872 and published in Rangoon in 1875. In this census of nationalities and races of Burma, a distinction was made between mountain and valley populations. The Karen are mentioned as one of the first tribes arriving, perhaps the first, 'as ancestors of the present hill-men'. This 'fact' was established by the Baptist missionaries in their interpretation of Karen mythology. The colonial government had recognized and used the ethnic differences soon after the first conquest in 1826. In Tenasserim the Karens were recognized as a particular object of taxation, and as the chief producers of valuable cotton.[31] The importance of the census, as seen by the KNU, is both the figure and the fact that the Karen from this date were officially classified with a name and degree of aboriginal status.[32] The other criterion in the British census which became important to the KNU was religion. The 'Case for the Karens' claims that 33 per cent were Christians in 1946; the British said 25 per cent; missionary sources varied between 15 and 20 per cent.

Religion

Religion has a crucial role in the Karen self-presentation as their cultural foundation and in their national identity. And in the end religion has divided the Karen nation. In the 'Case for the Karens' historical proofs are mainly derived from missionary sources. The Baptist missionary Ellen B. Mason's book *Civilizing Mountain Men*, 1862, is quoted in the 'Case for the Karens' for the following: 'they [the Karen] are neither a scanty nor a scattered people ... in number at least five millions'. Francis and Ellen B. Mason supported the thesis that the Karen were the 'Lost tribe of Israel of the Old Testament',

30. See *Karen's Political Future*, pp. 262, 614.

31. John S. Furnivall, 'Fashioning Leviathan', *Journal of the Burma Research Society*, vol. 29, no. 1, 1939, pp. 1–138; James Low, 'The History of Tenasserim', *Journal of the Royal Asiatic Society* of Bengal, vols 2–5. 1835–37 & 1839.

32. Cf. Benedict Anderson, *Imagined Communities. Reflections on the Origin and Spread of Nationalism*, London: Verso, 1991, on the role of the colonial census in the making of nations. In Burma census was important to the collection of poll tax, to village administration, and to law and order of 'pacification'.

Figure 5: The legendry home of the Karen (source: KNU, 'The Karens and Their Struggle'). The original title of this map states 'Htee Hset Met Ywa – Land of Karen Forefathers (Migrated South about B.C. 2615, and arrived Yunnan about B.C. 1385)'.

and that they came from China. Moreover, what was referred to in a Karen myth as the River of Flowing Sand, which they crossed, was said to be the Gobi desert (see Figure 5). Mrs Mason's book is one among many about the Karen written by missionaries. It uses the Karen myths as historical facts and as remnants of the Old Testament to prove that the Karen had contact with Jews in China in 258 BC before emigrating to Burma.[33]

Ellen B. Mason is cited for the historical fact that the ancient city Toungoo was founded by Karens in the fourteenth century and that 'The Karens once occupied the plains of Toungoo but the Burmese ... drove them

---

33. Ellen B. Mason, *Civilizing Mountain Men*. London: James Nisbet & Co. 1862, p. 371.

back and took their lands.'[34] The importance of Toungoo as 'the cradle of Karen tradition' was established by Francis Mason and has been reiterated by Karen nationalists. One of the myths published by the Baptist missionaries became the foundational narration of primordial relation between the White Brother and his elder Karen brother. It defines the ethnic-religious essence of Karen identity in opposition to the Burmans. It is about the creation of the world, the first man and woman, and how they lost both the love of God (Yuah in Karen or Yahweh in Baptist translations) and the Golden Book of Knowledge:

> God departed with our younger brother,
> the white foreigner ...
> God gave them power to cross waters and reach lands,
> Then God went up to heaven.
> But he made the white foreigners
> More skilful than all other nations.

When God departed, the myth says, the Karens became slaves to the Burmans. They lost the Golden Book of Knowledge. But one day the younger White Brother will return with that book and God will yet save them:

> The Talien (Mon) Kings had their season;
> The Burman Kings had their seasons;
> The Siamese Kings had their seasons;
> And the foreign Kings will have their season;
> But a Karen King will yet appear.
> When he arrives there will be only one King,
> And there will be neither rich nor poor.
> Everything [sic!] will be happy,
> And even the lions and leopards will lose their savageness.[35]

In the 'Case for the Karens' this prophecy is made a part of the Karen ethos:

> An intuitive feeling born of tradition and prophecy that their White Brother would come to them for help [*sic*] had long taken root in them, and this prophecy has to a large degree been fulfilled in the advent of British rulers with the American and European Missionaries.

---

34. Mason, *Civilizing Mountain Men*, p. 85. The theory on the lost tribe was gradually abandoned by the Baptist missionaries in Burma; see A.R. McMahon, *The Karens of the Golden Chersonese*, London: Harrison, 1876, p. 95. It is still mentioned in the literature and in political pamphlets; see Jonathan Falla, *True Love and Bartholomew. Rebels on the Burmese Border*, Cambridge: Cambridge University Press, 1991, pp. 230–231; Smith, *Burma*, p. 45,

35. Mason, *Civilizing Mountain Men*, pp. 366–367.

The myth and the prophecy of the return of the White Brother has been repeated by almost all later writings about the Karen as a central point of identification – which it has become, indeed. The obvious conclusion to this tale, even in 1946, has been: after the foreign kings, a Karen nation will appear!

Now, its parallel but contrary Buddhist version is rarely cited as historical evidence. In that version 'the Lord of the Pagoda' (Buddha) gave wisdom. It is still told among the Buddhist Pwo Karen in Thailand as a metaphorical presentation of their minority situation: 'we are like the orphan without a leader'. The Buddhist Karens in Thailand and in Burma from Tavoi to Papun have been waiting for the next Buddha (*Ariya Metteya*). Before the arrival of *Ariya* the universal ruler (*cakkavatti* or *setkyamin* in Burman) is going to establish peace and order.[36] Thus, the great expectations of the Karen expressed in their different myths were indeed not very different from Mon, Shan or Burman ideas of a *mìn làung* (a pretender, embryo ruler), a righteous leader and a culture hero who could re-establish a relatively fair social order regardless of ethnic identity.[37]

Ellen and Francis Mason did not use the Buddhist version. Their valuable and loyal Sgaw Karen assistant, Saw Quala, collected, translated and selected the version used by Ellen Mason. She quotes Saw Quala for saying that the Karen, are 'the children of the forest without books, without a king and with no common name' ... 'we had no knowledge, no understanding, no power.' And Saw Quala suggested that the Karen nation should have a flag with the Bible and a sword as God's weapon for a Karen victory: 'Let us erect the National banner, as other book nations have done. Let us follow the white foreigners and learn from them'.[38]

Ethnic identity with a fundamental Protestant substance was the first step towards the common Karen nationality which is still upheld by the KNU and probably by many Karens in Burma. Knowledge, organizational self-reliance and power are the main themes in the Baptist Karen literature: 'to pray is to obtain' as a Karen wrote in *The Morning Star*, a Karen language

36. The *Ariya*-oriented Buddhism among the Pwo Karen in Western Thailand was studied by the present writer and two colleagues 1970–72. See Kirsten E. Andersen, 'Elements of Pwo Karen Buddhism,' in Søren Egerod and Per Sørensen (eds), *Lampang Reports*, Copenhagen: The Scandinavian Institute of Asian Studies 1976, pp. 269–274; K.E. Andersen, 'Two Indigenous Karen Religious Denominations', *Folk*, vol. 23, 1981, pp. 251–261; Gravers, *Pwo Karen Ethnic Minority*. This version of Buddhism is still active and is often reported in Thai English language newspapers.
37. See Gravers, *Pwo Karen Ethnic Minority*, p. 33; Gravers, *Nationalism as Political Paranoia*, p. 22.
38. Mason, *Civilizing Mountain Men*, p. 265.

newspaper established in 1842. And the Christian religion was not seen as an alien construction. It was, and still is, considered to be the return of the original, but lost, Karen religion.[39] This is an important point since it established Karen (Christian) identity as authentic and as separate from other ethnic groups in Burma.

Another myth of importance is the tale about the culture hero Phu Htaw Meh Pah (Phu Tho' Mè Pha) 'Grandfather Wild Boar Tusk', who led his people from the 'River of Flowing Sand' to Burma. He went ahead while his family were cooking. His children lost his trail and are now waiting for him to return to the 'orphans'. This myth has the same theme as the *Ariya* myth but with a non-religious legendary narration. It has also been used in official KNU publications to establish the identity of a Karen as a descendant of Htaw Meh Pah.[40] It has often been used to confirm the Karen as the indigenous people of Burma as related in the KNU edited history. The first migration of Karens is said to have taken place in 1125 BC and the second in 739 BC. Htaw Meh Pah is not mentioned in the 'Case for the Karens' but the tale was used widely in 1946. The controversial Baptist and Karen politician, San Po Thin, founded a Htaw Meh Pah Association during the war.[41] The significance of the Htaw Meh Pah myth is that, as a non-religious tale, it is used as the genealogical foundation of a common Karen national identity despite religious and cultural differences. When asked 'Who is a Karen?', the KNU publications will answer that a Karen is one who claims ancestry back to Htaw Meh Pah. It is used as a metaphor of ancestry and evidence of the historical migration and origin. The narration is partly biblical by using the Exodus. At the same time it is genuinely Karen and still a very active part of Karen identification in conversations with 'the White Brother'.

In other words, the Karen mythology is important as the *public image of national identity* with a primordial ethnic essence established by the Christian Karens and congruent with the category used by the colonial power and at present by world media. Even though many Karens do not use this cultural content of the myth as the only means of subjective identification,

---

39.   This was emphasized by Saw Tha Din during his personal lectures on Karen history in Sangkhlaburi 1970. His grandparents belonged to the Talakhoung sect, one of several Buddhist-inspired utopian sects still active in Thailand and Burma.

40.   See Falla, *True Love*, pp. 12–15, for one version of the myth and its present use by the KNU. After the war the KNU published a Htaw Meh Pah journal.

41.   See Ian Morrison, *Grandfather Longlegs. The Life and Galant Death of Major H.P. Seagrim*, London: Faber & Faber, 1947, p. 187. San Po Thin's cooperation with Aung San and the formation of a Karen unit, with a Htaw-Meh-Pah Band, of the Burma Defence Army is recounted by Morrison.

the substance cannot be evaded when used by Amnesty International, anthropologists or even SLORC in the political discourse.

Saw Tha Din read a paper on the Karen People in the Royal Anthropological Institute in 1946. I have not seen the paper but I find it safe to assume that he presented the historical and ethnological ideas based on the mythology published by F. Mason's work. In this way an anthropological circle of primordialism was completed combining the subjective presentation of a nation with the objective, scientific data.[42] In 1946–47 it had the effect that a major part of the British public felt unhappy in letting down their 'loyal Karens', as for example expressed in *The Times* on 14 November, 1947.

Modernization of Tradition

> The East still wants help and guidance and understanding from the West – but not domination.[43]

The Christian Karens claim that they are more civilized and modern than other ethnic groups in Burma. The older generation had their education in Christian schools and colleges in Burma. The political leadership in 1946 was mostly wealthy landowners from the Irrawaddy Delta, barristers, teachers and traders – like, for example, the members of the Goodwill Mission to London. They formed an influential faction of the middle class in colonial Burma and a relatively large number compared to Burman members of this middle class. The renowned Karen leader, Sir San C. Po, wrote: 'Christianity has satisfied a great national religious need, and doing so has developed a national civilization.'[44] The Karen leaders see the combination of Christianity and a comparatively high level of education as proof of a modern national identity and consciousness. At the same time they have preserved their cultural identity: 'Through the centuries the Karens had preserved themselves as a race distinct from the Burmese and other peoples. Characterized by qualities such as reserve, unobtrusiveness, steadiness and simplicity ...'[45] The Karen are often characterized as 'a timid race' in missionary literature and these special qualities are repeated in recent KNU publications:

42. F. Mason was a member of The Royal Asiatic Society and returned ethnological queries to the British Association for the Advancement of Science. See Francis Mason, 'Religion, Myth, and Astronomy Among the Karens', *Journal of the Asiatic Society of Bengal*, vol. 34, no. 3, 1865; see also McMahon, *The Karens*.

43. 'Case for the Karens', p. 4.

44. San C. Po, *Burma and the Karens*, p. 60.

45. 'Case for the Karens', p. 5.

By nature the Karens are simple, quiet, unassuming and peace-loving people, who uphold the high moral qualities of honesty, purity, brotherly love, cooperative living and loyalty, and are devout in their religious beliefs.[46]

When Karen leaders sent what they termed 'memorials' to the colonial government, they often made an initial presentation like the following from the Karen National Association in Toungoo 1935: 'Wherefore your humble memorialists, on behalf of the poor, timid and simple Karens inhabiting the hill tracts … The Karen desire to re-establish a national home of their own like the Jewish race.'[47] Other documents reveal that the Buddhist Karens did not ask to be considered a 'separate race' in the 1930s as part of a special electorate.[48]

The important point here is that the Karen, according to the KNU, preserved their tradition and ethos while progressing towards modernity (with the exception of some of the Animist hill Karen). But they felt that their British masters did not honour their achievements: 'But tradition die hard in the East; despite their considerable achievements in Religion, Medicine, Law, Politics and Commerce, the Karens were still an "inferior race".'

As participants in modern education and the law-and-order functions of the Empire, the Karen had become part of plural society and its cultural mix which, according to Furnivall, could never combine. Modernity and its 'spirit of nationalism' were not sufficient remedies to overcome cultural differentialism and its colonial hierarchy.

The Making of a Karen National Identity

Karens have meticulously preserved their race, creed and culture in spite of all changes … The national consciousness of the Karens has passed its embryonic stage.[49]

They kept aloof as a race, jealously preserved their National Identity, and anxiously nurtured their National Virtue and National Morals[50]

---

46. KNU, *The Karens and Their Struggle*, p. 3.

47. Memorials M/1/33, OIOC. This memorial asked for Toungoo area to be part of Salween excluded area under the direct power of the governor.

48. See Memorials M/1/120, OIOC, p. 4.

49. 'Case for the Karens', p. 7.

50. 'The Humble Memorial of the Karens of Burma September 26, 1945', 'Karen's Political Future', p. 22. Today the tone is more defensive: 'Culturally [the Burmese government] has attempted to absorb and dissolve our language, literature, traditions, and customs', KNU, *The Karens and Their Struggle*, p. 1.

The Karen leaders emphatically tried to assure their former masters and their Burman adversaries of their status as a nation and not merely as an ethnic minority or hill tribe. The definitions are very bombastic. However, they are attempts to represent the Karen case as based on an authentic national identity and on indisputable historical realities, as real as the claims of any other nation:

> Karens are a nation according to any definition. We are a nation with our own distinctive culture and civilization, language, literature, names, nomenclature, sense of value and proportion, customary laws and moral codes, aptitudes and ambitions; in short we have our own distinctive outlook on life. By all canons of international law we are a nation.[51]

Such a definition leaves little to add. It is the clearest example of how the KNU leaders used the cultural differentialism of their colonial masters and combined it with their own cultural particularism. In the same document Karen and Burman are defined as two different races (Karen = Mongolian; Burman = Tibeto-Burman), and as different civilizations. It is a dream that they can ever evolve a common nationality, writes Saw Po Chit. The same wording can be found in recent publications from the KNU.[52] The conclusion of Saw Po Chit's analysis is that democracy is impossible in a country with several nations of which one, the Burman, is a dominating majority. Thus, in the analysis of the KNU, the colonial plural society could never become a nation due to the oppositional qualities of the ethnic (racial) groups.

It became of urgent importance to the KNU leadership to underline the common national identification as the political situation evolved in 1946–47 and a split within the leadership of the KNU became evident. Saw Tha Din stepped down as the leader and another member of the Goodwill Mission, Saw Ba U Gyi, took over. The young and the militant leadership of the KNU extended the area of the contested Karen state.

A majority of Karens supported an independent state while the Karen Youth Organization (KYO) allied with Aung San's organization the Anti-Fascist People's Freedom League (AFPFL). These Karens did not make the same exorbitant claims and wished to negotiate a solution including special constitutional rights within a federation. The Karen Youth Organization

---

51. Saw Po Chit, 'Karens and the Karen State', p. 170.

52. KNU, *The Karens and Their Struggle*; Ananda Rajah, 'Ethnicity, Nationalism, and the Nation-State. The Karen in Burma and Thailand,' in Gehan Wijeyewardene (ed.), *Ethnic Groups Across National Boundaries in Mainland Southeast Asia*, Singapore: Institute of Southeast Asian Studies, 1990, pp. 102–133.

seems to have mobilized among the Buddhist Pwo Karen, but had among its leaders Christians and also former Force 136 guerrillas.[53] Thus, the split did not explicitly occur along religious lines. Political sympathies of left and right, differences between young and old, conflicts between well-to-do urban elite and poor hill peasants from the mountains worked against unity. And from the Salween and Shwegyin areas came memorials with confusing messages – some supporting an autonomous state in the Salween district as part of the British Commonwealth, others wishing to be a part of Burma. A group of Christian Karens from Salween formed their own organization outside the KNU. Their leader, a former Force 136 guerrilla, signed a copy of the draft constitution on behalf of the Karen even though there was no firm guarantee of an autonomous Karen state. He was later executed by the KNU.[54] This was a very confusing development for their British patrons who anticipated that the Karens would behave *as one ethnic group* with a common national interest.

The British saw the confusion as an indication of lack of leadership and had increasing doubts about the Karen case. Saw Tha Din believed that it suited the British well to be confused and use this as a excuse for supporting the former allied of the Japanese, Aung San, in establishing a unified Burma. However, the internal split among the Karens is not the negation of the existence of an ethnic category. On the contrary, it is the failure of colonial ethnicism. The many local as well as national political struggles between Karens for power, representation and resources were all elements in the formation of the category, Karen.

The KNU replied to British doubt in a resentful statement with the title 'Karen Unity'. They claimed that the KNU also did have the support of Buddhist or hill Karens:

> No matter whether a Karen lives in the mountains or in the plains, whether Animist, Buddhist, Christian ... Sgaw, Pwo ... A KAREN IS A KAREN; one in blood and brotherhood; one in sentiment; one in adversity and one mass of Karen nationhood.[55]

---

53. Force 136 was the Southeast Asia section of the British Special Operation Executive (SOE), which parachuted arms to Karen guerrillas during the Japanese occupation. The Karen insisted on keeping their weapons, about 12,000, after the war. On Force 136 and the Karen, see Morrison, *Grandfather Longlegs*.

54. Smith, *Burma*, p. 86. Unfortunately, the divergent economic and political interests among the Karen leaders and their local differences have not yet been thoroughly analysed.

55. *Karen's Political Future*, p. 350. The disunity became accentuated during the enquiry of the Frontier Areas Committee, see 'Frontier Area Committee', M/4/2854, OIOC.

In the last instance, all Karens had to support an image of common identity, no matter to what faction they belonged.

Territorial Claims

The Goodwill Mission of 1946 presented the territorial claims by giving credit to the Empire for safeguarding the minorities by grouping them in scheduled areas. However, the Karens were disappointed by not having access to the sea. The Goodwill Mission asked for a state comprising the scheduled area of Salween, Tenasserim division and part of the Pegu area (see Map 6). They did not ask for any part of the Irrawaddy Delta. The state would be a member of the Commonwealth under a British governor. Alternatively they proposed a Federation of Autonomous Frontier States (Kachin, Shan, Chin, Karen) with full dominion status.

When Saw Tha Din withdrew as leader of the KNU, his successor Saw Ba U Gyi demanded a state comprising large parts of the Delta including the Irrawaddy division. And since Thailand was among the losers in World War II, the KNU even demanded the inclusion of areas in Thailand inhabited by Karens. Probably the elite and landowners from the Delta, where Saw Ba U Gyi came from, realised that the majority of the Karens living in the plains and towns would never move up into the mountain areas. In the plains the Karen did not form a majority of the population as in some parts of Salween district. However, to the KNU leaders their political status and claim to a separate state was seen as *natural according to the Western criteria of a nation*. They had demonstrated that the Karens had evolved as a modern nation on par with their Burman adversaries: 'Righteousness Exalteth a Nation' was the theme of a KNU conference in 1947.

When Saw Tha Din referred to the 'Case for the Karens' in 1970, I think he considered the proposal to be fair and reasonable as compared to the KNU claims in 1947: 'The Karens look to the good sense and fair-play of the British public and the wisdom of His Majesty's Government to review the situation of the Karens (& other tribal peoples) ...' The 'Case for the Karens' was the last attempt to negotiate a settlement and to cooperate with the AFPFL and Aung San. Saw Tha Din explained that this effort failed and he foresaw the consequences: a rebellion was impossible to avoid. His personal project had failed, the case had been lost, and he stepped down. Saw Tha Din and the KNU had followed the rules of their white brother and his ideals of a modern nation, but they never received a reply from him! The British angered all Karen leaders and especially the more

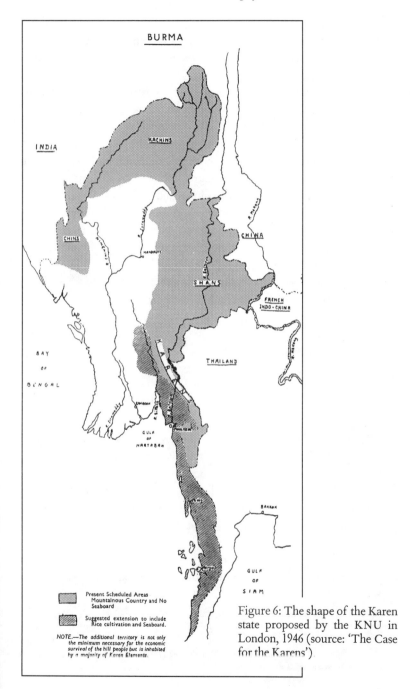

Figure 6: The shape of the Karen
state proposed by the KNU in
London, 1946 (source: 'The Case
for the Karens')

militant ones by not responding directly and officially upon their proposals for a state. Saw Tha Din emphasized that he was against the rebellion in 1949. However, it is clear from the process presented above that the ethnicism in the colonial society combined so many social and cultural contradictions that it would inevitably lead to a violent conflict – particularly as ethnic differences were to the fore during the negotiations on the Constitution.

The nationalist KNU model of a Karen society in the discourse of 1946–47 was an attempt to represent all groups within the category 'Karen'. This is precisely the nature of ethnicism as I defined it in the first section: the imagination of a social and cultural entity is created by a long inculcation of differentialism (race, culture and religion). This essence of ethnic and national identity has become ingrained in every individual. And now the Karen demanded that their nation, 'which has passed its embryonic stage' be situated in their historical territory as an autonomous state. Against this model the Burmans saw perhaps only one remedy as suggested by Furnivall: the national corporative model 'a union state transcending ethnic division' as Aung San emphasized in 1946:

> A nation is a collective term applied to a people irrespective of their ethnic origin, living in close contact with one another and having common interests and sharing joys and sorrows together for such historic periods as to have acquired a sense of oneness. Though race, religion and language are important factors it is only their traditional desire and will to live in unity through weal and woe that binds a people together and makes them a nation and their spirit a patriotism.[56]

The Burma Socialist Programme Party adhered to this definition although the BSPP transformed Burma to a unitary state dominated by Burman culture. However, the ideas of Aung San are still repeated by SLORC and this regime has taken the model further towards its unitary extreme despite their strategy of local ethnic autonomy. Aung San Suu Kyi seems to hold to the ideal of a union state, as indicated in the statement quoted on the first page of this chapter.[57]

Aung San agreed to let the minorities decide on cultural matters and even agreed to a clause in the Constitution of 1947 making it possible for the

---

56. Quoted in Burma Socialist Programme Party (BSPP): *The System of Correlation*, p. 50. See also Gravers, *Nationalism as Political Paranoia*, p. 44. The same definition was cited in the Constitution of 1974.

57. I have discussed the implications of these opposing nationalist models and strategies in Gravers, *Nationalism as Political Paranoia*.

Shan states to withdraw from the Union. Thus, the Burman and the Karen models of a nation came to suffer from the same problems created by the ethnicism of the colonial era, although definitions and strategies were indeed very different. When the British colonizers left Burma, the ghost of plural society lingered on as a historical medium through which present practice had to be identified.

The KNU 1949–94: a Nation in Exile – the Consequences of Ethnicism

The KNU rejected Aung San's definition of a nation and added that the 'homogeneous Burmese nation has gone far beyond the limits, is the cause of most of the troubles, and will lead to Burma's destruction.'[58] In 1945 a British government White Paper endorsed an autonomous Karen state and member of the Commonwealth; in 1947 the Karen had not obtained autonomy and felt betrayed. The KNU boycotted the Constitutional Assembly and the elections in April 1947 while the KYO participated and won 20 of 24 seats reserved for the Karen, uncontested. The rest of the seats went to independent Karen candidates. Obviously, the KNU had overestimated its influence. However, all Karen organizations except the KYO leadership did agree on an autonomous state at joint meetings in 1947, but they could not agree on its status and its extension. With the murder of Aung San in July 1947 the last chance of a settlement faded.

However, the feeling of betrayal by the British and the Burmans seems to have imbued the KNU with renewed expectations of help from the 'younger White Brother'.[59] Sympathizers among missionaries and British officers gave support to KNU separatism, and great expectations of shiploads of weapons from Britain may have triggered many of the disastrous events after Burma's independence in 1948.[60] KNU supporters stole money and weapons in Moulmein and Burman auxiliary troops killed eighty Christian Karens in Palaw near Mergui during Christmas. The Karen rebellion, which began in early 1949, involved three battalions from the Karen Rifles and Karen military police, all drilled by British officers since 1945. Karen forces surrounded Rangoon before they were driven back. The cost in lives and

58. Saw Po Chit, 'Karens and the Karen State', p. 170.

59. The feeling of betrayal is still emphasized as in KNU, *The Karens and Their Struggle*, p. 6.

60. On the rebellion see Cady, *History*, Smith, *Burma*, ch. 6. A colonel and ex-Force 136 adventurer, Tulloch, was especially active as the 'younger White Brother'.

the economic losses have never been established but were huge and had a devastating impact upon Burma. The KNU were driven up into the mountains in the east near Thailand and to the west in Arakan during the early 1950s. In 1950 Saw Ba U Gyi and Saw Sankey, the leaders of the KNU, were killed in an ambush on their way to Thailand. Again there were rumours of British officers travelling with the KNU leaders. One of them was Captain Vivian, who was jailed for supplying weapons to the right-wing assassins of Aung San. The KNU had set Vivian free during the rebellion.

When the British failed to return, the KNU allied with the remnants of the Guomindang armies driven out of China. They had settled in Burma and got weapons from the USA via Taiwan. But again the Karens were disappointed when the weapons did not arrive. In 1955 a new Karen leadership under a Karen Revolutionary Council was formed. It was a left-wing group inspired by Mao's theses on people's war. One of the new leaders was a deputy schoolmaster, Saw Hunter Tha Hmwe, who adopted the traditional title of 'Lord of the Land' (*kaw ka sa* in Sgaw Karen). He gained support from the hill Karens but was opposed by the older leaders like Saw Tha Din who withdrew from politics and settled as a teacher and missionary in Thailand.

The left-wing period ended in 1976 when Bo Mya, who is still president of the KNU, took power. Bo Mya is an Animist Karen who became a Seventh-day Adventist when he married (a Karen husband must follow his wife's religious denomination). As a fervent anti-communist, he was able to obtain weapons from the USA. In the 1960s and 1970s the KNU gained support from a variety of dubious foreign friends like the World Anti-Communist League (a part of the Moon religious empire), Baptist missionary organizations, *Soldier of Fortune* mercenaries, and tacit support from SEATO and the Thai army.[61] The KNU became important to Thailand and SEATO as a buffer against the communist parties in Thailand and Burma.

During this period the KNU bases along the Thai-Burma border prospered from a 5 per cent taxation of border trade and from the sale of timber and cattle. Maintaining this semi-permanent nation-in-exile identity, while entering several alliances with the other minorities in Burma and with the rebels of former prime minister U Nu, made the Karen nation *a reality in space and time* to a majority of Karens in Burma. At the same time it was confirmed that the outside world responded positively to the Karen case. However, since 1987 the KNU has lost all of its bases on the border. The

---

61. See the journal *Soldier of Fortune*, April 1984 and March 1990.

mutual understanding between SLORC and the Thai military has drastically reduced the support and the strategic options for the KNU. The Karens have recently been forced to enter into negotiations with Rangoon with the Anglican Bishop of Rangoon as go-between. Federalism is on the agenda in these contacts, but the KNU has taken the vow never to surrender its weapons and they want to keep an armed Karen force if they enter a new Union of Burma.

During the rebellion in 1949 a Karen state in the eastern part of Burma was formed and baptized *Kawthoolei* (or *Kawthulay*): a poetic term for 'The Old Land' as Saw Tha Din explained in 1970. *Kaw* means land/country; the rest of the name has been translated in many different ways, 'Flowerland' for example.[62] Saw Tha Din said it means 'cicada'. But the significance is not the meaning of the words but the metaphor and its sound of common place, common culture and identity. Today it is still the name of the Karen nation led by the KNU and of a future independent state within a federal union.

> We desire the extent of Kawthoolei to be the areas where the Karens are in majority ... All the people in Kawthoolei shall be given democratic rights, politically, economically, socially and culturally ... freedom and equality of all religions ...[63]

The consequences of fifty years of rebellion, perhaps the longest in the world, are difficult to estimate. The struggle, the history and the ethnicism which have united the Karen also contain serious antagonisms. Animist and Buddhist Karen form the majority of the subalterns fighting and suffering, about 70 per cent of an estimated force of 4,000–5,000 while an elite of Christian officers, the oldest trained by the British, are the top leaders. The Burmese language is the daily lingua franca. And many Karens in the Delta speak only Burmese. Cultural, religious and economic differences have grown, especially the differences between those long in exile and those living in fear of the Burmese army.

According to Falla, the exiled Karens are still waiting for a leader like Htaw Me Pah to come and fulfil the expectations of their mythical traditions. However, younger generations are probably not going to spend another fifty years in jungle war for a state which is quickly depleted of its resources (including the jungle!) and which may never be recognized internationally. The young may prefer to enjoy peace, urban life and modern consumption

---

62. Falla, *True Love*, p. xvi; another translation is the not so poetic 'Country Burnt Black'. The precise translation is uncertain.

63. KNU, *The Karens and Their Struggle*, p. 13.

like their cousins in ASEAN to a life in fear of torture and death.[64] The KNU cling to the illusion of help from the 'White Brother' and repeat that ethnic opposition to the Burmans is the main problem, and that they were independent in pre-colonial times.[65]

In December 1994 the internal antagonism in the KNU surfaced when 400 Buddhist Karen soldiers mutinied. They were influenced by a charismatic senior monk (*sayadaw*) U Thuzana who is a Karen from the Salween area. He and his Buddhist sect preach vegetarianism and pacifism. His followers have been building pagodas on the front line between KNU forces and the Burmese army to stop the fighting.[66] Leaflets accusing the KNU of oppressing Buddhist Karens were distributed. This conflict may result from a SLORC plot. However, the mutiny and the sect are clear signs of a widening split between Buddhist and Christian Karens.[67] The Buddhist Karen mutineers are organized in the Democratic Karen Buddhist Organization (DKBA) with their own armed unit supported by SLORC. In April 1995 soldiers from DKBA with yellow headbands (the colour of Buddhism) attacked Christian Karen refugees in Thailand. They killed, burned, looted and took hostages in an attempt to force the 70,000 refugees back across the border. These attacks were led by the Burmese army and its regular Karen soldiers and may also be viewed as a Burmese attempt to humiliate Thailand as 'host' to the KNU for forty years. The KNU leadership is about to be over-taken by younger officers, and the old vision of a Karen nation and state may be losing ground as it becomes exiled from the realities inside Burma.

The mutiny and the religious sect are clear signs of a widening split between Buddhist and Christian Karens that had been submerged since 1949. When 2,000 Karen families gather around U Thuzana's temple, it is certainly also a sign of a genuine longing for peace among the subaltern and civilian Karen who have suffered incredible hardship for almost half a century. Among

---

64. Falla, *True Love*, pp. 291–299. The young KNU people look to modern life in Bangkok and to brisk trade.

65. IWGIA Newsletters 1987, no. 50; 1988, no. 51.

66. On this type of Buddhist sects among the Karen, see Gravers, *Pwo Karen Ethnic Minority*.

67. Such splits are not new and reflect Karen political diversity. For instance, the Karen Central Organization, formed in 1942 to group all Karen organizations, split in 1947 into the Christian KNU, the Karen Youth Organization (affiliated to Aung San's AFPFL) and the Buddhist-oriented All Burma Karen National Association. Karens remaining loyal to the Union formed the Union Karen League within the AFPFL while in Salween District the hill Karen formed a United Karens Organization vowing to keep the KNU out of their area. A minor faction within the KNU, the Karen Congress, also did not rebel in 1949. The pro-communist and anti-religious Karen National United Party, formed in 1953 by left-wing KNU leaders, played an important role in the KNU's struggle until the mid-1970s.

those who have been hardest hit are the Buddhist Karen, who have witnessed the Christian-dominated KNU taxing the border trade, depleting the forests and conscripting their young men into the KNU while they remained poor and terrorized by the Burmese army.[68] It may be the beginning of the end for the KNU rebellion but not to the problems created by the process of ethnicism.

Ethnic hatred and violence are deeply ingrained in generations of Karens and Burmans. Although colonial plural society belongs to the past, the process of violence in the name of cultural and religious differences continue, adding new experiences to the historical memory. This historical memory as the basis for the making of ethnic and national identity is a serious obstacle to a reconciliation. Then, should we dismiss the KNU concept of a nation as a mere inauthentic colonial construction?[69]

> In fighting against the Burmese Government, we are not being motivated by narrow nationalism, nor by ill-will towards the Burmese Government or the Burman people. Our struggle was instigated neither by capitalist world nor by the communists... *It has an originality completely of its own.*[70]

Blurred Imaginations and Concepts: Karen or Anthropologists?

Recently anthropologists have come to see the Karen imagination of a nation as a 'construction', an 'invention of tradition', and have 'deconstructed' the discourse and narration. In the concluding pages I shall briefly attend to this theme which is crucial to the debate of ethnicity and nationalism in former colonies. Chatterjee has raised the question of making history as an authentic self-identification in colonial and post-colonial contexts.[71]

Authenticity is an act of self-representation of identity. It means that a relation exists between subjects, their historical practice and the way they model and relate their experience of past and present, including categorization made by 'others'. It is a mode of presenting and representing identity in the

---

68. See, for instance, *The Bangkok Post*, 1 May and 5 May, 1995.

69. As for example Salemink has concluded in his analysis of the Montagnards in the Central Highlands of Vietnam: 'Montagnard identity was merely a construction on the part of outside powers, which supported, protected and exploited this distinct identity for its own purpose.' Oscar Salemink, 'Primitive Partisans: French Strategy and the Construction of a Montagnard Ethnic Identity in Indochina,' in Hans Antlöv and Stein Tønnesson (eds), *Imperial Policy and Southeast Asian Nationalism, 1930–57*, London: Curzon Press, 1995, p. 264.

70. KNU, *The Karens and Their Struggle*, p. 2, my italics.

71. Chatterjee, *Nation and its Fragments*. On the debate of authentic identity, see Jonathan Friedman, *Cultural Identity and Global Process*, London: Sage Publications, 1994. It is significant that this issue is to the fore among Christian ethnic groups in former colonies: Fijians, Solomon Islanders, Moluccans, Montagnards of Vietnam among others.

history and as a meaningful basis of social interaction. Thus, it is necessarily related to political processes. The revelation of the properties of a cultural identity also exposes these in the struggles for symbolic power. Obviously, we may question the historical evidence used in presenting the history of an identity, as in the case of the Karen. But authenticity as an act of identification in itself cannot be falsified or denied its historical role in establishing a fulcrum of social practices. However, the complex questions of authenticity and legitimation have been confused in the recent debate on the Karen nationalism.

When the anthropologist Peter Hinton asked 'Do the Karen really exist?', his conclusion was that they do not possess a common identity. None of his Karen informants in Thailand was able to define the content of a common cultural identity. To answer the question 'What is a Karen?' Hinton found that his difficulty was 'due to the fact that I was assuming cultural distinctiveness where there was none, at least as correlates of ethnicity or tribal identity'.[72] He is certainly right in concluding that there are great cultural and linguistic variations among the population categorized as Karen. However, he seems to have fallen into the culturalist trap of assuming that cultural distinctiveness is equal to a common cultural essence as the core of ethnic (or national) identity. Common identification may exist in political models based on cosmologies, rituals and myths. Leach has demonstrated that such models may combine groups despite cultural and linguistic differences within the ethnic category Kachin and between Kachin and Shan.[73] Although Hinton cites Leach, he implies that the religious ideas, which the Karen share with their Buddhist neighbours, and which are expressed in various religious movements, are not criteria of a Karen identity. Hinton takes his analysis even further and concludes that the concept 'Karen' is a colonial construction based on European ideas of culture, nation and society: 'The conventional classifications may be wrong, but nevertheless they have far-reaching consequences for the practical politics of the region: paradoxically they have helped to make *real* the very facts which they inaccurately describe'.[74]

Hinton adds that this misconception had tragic dimensions in post-colonial Burma. However, the tragedy of the Karen (and Burma) is not ethnicity but the politics of ethnicism which has produced a wide gap between

72. Hinton, 'Do the Karen Really Exist?', p. 165.

73. Edmund R. Leach, *Political Systems of Highland Burma. A Study of Kachin Social Structure*, London: Bell & Sons, 1964.

74. Hinton, 'Do the Karen Really Exist?', p. 166.

the political demands made by the KNU and the realities inside Burma. What is also deplorable is that Hinton gives the unfortunate impression of an ambiguous and even inauthentic Karen identity, something unreal made real by colonialism. That is not the case. The point is that precisely the elitist model and its concepts can be authentic even though trying to represent the whole ethnic category. Perhaps Hinton's conceptions of ethnic and national identity are blurred by the subjective and primordialist phrases of the Karen? But the KNU is making ethno-history and creating its own anthropological model as an authentic one. They can quote several missionaries, anthropologists and officials proving the authenticity, and they can demonstrate their theses empirically. And at the same time they can claim that the construction is their own making in the history.

In an article by the anthropologist Ananda Rajah, the KNU model of a nation is characterized as an 'invention of tradition'. Rajah analyses the KNU as a "nation-state" (in quotes) and relates it to Burma and Thailand. He concludes:

> It is not difficult to see how that Karen identity, as it is made to be by the KNU is an invention rather different from the way the village communities identify themselves, and that the Karen 'nation-state' is, to use Anderson's term, an imagined political community.[75]

The problem with this conclusion is an implicit contention that the village represents the authentic and 'uninvented' tradition. This interpretation is perhaps a blurred understanding of 'imagined community' since that concept does not make any distinction of authenticity.[76] Even in a hill Karen village an imagination of a nation is possible although they may disagree with the KNU version! At the local level people obviously interact more directly than at the 'national' level where interaction and its simultaneity have to be imagined. The formation of identity is neither singular nor exclusive. The KNU concept of a nation may be shared not only by Christian Karens but even by Animists in Burma, while most Karens in Thailand may share a common ethnic identity but emphasize that they are Thai citizens. The Karen in Thailand may sympathize with the idea of autonomy but rarely give direct support to the KNU rebellion. In other words, place, status and

---

75. Rajah, 'Ethnicity, Nationalism, and the Nation-State', p. 121. He takes up several important issues such as the role of the borders in relation to ethnic and national identity and the KNU control of schools as decisive in communicating their vision of a nation.

76. Anderson, *Imagined Comunities*, p. 6, criticizes Gellner for assimilating invention to 'fabrication' and 'falsity'.

situation may implicate variations of identification.[77] The problem is perhaps located within another category: we, the anthropologists who have become obsessed with revealing 'constructions' and inventions' and after deconstructing leave the unfortunate impression of something false and not authentic. The discussion is based on a fiction: that a sharp distinction between 'invented' (spurious) and 'real' (original) can be made concerning identity.

The Karen have been engaged in a struggle over ethnic and national classifications in the history of Burma. Subjective as well as objective properties are ingredients of this process of representation. However, both Hinton and Rajah fail to recognize the complexity of the process. In the words of Pierre Bourdieu:

> When, as their education and their specific interests incline them, researchers try to set themselves up as judges of all judgement and as critique of all criteria, they prevent themselves from grasping the specific logic of a struggle in which the social force of representations is not necessarily proportional to their truth-value ...[78]

Obviously the missionaries have re-edited the Karen myths. But they made them available to many Karens by constructing a Sgaw and Pwo alphabet and printing thousands of school books, journals and magazines in Karen dialects: print-capitalism and the Baptist interpretation of the Holy Ghost worked in a remarkably effective way *for* the Karen case. A communal Karen imagination of a nation has been in the making since 1830, and it is not merely a foreign creation. The Karen have indeed been active participants in the making of their own history.[79] And during the post-war negotiations the Karen leaders appeared as the traditional Karen elders and were able to communicate the message of a separate nation and state via several mass meetings and the memorials in which proposals and motions were published. When the strategy failed, the leaders left the subaltern Karen in a predicament: there was no neutral position available between separatism and inclusion with which to identify.

Chatterjee has emphasized that 'elite' and 'subaltern' politics have shaped each other and that populism ought not to be read as a sign of unauthenticity:

77. On the process of ethnic categorization see the important theoretical article by Richard Jenkins, 'Rethinking Ethnicity: Identity, Categorization and Power', *Ethnic & Racial Studies*, vol. 17, no. 2, 1994, pp. 197–223.

78. Pierre Bourdieu, *Language and Symbolic Power*, Cambridge: Polity Press, 1992, p. 226.

79. Cf. Ranajit Guha, *Subaltern Studies 2*, 1983, p. 33.

Now, the task is to trace in their mutually conditioned historicities the specific forms that have appeared, on the one hand, in the domain defined by the hegemonic project of nationalist modernity, and on the other, in the numerous fragmented resistances to that normalizing project.[80]

The KNU elite grew out of a colonial middle class, a modern development largely denied to the Burmans – a middle class imitating the British and at the same time being an excluded and scheduled race/ethnic group outside the domain of their white *thakin* ('master') and his Commonwealth Club.[81] The Karen in the KNU reformulated the model of their White Brother within their own imagining. The Burman nationalists, and even SLORC, have rejected the colonial past and the cultural concepts of the white *kala* (foreigner) including democracy and human rights. In both models and conceptions the ethnicism of their former colonial masters are reappearing *as if* it were the existential substance of social life, culture, identity and a precondition of nation and state. Both are undeniable authentic representations of identity in the history of colonial, anti-colonial and post-colonial imaginations of nation and state in Burma.

The problem of those who struggle for democracy in Myanmar is that an antagonistic cultural differentialism has become deeply rooted in every model of nation and state and in social relations and practices. In this process the combination of ethnicism, nationalism and violence has become a decisive substance of individual and social identification – indeed, deadly designations with an impact which we cannot dismiss as unauthentic. The connected trend in the ethnicism of high modernity is the tendency of some Western countries and organizations to support ethnic rebellion and ethnic autonomy whenever they criticize a non-democratic state. Western support to ethnic autonomy is often based on such subjective representations of history as those made by the KNU and other rebel organizations. Their versions of history are more or less based on the colonial Plural Society. This bitter irony of historical imaginations is precisely what Aung San Suu Kyi and her supporters may be up against: one-dimensional identities as dogmatic political models of society preventing a civic pluralism.

---

80. Chatterjee, *Nation and Its Fragments*, pp. 12–13.
81. See Gravers, *Nationalism as Political Paranoia*, on the role of the club in colonial Burma.

CHAPTER TEN

Nationalism Transcending the State: Changing Conceptions of Chinese Identity

Torbjörn Lodén

To discuss 'nationalism' is, as Benjamin Akzin pointed out thrity years ago, to enter into a terminological jungle in which one easily gets lost.[1] Different scholarly disciplines have their own more or less established and more or less peculiar ways of dealing with nationalism. In Chinese studies in the West, the 'culturalism-to-nationalism' thesis provided for a long time the core of a dominating discourse.[2] According to this thesis, China in imperial times was essentially a cultural entity, defined in terms of the traditional, predominantly Confucian high culture, and to be Chinese was in the final analysis the same as to be civilized. The boundaries of the Chinese state were contingent, since the emperor's mandate was to rule 'under heaven', i.e. the

1. Benjamin Akzin, *State and Nation*, London: Hutchinson, 1964, pp. 7–10.

2. This paradigm, which was perhaps most eloquently formulated by Joseph Levenson in his *Confucian China and Its Modern Fate. A Trilogy*, 3 vols, Berkeley: University of California Press, 1968, has informed the mainstream of China scholars dealing with 'China's modern transformation', e.g., John K. Fairbank, Benjamin Schwartz and Mary C. Wright. See Paul A. Cohen, *Discovering History on China: American Historical Writing on the Recent Chinese Past*, New York: Columbia University Press, 1984, and James Harrison, *Modern Chinese Nationalism*, New York: Hunter College of the City of New York, Research Institute on Modern China, n.d. (1969). Also outside the China field many scholars have accepted this thesis as an authoritative interpretation of modern Chinese history; see, e.g., Hugh Seton-Watson, *Nations and States: An Inquiry into the Origins of Nations and the Politics of Nationalism*, Boulder: Westview Press, 1977; Selig S. Harrison, *The Widening Gulf: Asian Nationalism and American Policy*, New York: The Free Press, 1978.

whole world. The ideology of the Chinese empire was universalistic culturalism. Only in the wake of China's encounter with the European powers and
with Japan in the nineteenth century did it become possible to conceptually
separate 'China' and 'Chinese culture'. To save China, even at the possible
expense of traditional high culture, became the first priority. In the language
of the thesis this was the essence of the transition from culturalism to
nationalism.

Only rather recently have scholars started to reconsider the culturalism-
to-nationalism thesis critically. It is the great changes in China after Mao
Zedong and in Europe after the collapse of the Soviet Union that have
triggered this critical re-examination which, from a scholarly point of view,
may seem long overdue.[3]

While highlighting significant aspects of China's historical development,
important issues are also concealed underneath the generalities of the
formulation of the culturalism-to-nationalism thesis; for example, what
roles have in fact ethnicity, culture and politics played in the definition of
Chineseness during various epochs of Chinese history?

Culturalism was indeed a central aspect of Chinese thought from very
early times. For example, the philosopher Mencius (c. 371–c. 289 BC) stated
that the sage-king Shun as well as Duke Wen of Zhou, two major paragons
of virtue in Chinese tradition, came from respectively the Eastern and
Western Yi barbarians; in other words, ethnically foreign they adopted and
developed Sinitic culture.[4] In the words of Professor Ping-ti Ho, this
suggests that:

---

3. See, e.g., James Townsend, 'Chinese Nationalism', *The Australian Journal of Chinese
Affairs*, no. 27, 1992, pp. 97–130; Lucian W. Pye, 'How China's Nationalism was Shang-
haied', *The Australian Journal of Chinese Affairs*, no. 29, 1993, pp. 107–133; Prasenjit
Duara, 'Deconstructing the Chinese Nation', *The Australian Journal of Chinese Affairs*, no.
30, 1993, pp. 1–26. For more recent writings on Chinese nationalism, see also Fong-ching
Chen, 'On Chinese Nationalism: A New Global Perspective', *The Stockholm Journal of
East Asian Studies*, no. 6, 1995, pp. 1–18; K.S. Liao, *Antiforeignism and Modernisation in
China*, Hong Kong: Chinese University Press, 1986; Lucian Pye, 'The Challenge of Mod-
ernization to the Chinese National Identity', *Wei Lun Lecture Series* I, Hong Kong: The
Chinese University, 1992; Jin Yaoji [A. King], 'Minzuzhuyi yu xiandai Zhongguo'
[Nationalism and Modern China], in *Zhongguo shehui yu wenhua* [Chinese Society and
Culture], Hong Kong: Oxford University Press, 1992; Jin Guantao, 'Bainian lai Zhongguo
minzuzhuyi jiegou de yanbian' [Development in the structure of Chinese nationalism during the past century], *Ershiyi shiji* [Twenty-First Century], no. 15, 1993. pp. 50–59. The
contributions to the 1992 conference in Hong Kong have been published in condensed
form in *Ershiyi shiji* [Twenty-First Century], nos. 15 & 16, 1993.

4. *Mong Zi*, 4 B: 1. Cf. *Mencius*, translated with an introduction by D.C. Lau, Harmonds
worth: Penguin Books, 1970, p. 128.

... long before the rise of the Chou [Zhou], the fundamental criterion for defining membership in the Sinitic world was the awareness of a common cultural heritage rather than of true racial or ethnic affinity; for in all likelihood the majority of the ancient peoples of North China took their ethnic affinity for granted.[5]

Now someone might object that since dynastic appellations rather than the word *Zhongguo* (in modern times the most common word for 'China') or some equivalent, was used to refer to the Chinese state in pre-modern times, it is misleading to use English words as 'China' and 'Chinese' to discuss the identity of the people of the Zhou dynasty or of the later unified celestial empire. Even Liang Qichao (1873–1929), a towering intellectual figure of the late nineteenth and early twentieth centuries, deplored the fact that the Chinese themselves had not managed to invent a proper national name for China. In recent times Professor Wang Ermin in Taipei has carefully analysed the occurrences of *Zhongguo* in pre-Qin sources, and he has identified five different meanings of this word.[6] The most frequent meaning turns out to be *Zhuxia*, i.e. the central states of the Zhou dynasty surrounded by barbarian tribes. He finds that 83 per cent of all occurrences carry this meaning. In the early philosophical texts *Mo Zi*, *Mencius* and *Zhuang Zi*, he finds examples of *Zhongguo* referring to China as an area inhabited by one and the same ethnic group tied together by kinship and culture. He concludes that although never an official appellation of the Chinese state, the word *Zhongguo* was in fact used to designate the Chinese people united by kinship and culture as early as before China's unification under the Qin dynasty in 221 BC and that it has then been so used throughout history.

The early legends about the ancient world describe the transition from succession according to kinship to succession according to competence. The sage-king Yao considered his own son too incompetent and therefore abdicated in favour of the virtuous Shun, who in turn was succeeded not by his son but by Yu who regulated the flood. The principle of succession according to competence rather than kinship served to reinforce the idea that cultural affinity is more important than ethnic community.[7]

---

5. Ping-ti Ho, *The Cradle of the East*, Hong Kong, Chicago & London: The Chinese University of Hong Kong and the University of Chicago Press, 1975, p. 344.

6. Cf. Wang Ermin, '"Zhongguo" mingcheng suyuan ji qi jindai quanshi' [The origin of the notion 'China' and its modern interpretation], in Wang Ermin, *Zhongguo jindai sixiangshi lun* [Essays on Modern Chinese Thought], Taipei: Huashi chubanshe, 1977, pp. 441–482.

7. For a classical formulation of the legend of Yao, Shun and Yu, see the first chapter 'Wu Di benji' [The basic annals of the Five Emperors] of Sima Qian's *Shiji* [Records of the Historian]; French translation Édouard Chavannes, *Les mémoires historiques de Se-ma Ts'ien*, reprint Leiden: E.J. Brill, 1967, pp. 42–96. See also Fan Wenlan, *Zhongguo tongshi jianbian* [A simplified general history of China], vol. 1, fourth edition, Beijing: Renmin chubanshe, 1964, pp. 92ff.

Indeed, this kind of culturalism is also an essential aspect of the notion of the Mandate of Heaven. He who was most qualified to emulate the Way of Heaven and implement the Kingly Way should receive the Mandate of Heaven to rule as Son of Heaven, irrespective of his ethnic identity. (In this context, 'she' was just not conceivable.)[8]

In terms of space, the mandate was to rule under Heaven (i.e. the whole world), and the world over which the Son of Heaven ruled was conceived as a number of quadratic domains, like Chinese boxes, with the royal domain in the middle. In sources dating back to the first millennium BC this idea of a series of domains is formulated in slightly different ways, but the basic idea is the same: the rule of the Son of Heaven radiates from the centre and 'extends to the four seas', which mark the end of the known world, while in the outer boxes reside barbarian peoples who remain to be civilized, i.e. sinicized.[9]

Throughout pre-modern Chinese history the acculturation of barbarians remained a recurring theme. Obviously this kind of culturalism could well serve an empire with universalistic pretensions. For a ruler in possession of the Mandate of Heaven, no ethnic diversity could justify political division. Yet there is something paradoxical here: the view of cultural commonality as more important than ethnic affinity co-existed in Chinese tradition with a focus on lineage and family relations. The Confucian tradition, which provided the major ingredients of the official discourse in the Chinese empire, took the family as a microcosm of the world. The ideal relations within the family provided a model for social relations. Ruler and subject should relate to one another as father and son.

---

8. Concerning the Mandate of Heaven, see Benjamin I. Schwartz, *The World of Thought in Ancient China*, Cambridge: Harvard University Press, 1985, pp. 39ff.

9. The *Shujing* [The Book of Documents] speaks about 'five domains' [*wufu*], the outermost of which was the 'wild domain' inhabited by the the the Man barbarians and by criminals undergoing banishment. The *Guoyu* [Narratives of the States] speaks about seven domains out of which the four outermost are inhabited by barbarians. The *Zhouli* [The Rites of Zhou] identify ten domains. See Bernhard Karlgren, *The Book of Documents*, Stockholm: The Museum of Far Eastern Antiquities, 1950, p. 18, reprint from *The Bulletin of the Museum of Far Eastern Antiquities*, no. 22, 1950; Bernhard Karlgren *Glosses on the Book of Documents*, Stockholm: The Museum of Far Eastern Antiquities, 1970, pp. 158ff., reprint from *The Bulletin of the Museum of Far Eastern Antiquities*, no. 20, 1948; James Legge, *The Chinese Classics*, vol. III The Shoo King, Taipei: Southern Materials Centre Inc. 1985, pp. 142–151, reprint of the original edition published by Henry Frowde in London, 1865. See also Claudius C. Müller, 'Die Herausbildung der Gegensätze: Chinesen und Barbaren in der frühen Zeit (1. Jahrtausend v. Chr. bis 220 n. Chr.)', in Wolfgang Bauer (ed.), *China und die Fremden. 3000 Jahre Auseinandersetzung in Krieg und Frieden*, München: C.H. Beck'sche Verlagsbuchhandlung, 1980, pp. 43–76 and Lien-sheng Yang, 'Historical Notes on the Chinese World Order', in John K. Fairbank (ed.), *The Chinese World Order*, Cambridge: Harvard University Press, 1968, pp. 20–33.

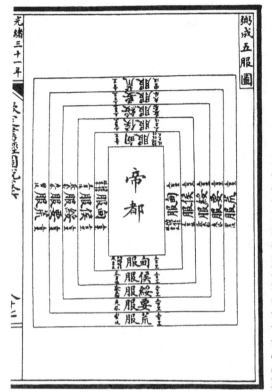

Figure 5: Traditional conception of Chinese culture radiating from the imperial centre. Proceeding outwards from the metropolitan area, we have (1) the royal domains, (2) the lands of the tributary feudal princes and lords, (3) the zone of pacification, i.e. the marches, where Chinese civilization was in the process of being adopted, and (5) the zone of cultureless savagery.

The focus on the family naturally meant close attention to genealogy. The first chapters of Sima Qian's *Records of the Historian*, the major work on Chinese history from the earliest time to the Han dynasty compiled in the first century BC, begins with a genealogy of rulers beginning from the legendary ancient past. In written sources as well as in the consciousness of Chinese people throughout the centuries, Huangdi (the Yellow Emperor with the clan name Ji) and Yandi (Emperor Yan with the clan name Jiang) have been conceived as the forefathers of the Chinese people. The descendants of Huangdi and Yandi were considered to have later amalgamated with parts of the barbarian peoples Yi, Li, and Miao and then formed the people which in the Zhou was sometimes called *Hua* and which from the Han dynasty has been referred to as *Han*.[10]

The ethnic distinction between the sedentary lineages of central China, engaging in agriculture, and the barbarian nomadic tribes on the

---

10. See Fan Wenlan, 'The origin of the notion "China"', pp. 88–92.

frontiers of Chinese society was most probably an important part of Chinese consciousness throughout the pre-modern period.[11] The ethnic and cultural distinctions tended to coincide, so the difference between the two was a difference of connotation rather than of denotation. It thus seems that to the extent that the culturalism-to-nationalism thesis leaves out the ethnic dimension under culturalism, this is misleading; rather one could say that culturalism meant that the cultural distinctions were considered by some chroniclers and philosophers to be more important than the ethnic ones.

We may discern a polarity or a tension between an ethnic and a culturalistic orientation which have co-existed throughout Chinese history and have been given different emphases at different times according to the needs of powerholders and ideologists. We may speak of a movement between the pole of ethnicity, stressing the importance of common descent, and the pole of culturalism, emphasizing cultural qualities that can be acquired. More research on the interplay of these orientations in pre-modern Chinese thought is much needed, but we may still surmise that in the official discourse of the empire throughout the centuries the culturalistic orientation has been dominant.

The orientation of ethnicity has often, but not exclusively, found expression in attacks on the legitimacy of 'barbarian' rule in China. For example, Zhu Yuanzhang (1328–98), later to become the first emperor of the Ming dynasty (1368–1644), questioned the rule of the Mongolian Yuan dynasty (1260–1368) in such terms: 'As for our Chinese people, Heaven must appoint a person from China to achieve stability – how could they be ruled by barbarians?' Hsiao Kung-ch'üan (Xiao Gongquan), a leading scholar in the field of Chinese political thought, refers to this statement as 'the first proclamation in two thousand years of a national revolution' and 'the first expression of a concept of a national state in China'.[12] Zhu Yuanzhang's notion was later elaborated by the scholar Fang Xiaoru (1357–1402).

In the sixteenth century the ethnic orientation found forceful and philosophically sophisticated expression in the thought of Wang Fuzhi (1619–92), who emphasized the distinction between 'Chinese' (here *Huaxia* in his parlance) and 'barbarian' (*yidi* or *rongdi*) as different in a way that tempts people in the modern world to use the word 'race' to characterize this distinction:

---

11. The classical work on the relationship between the Chinese and the nomadic tribes surrounding them is Owen Lattimore, *Inner Asian Frontiers of China*, London and New York: Oxford University Press, 1940.

12. See Xiao Gongquan, *Zhongguo zhengzhi sixiang shi* [A History of Chinese Political Thought], Taipei: Zhongguo wenhua xueyuan chubanbu, 1970, vol. 2, p. 544.

> Now man partakes of yin and yang, food and breath, equally with other things, and yet he cannot but be distinguished absolutely from other things; the Chinese in their bone structure, sense organs, gregariousness and exclusiveness, are no different from the barbarians, and yet they must be distinguished absolutely from the barbarians. Why is this so? Because if man does not mark himself off from things, then the principle of Heaven is violated. If the Chinese do not mark themselves off from the barbarians, then the principle of earth is violated.[13]

Wang's ideological purpose was no doubt to question the legitimacy of Manchu rule in China.[14]

The twin themes of ethnicity and culturalism were articulated by the Confucian elite, either by powerholders who were preoccupied with the legitimacy of the prevailing order or by critics who questioned this legitimacy. Statements regarding identity were ideological and designed to serve social and political interests.

Conceptions among the elite of Chinese identity in pre-modern China may be studied from the texts handed down from traditional Chinese high culture. Much work remains to be done, however. In particular it seems important to analyse in much greater detail than has yet been done the actual meaning of key concepts – such as *Zhongguo*, *Hua*, *Xia*, *Han*, etc. – at different times in Chinese history.[15] As for identity conceptions outside the elite, we know rather little, and this lacuna in our knowledge will be exceedingly difficult to fill because of the paucity of material reflecting the attitudes of ordinary people. It is important not to forget about this lacuna since it should alert us to the possibility that some of the attitudes we do meet in the historical material may have been of little or no concern to the population at large.

In the modern period, when China has been in the process of finding her place as a member of the family of nations, the twin themes of ethnicity and culturalism in pre-modern China have provided sources for articulating different kinds of nationalism.

---

13. Quotation from the opening sections of Wang Fuzhi's *Huangshu* [The Yellow Book]; I have here used the rather free but not misleading translation found in Wm. Theodor de Bary, Wing-tsit Chan and Burton Watson (eds), *Sources of Chinese Tradition*, vol. I, New York: Columbia University Press, 1960, pp. 542–543.

14. Concerning Wang Fuzhi's proto-nationalism, see Ernstjoachim Vierheller, *Nation und Elite im Denken von Wang Fuzhi* (1619–1692), Hamburg: Mitteilungen der Gesellschaft für Natur- und Völkerkunde Ostasiens, Band XLIX, 1968.

15. In this context we have reason to look forward to the results of the research that Harald Bøckman of the University of Oslo is carrying out on conceptions of Chineseness in Chinese history.

Entering the Family of Nation

China's confrontation with the Western Powers and Japan in the nineteenth century made it necessary to relinquish the universalistic pretensions of the empire and to seek entrance into the family of nations, or the international system of states, as one sovereign state among others.[16] This process, which began in the latter half of the nineteenth century, is a key aspect of that transformation and search for modernization which John King Fairbank referred to as the Great Chinese Revolution, and which has set the agenda for politics and culture in China up to the contemporary period. During the last two decades it has been fashionable, and fruitful too, to attempt to revise Fairbank's view of China's modernization as largely a response to the West and to seek for the roots of China's modern transformation in indigenous tradition rather than in foreign influence in much the same way as in other former colonies in Asia. Yet as far as I can see, the search for modernization has, in this fundamental sense, indeed been 'a response to the West'.[17]

In the cultural arena there developed increasingly radical calls for a re-evaluation of indigenous traditions and for Westernization. In an early phase of this process of radicalization, dating back to the latter half of the nineteenth century, we meet the formula of preserving 'Chinese learning' (*zhongxue*), mainly Confucianism as 'essence' (*ti*) while adopting 'Western learning' (*xixue*), mainly the natural sciences and technology, as a 'means' (*yong*).

In this early phase we find the tendency to project Western ideas, particularly the notions of cultural and social evolution, on to classical Chinese texts and even attempts to derive Western culture from China: one prominent scholar pointed out that the famous Westerner Moses was none other than the ancient Chinese philosopher Mo Zi; while another scholar attributed the success of Christianity in the West to the 'fact' that Jesus had somehow got hold of the Confucian classics and translated them into Latin.[18] This was a few years before August Strindberg in Stockholm was busy deriving the Chinese language from Swedish.

---

16. For an illuminating study of the diplomatic aspects of this process, see Immanuel C.Y. Hsü, *China's Entrance into the Family of Nations: The Diplomatic Phase, 1858–1880*, Cambridge: Harvard University Press, 1968.

17. Cf. John King Fairbank, *The Great Chinese Revolution, 1800–1985*, New York: Harper & Row, 1986.

18. The former view was espoused by Wei Yuan (1794–1856) and the latter by, among others, Xue Fucheng (1838–94). See Jerome Ch'en, *China and the West: Society and Culture 1815–1937*, London: Hutchinson & Co., 1979, pp. 65ff.

In the 1910s this process ushered in the call for the rejection of Confucianism and even for 'total Westernization'.[19] In 1918 Professor Qian Xuantong (1887–1939), a leading scholar at Beijing University, went so far as to suggest in a letter to Chen Duxiu (1880–1939), later to become the first leader of the Chinese Communist Party, that the Chinese script was not fit to convey the ideas of the modern age. And Chen Duxiu agreed: 'The Chinese script can hardly convey new things and new ideas, and it is the nest of rotten and poisonous thought. Abandoning it is no cause for regret.'[20]

Beginning in the late nineteenth century, Western intellectual currents were discussed as possible ingredients of a recipe for the regeneration of a wealthy and powerful China. Numerous Western works were translated into Chinese. Yan Fu (1853–1921) translated scholarly writings by Adam Smith, John Stuart Mill, Herbert Spencer and others.[21] Lin Shu (1852–1924), basing himself on oral translations made by his collaborators, translated literary works by Dickens, Alexander Dumas (his rendering of *La Dame aux Camélias* became particularly famous), H. Rider Haggard, Sir Walter Scott, Shakespeare and others.[22]

A number of Western concepts – society, nation, citizen, individual, etc. – were rendered into Chinese by means of characters whose original meanings were more or less distant from the new concepts. Even if these concepts were more or less sinicized when rendered into Chinese, this cultural translation must still be understood as a process of Westernization. Around 1920 a language reform was undertaken replacing the classical written language *wenyan*, which had been the main vehicle of high Chinese culture, with a new written language based on the classical vernacular *baihua*, which had been the medium of classical fiction as we meet it in, for example, novels such as *The Dream of the Red Chamber* and which was close to the spoken language of northern China. The language reform and the

19. See in this context Chow Tse-tsung, *The May Fourth Movement: Intellectual Revolution in Modern China, 1915–1924*, Cambridge: Harvard University Press, 1963.

20. Qian Xuantong, 'Zhongguo jinhou zhi wenzi wenti' [The Question of the Script in China in the Future], letter to Chen Duxiu dated 14 March 1918 and published in *Xin Qingnian* [New Youth], vol. 4, no. 4, 15 April 1918; pp. 350–56. Chen Duxiu's answer dated 15 April was published in the same issue of *Xin Qingnian*. Both letters are reprinted in *Duxiu wencun* [(Chen) Duxiu's Collected Writings], vol. 3, Shanghai, Yadong tushuguan, 1922, pp. 150–160.

21. Concerning Yan Fu, see Benjamin Schwartz, *In Search of Wealth and Power: Yen Fu and the West*, Cambridge: Harvard University Press, 1964.

22. Concerning Lin Shu, see Leo Ou-fan Lee, *The Romantic Generation of Modern Chinese Writers*, Cambridge: Harvard University Press, 1973, pp. 41–57.

emergence of a new written medium, which came to be referred to as 'the national language' (*guoyu*) served to underline the separation between traditional Chinese high culture and China.[23]

Entering the family of nations, China needed a new identity: the various attempts to construe this within the international system provide the content of Chinese nationalism, as understood by the advocates of the culturalism-to-nationalism thesis and others, from the late nineteenth century up until our own time. As John Fitzgerald convincingly argues in a recent article, the ruling elite needed to define a national identity as a means to regenerate a strong and unified state.[24] In other words, nationalism emerged as part of the new state formation. Varieties of this state nationalism, for which national identity is a means and a strong state is the end, has dominated political discourse in China in this century. In twentieth-century China one does not find so much a nation seeking to set up a state but rather the state needing to find a nation.

The advocates of the culturalism-to-nationalism thesis captured one essential aspect of the emergence of state nationalism by drawing attention to the fact that this was a process of separating, for the first time in Chinese history, the concepts of China and Chinese identity on the one hand and traditional high culture on the other: 'saving China' was given the highest priority and it became conceivable that China could be saved at the expense of traditional Chinese culture. However, this separation should not be understood to mean that state nationalism did not make use of traditional high culture to define the Chinese national identity. If we consider the various attempts to construe a new identity for China as a nation-state, we shall see that the twin themes of ethnicity and culturalism appeared again, with new significance.

A school of early culturalistic nationalists, with Liang Qichao as the most eloquent spokesman, defined the national identity primarily in terms of the consciousness of the Chinese citizen. He explicitly and in polemics against Zhang Taiyan (1869–1936) and others took exception to the idea of an ethnically or racially defined national identity and proposed a 'great nationalism' which would encompass the several ethnic groups of China.

---

23. Concerning the language reform, see John De Francis, *Nationalism and Language Reform in China*, Princeton: Princeton University Press, 1950. See also Edward Gunn, *Rewriting Chinese: Style and Innovation in Twentieth-Century Chinese Prose*, Stanford: Stanford University Press, 1991.

24. See John Fitzgerald, 'The Nationless State: The Search for a Nation in Modern Chinese Nationalism', *The Australian Journal of Chinese Affairs*, no. 33, 1995, pp. 75–104.

This notion of a 'Chinese nation' including several ethnic groups has later been made use of by the communists, according to whose ideology the Han people and the national minorities together form the Chinese identity.[25]

On the other hand a school of ethnicist nationalists, with Zhang Taiyan as the pioneering figure, have argued, much in the vein of Wang Fuzhi, that Chinese identity is primarily based on ethnic commonality. A fierce opponent of Manchu rule in China, he criticized the culturalistic school of Liang Qichao and others for not emphasizing sufficiently the distinction between the Chinese and barbarians. In his famous article 'Zhonghua minguo jie' (Explaining the Republic of China), published in 1907, he wrote:

> During the Han and the period before that, the Chinese did not regard the barbarian tribes as peers and therefore there is no example of barbarians being referred to as men in the records ...

> The Spring and Autumn Annals cite instances of degrading *Xia* states to the level of barbarians, but there is no example of barbarian states being included among the *Xia* states. When the Qi state used barbarian rites, there was a record of it being demoted as a barbarian state. In this respect, how could there be a case of regarding the Manchus as Chinese? [26]

However, Zhang's complex arguments about the Chinese identity demonstrate that he was also aware of and wished to uphold cultural characteristics of the Chinese identity, and he did not reject the notion of Chinese assimilation of barbarians:

> It is only possible to allow alien races to assimilate with us when the sovereignty is in our hands; that would be sufficient for accepting them. The assimilation of the Manchus has not been achieved because they have been subject to our control but because they have overthrown and suppressed us. These two things cannot be compared, it is similar to the difference between marriage and robbery. According to the logic of marriage, the bride belongs to us and she will have to assimilate with us. According to the logic of robbery, they occupy the

25. Concerning Liang Qichao, see Hao Chang, *Liang Ch'i-ch'ao and Intellectual Transition in China, 1890–1907*, Cambridge: Harvard University Press, 1971; Joseph Levenson, *Liang Ch'i-ch'ao and the Mind of Modern China*, Cambridge: Harvard University Press, 1953; and Philip Huang, *Liang Ch'i-ch'ao and Modern Chinese Liberalism*, Seattle: University of Washington Press, 1972.
26. Zhang Taiyan, 'Zhonghua minguo jie' [Explaining the Republic of China], in *Zhang Taiyan quanji*, vol. 4, Shanghai: Shanghai renmin chubanshe, 1985, pp. 254–255. This article was originally published in *Minbao* , no. 15, 5 July 5 1907, pp. 1–17. Pär Cassel, a student of Chinese in Stockholm, has prepared a complete and annotated, as yet unpublished, translation of this article which I use here with his permission. Concerning Zhang Taiyan's nationalism, see also Kauko Laitinen, *Chinese Nationalism in the Late Qing Dynasty: Zhang Binglin as an Anti-Manchu Propagandist*, London: Curzon Press, 1990, NIAS Monograph Series, no. 57.

house of our emperor and penetrate the innermost rooms of his concubines, and in this way they can assimilate with us, but it is self-evident that we will hate them ... If we beat the enemy and win a victory so that the Manchu *Khan* leave ... then we could do the same thing as in Japan and in Siam, i.e. regard them as people of our race.[27]

In Zhang's writings we may hear echoes of the ancient notion of China as being made up of a series of domains with the emperor in the middle. Territories bordering on China proper and inhabited by barbarians should be incoporated and the peoples assimilated with the Chinese. But Zhang is concerned with the order of priorities:

> Thus, from the standpoint of regulating the borders of the Republic of China, the two prefectures Vietnam and Korea must be recovered and the district Burma follows slightly behind in priority; as for Tibet, the Hui areas and Mongolia, let them decide themselves if they want to be incorporated or rejected.

> However, this task has both easy and difficult aspects. To complete this task is not a straightforward, but a tortuous process, and what is easy to achieve might be somewhat contrary to our priorities. Today I am afraid that the Republic of China is unable to restore the borders of the pre-Han period, and it is necessary to take the provincial division of Ming as the basis, except with regard to Burma. The restoration of Vietnam and Korea is not an easy task. Not even the restoration of Burma can be accomplished at once ... Their assimilation also has different degrees in difficulty.

> As regards the assimilation of language and writing, there are a lot of Hans in Xinjiang and the Huis are more intelligent than the Mongols, so the teaching will easily penetrate their region.[28]

The different approaches to Chinese identity of Liang Qichao and Zhang Taiyan implied a difference in political focus: Liang was concerned with fostering as broad a Chinese unity as possible to resist foreign threats while Zhang was more preoccupied with throwing off the yoke of barbarian Manchu rule.

The Formation of National Identity

The ethnic approach to Chinese identity was also a key feature of Sun Yat-sen's nationalism as advocated in his Three Principles of the People, which have played a central role for the Guomindang ideology. While Liang Qichao deplored the lack of an explicit distinction in Chinese tradition between state and nation, Sun Yat-sen argued that race and state had been

---

27. Zhang Taiyan, 'Zhonghua minguo jie', pp. 255–256.
28. *Ibid*, pp. 256–257.

congruent in pre-modern China: 'China, since the Qin and Han dynasties, has been developing a single state out of a single race, while foreign countries have developed many states from one race and have included many nationalities within one state.' Sun maintained that his own Principle of Nationalism was the same as the 'doctrine of the state'.[29] Defining the national identity, whether in terms of culturalism or ethnicity, was seen as a central aspect of building a strong state as a means to save China.

In the ideology of the Chinese communists, the concept of class has from the beginning played a key role in defining Chinese identity, and class came increasingly to be defined in terms of consciousness rather than actual position in the production process. One might think that emphasizing class distinctions would threaten the sense of national identity.[30] Indeed, class analysis as undertaken by Marx and Engels construed class identity as international and transcending national boundaries and, to be sure, in China the Guomindang criticized the communists' focus on class as unpatriotic. For example, Chiang Kai-shek said: 'It is only too clear now that Communists can never have any sense of loyalty to their own country: they are devoid of patriotism or national consciousness. In fact they have no love for their country but they will deliberately work against national interests.'[31]

The Guomindang even went so far as to consider it more patriotic to fight the communists than the Japanese invaders. However, the communist class analysis was in fact used to define a national identity and to serve nationalistic purposes. For example, in their explication of the concept of class, the communists sometimes emphasized that class identity transcended regional differences. So although in theory there is certainly a tension between the idea of antagonistic class contradictions and national unity, in practice class analysis was an instrument for defining a national identity that could serve as a basis of a strong Chinese state represented by the one-party dictatorship exercised by the Communist Party. Indeed, it remains a widely shared belief that the patriotism that the communists demonstrated in fighting the Japanese invasion contributed decisively to their victory over the Guomindang.[32]

29. Sun Yat-sen, *San Min Chu I, The Three Principles of the People*, translated by Frank W. Price and edited by L.T. Chen, Chungking: Ministry of Information, 1943, p. 6; quoted from Fitzgerald, 'The Nationless State', p. 88.

30. Concerning Marxism and nationalism, see Germaine A. Hoston, *The State, Identity, and the National Question in China and Japan*, Princeton: Princeton University Prress, 1994.

31. Chiang Kai-shek, *Soviet Russia in China*, New York: Farr, Strauss and Cudahy, 1968, pp. 88–89; quoted from Fitzgerald, 'The Nationless State', p. 97

32. For a classical formulation of this thesis, see Chalmers A. Johnson, *Peasant Nationalism and Communist Power: the Emergence of Revolutionary China, 1937–1945*, Stanford: Stanford University Press (2nd rev. ed. 1966).

The use of class as a defining characteristic of national identity was an expression of the extreme politicizing of the Maoist discourse. As we have seen, even before the communist era, nationalism appeared mainly as a tool for the state: the national identity was defined so as to contribute as effectively as possible to strengthening the state. Politics took precedence in defining national identity. To define the political identity in national terms signified even more extreme politicizing.

The period in Chinese history from the break-up of the empire to the establishment of the People's Republic of China was largely a period of dissolution of the traditional order. During these decades there was no unifying intellectual orthodoxy other than the search for a recipe for the regeneration of a powerful, affluent and respected China. After 1949 a new order with a new ideological orthodoxy emerged. 'Marxism Leninism Mao Zedong Thought' with its peculiar blend of elements from Chinese and Western traditions meant the return to a kind of imperial normality. Just like the role Confucianism had played earlier, the new orthodoxy provided the source of legitimacy for the state and its actions and also the basic discourse for scholarship and literature. But whereas the Confucian orthodoxy had been the ideology of a universalistic empire, in theory not recognizing China as a member of an international system, the Maoist orthodoxy, while also providing a universalistic model of social development, was 'nationalistic' in the sense that it was first and foremost preoccupied with saving China from foreign domination and with developing China into a strong and respected member of the international system of states.

Although the state nationalism of the communist party-state was primarily concerned with the wealth and power of the People's Republic of China as a member of the international system of states, it was also important for the ideologues of the communist party-state to provide space within the official discourse for the 'Chinese compatriots' in Taiwan and Hong Kong and Macao as well as for the 'overseas Chinese'. According to the Maoist discourse, Taiwan, Hong Kong and Macao should properly be part of the People's Republic and people there were considered Chinese.[33] In the case of the overseas Chinese in other parts of the world, they were defined as Chinese by means of ethnic and cultural criteria. It is probably fair to say that there was a tension between the Maoist discourse of state nationalism

---

33. Another thing is that the PRC regime was not eager at first to retrieve Hong Kong and Macao as soon as possible. In the case of Macao, the regime seems even to have turned down an offer by the new Portuguese regime after the fall of the Salazar regime to return Macao immediately to the PRC.

and the classification of the overseas Chinese, but the regime was generally cautious not to sever ties with the overseas Chinese community.[34]

National Identity and Chinese Culture

Nationalism in China as in Europe is associated with the emergence of a sovereign state, often called 'nation-state', which together with other nation-states constitute 'the family of nations' or an international system of states. But the contexts are different.

The European 'nation-states' emerged in the context of the splitting-up of a larger unit into sub-units. The larger unit was the Roman empire and its successors, and the division referred specifically to a kind of 'national liberation' from the supranational kings, emperors and churches. The nation-states may be seen as new organizational forms emerging in the wake of (a process of several centuries) the break-up of the universalistic Roman empire.

In China the emergence of the 'nation-state' (in fact a multinational state) was not connected with the division of the larger unit of China into sub-units. Rather the Chinese nation-state should be seen as the response to a perceived threat to China's survival, a threat which was manifested most acutely as foreign aggression, but which was also rooted in the internal weaknesses and problems of late imperial China.

In Europe, nationalism has drawn on local European sources for defining the nation within the larger context of Europe in terms of a national culture, often in terms of a national language. At the time of the New Culture Movement in the early twentieth century, Chinese intellectuals often pointed to Europe as a model to emulate, particularly when it came to replacing the old literary language *wenyan* – the Latin of China – with the vernacular *baihua* which was compared to the national languages in Europe.[35] But this comparison was rather strained, since in China it was never really the question of splitting up the unifying high culture of the empire into local, national cultures which would define new nation-states.

---

34. Concerning the overseas Chinese, see, e.g., Stephen FitzGerald, *China and the Overseas Chinese: A Study of Peking's Changing Policy*, Cambridge: Cambridge University Press, 1972; Wang Gung-wu, 'Greater China and the Chinese Overseas', *China Quarterly*, no. 136, December 1993, pp. 926–948; Yeu-farn Wang, 'The National Identity of the Southeast Asian Chinese', Working Paper 35, Stockholm: Centre for Pacific Asia Studies, 1994.

35. Hu Shi (1891–1962) is probably the best example of this. See, e.g., his *The Chinese Renaissance*, Chicago: Chicago University Press, 1934.

In Europe the nation-state provided the setting for the development of individualism. Not that the European nation-state necessarily produces individualism, but, fortuitously or not, it was the nation-state that saw the emergence of industrialism, urbanization, the rise of a bourgeoisie and of a liberal ideology built on the rights of the individual citizen. In China, on the other hand, nationalism has rather been a weapon to combat individualism. The necessary focus on the state was considered to preclude individualism. To paraphrase the Chinese historian Li Zehou, the ideals of the liberation of the individual associated with the European Enlightenment were sacrificed in China in the name of national salvation.[36]

To repeat, the emergence of Chinese nationalism has been a process of conceptually separating China and traditional Chinese high culture, which would make it possible to reject those aspects of the cultural legacy that stood in the way of China's development and entrance as a respected member into the family of nations. However, this must not be understood as a continuing process of de-sinicization. First, the very preoccupation with saving China – albeit at the expense of acertain spects of Chinese culture – was rooted in a strong sense of ethnic *and* cultural identity; in other words, why the fuss about saving China, if Chineseness were unimportant? Second, in the process of conceptually separating China from traditional Chinese high culture, aspects of this high culture, as re-interpreted according to the formulas of intellectual currents imported from the West (pragmatism, analytical philosophy, Liberalism, Marxism, etc.), were integrated with the various alternatives of a New Culture proposed for a New China. This dialectic of keeping by rejecting is a central theme in twentieth century Chinese intellectual history; this was also the profound insight of Joseph Levenson in his once very influential, now often neglected, *magnum opus*, the *Confucian China and its Modern Fate*.[37]

The sense of ethnic and cultural identity has been and remains a source of Han Chinese identity. The relationship between the Han Chinese and the so-called national minorities is to this day perceived as a relationship between different cultures; too often it is seen as a relationship between a superior Han culture and inferior minority cultures. Officially, attempts are made to construe a unifying discourse of national identity to encompass the whole of China, but such definitions are only part of a very thin layer of

---

36. See Li Zehou, 'Qimeng yu jiuwang de shuangchong bianzou' [Double Variations on Enlightenment and National Salvation], in Li Zehou, *Zhongguo xiandai sixiangshi lun* [Essays on Modern Chinese Thought], Beijing: Dongfang chubanshe, 1987, pp. 7–49.

37. Three vols, Berkeley: University of California Press, 1958–65.

ideology. The relationship between the Han Chinese and the national minorities remains unequal and largely characterized by attempts of the Han Chinese to 'civilize' the minorities by inculcating them with Han Chinese national culture.

Contradictions in Contemporary Identity

The modernization programme enacted in the late 1970s after Mao Zedong's death, with its dual emphasis on internal reform and opening up to the outside world, has unleashed forces that are bringing about a transformation of Chinese culture and society which may be more revolutionary than the accomplishments of any previous revolution. China has entered into a phase of deconstruction of the prevailing intellectual and cultural orthodoxy, and this deconstruction concerns, among other things, state nationalism.

The modernization programme prescribed a series of measures which broke radically with the earlier line of 'regeneration through self-reliance' (*zili gengsheng*) by, for example, focusing on the importance of foreign trade and particularly the import of advanced foreign technology.

As a result of this programme, China has now entered a new phase of modernization, which is characterized externally by relations and cooperation with foreign countries or industries which lead to interdependence rather than total independence and sovereignty. Internally, there is a greater degree of pluralism and a shift of emphasis away from the party-state to localities and to certain groups, organizations and enterprises situated between the state and the individual, in the sector often loosely referred to as 'civil society'.

The modernization programme meant a radical departure from the Maoist policies of the mid 1970s. The shift was initiated from the top echelons of power whose ideologues attempted to anchor the reforms in Mao Zedong Thought, which they described as not totally identical with all ideas of the person Mao Zedong. This was probably done in order to maintain stability; for anyone familiar with Chinese politics it was obvious that the content of the modernization programme was radically different from the earlier Maoist orthodoxy. But the new leadership considered it crucial to maintain the political and ideological control of the Communist Party, and so it also needed an ideological orthodoxy. Endless efforts went into formulating the ideology legitimizing the new policies. For the formulation of the new ideological tenets the party made use of veteran ideologists such as Hu Qiaomu and Zhou Yang but also of more independent and free-thinking scholars, intellectuals and writers such as Su Shaozhi and Yan Jiaqi. One reason why the party leaders offered the intellectual community more freedom than ever before in the People's Republic of China was probably that they expected that the new ideas could be used to formulate the intellectual orthodoxy of the post-Mao era. To a certain extent this was a successful strategy: the think-tanks of Deng Xiaoping, Hu Yaobang, Zhao Ziyang and other top leaders did produce policy formulations that were on the one hand innovative while, on the other, they found legitimacy in the terms of 'Marxism Leninism Mao Zedong Thought'. But in the process, forces were set free that the party could no longer control. So for the first time in the history of the People's Republic of China there emerged in the 1980s a dichotomization between the official ideological discourse which, for that matter, expressed contradictions within the party elite, and various forms of more or less independent discourse outside the control of the party.

One way to describe the thrust of the modernization policies is to say that they have shrunk the realm of the party-state. Agriculture has in practice been decollectivized, and in the industrial sector the sphere of state enterprises is shrinking year by year, month by month, day by day. A shrinking arena for the party-state does not necessarily mean a *weakening* of the party and the state. A strong economy, although not directly controlled by the party and the state, could serve to strengthen the party-state, just as economic difficulties in a country often tend to weaken the government. In the Chinese case, however, it seems that the Communist Party *is* paying a high price for the implementation of its modernization programme in terms of decreasing power and diminishing influence.

As I have already suggested, the shrinking of the party-state has some very important consequences for intellectual and cultural life in China. It has opened up space for different voices to engage in debate. In the words of Liu Zaifu, the monologue of the years of the Maoist orthodoxy has given way to polyphony.[38] The party-state no longer monopolizes cultural discourse.[39]

One central feature of post-Mao Chinese thought is the problematization of the relationship between the strength of the state, on the one hand, and the well-being of the people, on the other hand. Modern Chinese history up until the death of Mao Zedong had largely been a quest for the

---

38. Liu Zaifu, 'Cong dubai de shidai dao fudiao de shidai' [From the Era of Monologue to the Era of Polyphony], in Liu Zaifu, *Fangzhu zhushen* [Exiling the Gods], Hong Kong: Tiandi tushu youxian gongsi, 1994, pp. 3–24.

39. For a stimulating collection of articles on contemporary Chinese identity, see 'The Living Tree: the Changing Meaning of Being Chinese Today', special issue of *Daedalus*, Spring 1991.

wealth and power of the state as a means of saving China, and communist
nationalism recognized no conflict between the wealth and power of the state
and the well-being of the Chinese people, let alone individual human beings
in China. In post-Mao China, on the other hand, the tension between these two
dimensions of the modernization process has very much come to the foreground,
and this problematization undermines the state nationalism of earlier years.

The state hegemony is questioned in different fields of culture. From
his position as a cultural exile, Liu Zaifu goes so far as to call for 'the exiling
of the Chinese state'.[40] This call challenges the very core of state nationalism:
the idea that nationalism and state relate as means and end; that national
identity should be defined so as to contribute as effectively as possible towards
strengthening the state. Liu's call for exiling the state is a call for a reversal of
priorities and for recognizing the state as a means rather than an end. It is my
belief, and the main idea in this chapter, that this reversal heralds profound
changes in the Chinese discourse on nationalism and that these changes may
have far-reaching impact, also beyond issues related directly to nationalism.

Globalization is one central feature of post-Mao China. Of course, no
matter how we define 'globalization', we can hardly claim that it refers to
phenomena that began only in the last two decades. But during these years
the contacts between China and the outside world have increased so rapidly
and taken on such dimensions that China's integration with the rest of the
world is acquiring new significance. As far as nationalism is concerned,
globalization finds different and conflicting ideological expressions.

In order to interpret the different views of globalization, Westernization, Chinese traditions, etc., articulated in post-Mao China, it is essential to
keep in mind the dichotomization between official and unofficial forms of
discourse. In practice it may be difficult to draw the line between these two
arenas of discourse; many scholars and intellectuals still try to accommodate
to the party-state. Yet this separation is an important distinguishing feature
of post-Mao China. Until the late 1970s hardly any intellectual dialogue
took place in the People's Republic of China outside the framework defined
by the party-state, whereas the fervent search for authentic expression of
personal views among intellectuals is one characteristic feature of post-Mao
culture. Party-state ideology is becoming increasingly divorced from
individual human beings. Even officials who professionally represent the
state tend in private conversations to 'open up a distance' – to use a

---

40. Liu Zaifu, 'Literature Exiling the State', *The Stockholm Journal of East Asian Studies*,
vol. 5, 1994, pp. 13–24.

frequent phrase from the present intellectual jargon – *vis-à-vis* the official discourse. Of course, the linkages between various forms of official and unofficial discourse are complex and intricate.

'Reform and opening up to the outside world' is the phrase of the official discourse for designating the modernization programme pursued since the late 1970s, and this suggests a positive attitude to globalization. But according to official ideology, opening up to the outside world is primarily a means to develop the wealth and power of China and therefore only too compatible with state nationalism. It is also obvious that the Chinese government is doing its best to uphold state nationalism, although the way of defining Chinese nationality has changed and is changing as compared with the Maoist era. Symptomatically, when foreign observers criticize the Chinese authorities for not complying with international standards on human rights, the Chinese government refers to such criticism as interfering with the internal affairs of China.[41] According to the official line, human rights standards in China and the Western world must necessarily be different since the cultural traditions are different. This line of argument suggests the return to a kind of culturalism; cultural criteria, at the expense of political criteria, seem to play an increasingly important role in the conception of national identity.

Indirectly, official culturalism lends some support to Samuel P. Huntington's contention that a 'clash of civilizations' is taking precedence over other forms of conflicts in the post-Cold War era.[42] But while globalization means more contacts and more opportunities for clashes, this is by no means an iron logic and one has good reason to question why cultural differences as such should lead to conflict. In the words of two of Huntington's critics, 'why indeed, unless basic human needs are unfulfilled, should those who participate in different cultures fight?'[43]

In the various forms of unofficial discourse, the culturalistic tendencies are even more conspicuous. Proponents of so-called New Confucianism suggest that traditional Chinese culture should be revived and preserved as a source of identity for the Chinese wherever they happen to live. Professor Tu Wei-ming defines a new kind of culturalism, defining 'China' as essentially

41. See, e.g., *Human Rights in China*, Beijing: Information Office of the State Council of The People's Republic of China, November 1991.

42. Samuel P. Huntington, 'The Clash of Civilizations', *Foreign Affairs*, vol. 72, no. 3, Summer 1993, pp. 21–49; 'If Not Civilizations, What? Paradigms of the Post-Cold War World', *Foreign Affairs*, vol. 72, no. 5, November/December 1993, pp. 186–194.

43. Richard E. Rubenstein and Jarle Crocker, 'Challenging Huntington', *Foreign Policy*, no. 96, Fall 1994, pp. 113–128.

'Cultural China', and draws a parallel with Judaism: 'China' is essentially a cultural concept and thus conceivable without its own country.[44]

Interestingly, Tu Wei-ming discusses the meaning of 'Cultural China' in a way that is somewhat reminiscent of the ancient notions of domains described above. The first domain (to use the ancient discourse) of Cultural China is made up of the world inhabited mainly by Chinese people: the Chinese mainland, Hong Kong and Macao, Taiwan and Singapore. The second domain is made up of Chinese communities residing outside this core area in East, Southeast and South Asia, on the Pacific rim, in North America, Europe, Latin America and Africa. Finally the third domain is made up of people all over the world who are engaged in research on China and of scholars, intellectuals, writers, journalists and others interested in China and Chinese culture.[45]

This kind of culturalism is clearly at odds with the communist state nationalism. Although New Confucianism as such remains a concern of a very limited number of Chinese, the idea of China as a cultural rather than a political unity is gaining momentum, and though avowedly apolitical, it certainly has political impact in reinforcing the sense of common identity of Chinese people all over the world. In this sense, the notion of Cultural China serves to promote integration within the Chinese world. And although the New Confucianism of Tu Wei-ming seeks to maintain a distance to political power, we can see that the Chinese government now increasingly appeals to the sense of a cultural (and ethnic) identity of the Chinese people globally. Particularly vis-à-vis Taiwan, this is becoming a hot issue. On Taiwan the idea of an independent cultural Taiwanese identity is gaining momentum and takes expression in increasingly forceful demands for establishing a sovereign Taiwanese state, formally separate from China. This must be a source of grave concern to the leaders in Beijing, and then it becomes natural in the propaganda from Beijing to emphasize the cultural dimension of Chinese identity. Thus, what was at one level conceived as a concept to divorce Chinese identity from politics takes on political significance at another level.

Outside the arena of official discourse, 'transcendence' (chaoyue) and 'the reclusive spirit' (yinyi jingshen) have become catchwords for several

---

44. See Tu Wei-ming, 'Guanyu wenhua Zhongguo de hanyi' [On the Meaning of Cultural China], in Su Xiaokang (ed.), Cong Wusi dao Heshang [From the May Fourth to the Yellow River Elegy], Taipei: Fengyun shidai chuban youxian gongsi, 1992, pp. 1–13.
45. Ibid.

intellectuals, such as Liu Zaifu, to mention but one of the most prominent.[46] He argues that Chinese literature and culture in modern times have suffered greatly from not transcending 'the homeland of reality':

> After 1942 and particularly after the nationalization of literature in 1949 and the demand that literature should immediately serve politics, there remained even less right for literature to maintain a distance from the actual struggle, i.e. the right of reclusion. Losing this distance, the soul of the writers also lost the possibility to transcend. Thus the very rich spiritual space had to pander to the simplest secular life, the freest forms of feeling became transformed into the most mechanical cogs in the wheels of the state machine, and the spiritual production of the world of the imagination became totally absorbed by the world of reality. The writers did not even have the right to seek exile in their own spiritual garden (self-exile), not to mention the right to 'exile the state'. This not only signifies the complete loss of private space on the part of contemporary Chinese writers, but also lack of imagination as a fundamental deficiency of modern Chinese literature.[47]

The ideological thrust of this use of transcendence is certainly anti-nationalistic. The state and nation as geographically defined concepts are to be transcended and even 'exiled' for the individual to attain freedom.

In Tu Wei-ming's definition of 'Cultural China', Confucianism constitutes the essence of Chinese culture. However, the search for identity in indigenous cultural sources by far transcends the confines of the Confucian tradition. The root-seeking literature which emerged in the 1980s rather focused on local cultural traditions. Among the representatives of this trend we find writers such as Ah Cheng, who largely focuses on the tradition of Daoist philosophy; Han Shaogong, who writes about the southern Chu culture; Zheng Yi, who writes about the Taihang mountains; Jia Pingwa, who writes about Shangzhou; and Li Hangyu, who seeks roots in the the culture of the lower Yangzi Delta.[48] And there are other writers who explore minority cultures and regions; for example, Zhang Chengzhi writes about Muslims in Inner Mongolia and Xinjiang, and Zhaxi Duowa writes about Tibet.[49]

There are examples of writers and intellectuals who combine their search for identity in indigenous cultural traditions with a rather negative

---

46. Concerning 'the reclusive spirit', see Gao Jianping, 'The Reclusive Spirit in Ancient Chinese Painting', *Stockholm Journal of East Asian Studies*, vol. 6, 1995, pp. 102–124.

47. Liu Zaifu, 'Literature Exiling the State', *The Stockholm Journal of East Asian Studies*, vol. 5, 1994, pp. 13–24.

48. 'Shangzhou' is an expression that goes back to the time of the Three Kingdoms (A.D. 221 – 280) and refers to the area of the Shang Mountain and Luo River in Shaanxi province.

49. For an anthology of so-called root-seeking literature, see Li Tuo (ed.), *Zhongguo xungen xiaoshuo xuan* [Selected Chinese Root-Seeking Stories], Hong Kong: Sanlian, 1993.

and critical view of Western attitudes to China. For example, Edward Said's book *Orientalism* has recently attracted much attention among younger intellectuals who consider it important to resist Western cultural hegemony. In a recent article, the writer Han Shaogong even uses the word 'Han traitors' to refer to Chinese writers and artists who deliberately cater to the tastes of Westerners. In a Han nationalistic vein, he questions the motives of Western advocates of Tibetan independence, since they do not demand that America be returned to the Red Indians.[50] I bring this up as an example of how the search for identity in indigenous Chinese traditions as articulated seriously in unofficial discourse might sometimes degenerate into almost chauvinistic nationalism, defined in ethnic and cultural terms.

The culturalistic trends are also visible in popular culture. Historical novels, advertisements in magazines and television commercials, etc. often make use of themes from China's cultural tradition.[51] Not infrequently magic powers are ascribed to traditional techniques and medicine such as *qigong* and ginseng. In scholarship, culturalism has found expression in renewed interest in classical studies. And the term 'national studies' (*guoxue*), which was in vogue in the early twentieth century, is now used again. Recently a Centre for National Studies was set up at Beijing University.

New culturalism has emerged in post-Mao China in close connection with pleas for globalization and Westernization. In some fortunate cases a happy synthesis of the two appears possible. A good example of this is Gao Xingjian who, like a Chinese Kenzaburo Oe, creatively combines elements from the West and China in his interpretation of Chinese cultural traditions.[52] But more often they appear as poles of a contradiction in post-Mao intellectual discourse.

In line with the trend of globalization, several Chinese intellectuals argue that China should 'Westernize' and that national boundaries should be transcended as far as possible; for intellectuals in China it is still mainly if not exclusively North America and Europe that represent non-Chinese culture. They consider nationalism a thing of the past. Chinese cultural

---

50. Han Shaogong, 'Shijie' [The World], *Huacheng*, no. 6, 1994, pp. 89–97.

51. For an introduction to popular literature in contemporary China, see Marja Kaikko-nen, 'From Knights to Nudes: Chinese Popular Literature since Mao', *The Stockholm Journal of East Asian Studies*, vol. 5, 1994, pp. 85–110. For information about the the content of advertisements and commericals in China, I am indebted to Perry Johansson, a research student in sinology in Stockholm, who is prepraring a PhD dissertation on advertising in post-Mao China.

52. Cf. my article 'World Literature with Chinese Characteristics: On a Novel by Gao Xingjian', *The Stockholm Journal of East Asian Studies*, vol. 4, 1993, pp. 17–39.

traditions are considered as impediments to modernization and largely to be rejected in favour of modern Western culture. Even the unity of China as a supreme value has been questioned. The scriptwriters for the television series *Yellow River Elegy,* which attracted a lot of attention in the late 1980s, contrasted the unity of China with the break-up of the Roman empire in Europe and associated what they perceived as China's inertia and Europe's dynamism with this difference.[53] Often, as in the case of *Yellow River Elegy,* this current advocating Westernization appears extreme and exaggerated. Perhaps this is one reason why advocates of Westernization when coming to the West sometimes experience deep disillusionment and move to the other pole of the contradiction: chauvinistic culturalism.

Conclusions

At the outset I quoted Benjamin Akzin as saying that to discuss nationalism is to enter into a terminological jungle in which one easily gets lost. So far I have deliberately avoided giving a general definition of the concept of nationalism. Instead I have tried to analyse some aspects of identity in pre-modern, modern and contemporary China that appear relevant, no matter how we define this elusive concept. In this final section, when I try to draw some conclusions, it may be appropriate to attempt a general definition of 'nationalism' relevant for China. I therefore propose the following definition: 'nationalism' refers to the identification of a group of people as a nation, in terms of criteria that may be ethnic, cultural and/or political, and the commitment to the special interests of this nation, particularly in building a nation-state. 'Nation' may refer to any group of people which serves as the basis of a state or which claims the right of its own state.[54] Let me now

---

53. See *Deathsong of the River: A Reader's Guide to the Chinese TV Series 'Heshang'* by Su Xiaokang, Wang Luxiang et al. Translated by Richard W. Bodman and Pin P. Wang, Ithaca: Cornell University East Asia Program, 1991.

54. This definition is not to be understood as an attempt at an essentialist *Realdefinition* but merely as a heuristic device for analysing and explaining dimensions of Chinese identity that are relevant for questions which are frequently and loosely discussed in terms of 'nationalism'. In particular, I have been anxious to spell out explicitly the distinction between ethnic, cultural and political orientations in defining Chinese identity in general and a Chinese nation in particular. There exist innumerable definitions of nationalism. Recent and influential definitions have been given by, for instance Anthony D. Smith, who defines nationalism as 'an ideological movement for attaining and maintaining autonomy, unity and identity on behalf of a population deemed by some of its members to constitute an actual or potential "nation"' (Anthony D. Smith, *National Identity,* London: Penguin, 1991, p. 73) and by Ernest Gellner, who says that '[n]ationalism is primarily a political principle, which holds that the political and the national unit should be congruent' (Ernest Gellner, *Nations and Nationalism,* Oxford: Blackwell, 1983, p. 1). These definitions may also well be used for analysing nationalism in China, but neither of them includes the distinction between the ethnic, cultural and political orientations.

recapitulate and develop some of the points that I have tried to make in this essay.

In pre-modern times, Chinese identity was defined in terms of ethnic and cultural characteristics within a universalistic philosophy which defined the Son of Heaven as ruler of all under heaven. Thus there was never any question of using Chinese identity to legitimate the existence of a Chinese state independent of, or co-existing on equal terms with, other states. Yet, I suggest that we may speak of a kind of proto-nationalism in imperial China, which was accentuated in recurrent criticism of barbarian rule in China but also in general descriptions of barbarians.

In modern times, ethnic, cultural and political criteria have been used to define a Chinese nation as the basis of the Chinese state which could gain entrance as a respected member into the family of nations. Joining the family of nations as an equal and respected member was perceived as a necessity by the Chinese elite in a situation when the imperial order had been proven non-viable. Consequently, it was the new Chinese state-builders who needed a nation rather than a particular nation that called for a state. State nationalism has also taken different forms in twentieth-century China. For example, the national identity has been defined in cultural terms by early reformers such as Liang Qichao (who as a result was criticized for being too 'soft' on the Manchus); in ethnic terms by nationalist revolutionaries such as Sun Yat-sen (who had to pretend that there was no ethnic distinction between the Han Chinese and the Mongols, Tibetans, Uighurs and the other groups which today are referred to as national minorities); and even in political (although not exclusively political) terms by the communists, who defined class criteria as prerequisites for inclusion among 'the Chinese people'.

In contemporary China, as a result of the implementation of the modernization programme and the dismantling of the Maoist orthodoxy, the public discourse, as we meet it in newspapers, journals, books, etc., has become polyphonic. While the Maoist orthodoxy defined in great detail all important truths about man, society and the universe as well as the themes and subjects to be treated by writers, scholars, etc., people now have considerable freedom to articulate their own perspectives.

One tendency in post-Mao unofficial high-culture discourse is a change of focus away from the state towards society and the individual. It is often pointed out that since the individual has had to sacrifice so much for the state, the freedom and welfare of the individual or of families ought to receive the highest priority. For example, the poet Bei Dao laments the fact that questions concerning the state and country have taken precedence over questions concerning the individual human being, which he sees as a reversal of the natural order, just as when a Chinese writes the address on an envelope: first he writes the name of the country, then the place and only finally the name of the person.[55] In Bei Dao's view, Chinese intellectuals have to try to get away from 'saving the country and saving the people' and concentrate on saving themselves – 'everything else is empty talk'. He explicitly warns against nationalism:

> Nationalism's great attraction is dangerous, particularly when the nation is rising or falling. This cry based on blood relationship often erodes the existence of the individual. It easily becomes a part of the state discourse, forcing people – even dissidents – to give up their revolt.[56]

Another tendency in unofficial discourse is to seek to 'transcend reality' which, among other things, means to seek one's homeland beyond the state in a metaphysical realm. A third tendency in unofficial discourse, mainly high culture but also popular culture, is the rejection of Chinese tradition and the plea for Westernization. A fourth tendency, which finds expression in official discourse as well as in unofficial high and popular culture discourse is a new culturalism, which means a return to cultural tradition or traditions as a means to define China and Chineseness.

These tendencies all seem to break with that major current in modern Chinese history which in its search for 'wealth and power' for China has sought to divorce or liberate the notion of China from the cultural heritage and which has provided the core intellectual content of state nationalism in twentieth-century China. Therefore, the present tendencies suggest that Chinese state nationalism, in the forms we have become used to, is coming to an end.

The polyphonic discourse in post-Mao China emerges against the background of China rapidly developing its contacts with the outside world into a net of interrelations which inevitably infringes on the independence of the state and which necessarily entails interdependence. However, the regime in China continues to be as concerned as ever with its own wealth and power. No doubt, it tries to uphold state nationalism, but rather than using class analysis it is reverting to culturalism and ethnicity for the definition of Chinese identity. The culturalism of the official discourse often

---

55. Bei Dao, 'Suixiang: Cong geren chufa' [Random Thoughts: Proceeding from the Individual], paper presented paper at the International Conference on State, Society and Individual in Contemporary Chinese Thought held in Stockholm in June 1993 (to be published).
56. *Ibid.*

tends to make use of popular sentiments to serve the state. This becomes manifest in reactions to foreign criticism. Official reactions to international criticism of the human rights situation in China provide one example of this. But the government can even use rather innocent defeats in the international arena to encourage such sentiments. Semi-official statements after Beijing's failure in the bid to have the Summer Olympics in the year 2000 are rather ominous in this respect. One can just hope that the government will show restraint in stirring up xenophobic sentiments in order to strengthen its domestic authority.

In the wake of the break-up of the totalitarian discourse of Maoism and the emergence of the new polyphony, we may expect increasingly forceful attacks on the notion that the Han Chinese and the national minorities constitute one big Chinese nation, and hear renewed calls for national independence for several minorities. The form and extent of such demands will largely depend on the policy that the Beijing government implements in the minority areas but the issue as such can hardly be concealed or avoided in the present era.

State nationalism, as we have come to know it during the decades of Maoist rule in China, is coming to an end together with the totalitarian order of that era. In its wake we may expect to see a cultural nationalism which in the hands of the government may degenerate into chauvinism and, at worst, even confirm the fears of an emerging clash of civilizations. On the other hand, the pursuit of authenticity, truth, freedom and human dignity, which is also a salient feature of contemporary Chinese culture, gives us reason to hope for increasing and mutually enriching contacts between Chinese and other cultures in a global context.

CHAPTER ELEVEN

The Construction of the Post-Colonial Subject in Malaysia

C.W. Watson

The issue of a national identity, what it is that comprises those unique and definitive characteristics of the nation which all citizens are happy to recognize, constitutes a major element in political discourse in Malaysia. As well it might, since of all the problems facing the country since independence, creating national unity within a heterogeneous plural society has been the most intractable, and the proposed remedy of cultivating a sense of pride in a national identity has been, and continues to be, elusive. Below, I shall examine some of the ways in which successive governments, colonial and post-colonial, have dealt with the issue, and in particular I shall consider how Malay intellectuals and politicians have tried with only limited success to reach agreement on what a Malaysian national identity might be.[1]

One way to approach the debates which are specific to Malaysia is to begin by contrasting the situation in Malaysia with that in neighbouring countries, Singapore and Indonesia in particular, where superficial similarities at least suggest useful comparisons. In relation to Singapore, for example, both countries share a common legacy of British colonial institutions and it is consequently no surprise to see the similarities between the two governments in terms of their view of the future economic development of the countries and the type of polities and citizens which they hope to create. Both countries superficially espouse liberal democratic principles, yet both

1. I should like to thank the British Academy for its support which made possible my attendance at the conference at which this paper was originally presented.

are more than ready to employ strong-arm tactics in the form of curbs on the press and use of the colonially created Internal Security Act when they feel that their plans for the economic prosperity and political stability of the nation are being threatened or challenged by oppositional voices. Furthermore, precisely in relation to this issue, that is, the degree to which debate on the objectives of policy must be an open one, both countries also face a common dilemma: on the one hand the citizenry of the country needs to be propelled in the direction of an open free-market liberal economy, regarded as the only route to travel in the pursuit of economic prosperity, and on the other that very encouragement to liberal thinking and Western capitalist lifestyles creates an environment of challenge to the nation's collective goals. To put it crudely, then, the problem is how to create a climate of 'rugged individualism', without at the same time destroying that commitment to the 'imagined community' of common values and a caring society so clearly absent in the economically successful Western countries to which Asian leaders frequently turn their baleful glance.

Enough has been written about the way in which Singapore has dealt with the situation by trying to temper aspirations to a Western capitalist lifestyle by reference to Asian and Confucian ethics, and the difficulties it has encountered along the way.[2] Less well understood, it seems to me, is the manner in which successive Malaysian governments have trod the same path but in the course of their progress have had to deal with a different set of obstacles, the foremost of which is the peculiar nature of the plural society of Malaysia.

Whatever the difference of the obstacles, however, both governments have felt that fundamental to the intellectual armoury, which they require to pursue their objectives and win national support for them, is the construction of a post-colonial identity to which their citizens can relate. By this I mean a universally accepted representation of the collectivity of the nation which explains the present in terms of a peculiar concatenation of historical circumstances, and which projects a future in terms of a unique cultural and social constellation already existing within the country. There are thus two components to the construction of the post-colonial identity: first, the evaluation and interpretation of the immediate colonial past, which

---

2. See, for example, S. Gopinathan, 'Education', in Jon S.T. Quah, Chan Heng Chee and Seah Chee Meow (eds), *Government and Politics of Singapore*, Singapore: Oxford University Press, 1987, pp. 220–231; and Robert Iau, 'Culture and Society', in Tan Teng Lang (ed.), *Singapore. The Year in Review 1990*, Singapore: The Institute of Policy Studies, Times Academic Press, 1991, pp. 56–68.

is flexible enough to allow the attribution of shortcomings in the present system to the adverse effects of colonial experience, while at the same time celebrating a triumphant nationalist subversion of colonial aims; second, the promulgation of a set of values and aspirations which will constitute the features of a unique identity to which reference can constantly be made when soliciting support for government initiatives.

Of course, there is nothing peculiar to Singapore and Malaysia in having to pursue a post-colonial imperative of this kind. To some extent, all the former colonies of South and Southeast Asia have followed a similar strategy, and the writing of nationalist histories in the immediate aftermath of colonial experience is a well-known phenomenon. We are also familiar (although the analysis in this area has not been quite so perceptive) with the manner in which post-independence and revolutionary governments have devised powerful and enduring political symbols which have caught the imagination of the nation and inspired the people with a sense of common endeavour. To give one example from Indonesia, the other neighbouring state with which we may usefully compare Malaysia, *Pancasila*, the five sovereign principles of the Indonesian state, has been extraordinarily successful as an enduring political symbol which has transcended two very different political regimes, the Orde Lama (Old Order) of Sukarno, 1954–66, and the Orde Baru (New Order) of Suharto, 1966 to the present. At the same time Pancasila has managed to convince the Indonesian people of the continuity between the two regimes.

The very success of the Indonesian manipulation of political symbols and the state's construction of the post-colonial subject – the ideally politicized citizen-individual – must inevitably lead one to question why Malaysia, with cultural and historical ties to many Indonesian ethnic groups, has never been able to emulate Indonesia's achievement in this respect. The answer is long and involved, and there can be no single explanation given the great differences between the experiences of the two countries. Nonetheless, there are comparisons that can fruitfully be made which bring into sharper relief the peculiar dynamics of the political developments of the two countries over the last five decades.

One possible explanation for the different articulation of the post-colonial subject in the political processes of both countries may simply be the relatively late politicization of the Malaysian society which, when it eventually did begin to take root, encountered a scepticism and distrust of political symbols at grass-roots levels which it has never been able to remove. According to such an argument, national consensus was forged in

Indonesia in the crucible of the Indonesian Revolution between 1945 and 1949, and, however great the differences between proponents of different political parties right and left, religious and secular, there was a strong core commitment to a national, egalitarian ideology, which not only submerged local particularistic interests but also denied economic development absolute priority over other social and political goals. Even under the Orde Baru that consensus remained in place. The Orde Baru, it is true, emphasized the task of economic reconstruction and succeeded in its plans for development, but despite appearances it was not this which was the basis of its legitimacy, but rather its claim to be the true heir to the spirit of 1945, safeguarding the stability of the nation. Thus, it could be argued, the overwhelming electoral success of Golkar (the state-supported party) in the 1970s does not so much represent a triumph of the intimidation of the population by the state – although of course there was intimidation too – but a genuine reflection of the people's will to be governed by the political acumen of people who still strongly espoused nationalist principles. The acceptance of, and commitment to, Pancasila over five decades could, then, be seen as confirmation of and contributory to a strong shared sense of national identity.

In Malaysia by contrast there was no revolution, no political consensus. True, there were anti-colonial demonstrations, in particular around the time of the abortive Malayan Union proposals put forward by the British in 1946, and there was armed resistance over a number of years on the part of the communists to the British administration during the so-called Emergency (1948–60). At best, however, this created a sense of common identity only among the Malays, and that identity was defined not so much in opposition to the British as in opposition to the Chinese and the Indians. In relation to the latter two groups, although there was an attempt to forge a common identity among them by referring to them as Malayans – at one strong stroke cleverly suggesting a communality with the Malays while simultaneously denying complete identification by the adding of another syllable – this ploy was in fact rejected by the Malays who saw contained within it the subtle undermining of their special position within the nation.

The Chinese and the Indians were, then, excluded from participation in the political discourse and the ideological formulations of the period and were, by and large, content with guarantees and safeguards in relation to economic opportunities and rights of citizenship. The Malays consequently monopolized the debates and these remained largely confined to issues surrounding the position and status of the Malay monarchy, and the development of a national Malay language.

Even as the polity developed and the Federation of Malaysia was created in 1963 no real politicization occurred. The new concept of 'Malaysian' accomplished part of what was intended by the Malay/Malayan distinction by giving the Chinese and Indian populations a sense of being at least stake-holders in the country. But as debates about rights and privileges increased in intensity, the further formulaic distinction between the *bumiputera* (sons of the soil), used to refer to the Malays and other indigenous peoples, and the *non-bumiputera* (the rest of the citizenry), served only to accentuate the lack of consensus. Thus when politicization began to impinge on political and economic development in the late 1960s, the consequence was to imperil rather than, as in the Indonesian case, cement national unity.

It was the realization that this had occurred which led the Malaysian state after the race riots of 13 May 1969 belatedly to give greater thought to the need to create a sense of ownership and commitment throughout the society. In other words the construction of the post-colonial subject was recognized as being a project of pressing urgency. The problem, however, was that this construction had not, as in the Indonesian case, emerged almost organically out of the day-to-day struggles of the nationalist move-ment. In the Malaysian case it had to be created more or less *ex nihilo* – more or less, because there were already some potential elements, again the monarchy and the language, which could be reused. A further difficulty was that by that time in the history of the global developments in post-colonial societies, enough was known by ethnic minorities and oppositional voices to make them sceptical of state-inspired constructions of nationhood – one thinks immediately in the Southeast Asian context of Burma. Thus both at the level of evaluation of the past, and in terms of constructing a national consciousness, the authorized and authoritative versions promoted by the institutions of the state were – and still are – constantly open to challenge. As a consequence of these challenges, and also as a response to rapidly changing national and international circumstances which cannot be accom-modated within these original paradigms of what are substantive features of a Malaysian past and present, the construction of the post-colonial subject has been especially susceptible to rapid transformation. Authorized versions succeed one another with bewildering rapidity.

In what follows I shall try to chart some of the shifts that have taken place in the key dimensions of both interpreting the colonial past and re-cuperating a sense of Malay identity. In the second part of the chapter I demonstrate how under the present prime minister, Mahathir Mohamad, there has been a renewed vigour in attending to the issue of a national identity. But underlying that vigour there is in Mahathir's rhetoric an ambivalence, in relation both to an evaluation of the construction of the subject in Malaya's colonial and pre-colonial past and also in relation to the creation of the post-colonial Malaysian subject.

The Evaluation of the Colonial Past

The use of the term 'post-colonial' both in this chapter and in recent Malaysian historiography (where it is translated *pasca-penjajahan*) is of course instantly problematic, both in its general implications and in reference to Malaysia, since it assumes that a certain critical weight and significance be attached to colonialism.[3] Furthermore it implicitly excludes other categories relevant to a discussion of historical change (e.g. world-systems), and suggests an emphasis on the specification of the mechanisms of colonialism and their variance from one colonial power to another. A paper, if not a book, then could be written about the relevance of colonialism as a category to an understanding of Malayan history. Much could be learned in this respect from recent controversies concerning Indian historiography.[4] However, rather than pursue the issue of the appropriateness of the category, I want to take it as a given for the purposes of this chapter – a given, in as much as Malaysian politicians and intellectuals, either by implication or by explicit avowal, concede the significance of the colonial period for the understanding of contemporary Malaysian politics. In current debates, that is, the colonial period is almost invariably the *terminus a quo* from which discussions are launched concerning what constitutes identity and ethnicity within Malaysia today. There are, of course, different evaluations of policies pursued, of actions taken, and of the significance of specific historical turning points. However, the terms of the discussion, the criteria to be applied, are agreed: the political period of colonialism both ruptured continuity with the past and critically determined the shape of what followed.

---

3. For a good recent overview of what is meant by post-colonialism and how the term has been used in recent discussions see Arif Dirlik, 'The Postcolonial Aura: Third World Criticism in the Age of Global Capitalism', *Critical Inquiry*, vol. 20, no. 2 (Winter), 1994, pp. 328–56; Gyan Prakash, 'Postcolonial Criticism and Indian Historiography', *Social Text*, no. 31/32, 1992, pp. 8–19.

4. See Partha Chatterjee, *Nationalist Thought and the Colonial World*, London: Zed Books, 1986; Gyan Prakash, 'Writing Post-Orientalist Histories of the Third World: Perspectives from Indian Historiography', *Comparative Studies in Society and History*, vol. 32, no. 2, April, 1990, pp. 383–408; Rosalind O'Hanlon and David Washbrook, 'After Orientalism: Culture, Criticism and Politics in the Third World', *Comparative Studies in Society and History*, vol. 34, 1992, pp. 141–167.

It is not the place here to rehearse the different ways in which the agency and effectiveness of colonial policy have been perceived, reconsidered and reframed over the last forty years or so, nor to document how each re-positioning of colonialism as an essentialized object of discourse has affected and been affected by that other historiographic essentialized object, Malay nationalism. It is, however, necessary to try to summarize what the current stage of the debate is – how the discourse seems recently to have taken shape. In particular what I want to argue is that within Malaysia there are compet-ing interpretations of the past. One of these can be labelled the 'accepted version', because it is this version which is promoted by the state and, as any perusal of ministerial speeches reveals, often serves as a point of reference to justify both domestic and foreign policies. The others I would describe as 'alternative', because in one way or another they challenge the accepted version. However, one word of caution is required here. The various interpreta-tions are not always at odds with one another, and there is frequently a degree of overlap among them. Thus, as I shall show, the accepted version is at times happy to make use of notions of the Malay hero as constructed by the historians and intellectuals both within and outside Malaysia who belong to the alternative schools, and, conversely, the latter will occasionally support the anti-neo-imperialist rhetoric of the government which relies on the acknowledged reference points of the accepted version of history. In all cases, as we might have expected, it is present concerns which drive how the past is interpreted. Trying to identify how the present both determines and relies on the past and how the various interpretations compete, combine and diverge in this enterprise is one of the aims of this chapter.

There are, in fact, two interwoven but separable sub-themes within the arguments concerning the determining effects of colonialism in Malaysia: one relates to the policy devised by the colonial authorities for the governance of Malaya in the period 1942–57; the other concerns the notion of the Malay subject, that is the conceptualization of the character of the ideal-typical Malay as historical agent. Both themes are directly addressed in Mahathir's polemical work, 'The Malay Dilemma', though, as Syed Hussein Alatas has shown, it is the second of the themes, that of the Malay subject, which is at the heart of the book.

The interpretation which ascribes Machiavellian cunning to the colonial office – a form of conspiracy theory – although still occasionally rehearsed when references are made to *divide et impera* for popular consumption[5] are

5. Ibrahim Anwar, *Menangani Perubahan*, Kuala Lumpur: Berita Publishing Sdn. Berhad, 1989.

rarely invoked nowadays in serious debate. Tony Stockwell gives sound reasons for concluding why such interpretations are rather facile,[6] and Albert Lau in his recent book[7] confirms the variety of 'colonial' positions which existed, and the almost serendipitous formulation of policy. Lau's account of the dynamics of what went on – the letters, reports, minutes and discussions – is very helpful, not necessarily for the importance it attributes to certain individual interventions, but for its account of the way in which the aim of the policy was to balance the various demands and rights of the ethnic groups within Malaya which were regarded as having been left too much to their own separate devices rather than integrated during the pre-war period. Neither Lau nor Stockwell, then, has much truck with the colonial government as being devilishly cunning and far-sighted, or even for the idea of a single colonial ideology.

The accepted account, then, runs more or less as follows.[8] About 1940, the British government realised that, as a consequence of the colonial policies which they had pursued until then and as a result of the economic and social developments which had taken place, there were in Malaya separate ethnic communities of Malays, Chinese and Indians. The latter two had been encouraged to come to Malaya to provide the necessary cheap labour for the extractive plantation and mineral economy of the country. Whereas in the past this pluralist system – which relied on the complementarity of these groups within the economic structure of the country – had operated efficiently and without any major indications of political tension, it was evident during the Japanese occupation of 1942–45 that there would have to be a political restructuring after the war. This restructuring was needed to accommodate the demands of the various groups, in particular the demands of the large Chinese minority who from originally being sojourners and uncommitted to Malaya had now become permanent residents anxious for rights of citizenship, and who, as a consequence of their anti-Japanese

---

6. A.J. Stockwell, 'The White Man's Burden and Brown Humanity: Colonialism and Ethnicity in British Malaya', *Southeast Asian Journal of Social Science*, vol. 10, no. 1, 1982, pp. 44–68; 'British Imperial Policy and Decolonization in Malaya, 1942–52', in *The Journal of Imperial and Commonwealth History*, vol. XIII, no. 1, October 1984, pp. 68–87.

7. Albert Lau, *The Malayan Union Controversy 1942–1948*, Singapore: Oxford University Press, 1991.

8. A good brief example of the accepted account is that of Professor Zainal Abidin bin Abdul Wahid, for many years a senior figure in the History Department of the National University of Malaysia and closely associated with the ruling Malay party, 'Semangat Perjuangan Melayu', *Jebat*, Bl. 7/8, 1977/8–1978/9 (Jabatan Sejarah, Universiti Kebangsaan Malaysia), 1978.

stance during the war, had won considerable British support. Ideally it
would have been best if political, cultural, economic and social integration
had occurred earlier, but the reverse had been the case and ethnic divisions
had become entrenched. How to dissolve the divisions, integrate the communities and reverse the previous policy therefore became the critical issues
of the moment.

The original solution proposed by the British in 1945–46, the Malayan
Union, ran into unexpectedly strong opposition from the Malays. They were
hostile to the effective dissolution of the Malay monarchy and alarmed at the
prospect of being overwhelmed politically and economically by the Chinese,
who were to be given rights equal to their own. This led the Malays to vigorously attack British proposals, thus acquiring a new political and nationalist
consciousness under the leadership of the Malay aristocratic elite.

The compromise proposal, the Malayan Federation of 1947, effectively
satisfied the demands of all interested parties – British, Malays, Chinese and
Indians; it seemed to safeguard Malay political privileges while at the same
time providing political security in the form of citizenship for the Chinese
and Indians and preserving for the Chinese the economic opportunities they
had always enjoyed. It also left the British secure in the possession of their
overseas investments. Thus in 1957 with the achievement of independence,
the first wave of decolonization, to use Mahathir's terms, had passed. If in
the eyes of the Malays there was blame to be attached to colonial policy up
to this point, it lay not so much in deviousness, although that had been
present in the original negotiations concerning the Malayan Union, but in
the muddle-headed *ad hoc* approach which had characterized the pre-war
policy of colonial pluralism, and the short-sightedness of the British vision
of Malaya's future which had not contemplated independence for Malaya in
the foreseeable future.

Of course, with the hindsight of what may be called the second wave
of decolonization which began to accelerate from the mid-1970s, in the eyes
of Malay intellectuals of the Mahathir mould the principal British failure in
the immediate post-war period lay in limiting Malay representation in
negotiations to those Malays who had been sponsored by the British – that
is those who came from an aristocratic elite and did not in effect know how
to, nor indeed wish to, articulate the economic interests of the majority of
the Malay population. The Malay elite and the British were, in this interpretation, guilty of collusion which suited their selfish interests, and a second
wave of decolonization was required as a rectification of this situation, one

which would wrest political power – and the limited economic patronage which went with it – from the old Malay elite, at the same time as challenging the monopoly of British business interests. It also meant a vigorous programme of affirmative action on behalf of the formerly unrepresented Malays. This at least is the thinking which runs through 'The Malay Dilemma' written in 1970 and which, with the addition of an incorporation of an Islamic dimension and a new post-Said critical vocabulary,[9] continues to inform the Malaysian prime minister's strategy today.

Most observers would, I think, accept this summary of the account which is now the dominant discourse articulated throughout the system and given voice in the hegemonic institutions of Malaysia: the media, the education system and the party machines of the ruling Barisan Nasional coalition of parties. Such an acceptance would not, of course, imply agreement with the argument of the discourse nor, even less, an acceptance of those political actions that find their justification in an appeal to the discourse – actions, for example, such as the intermittent use of the Internal Security Act (ISA), a legacy of the colonial period allowing for arbitrary detention of political opponents.

Leaving aside for the moment controversies concerning the *realpolitik* of present-day Malaysian politics and confining ourselves to the alternative versions which challenge the historical reconstructions of the dominant discourse, we find increasingly that two critical areas of investigation are drawn to our attention because, it is argued, their insertion into the narrative is fundamental to our understanding of the history and requires a rewriting of it. The first of these might be labelled, to borrow a term from contemporary Indian studies,[10] the subaltern voice, that is the documenting of the progress and development of non-elite movements, peasant resistance, women's groups and religious protests, which are seen to have been major actors within the history, and not simply, as the dominant discourse suggests, history's passive victims. The other neglected area of study is that of the formation of Malay consciousness and how and when its emergence can be identified.

---

9. The reference here is to Edward Said, the author of *Orientalism* (first edition 1978), which Mahathir is fond of quoting, as for example in *Holier Than Thou – A Mild Critique*, a speech delivered at All Souls College, Oxford, Friday 19 April 1985. Said's work has been extremely influential not only in terms of particular historical interpretations but also for its tone and rhetoric which many Malaysian intellectuals strive to emulate.

10. See Ranajit Guha (ed.) *Subaltern Studies I. Writings on South Asian History and Society,* Delhi: Oxford University Press, 1982.

The debate about the submerged/subaltern voice in Malaysian history – constructed largely, it should be noted, by non-Malaysian scholars[11] – needs careful unravelling. Malaysian scholars have noted the phenomena and indeed have frequently celebrated the acts of resistance to colonialism, but they have seen such incidental protests as peripheral rather than central to the main historical narrative, colouring it but not changing its contours. The one major exception is Shamsul,[12] where the subaltern's resistance is central to the understanding of the dynamics of historical development in Malaysia. In general, then, the way in which the new direction of attention to micro-political processes at village level within the colonial and post-colonial state potentially allows us to recast our whole understanding of Malaysian history remains largely to be explored.

There has, however, been a more sustained attempt on the part of Malaysian scholars to establish a subaltern tradition of a different kind in the socialist pan-Malay ideas of the PKMM (Parti Kebangsaan Melayu Malaya) and the earlier KMM (Kesatuan Melayu Muda). Their role in the historical trajectory towards independence has always been considered to be relatively minor, if not ignored altogether, within the dominant discourse. Within Malay academia, however, there has always been room for this tradition both precisely because it is an alternative to the dominant discourse and because it allows one to move the origins of Malay nationalism further back into history and deny its aristocratic origins. Rustam Sani[13] has been the most recent proponent of a realignment of the narrative in favour of this socialist tradition which, interestingly, he sees as continuous with the small but important socialist tradition of the Partai Rakyat, numerically insignificant but of great importance in the formulation of the terms of the debates and the defining historical issues.

These arguments about subalternity are intimately linked with the second contested issue mentioned above, the definition of Malay conscious-

---

11. See Donald M. Nonini, *British Colonial Rule and the Resistance of the Malay Peasantry, 1900–1957*, New Haven: Monograph Series 38/Yale University Southeast Asia Studies, 1992; Patrick Sullivan 'A Critical Appraisal of Historians of Malaysia: the Theory of Society Implicit in their Work', in R. Higgot and R. Robison (eds), *Southeast Asia. Essays in the Political Economy of Structural Change*, London: Routledge and Kegan Paul, 1985, pp. 65–92.

12. See Shamsul A.B., *From British to Bumiputera Rule. Local Politics and Rural Development in Peninsular Malaysia*, Singapore: Institute of Southeast Asian Studies, 1982.

13. See Rustam A. Sani, 'Tradisi Intelektual Melayu dan Pembentukan Bangsa Malaysia: Beberapa Persoalan Sosial', in Ahmat Adam, Kassim Ahmad and Rustam A. Sani, *Intelektualisme Melayu: Satu Polemik*, Bangi: The Faculty of Social Sciences and Humanities, Universiti Kebangsaan Malaysia, Kertas Kadangkala Bil. 5, 1989, pp. 73–105.

ness (an issue which, in its turn, as we shall see, directly affects contemporary constructions of nationhood), since those who seek to recuperate the subaltern often do so with the implicit justification that the subaltern's voice is authentically that of the Malay subject. Certainly, for example, that is the argument of those who argue the case for the KMM. The search for authenticity, however, is fraught with epistemological contortion. The difficulties at one level may not be so great as comparable constructions of the indigenous subject in India, say, where regional, religious and economic, ethnic and linguistic difference makes a mockery of every attempt to define an essentialist India,[14] or in Indonesia, where there is again difference, and where the difficulty lies in the recent coinage of the Indonesian subject constructed as a recent post-1928 invention and therefore lacking in any historical authenticity. Nonetheless Malaysian difficulties in this area are palpable enough.

At the level of superficial homogeneity – mutually intelligible dialects of Malay, a common religion, Islam, experience of similar political structures and a sharing of the same cultural universe of aesthetic and literary forms – the Malay subject would appear relatively easy to identify. Indeed, it has been precisely this which Gullick accomplishes in his early work.[15] However, as Sullivan convincingly argues,[16] this creation of an ideal type fails to account for the variation between Malay states and subjects, even at a synchronic level, where at the same historical moment Malays in different geographical and economic sites were exposed and reacted to a host of external influences generating a differential rate of change and development: what was happening in Johor was very different from circumstances in Pahang or Kedah, affecting the culture and self-perceptions of Malays in very different ways and differentiating rather than assimilating them.

Under these circumstances, where there is no obvious single source of Malay culture and identity, who speaks for Malay consciousness and why should their claim be more legitimate than any other? In post-colonial terms, in response to these questions there has been an extraordinary flowering of different debates which at first sight seem unrelated, but all of which in fact hinge upon this issue of who or what was a Malay during the colonial period. Let me mention some of these simply to indicate the variety.

---

14. On this point see the very pertinent essays by Ashis Nandy, *The Intimate Enemy. Loss and Recovery of Self Under Colonialism*, Delhi: Oxford University Press, 1983.

15. See J.M. Gullick, *Indigenous Political Systems of Western Malaya*, London: The Athlone Press, 1965.

16. Sullivan, 'A Critical Appraisal'.

In a recent article, Michael Peletz argues cogently that the codification of the Malay *adat* in Rembau in 1910 by Parr and Mackray led to the ossification of a cultural tradition which having been inscribed in print has taken on a quasi-sacral ontological status. 'If it is not in Parr and Mackray, it is not adat', as one of Peletz's informants pointed out.[17] We have here then the reification of *adat*. Of course, one could legitimately argue that this inscription of *adat* is simply another of those metamorphoses through which a living tradition passes and out of which it will emerge, just as it has emerged through other changing forms. That, however, is not really the point at issue here, which is rather both the manner in which appeal is being made to capture the 'eternal Malay' and the fact that such an appeal is made at all.

In a very different domain, literary criticism, a similar argument over the true nature of Malay identity is pursued by opponents who contest the nature of that identity but not the fact that the identity is there open to disclosure. The best-known of such debates in post-colonial Malaya has been that surrounding the figures of Hang Tuah and Hang Jebat of the Malay epic *Hang Tuah* and how they should be evaluated. One of the most recent examples of the debate is an article by Muhammad H. Salleh on the 'Traditional Malay Hero'[18] where he usefully describes the origins of the controversy in Kassim Ahmad's famous analysis[19] in which the traditional evaluation of the two characters is reversed. In other words, Jebat, the *hulubalang* (the soldier) who takes up arms against the tyranny of the sultan, is regarded as the rightful hero of the story, rather than his opponent Tuah whose blind obedience to the monarch is critically reappraised and whose character is judged to be wanting in fundamental human qualities. Muhammad endorses this reading of the story, drawing out in more detail what the particularly attractive qualities of Jebat were and comparing them favourably with the one-dimensional attributes of Tuah.

More relevant to the immediate discussion of the way in which the construction of a Malay subject emerges out of historiographical re-evaluation of the colonial period, is to notice how Muhammad links the discussion of Jebat's character to the need for a hero of modern times – by

17. Michael G. Peletz, 'Sacred Texts and Dangerous Words: The Politics of Law and Cultural Rationalization in Malaysia', *Comparative Studies in Society and History*, vol. 35, no. 1, January 1993, pp. 73.

18. Muhammad H. Salleh, *Cermin Diri. Esei-Esei Kesusasteraan*, Petaling Jaya: Fajar Bakti Sdn. Berhad, 1986.

19. Kassim Ahmad, *Characterization in Hikayat Hang Tuah*, Kuala Lumpur: Dewan Bahasa dan Pustaka, 1966.

which he means the period of colonialism up to the present – a hero who, unlike Tuah, is prepared to be a rebel and oppose tyranny in order to render safe the Malay people. In this context he draws the analogy between Jebat and Kassim Ahmad, the poet, who has celebrated him and who, like him, was prepared to resist.[20] In fact, here Muhammad's argument follows a similar course to Rustam Sani's, in charting a continuity from the ideal rebel figure of the colonial period to the socialist hero of the post-colonial political world after independence. Contemporary Malay understanding of the colonial period as a period of struggle and confrontation, then, as well as leading to the discovery – one is almost tempted to say invention – of an energetic tradition of resistance and rebellion, pushes cultural analysis to the point of reinterpreting the canon of classical Malay literature along post-colonial lines.

A final example and, arguably the most striking of all, of the Malay subject as a contested site of post-colonial debates concerns the endorsement and refutation of the colonially created Malay. What is at issue here are two points: first, the reality and acceptability of the image of the Malay, that is, the character ascribed to the Malay personality by the colonial scholar-administrator, and second, the extent to which colonial policy consciously worked to fix and perpetuate the image once fashioned.[21] In this respect several writers have demonstrated that those scholar-administrators most closely associated with Malaya, and all of whom are acknowledged to have had an intimate acquaintance with Malay culture and society, were disposed, in accordance with what one might describe as the anthropological ideas of their time, to endorse and contribute to the creation of images of national character. In their capacity as administrators, they acted and reacted according to what they took the implications of that character to be for everyday behaviour, and as scholars they found evidence for what the constituent features of the Malay (and the Chinese) were and then pontificated about these essential features in their documentary accounts, in their official reports, in their fictional writings and in their public lectures. The best-

---

20. Muhammad, *Cermin Diri*, p. 42.

21. This is well-trodden ground and there is no need to go over it in detail. The interested reader can follow up the fascinating references provided in Stockwell, 'The White Man's Burden and Brown Humanity'; H.M.J. Maier, *In the Center of Authority: the Malay Hikayat Merong Mahawangsa*, Ithaca, NY: Southeast Asian Program, Cornell University, 1988; Michael G. Peletz, 'Sacred Texts and Dangerous Words: The Politics of Law and Cultural Rationalization in Malaysia', *Comparative Studies in Society and History*, vol. 35, no. 1, January 1993, pp. 66–109; Muhammad, *Cermin Diri*; P. Wicks, *Literary Perspectives in Southeast Asia: Collected Essays*, Toowoomba: University College of Southern Queensland, 1991.

known and most influential of these writers were Swettenham and Clifford, who wrote books with such titles as 'The Real Malay' and 'In Court and Kampong'. But there were other writers, too, who were caught up unconsciously in the orientalist fabrications of their day, and in different literary modes enhanced contemporary colonial notions. Henri Fauconnier's novel, *Malaisie* – translated as 'The Soul of Malaya' – for example, was required reading for all Malay Civil Service (MCS) cadets going out to Malaya in the inter-war years.[22]

The collective fashioning of these writers represented the Malay – usually a man, although, in some of the fictional accounts in particular, sometimes a woman – as an easy-going, happy-go-lucky peasant or prince by inclination rather idle, but fond of sport and pastimes (a characteristic which endeared him to the English); a person whose natural inclination was to be polite and not to give offence, and a person who valued his leisure time in the company of friends above the possession of material comforts. Consequently, it was very difficult to convince a Malay of the value of long-term, or even medium-term, goals, or the need for lengthy preparation and planning. In terms of temperament he was not violent by nature nor quick to take offence but once roused he was prepared to act violently in that suicide attack which we know through the original Malay word *amok*.

To substantiate this construction – and I have given only the bare outlines of it here – the writers referred to their own experiences and observations claiming for themselves, to the satisfaction of their expatriate audiences at least, that ethnographic authority which contemporary anthropologists, often upon much shorter acquaintance, still claim in their descriptions of other cultures – or at least did until quite recent post-modernist times. But in addition to referring simply to their personal observations, they also claimed authority for their depictions of Malay culture and personality by directly analysing Malay sayings and proverbs. These, they argued, were an unrivalled source of information about things Malay. Their subsequent claims to be, as it were, simply allowing the Malays to speak for themselves, were then ironically endorsed by post-colonial Malays – or at least some of them. One example of this should suffice.

There is a Malay expression '*kais pagi makan pagi kais petang makan petang*'. The literal meaning refers to a hen who is said to 'scratch around in the morning when it wants to eat in the morning, and scratch around in the

---

22. See, for example, the reference in B. Lockhart, *Return to Malaya*, London: Putnam, 1936, p. 109.

afternoon when it wants to eat in the afternoon'. In other words, it proverbially alludes to people who do not have much foresight, who live from hand to mouth, from day to day, and are not prepared to work and save for a prosperous future. This proverb which is clearly a didactic warning is paradoxically taken by the colonial expatriate to characterize the Malay attitude to work. The manufacturing of the image does not, however, cease with the demise of the colonial presence. Insidiously, as Alatas demonstrates so effectively,[23] 'the myth of the lazy native' is perpetuated by the native himself, in this case the post-colonial heir of the British administrator. Alatas writes excoriatingly of the way in which books such as *Revolusi Mental* by a collective authorship of senior Malay figures and Mahathir's *The Malay Dilemma* unquestioningly take over the colonial images, and how their authors have been methodologically duped by failing to understand that the function of a proverb such as the one quoted is not to characterize a culture but to provide simple lessons and rules for the individual.[24] This is a very telling point, particularly when applied to Mahathir who himself had criticized the earlier generation of Malay leadership because they were too comfortable with British ideas.

It is, furthermore, a point which needs constant reiteration. Intellectuals and politicians still appear to be easily seduced by the colonial imagination.[25] Musa Hitam, for example, a senior Malay political figure for a long time close to Mahathir, was still warning in 1985 about the attitude of '*kais pagi, makan pagi*', as an example of the '*sikap Bumiputera*' (attitude of the indigenous people) which had to be changed.[26] The curious ambivalence which lies at the heart of this discussion of the '*sikap bangsa*' ('the attitude of the [Malay] people'), is reflected in the way in which the discourse (as found passim in *The Malay Dilemma*) hesitates between assigning the blame for the 'attitude' on Malay culture and genetic heritage, and denouncing as culprits the British who engineered the Malays into positions of subordination.

To recapitulate, within Malaysia today public discussions and arguments about the way forward in political, economic and cultural spheres hinge

---

23. See Syed Hussain Alatas, *Siapa Yang Salah. Sekitar Revolusi Mental dan Peribadi Melayu*, Singapore: Pustaka Nasional, 1974 (1972), and *The Myth of the Lazy Native*, London: Frank Cass, 1977.

24. Alatas, *Siapa Yang Salah*, p. 46.

25. See, for example, the work of Tham Seong Chee, *Language and Cognition: An Analysis of the Thought and Culture of the Malays*, Singapore: Chopmen, 1977.

26. Musa Hitam, *Nasionalisme, Krisis dan Kematangan*, Petaling Jaya: Pelanduk Publications, 1986.

implicitly upon how participants within the debates conceptualize Malay and Malaysian identity. The notion of identity in its turn is highly dependent on an evaluation of the past: it is one's account of what one argues has occurred in the period of recent history that substantiates one's analysis of the present. Central to all such accounts is an assessment of the intentions and policies of colonial administrators. The former accounts of devious British imperialists deliberately devising a policy of divide and rule have now been replaced by denunciations of British short-sightedness, incompetence and high-handedness. Also significant for contemporary discourse is the attempt to expose the manner by which traditions and images became established and in their rigid forms resisted re-analysis at the same time as determining future agendas. Thus Peletz has shown the pitfalls underlying the use of colonial notions of *adat* as a repository of Malay culture, and Alatas has usefully alerted us to the way in which even the most anti-colonial of writers unconsciously, and dangerously, subscribe to what are in effect the caricatures of colonial rhetoric.

At another level, however, we have observed above that one of the ways in which intellectuals have tried to think through colonial categories, and by this I mean interrogating the validity of these categories as valid tools for historical analysis, has been through giving attention to the subaltern voice. The identification of the authentic subaltern voice for appropriate commendation, however, remains problematic. For some historians the invention of new categories and the task of reinterpretation can be accomplished by reading 'against the grain', and demonstrating, for example, how colonial reports signally fail to grasp the dynamics of the process which they aspire to record.[27] Others look to a revalorization of peasant resistance and rebellion to illustrate a very different narrative trajectory to the one commonly recited. Thus Rustam Sani redirects our gaze to the half-forgotten Kesatuan Melayu Muda (KMM); Nonini argues for a greater historical importance to be attributed to the many instances of peasant rebellion he documents; Shamsul meticulously chronicles the continuity from colonial to post-colonial times, thus implicitly at the level of micro-history challenging the macro-historical explanation; and Sullivan recalls for us the several flaws of the narrative of the nation as generally accepted.[28]

---

27. Anthony Milner writes perceptively on this in 'Colonial Records History: British Malaya', *Modern Asian Studies*, vol. 21, no. 4, 1986, pp. 773–792.
28. Rustam Sani, 'Tradisi Intelektual Melayu'; Nonini, *British Colonial Rule*; Shamsul A.B., *From British to Bumiputera Rule*; Sullivan, 'A Critical Appraisal'.

Caught up within this same endeavour to establish some sort of legitimacy by means of identifying an authentic subaltern voice, not only to set against the self-aggrandizing narrative of imperial history but also to reaffirm or rediscover a sense of cultural uniqueness, which might serve as a source of national pride, Muhammad's – and Kassim's – search for the Malay hero in the classical texts of Malay literature can be construed as a reaction to the colonial dismissal of aesthetic and cultural worth in Malay literature. They argue against both colonial and post-colonial commentators, and reject the version of the Malay hero (Hang Tuah) as blindly obedient, in favour of a more dynamic oppositional figure (Hang Jebat). Thus they consciously work to create a model hero for the times – one, however, who cannot be endorsed by the post-colonial governments because of that hero's socialist aspirations.

Indeed, the problems which Malay politicians of the ruling elite have in endorsing Jebat as hero nicely indicate the nature of a more general dilemma which they face. It is their constant plea to Malays that they should be more active and vigorous, more independent, more assertive, more dynamic, less dependent on government protection. Musa Hitam warns them of the need to rid themselves of their *'mentaliti subsidi'* (their subsidy 'mentality'),[29] Mahathir tells them they have been protected long enough and that they must fight their own way in the marketplace towards 2020 (Jebat). However, assertiveness, argument and a challenge to their authority is what they most fear: criticism will lead to political instability and therefore Malays must be prepared unconditionally to surrender authority to their political leaders (Tuah) – participatory democracy is not really affordable, however desirable.[30]

The continuing difficulties which the present government has with this issue are reflected in its ambivalence towards the monarchy. Although seeing the monarchy's continued usefulness as a symbol of Malayness, Mahathir now seems to have come round to the old colonial view that its powers should be curtailed.[31] In taking action against the monarchy, he too

---

29. Musa Hitam, *Nationalism*, p. 48.

30. See the comments in Mahathir, *Holier Than Thou – A Mild Critique*, passim. In another context, Clive Kessler makes a similar point to this with respect to Tuah and Jebat which turns nicely on the punning possibilities of *merdeka* (freedom) and *menderhaka* (to be treacherous) in 'Archaism and Modernity: Contemporary Malay Political Culture', in Joel S. Kahn and Francis Lok Kok Wah (eds), *Fragmented Vision. Culture and Politics in Contemporary Malaysia*, Sydney: Asian Studies Association of Australia/Allen and Unwin, 1992, pp. 133–157.

31. See Mahathir, 'Pindaan untuk Kekalan Raja', *Dewan Masyarakat*, February, 1993, pp. 17–24.

risked a popular backlash, but his position is much more secure than the British. This last example is a good illustration of the intricate enmeshing of the past with the present, which as I have been arguing, characterizes much of the Malaysian political discourse today. The reason why such importance is attached to these issues relates to the acknowledged urgency of creating a sense of national identity, something which can only be accomplished if there is general agreement about the past. However, while different interpretations of the past compete for acceptance, the state cannot afford to wait upon consensus before devising a strategy for nationhood. There is a recognisable imperative to create a nationalist consciousness, that is, not only a sense of national identity but a commitment on the part of the citizenry to a common set of national goals as well as a sense of ownership of the nation. In the second part of this chapter, then, I want to show how the state is at present setting about its task, and the peculiarities of the Malaysian situation in this respect.

The Creation of a Nationalist Consciousness

Nationalism – *le désir d'être ensemble*, as we all know – precedes the formation of the nation, and relies for its force upon the evocation of symbols and myths of linguistic and cultural unity. When the nation is in place those symbols and myths are celebrated. At least that is the usual course of history. The Malaysian case, however, is somewhat exceptional for the reason that the *désir d'être ensemble* was never really a pronounced feature of the late colonial period. Not only was there no sense of common purpose among the different ethnic groups, but even among the Malays themselves there was a stronger commitment to local sultanates than to the idea of a nation-state. In other nations one sees a long lead-time between the emergence of nationalist sentiments coupled with the creation of powerful symbols of the nation by politicians and intellectuals, and the eventual achievement of nationhood. It is during this lead-time that the people acquire an understanding of and a commitment to the nation. We see this happening during the later colonial period in India and Burma as well as in Indonesia, Vietnam and the Philippines. The idea of the nation, it is true, is stronger in some of those countries than in others, and is held more enthusiastically by some of the minority groups in these countries than by others, but nonetheless the point at issue is the importance of a period during which there is the opportunity to consolidate the symbols of nationalism. In contrast to the other nations of South and Southeast Asia, this lead-time in Malaya was foreshortened because in effect nationalism was a post-1945 phenomenon, and nationhood was conceived and achieved before the symbolic discourse was in place. National identity, consequently, had to be created on the hoof.

In the case of Malaysia there is a further twist to the evolution of ideas about a national identity in so far as the effects of specific historical events – which always determine and change the character of the appeal to national identity from moment to moment – have meant that immediate concerns with political identity and international recognition have excluded any real discussion of cultural identity. This was despite the fact that the multi-ethnic composition of the citizenry would seem to have demanded that this issue be given priority in the development of the nation. At least this was the case until 1969, and arguably even today the framing of a discourse of unique Malaysian identity in cultural terms is woefully inadequate as a point of reference for nationalist consciousness.

The origins of the formation of a political identity in the disputes over the Malayan Union and the Federation have already been discussed above. It needs to be recalled here that, although there was of course considerable concern about rights and political status with respect to three major issues (the position of the Malay aristocracy, the primary importance of the Malay language, and the concept of the indigenous people),[32] the real debates of the time were about the political entity that Malaya would become and the fixing of its territorial boundaries. What I am suggesting, then, is that in the first place the arguments were about the maximization of political privileges and economic opportunities for the parties involved, the peoples of Malaya and the British, and that references to language and the *bumiputera* are to be understood in that context. Second, and following from that, national identity as a constellation of clearly defined symbols and attributes was, if not entirely neglected in the discussion, regarded as a residual category; only after political consensus had been achieved and become electorally operational, could it then be properly attended to. The implementation of that promise of attention, however, was continually postponed. There were immediate political reasons for this: the Federation was transformed into Malaysia which in turn went through various vicissitudes, for example, confrontation with Indonesia, the split with Singapore. In other words, the

---

32. This is well explained in Oo Yu Hock, *Ethnic Chameleon. Multiracial Politics in Malaysia*, Petaling Jaya: Pelanduk Publications, 1991, pp. 48–56.

issue of political identity was forever being renegotiated and never sufficiently settled to allow discussion of other things. In the second place, there seems to have been a failure of the imagination on the part of the ruling Malaysian politicians who, as has been said so many times before, were content with the compromises which they reached for themselves with respect to existing circumstances and took very little thought for the future. The forging of a national identity and the very necessary task of constructing a universally acceptable set of symbols were never really on the agenda, and in their place were desultory and sporadic discussions of language and literature. Then, as we know, the riots of 13 May 1969 occurred, which did prompt immediate discussions of national identity. It was clear, or so it seemed, that an appeal to the common goal of economic prosperity by itself was insufficient, and that, underlying the *modus vivendi* established since independence, there was a sense, not of togetherness, but of separateness. Consequently, the efficiency of the old symbols of nation would have to be critically reappraised, and new ones, if necessary, would have to be appropriately created. If a sense of commitment of all its citizens to the nation was to be properly inculcated, Malaysia would need to be fashioned anew.

The Refashioning of Malaysia

The urgency of the need to persuade the Malaysian population that they all shared a common identity of sorts was precipitated, as I have suggested above, by the riots of May 1969. It had been all very well, muddling through until then in the vague expectation that the euphoria of independence (*Merdeka*) would sustain a general feeling of cooperation and harmony, which would give rise to a sense of common citizenship, that all would be post-colonial subjects of Malaysia. The new set of circumstances indicated that a much more purposeful and organized political engineering was required.

Initially there appear to have been two prongs to the quickly devised strategy: the first was the invention of cultural political symbols to which it was hoped to attach a sense of common national purpose; the second was the creation of a new economic strategy, the New Economic Plan (NEP), which by constantly and repeatedly holding out the promise of a better future for all, would, it was hoped, bring about a fusion of interests in the long run, at least at the level at which it counted, the bureaucratic and commercial middle classes.

The political symbol on which greatest initial emphasis was placed was the *Rukun Negara*, a set of five principles of state, closely modelled on the Indonesian *Pancasila*.[33] The *Rukun Negara*, with its unexceptional and pious declarations of the importance of harmony among ethnic groups and loyalty and commitment to the sovereignty and welfare of the nation, was much trumpeted in the early years after 1969, but somehow it never caught on. The Malaysian political public was perhaps too sophisticated to see it as other than a set of platitudes, certainly not something to encourage a sense of commitment.[34]

It could, however, be argued that the reason for the decline of *Rukun Negara* as a national symbol was not so much a lack of public enthusiasm, as a failure of the government's vision in relation to how to pursue its potential. There was never any concerted attempt to advance *Rukun Negara*, not only as a set of political and ethical principles, but as a political and educational foundation on which an image of the nation could be constructed. In other words the Malaysian government failed to do what, for example, Suharto's New Order Government did with *Pancasila*, namely embed in the national psyche the concepts of the nation contained within the principles through a systematic programme of education and political restructuring. Ask almost any Indonesian what characterizes the Indonesian polity and differentiates Indonesia from other nations and the reply will be – whether the speaker wholly believes it or not – that it is the fact that Indonesia is ruled according to *Pancasila* democracy. There are no such resonances attached to *Rukun Negara* in Malaysia.

For whatever reason, then, *Rukun Negara* lacked substance, and rather than working towards the creation of a common set of political and moral values, the government in effect opted ultimately to promote the economic vision of wealth for all to the exclusion of almost everything else. One consequence of this, incidentally, was the rise of Islamic organizations including the Islamic Youth Movement, ABIM, once led by Anwar Ibrahim, the

---

33. It is interesting to note in parenthesis that there had been an earlier attempt to graft *Pancasila* on to political discourse in Malaya. Ariffin describes how Dr Burhanuddin Al Helmy of the PKKM, perhaps as part of his overall strategy of bringing the two countries together, as early as October 1945 was already devising a set of five principles clearly modelled on *Pancasila* for his party. See Ariffin Omar, *Bangsa Melayu, Malay Concepts of Democracy and Community 1945–1950*, Kuala Lumpur: Oxford University Press, 1993, p. 43.

34. Analogous to the reiteration of *Rukun Negara* on public occasions was the television programme *Potret Pekerti* where a weekly drama ritually celebrated expressions of inter-ethnic harmony. Viewers were well able to share the sentiment but the everyday practice was no nearer achievement.

current deputy prime minister, to fill the moral vacuum. The nature of the New Economic Policy, NEP, and its relative success and failure in achieving its enunciated and unenunciated objectives need not detain us here. One point that does, however, need stressing in relation to our concern with the pursuit of a sense of national Malaysian identity in that decade of the 1970s is that the specific rhetoric of the NEP was directed largely at the Malays, who were then able to see themselves as the visible beneficiaries of new educational and employment policies. Conversely, Chinese and Indians, or at least those within the senior level government sector, saw themselves as disadvantaged, and looked for opportunities for escape. By the end of the decade, then, it was clear that though the strategy of emphasizing economic prosperity for all was working successfully in so far as there were no major political upheavals, the manner of its articulation was in danger of being divisive. A new rhetoric was again called for and provided.

The most visible signs of this new rhetoric were Mahathir's policies and slogans of the early 1980s: 'Look East', 'Malaysia Incorporated', 'Buy British Last'.[35] At one level these slogans can be interpreted as moves in the direction of creating an international presence, that is, rejecting the label of ex-colonial by asserting an individual Asian identity, but, more importantly, it seems to me, they should be read as initiating a new concept of national identity which ruptures the continuity with the past.

In effect, the embracing of the international vocabulary of moderniza-tion, the new ethic of commercial values and practices, and the conscious exploitation of the metaphor of the company to describe the aims and operation of the state, all suggest a comprehensive reorientation of the notion of the subject and citizen within Malaysia. Questions of ethnic identity, symbols of cultural distinctiveness – apart from those manufactured for international consumption – are all now subordinated to the demand to integrate Malaysians into a global culture.

Particularly striking has been the hardening of Mahathir's political style since 1990. For foreign observers this has been most in evidence in relation to various international confrontations in which Mahathir has been increasingly at the centre of defending his, and *de facto* his country's, position against the allegedly defamatory and exploitative tactics of the countries of the North: the issues range from irritation at the epithet 'recalcitrant' which the Australian prime minister used of him, to the much greater reactions of

---

35. See, for an explanation of some of these concepts, Mahathir, 'New Government Poli-cies' in Jomo K. Sundaram (ed.), *Mahathir's Economic Policies*, Petaling Jaya: Insan, 1988, pp. 1–3,

the Pergau Dam Affair of 1993–94 in which, while criticizing British aid policy to Malaysia, the British press appeared to be casting aspersions on Malaysian politicians. Within Malaysia this particular type of robust approach interpreted as tweaking of the noses of Britain and Australia enhances his reputation as a statesman. A similar toughness in relation to opponents at home has caused rather more uneasiness, but, at least if election results are anything to go by, it too has been largely endorsed. That endorsement has in turn led to the confidence with which, ever since 1990, the new rhetoric has acquired a futuristic dimension.

It was in 1990 that the fourth five-year plan, and with it the strategy of the NEP, came to an end. The ostensible intention of the NEP had been a more equal distribution of wealth. It was widely interpreted as a move of positive discrimination in favour of the Malays, and it is, I think, fair to argue that, however inaccurate it may have been as an interpretation, not much was done to correct the impression that this was what was intended. The replacement for the NEP was the National Development Plan (NDP), which in addition to giving the same detailed attention to economic planning needed to be underwritten by a new ideology.[36]

It is precisely this ideological underwriting which Mahathir has provided in his so-called 'Vision 2020', the most remarkable feature of which is the way in which to all intents and purposes the issue of national identity has been side-stepped: Malaysia's identity in 2020 will be no different from that of any other advanced prosperous nation in the world, and Malaysian citizens will be no different from the citizens of other such nations. Note, for example, how the Malay symbols have been whittled away: the monarchy is reduced to performing a superficial ceremonial function; the English language, that is the language of international commerce, is now reinstated in institutions of higher education; Malays are informed that they must shed their attachment to irrelevant historical traditions, depend less on government handouts and stand on their own two feet.

There is, however, one great drawback to this strategy and it is one which Mahathir and Anwar Ibrahim both partially recognize: the internationalization of the Malaysian citizen cannot be accomplished without all the horrors that accompany the cultures of advanced capitalist societies. I say partially, because sometimes it does seem that Mahathir thinks that

---

36. The details are to be found in Chandran Jeshurun, 'Malaysia. The Mahathir Supremacy and Vision 2020', in *Southeast Asian Affairs 1993*, Singapore: Institute of Southeast Asian Studies, pp. 203–223.

Eastern materialism is of a different kind from Western materialism, and that it may be possible to borrow selectively. Writing, for example, about West and East, he suggests that the decline of moral values in West has been caused by the loss of self-confidence brought about by the loss of their colonies and the USA's defeat in the Vietnam War.[37] The West would have done well to preserve the old values of the colonial period, and in fact it is these old colonial values which the new nations should abide by. He writes:

> We have seen how by copying and practising the old values and systems of the West, the Eastern nations succeeded in regaining their independence. If the values and systems are preserved, the logical consequence is further success for these independent nations.

It would seem, then, that by a curious stroke of irony the second wave of decolonization of which Mahathir spoke has brought with it a repositioning of the post-colonial subject in Malaysia. The irony is to be found in the way in which a strategy designed at the levels of both economic policy and cultural rhetoric to lay the ghosts of the colonial period and inspire a self-confident and independent national identity ends with a shuffling hesitancy about both the past and the future. In terms of the past, it no longer seems clear how the old colonial institutions and values should be evaluated: perhaps there was something in them after all? And as for the future, as the post-colonial subject dissolves into the transnational subject, does this mean national symbols are now no longer important? It may, however, be possible to understand the direction of movement and the stages by which we have reached this paradoxical present situation through a realignment of analytical perspective. In the light of global capitalist imperatives, it becomes quite clear why nationalist movements needed to differentiate themselves in their immediate post-independent environments. It was to allow for a trans-itional period of global restructuring which would cushion the effects of de-colonization for the West, but once that restructuring had taken place then the survival of all within the new global structures would require a homo-genization of values, cultures and identities. In such a scenario Mahathir and Malaysia, far from being independent agents within contemporary political processes, are as much caught up by the juggernaut of global capitalism as other role-players on the international stage.

The construction of the post-colonial subject in Malaysia, that is the process of identifying the uniqueness of Malaysians in terms of a definitive legacy of historical and cultural practice and then creating a sense of national

37. Mahathir, *The Challenge*, Petaling Jaya: Pelanduk Publications, 1986, p. 47.

consciousness upon the basis of that identification, has over a period of fifty years come full circle. Post-colonialism has brought Malaysia to where colonialism always wanted it to be. And yet there remain some ambiguities. The dictatorship of the North over the South and the implicit evocation of a colonial past still regularly surface in political debates; the symbols of culture and language are still sometimes rattled; and alternative voices outlining visions of the future different from those found in official blueprints, are still occasionally to be heard. Despite appearances there is never a finality about political discourse. In politics as in all else, everything flows. The terms of the discussion change, and the categories and distinctions which once seemed to have such value become obsolete and need to be discarded. The category of the post-colonial subject has not quite exhausted its usefulness: there remains, for example, further work to do on the enduring effects of colonially created institutions of bureaucracy, law and education. Debates on the future of Malaysia, however, are likely to be more about post-modernist consumers and less about post-colonial subjects.

CHAPTER TWELVE

Nations-of-Intent in Malaysia

Shamsul A.B.

Introduction

At independence, Malaysian society comprised three major ethnic communities, namely, the indigenous community or *bumiputera* (lit. sons of the soil), who accounted for 50 per cent of the population, and two sizeable immigrant communities, one Chinese (37 per cent) and the other Indian (11 per cent). Since then, the censuses of 1970, 1980 and 1990 have shown that, in spite of the general increase in the population, from about 10 to 18 million, the ethnic composition has not changed significantly. However, to most Malaysians, it is the *bumiputera* and non-*bumiputera* ethnic divide that is perceived as significant, used in official government documents as well as in the idiom of everyday interaction, despite the fact that there is heterogeneity within both. Nonetheless, colloquially, the public refers to this ethnic divide simply as '*bumi* and non-*bumi*', reflecting the delicate demographic balance between the two categories, each constituting about 50 per cent of the population. This has important wider implications in the social life of Malaysians, especially in political terms.

One of those involves the question of 'national identity'. At the level of 'authority-defined social reality', which is *bumiputera*-dominated, the national identity question is perceived by the government as a non-issue because its basis and content has been spelt out in a number of policy documents within the framework of the Malaysian Constitution. It is a *bumiputera*-defined identity that has privileged many aspects of *bumiputera* culture as the 'core' of the Malaysian national identity while recognizing, if peripherally, the cultural symbols of other ethnic groups.[1]

---

1. See Kementerian Kebudayaan, Belia dan Sukan, Malaysia (KKBSM), *Asas-Asas Kebudayaan Malaysia*, Kuala Lumpur: KKBSM, 1973 and Aziz Deraman, *Masyarakat dan Kebudayaan Malaysia*, Kuala Lumpur: KKBSM, 1975.

On the other hand, at the level of 'everyday social reality', the authority-defined national identity has been challenged by three groups, namely, the non-*bumiputera* group, led by the Chinese, and two *bumiputera* ones, the non-Muslim *bumiputera* group and the radical Islamic *bumiputera* group, each offering its own nation-of-intent, i.e. its own vision of what the national identity should be, based on a particular ideological framework. The non-*bumiputera* reject the *bumiputera*-based and *bumiputera*-defined national identity in preference for a more 'pluralized' national identity, in which the culture of each ethnic group in Malaysia is accorded a position equal to that of the *bumiputera*. For instance, the Chinese suggest that Chinese language and rituals should be considered as an integral part of the national identity.[2] Although both the non-Muslim *bumiputera* and the radical Islamic *bumiputera* accept the authority-defined *bumiputera*-based national identity, the former suggest that Christianity and 'native religions' be accorded equal status to that of Islam, as components within it; the latter, on the contrary, rejects what it sees as the secular, modernist Islamic component of the identity in preference for a 'truer and purer' Islam. The Kadazan of Sabah argue forcefully for the non-Muslim *bumiputera* case and the Parti Islam of Kelantan for the radical Islamic *bumiputera* group.[3]

Those who believe that Malaysia is an authoritarian state, with *bumiputera* hegemony well entrenched, view the opposition to the authority-defined national identity as an anomaly, a social aberration, or as minority voices, which the state allows as an act of benevolence or a form of 'social tokenism'. This view is informed, conceptually, by a 'benevolent state' thesis which stresses the fact that *bumiputera* dominance is a foregone conclusion. Hence dissenting voices find space at the behest of the *bumiputera* ruling class, who, in turn, use this to demonstrate that 'democracy' is well and alive in Malaysia. I find that this approach, albeit unwittingly, favours a kind of master narrative that downplays and, in an ironic twist, belittles many of the oppositions and differences of human experience that characterize everyday human life in Malaysia. Their 'hegemonic developmentalist' approach,

---

2. See, for instance, Kua Kia Soong, *National Culture and Democracy*, Petaling Jaya: Kersani, 1985; and Lim Kit Siang, *Malaysia: Crisis of Identity*, Petaling Jaya: Democratic Action Party, 1986.

3. For elaborations of the Kadazan case, see Francis Loh Kok Wah, 'Modernization, Cultural Revival and Counter-Hegemony: The Kadazans of Sabah in the 1980s', in Joel Kahn and Francis Loh KokWah (eds), *Fragmented Vision: Culture and Politics in Contemporary Malaysia*, Sydney: Allen and Unwin, 1992, pp. 225–253. For some background on Parti Islam recent ideological shift, see Jomo K.S. and Ahmad Shabery Cheek, 'The Politics of Malaysia's Islamic Resurgence', in *Third World Quarterly*, vol.10, no. 2, 1988, pp. 843–868; and Alias Mohamed, *Malaysia's Islamic Opposition: Past, Present and Future*, Kuala Lumpur: Gateway Publications, 1991.

which is not dissimilar to O'Donnell's 'bureaucratic authoritarianism' approach, ignores most of what is going on behind the public scene.[4]

I think it is more instructive to give equal weight to the dominant and the dominated, each representing a different view or approach, and each articulating dissimilar interests. This opens the way for uncertainties, ruptures and tensions. With such an approach we are in a better position to highlight the alternatives, their attendant differences, however slight, the distances between them and, most significantly, the dialogue between them, fruitful or futile, eventful or mundane. This is the strategy of this chapter. It is an effort to make sense of dissenting voices in the Malaysian present-day social milieu with regard to the question of national identity.[5] In doing so, I am offering a discourse analysis on the origin, social roots and bureaucratic management of contemporary contestation regarding Malaysia's national identity: a Malaysia, or a nation, which is in a hurry to realise its 'modernization project'.[6]

4. For a discussion on recent forms of bureaucratic authoritarianism, see G. O'Donnell and P.C. Schmitter, *Transitions from Authoritarian Rule: Tentative Conclusions about Uncertain Democracies*, Baltimore: Johns Hopkins University Press, 1989. For analysis on the issue of authoritarianism in Malaysia, see Harold Crouch, 'Authoritarian Trends, the UMNO Split and the Limits of State Power', in Kahn and Loh (eds), *Fragmented Vision*, pp. 21–43; Simon Tan, 'The Rise of State Authoritarianism in Malaysia', in *Bulletin of Concerned Asian Scholars*, vol. 22, no. 3, 1990, pp. 32–42; and Johan Saravanamuttu, 'The State, Authoritarianism and Industrialisation: Reflections on the Malaysian Case', in *Kajian Malaysia*, vol. 5, no. 2, 1987, pp. 43–75.
5. For an elaboration on some aspects of this approach, see Anthony Giddens, 'Living in a Post-Traditional Society', in Ulrich Beck, Anthony Giddens and Scott Lash (eds), *Reflexive Modernisation: Politics, Tradition and Aesthetics in the Modern Social Order*, Oxford: Polity Press, 1994, pp. 56–109; Anthony Giddens, *Beyond Left and Right: The Future of Radical Politics*, Oxford: Polity Press, 1994, especially, ch. 4: 'Two Theories of Democratization', pp.104–133; and Michael Herzfeld, *The Social Production of Indifference: Exploring the Symbolic Roots of Western Bureaucracy*, Chicago: University of Chicago Press, 1993. For a useful application of such an approach based on a long-term anthropological research, see Clifford Geertz, *After the Fact: Two Countries, Four Decades, One Anthropologist*, Cambridge: Harvard University Press, 1995, especially, ch. 6, 'Modernities', pp. 137–168.
6. As background information, please note that I have discussed and analysed various aspects of what I call Malaysia's 'bureaucratic management of identity' in a series of recent papers, namely Shamsul A.B., 'National Unity: Malaysia's Model for Self-Reliance', in Shamsul (ed.), *Malaysian Development Experience: Changes and Challenges*, Kuala Lumpur: National Institute of Public Administration, 1994, pp. 3–26; 'The Bureaucratic Management of Identity in a Modern State: "Malayness" in Postwar Malaysia', paper for a conference on 'Minority/Majority Discourse', Honolulu, 11–13 August 1994; 'The Cultural Agenda of Malaysia's Economic Development: The Bumiputera Policy Re-Examined', paper for a conference on 'Market Cultures: Entrepreneurial Precedents and Ethical Dilemmas in East and Southeast Asia', Boston,, 1–2 October 1994; 'The Market and the Malays: The Materialist Dimension of "Malayness" Re-Examined', paper for a workshop on 'Social and Cultural Dimensions of Market Expansion', Batam, Indonesia, 3–4 October 1994; 'Orang Kaya Baru: Origin, Construction and Predicament of Malay Nouveaux Riches', a paper for a workshop on 'Cultural Constructions of Asia's New Rich', Perth, 8–10 July 1995; and 'From Melayu to Bumiputera: Bureaucratic Management of Identity in Malaysia', a paper for the 'Joint Seminar', National Museum of Ethnology, Osaka, 19 July 1995.

I have chosen this strategy for two main reasons. First, most analyses of Malaysia's modernization project tend to emphasize the material process. Whereas this, of course, is necessary, I believe that we should also try to grasp the ideological, and in many ways 'abstract' contestation that goes with moderniza-tion. There is a need to explore what happens in the political space, beyond politics of parties and numbers, particularly in the realm of ideas, symbols and perceptions. Second, in so doing I hope to outline some of the origins of the present 'abstract' ideological struggle over the definition of national identity, not only amongst elites but between people in the street. They are particularly concerned about the practical consequences of various concepts of community for their everyday lives and the future, such as their children's education, the usefulness of their mother tongue and other cultural practices. Such concerns, mundane as they seem, are closely linked to the larger issue of Malaysia's future as a nation.

I shall begin with an outline of Malaysia's effort to chart the trajectory of its modernization project, particularly its unfinished political agenda, namely to create 'a united Malaysian nation', a *Bangsa Malaysia*, by the year 2020. Then I move on to discuss the ongoing debate amongst various social groups, both *bumiputera* and non-*bumiputera*, regarding the kind of Malaysian nation that each is trying to promote. The origin and social roots of these nations-of-intent shall be discussed. Then, the impact of this contestation for the intentional construction of knowledge about Malaysia will be examined. Finally, some possible long-term implications of these continued states of contestation within Malaysia shall be discussed.

Malaysia's 'Modernization Project': an Unfinished Political Agenda

Broadly speaking, Malaysia's 'modernization project' has two interconnected main components, the economic and the political. If the economic component is driven by the need to industrialize, the political one is motivated by the need to realise a nation. To achieve both has been the central objective of Malaysia's modernization project.[7]

---

7. The best source for official policy statement and report on Malaysia's 'modernization project' is still the five-year plan documents published by the Malaysian government. The two important ones are Government of Malaysia, *Second Malaysia Plan 1971–1975*, Kuala Lumpur: Government Printers, 1971 and *Sixth Malaysia Plan 1991–1995*, Kuala Lumpur: Government Printers, 1991. I have analysed some of its basic features and theoretical orientation in Shamsul A.B., *RMK, Tujuan dan Pelaksanaannya, Suatu Tinjauan Teoritis*, Kuala Lumpur: Dewan Bahasa dan Pustaka, 1977.

Politicians, policy-makers and most informed observers on Malaysia seem to hold the view that the economic component of Malaysia's modernization effort, as of the last decade, is not as problematic as the political one. Such a view has emerged against the background of Malaysia's spectacular economic growth, particularly during the last eight years. But we do know that the Malaysian economy, successful as it is, has a number of difficulties.[8] However, it has been argued that the political difficulties are more serious than the economic ones and they are perceived as obstacles to Malaysia's further economic success. In other words, Malaysia's achievement thus far has been perceived as one-sided, heavily economic in nature, and not matched by a similar achievement in the political sphere.[9]

Against such a perceived background as well as a concern for the long-term survival of the society, Malaysia's prime minister, Dr Mahathir Mohamad, in 1991, introduced his famous *Wawasan 2020*, or Vision 2020, which simply means that in the year 2020 Mahathir wants Malaysia to be an advanced industrialized country with an established nation, hence a fully modern society.[10] He lists a number of challenges and obstacles that Malaysia has to overcome in order to achieve this vision. It is quite clear that, to him, the political challenge of creating 'a united Malaysian nation', or a *Bangsa Malaysia*, is the greater and critical one compared to the economic challenge of sustaining the current level of economic growth in Malaysia's effort to become modern.

The fact that Mahathir emphasized the need to create 'a united Malaysian nation' implies that Malaysia is still 'one state with several nations', meaning that in the broad economic sense it is a coherent variant of a capitalist entity,

8. For a useful discussion on Malaysia's economic performance and related problems in the last fifteen years, especially its effort at industrialization, see Jomo K.S. (ed.), *Industrialising Malaysia*, London: Routledge, 1993.

9. An interesting comment on this matter was made recently by a former special advisor to the Malaysian government in the 1960s, who is an American professor and political scientist: see Milton J. Esman, *Ethnic Politics*, Ithaca: Cornell University Press, 1994, especially, Ch. 3, 'Malaysia: Native Sons and Immigrants', pp. 49–74.

10. Subsequent reference and discussion in this chapter to Vision 2020 and the concept of *Bangsa Malaysia* is based on Dr Mahathir Mohamad's working paper, interestingly written in English and later translated into Malay, 'Malaysia: The Way Forward', delivered at the Inaugural Meeting of the Malaysian Business Council, Kuala Lumpur, 28 February 1991. Its content has now become a subject of public discussion and debate. In fact his Vision 2020 has developed into a kind of popular public idiom and has become an integral part of Malaysia's present-day political discourse. So popular is this phrase now, particularly, the figure 2020 and the word *Wawasan*, that both have been used in advertisements and billboards of food-stalls, such as *Warong Wawasan* or *Warong 2020*, cinema and entertainment centres, such as *Pawagam 2020*, *Wawasan Billiard Saloon* and *2020 Karaoke Centre*, or used even to name cakes, such as *Kuih Lapis Wawasan*.

but in the political and ideological sense it is still searching for a parallel coherence because there exist strong competing nations-of-intent.[11]

By nation-of-intent I mean a more or less precisely defined idea of the form of a nation, i.e. its territory, population, language, culture, symbols and institutions. The idea must be shared by a number of people who perceive themselves as members of that nation, and who feel that it unites them. A nation-of-intent may imply a radical transformation of a given state, and the exclusion or inclusion of certain groups of people. It may also imply the creation of a new state, but it does not necessarily imply an aspiration for political self-rule on the part of the group of people who are advancing their nation-of-intent. It may be an inclusive construct, open to others, and which is employed as the basis for a political platform voicing dissent or a challenge to the established notion of nation. In any case, the concept nation-of-intent depicts an idea of a nation that still needs to be constructed or reconstructed. It promises the citizens (or some of them) an opportunity to participate in a 'grand project' which they can claim as theirs. It therefore bridges the authority-defined and the everyday-defined idea of a nation. In the Malaysian case, as admitted by Mahathir, the 'united Malaysian nation' is yet to be born. Hence various social groups in Malaysia can still voice their different nations-of-intent.

In some aspects, conceptually, 'nation-of-intent' is not dissimilar to Anderson's concept of 'imagined political community'.[12] By 'imagined', he does not necessarily mean 'invented', but rather the members of the said community 'will never know most of their fellow-members, meet them, or even hear them, yet in the minds of each lives the image of their communion'.[13] However, nation-of-intent is a more open-ended concept. It is more positive,

---

11. I first came across the 'nation-of-intent' concept in the work of a former colleague, Rustam A. Sani, 'The Origin of the Malay Left: An Analysis of the Social Roots', MA dissertation, Faculty of Social Sciences, University of Kent at Canterbury, United Kingdom, 1975. He was examining *Melayu Raya* as a Malay nation-of-intent as proposed by the Malay left. Since then I have explored the applicability of this concept beyond the Malay left context. The concept, however, was introduced by Robert I. Rotberg, 'African Nationalism: Concept or Confusion?' in *Journal of Modern African Studies*, vol. 4, no. 1, 1966, pp. 33–46. Nonetheless, I am grateful to Rustam A. Sani for the discussions we have had on the usefulness of this concept, analytically. In refining it for the present essay I gratefully acknowledge comments made by Ben Anderson.

12. See Benedict Anderson, *Imagined Communities: Reflections on the Origin and Spread of Nationalism,* London:Verso, 1983. For some recent comments on Anderson's 'imagined communities', see, for instance, Partha Chatterjee, *The Nation and Its Fragments: Colonial and Postcolonial Histories,* Princeton: Princeton University Press, 1993, ch.1, 'Whose Imagined Community?', pp. 3–13.

13. Anderson, *Imagined Communities*, p. 6.

proactive and forward-looking. It has a programmatic plan of action articulated in *realpolitik* which has, in the Malaysian case, emerged not only from a historical context of anti-colonialism but also in the post-colonial era. In the latter it serves as an alternative way of formulating political intentions even though, mostly, it remains at the discourse level. However, in a number of cases, especially in particular localities, the idea of advancing alternative nations-of-intent has found concrete expression, hence political space. This is what has happened in the local states of Kelantan and Sabah. In both states, the local ruling party, which opposes the Malaysian UMNO-dominated government, has made serious attempts not only to continue to articulate its own nation-of-intent but also to implement some aspects of it locally. Even though these attempts have met with limited success, they have demonstrated that it is possible to have and hold on to one's nation-of-intent and implement it within the so-called 'authoritarian' political context in Malaysia.[14]

It is in this sense that the Malaysian situation, in some ways, is not unlike the African one. If the latter has been complicated by 'tribal nationalism' thus giving rise to a situation described as 'one state, many nationalisms', the Malaysian case could be described as a situation of 'one state, several nations', or more precisely, nations-of-intent.[15]

The concept of a united Malaysian nation, proposed by Mahathir, could be interpreted in two ways: first, to mean 'the nation as a cultural community', a kind of political innovation which suggests the idea of rural and urban, intra- and inter-ethnic, and inter-class solidarity,[16] (clearly, here Mahathir is not using the term 'nation' in the traditional 'aspiration for political self-rule' sense); and, second, to mean the construction of a 'national identity', hence 'national integration'. In fact, the latter has been the overriding, but as yet not realized, objective of the New Economic Policy, which was launched in 1971, implemented over two decades, and ended in 1990.

---

14. Beside contributions by Francis Loh, Jomo and Ahmad Shabery Cheek, and Nagata cited in footnote 3, it also useful to see James Ongkili, *Nation-Building in Malaysia, 1946–1974*, Kuala Lumpur: Oxford University Press, 1985; Jeffrey Kitingan, 'Thorny Issues in Federal and State Relations: The Case for Sabah and Sarawak', in *Reflections on the Malaysian Constitution*, Penang: Aliran Publications, 1987, pp. 149–168; and, on recent development of Malaysia's Islamic resurgent movement, see Shamsul A.B. 'Religion and Ethnic Politics in Malaysia: The Significance of the Islamic Resurgent Phenomenon', in Charles Keyes, Laurel Kendall, Helen Hardacre (eds), *Asian Visions of Authority: Religion and the Modern States of East and Southeast Asia*, Honolulu: University of Hawaii Press, 1994, pp. 99–116.

15. For the African case, see, Victor Olorunsolo (ed.), *The Politics of Cultural Sub-Nationalism in Africa*, New York: Anchor Books, 1977

16. See Mahathir, 'Malaysia: The Way Forward', pp. 2–5.

Some observers have said that Mahathir's concept of *Bangsa Malaysia* is not really different from the one proposed by Lee Kuan Yew in 1963, when he was chief minister of Singapore and Singapore was still in Malaysia. However, some Malay bureaucratic intellectuals have answered that Mahathir's concept is qualitatively different. Whereas Lee Kuan Yew argued for a nation in which everyone, irrespective of race, colour and creed, would enjoy equal status, Mahathir argues for a nation in which the constitutionally recognized *bumiputera*'s special position, hence *bumiputera* political dominance, is retained and accepted by all Malaysians.[17]

Therefore, it could be said that the shaping of the political agenda of Malaysia's modernization project, as outlined by Mahathir, is contextualized within the existing legal-bureaucratic structures, namely, the Malaysian Constitution and the federalist nature of the state. Lee Kuan Yew's 'Malaysian Malaysia' agenda, on the other hand, demands a radical constitutional reform and perhaps the formation of an 'absolutist' unitary state, such as the one in Singapore, which, according to many analysts, has not really been a 'Singaporean Singapore'.[18] In spite of that, the Democratic Action Party (DAP), the Chinese-controlled main opposition political party in Malaysia, has continued, from the late 1960s until the last general election of 1995, to call for a 'Malaysian Malaysia' as its nation-of-intent.

Since it is unlikely that a radical constitutional reform will take place in Malaysia, by implication the formation of a unitary state in the mould of 'Malaysian Malaysia' is improbable. But, in Mahathir's opinion, there is no reason why Malaysians should not strive to create a 'united Malaysia nation' and build their own 'national identity'. Ironically, it is this very suggestion that keeps the debate open, about what kind of *Bangsa Malaysia* we should have, or at least that is the perception of many social groups in contemporary Malaysia. Hence the dialogue between various nations-of-intent is alive and well in Malaysia at present, arguably, in a redefined political space. Therefore, it is not surprising that elites from various ethnic groups in Malaysia continue to articulate different nations-of-intent.[19] These notions

---

17. See Rustam A. Sani, *Melayu Baru dan Bangsa Malaysia: Tradisi Cendekia dan Krisis Budaya*, Kuala Lumpur: Utusan Publications, 1993.

18. For recent empirical evidence on this, see, for example, Tania Li, *The Malays in Singapore*, Singapore: Oxford University Press, 1989 and Lai Ah Heng, *Meanings of Multiethnicity: A Case-Study of Ethnicity and Ethnic Relations in Singapore*, Kuala Lumpur: Oxford University Press, 1995.

19. See, for instance, the collection of speeches by the present president of MCA (Malaysian Chinese Association), the largest Chinese political party in the ruling coalition party called the National Front, Ling Leong Sik, *The Malaysian Chinese: Towards Vision 2020*, Petaling Jaya: Pelanduk Publications, 1995.

cannot be dismissed as wishful thinking, because some are actively articulated and operationalized in various institutional forms, such as through
political parties, NGOs and cultural organizations.

Malaysia's Competing Nations-of-Intent

What are the origin and social roots of the plurality of nations-of-intent in
Malaysia? How does Mahathir's Vision 2020 figure in the overall picture?
How, for instance, has it influenced the shaping of social scientific know-
ledge about Malaysia?

As it is presently, Malaysia has all the features of a modern democratic
capitalist state. It has a Constitution, respects the rule of law and the
concept of citizenship, recognizes and staunchly guards its territory, has a
bona fide government, and conducts relatively free elections at regular
intervals. With its booming economy it has more than enough funds not
only to finance massive development projects but also to write off massive
leaks, otherwise known as 'economic mismanagement', in the system.[20] In
the Hobbesian sense, the Malaysian state is working well as 'an artificial
animal'. As long as the economy prospers, which it has for the last decade,
the state survives.

But Mahathir has clearly indicated that having a strong and active
Malaysian state and a thriving economy cannot really guarantee the state's
continued survival. It could easily be dismantled by centrifugal forces,
particularly ethnic disunity.[21] Therefore Mahathir believes that it is
imperative for Malaysians to persevere in the effort to create a united
Malaysian nation despite unsuccessful efforts over the last two decades. In
his mind, this is simply one of the better ways to avoid the rise of dismantling tendencies which could threaten the state. In my view, he has
unwittingly described Malaysia as a society in 'a state of stable tension'. The
concern to avoid Malaysia suffering the same fate as Yugoslavia was also in
his mind when he introduced his Vision 2020 in 1991. The ethnic problem

---

20. A number of publications on cases of economic mismanagement and political corrup-
tion in Malaysia are now available. The latest is by Edmund Gomez, *Political Business:
Corporate Involvement of Malaysian Political Parties*, Townsville, Australia: Centre for
Southeast Asian Studies, James Cook University, 1994.

21. Arguably, the best biography of Mahathir available to date is by Khoo Boo Teik, *Paradoxes of Mahathirism: An Intellectual Biography of Mahathir Mohamad*, Kuala Lumpur:
Oxford University Press, 1995. Subsequent reference to Mahathir's ideas on the economy,
politics, nationalism and the Third World are drawn from this book and Mahathir's
'Malaysia: The Way Forward'.

facing the former states of Eastern Europe was just then brewing and was brought live through 'direct CNN telecast via satellite' to the sitting rooms of Malaysian households.

What Mahathir was expressing through his Vision 2020 and the need to create a united Malaysian nation was essentially a new kind of ideology capable of bringing about cohesion and loyalty amongst Malaysians, a kind of antidote to the distruptive consequences that industrialization has brought to bear on Malaysian society. He saw that Malaysia needs to maintain, even improve, the present rate of growth of its industrial system of production which requires the 'homogenization' of the education, skills and conscious-ness of the people.[22] In other words, with the material aspect of Malaysian modernization almost in place, the state needs to redefine, even reconstitute, its 'imagined community' based on creating a shared culture that is strongly embedded in the state. Mahathir, therefore, wants the people's loyalty and attachment to be directed towards the state and the legislative system rather than to other social collectives. For this he needs popular support which he seems to have. His party won a resounding victory in the general elections of 1995. He claims that his government has offered security and stability to the people while the rest of the world has become fragmented and uprooted, and therefore his Vision 2020 should be accepted by all Malaysians.[23]

Herein lies the problem of his idea of a 'united Malaysian nation' both in a political and an intellectual sense. Politically, because of the delicate demographic balance that exists between the *bumiputera* and non-*bumiputera*; whereas the former dominate at the political level, the latter aspire to defuse this political dominance or free themselves of it. This has in turn encouraged them to entertain their own, old and new nations-of-intent and to strive hard, if not to achieve it, at least to get the state's recognition, especially in the current situation where the *bumiputera* are divided politically and the ruling party, particularly UMNO, has begun to depend more and more on the votes of non-*bumiputera* for its political survival.[24] Within the *bumiputera* community, as mentioned previously, Mahathir's idea of a united

22. See Khoo Boo Teik, *Paradoxes of Mahathirism*, pp. 327–331.

23. For a detailed analysis on UMNO's effort to woo Chinese support, see Ghazali Mayu-din, 'Menawan Hati Pengundi Cina: Pemerhatian di Pulau Pinang'; Lee Kam Hing, 'Parti-Parti Politik Cina dalam Pilihanraya 1995'; S.S. Pillay, 'Election 95: An Analysis', three papers from a seminar on Malaysia's 1995 general elections called 'Seminar Politik dan Pilihanraya di Malaysia', held at Universiti Kebangsaan Malaysia, Bangi, on 19 July 1995.

24. See *Information Malaysia 1995 Yearbook*, Kuala Lumpur: Berita Publishing, 1995, pp. 501–539.

Malaysian nation is being challenged, but on a different level, within the accepted *bumiputera* framework. As a result, the plurality of nations-of-intent in Malaysia persists.

Intellectually, Mahathir's concept of nation and national identity is beginning to be perceived as problematic by the so-called 'nationalist faction' within the *bumiputera* circle of bureaucratic intellectuals. The latter are beginning to express more openly than before their displeasure with Mahathir's attempt to reintroduce English language at the tertiary level and his recent attacks on the Malaysian royalty. His critics have perceived these moves as subtle attempts to 'deconstruct' Malayness and its three principal pillars, namely, *bahasa, agama dan raja* (lit. language, religion, royalty).[25] Since these intellectuals are influential in UMNO politics, their criticisms could lead to Mahathir's leadership within UMNO being challenged by his deputy, Anwar Ibrahim, who is closely associated with the bureaucratic intellectuals and seen by them as a defender of Malay ideological interests. In short, despite Mahathir's insistence that the 'united Malaysian nation' is to be created within the present political context of *bumiputera* dominance, he seems to have trouble convincing some of the influential supporters within UMNO that his idea of a *Bangsa Malaysia* is not undermining the very basis of Malayness.

The presence of a plurality of nations-of-intent in contemporary Malaysia demonstrates the fact that dissenting voices are present and heard, within and without government. The government may be controlling the mass media but this does not mean, as many foreign observers claim, that these voices are muted or silenced. The lack of lively intellectual discussions in the main English-language press, which have been the main source of information for the foreign observers, perhaps has made them arrive at this conclusion. However, dissenting voices in Malaysia are articulated in minor vernacular dailies, such as in the Malay, Mandarin, Tamil, Kadazan or Iban language; yet others can be found in the form of cassette and video tapes, pamphlets, 'poison letters', political party manifestos, and the like, hence inaccessible to most of these observers, whose dependence on English-speaking, Kuala Lumpur-based, middle-class *bumiputera* and non-*bumiputera* for information is a well-known fact. This trend partly has resulted in the flourishing of the 'benevolent state' thesis I mentioned at the outset.

---

25. See, for example, Ahmat Adam, Kassim Ahmad and Rustam A. Sani, *Intelektualisme Melayu: Satu Polemik*, Kertas Kadangkala Bil. 5, Fakulti Sains Kemasyarakatan dan Kemanusiaan, Universiti Kebangsaan Malaysia, Bangi, 1989.

Therefore, it is useful for us to examine in some detail the origin and social roots of these dissenting voices found both within the *bumiputera* and the non-*bumiputera* groups, in the past and at present. By applying a historical perspective we should be able to find out how the nations-of-intent of the various social groups in Malaysia have emerged and been articulated, some during the colonial period and others only after independence. Most of them were articulated through political parties but there were also those which were promoted by ethnic-based social organizations.

WITHIN THE BUMIPUTERA

We must recognize the fact that the authority-defined nation-of-intent which is promoted currently in Malaysia is a *bumiputera*-based one, but also only one of the many found within the *bumiputera* community. It is not Kadazan or Iban but one that emerged amongst the Malay community in Peninsular Malaysia some fifty years ago and was eventually institutionalized and endorsed by the British in the late 1940s and up to independence in 1957. This nation-of-intent belongs to the Malay 'administocrat' faction, which is one of the three nationalist elite factions within the Malay community in Peninsular Malaysia.[26]

This administocrat group organized itself as a political party, the United Malays National Organization (UMNO). Its rise to power had the support of the British. It is useful to trace briefly the general development of UMNO, particularly the content of its nation-of-intent and its implementation. This should give us an overall idea how Malaysia arrived at its present stage with a contested, or yet to be born, nation. This is relevant because it is UMNO's version of what Malaysia should be that has now become the object of reconsideration, even reconstruction, especially after Mahathir's grand Vision 2020. The latter has, in turn, increased the tempo of the discussion on the various nations-of-intent amongst the populace.

Since the end of the World War II, we have seen at least four phases of the implementation of the administocrats' (read UMNO's) nation-of-intent,

---

26. For detailed discussions of the political and social history of Malay nationalism, see William Roff, *The Origins of Malay Nationalism*, Kuala Lumpur: University of Malaya Press, 1967; Anthony Milner, *The Invention of Politics in Colonial Malaya*, Melbourne: Cambridge University Press, 1994; Ariffin Omar, *Bangsa Melayu: Malay Concepts of Democracy and Community, 1945–1950*, Kuala Lumpur: Oxford University Press, 1993. The term Malay 'administocrat', referring to Malay aristocrats and administrators, was introduced by Chandra Muzaffar in his important book, *The Protector?An Analysis of the Concept and Practice of Loyalty in Leader-led Relationships within Malay Society*, Penang: Aliran Publications, 1979.

made possible initially by British military and material support.[27] The first phase was during the reign of Onn Jaafar, UMNO's first president. His preferred 'nation' was a 'plural society nation'. It was hardly an original idea because its content was not dissimilar from the concept of nation proposed by the British in its Malayan Union project of 1946, which had failed because of opposition from a movement in which Onn Jaafar played a leading role.[28] Still Onn Jaafar's attempt to turn UMNO into a multi-ethnic party must be said to have been based on the 'plural society nation' idea which he thought suitable for the Malaysian multi-ethnic society. His adoption of such a concept of nation is not surprising in view of the fact that the Malayan Union concept was replaced by a federal concept, the Federation of Malaya Agreement in 1948, which, essentially, recognized the primacy of *negeri*-based *kerajaan* (provincial-based traditional Malay polity) and the *sultan* as its symbolic ruler.[29] In effect, UMNO then had no concept of nation in the sense articulated by Mahathir at present. Eventually, Onn Jaafar had to resign as UMNO's president when UMNO members rejected his 'plural society nation', which was perceived as abandoning Malay interests. He left UMNO and formed a short-lived multi-ethnic party. Tunku Abdul Rahman took over the leadership of UMNO from Onn Jaafar, which marked the beginning of the second phase. He adopted a similar viewpoint to that of Onn Jaafar, but advocated a 'Malay UMNO', retaining it as a communal party and thus emphasizing the primacy of Malay ethnic interests while recognizing the interests of other ethnic groups.

Abdul Razak, when he took over from Tunku Abdul Rahman soon after the Kuala Lumpur May 1969 racial riot, still retained the 'plural society nation' framework. He, however, further emphasized the primacy of Malay political hegemony, hence began the third phase. This was written into an amended Constitution and subsequently incorporated as a principle in the formulation of public policies and institutions, particularly in the form of the NEP, popularly known as the *bumiputera* policy. Hussein Onn, who succeeded Razak after his untimely demise in 1976, adopted the same framework. This constitutes the third phase.

---

27. The description here is based on the standard text on the history of UMNO and the Parti Islam: John Funston, *Malay Politics in Malaysia: A Study of the United Malays National Organisation and Parti Islam SeMalaysia*, Kuala Lumpur: Heinemann Asia, 1980.

28. For a recent detailed study on the political history of the struggle over the Malayan Union, see Albert Lau, *The Malayan Union Controversy, 1942–1948*, Singapore: Oxford University Press, 1991.

29. See Milner, *The Invention of Politics in Colonial Malaya*, ch. 4, 'Conceptualising a *Bangsa* Community', pp. 89–113.

It was not until 1981, when Dr Mahathir Mohamad took over from Hussein Onn, that the framework was modified to suit global changes and Mahathir's own vision of Malaysia's future as a Newly Industrialized Country. This commenced the fourth phase, which we are observing now. The pro-Japan 'Look East Policy' was born out of this ambition. However, Mahathir's vision of Malaysia's future, which was operationalized into policy initiatives in the late 1980s, did not alter the basics of Razak's version of a Malay-dominated plural society. Therefore, Mahathir's contribution was simply to turn Malaysia, a Malay-dominated plural society, into an NIC.

It is in this historical and ideological context that we should locate Mahathir's Vision 2020. To my mind it is really a restatement, if an upgrading, of his earlier commitment, made in 1981 soon after he became prime minister, to turn Malaysia into a modern state.[30] It is also a statement about what is to come after the NEP, which ended in 1990, especially regarding the future of the *bumiputera*'s role in the economy and of inter-ethnic relations and socio-political stability of Malaysia. In a historical sense, it could be argued that this is also the first time UMNO is promoting a clear concept of nation, beyond the *negeri*-based *kerajaan* framework nation and the British-initiated 'plural society nation'. But the fact remains that the present (UMNO) Malay-dominated Malaysian state is articulating only one version amongst the many of the nations-of-intent that exists within the *bumiputera* community.

Besides the administocrats, the other two factions within the Malay nationalist movement were the Malay Islamic faction and the Malay left, each with its own political agenda for the 'Malay nation' which they proposed to establish if they got into power.

The Islamic faction, represented by the Parti Islam (PI), offers an 'Islamic nation' as its nation-of-intent.[31] In fact, the PI briefly suspended its support for this idea in the early 1970s when the party joined the UMNO-dominated ruling coalition party, the National Front. However, the PI left the National Front in 1977 and has since been on its own. It has won back the majority in the State Legislative Assembly of Kelantan in the last two general elections of 1990 and 1995. It has also become more fundamentalist than before in the

---

30. For an elaboration on this point, see Shamsul A.B., *Malaysia's Vision 2020: Old Ideas in a New Package*, Working Paper 92–4, Development Studies Centre, Monash University, Melbourne, Australia, 1992.

31. For detailed informed discussion on Parti Islam's past, present and future strategies, see Alias Mohamed, *Malaysia's Islamic Opposition: Past, Present and Future*, Kuala Lumpur: Gateway Publications, 1991.

sense that it has rejected the notion of *assabiyah*, or ethnic group-based nation, and prefers an Islamic-based one, which considers every Muslim as equal in the eyes of Allah irrespective of colour, creed or race. So, the PI's concept of an 'Islamic nation' simply means a nation of Muslims and non-Muslims organized and administered using Quranic principles and Islamic laws. Perhaps the recent attempt to introduce and implement the strict Islamic *hudud* law in Kelantan is part of the strategy towards establishing a local prototype for the Islamic nation that the PI wants to establish throughout Malaysia. However, it has not been able to convince the non-*bumiputera* that it is not a *bumiputera* party using Islam as an ideological platform. Ironically, UMNO, in an effort to show how tolerant its 'Islam' is, has joined the non-*bumiputera* to condemn the PI for 'abusing' Islam.

The Malay left, active since before the war, had *Melayu Raya* (including all of what came to be Indonesia) as its first nation-of-intent, in which it imagined that 'all Malays in one region should come together and see themselves as One Race, speaking One Language, and belonging to One Nation'.[32] Like the Chinese-dominated Malayan Communist Party (MCP) the Malay left was disfavoured by the British for its Indonesian connections. Wary of the fact that the Dutch were humbled after the war by an army of indigenous freedom fighters, some motivated by socialist ideals, the API – (Angkatan Pemuda Insaf), the militant-oriented youth section of the Malay left – was banned by the British in 1948. Later, in 1950, Parti Kebangsaan Melayu Malaya (PKMM; Malay Nationalist Party), also part of the Malay left, was disbanded. As a result, the Malay left became considerably weakened. However, it reappeared in November 1955 in the form of the Malay-dominated Parti Rakyat Malaysia (PRM). Together with the non-*bumiputera*-controlled Labour Party it formed a loosely organized Socialist Front (SF) and won a number of seats in the general elections of 1959 and 1964 but split after 1967. The PRM continued to soldier on but with little success with its original idea of *Melayu Raya*. The party still exists today but more as 'conscience party', fighting for the poor and exploited, against corruption and nepotism in the government. However, it has failed to receive real political support

---

32. A useful study on the Malay left was carried out by Rustam A. Sani, 'The Origin of the Malay Left'. See also Firdaus Abdullah, *Radical Malay Politics: Its Origins and Early Development*, Kuala Lumpur: Pelanduk Publications, 1985. The above quotation is taken from Cheah Boon Kheng, *Red Star Over Malaya; Resistance and Social Conflict during and after the Japanese Occupation 1941–1946*, (2nd ed.), Singapore. Singapore University Press, 1983, p. 11.

from the mass of *bumiputera* and consists of a handful of academics, middle-class intellectuals and trade union elites, mostly *bumiputera*.

After the formation of Malaysia in 1963, *bumiputera* communities in the states of Sabah and Sarawak made their entry into Malaysian politics. In Sabah, the Christian Kadazan and the Muslim Dusun have dominated Sabah politics to this day. In Sarawak, it is the non-Muslim Iban and the Muslim Melanaus who have been dictating politics. However, in both states, the Chinese community has represented the critical third party whose support is much needed by any of the *bumiputera* groups aiming to control the local state.

Except for the small marginalized group of mainly non-Muslim *Orang Asli*, or the aborigines, the *bumiputera* community in the Peninsula is dominated by Malays, who are constitutionally defined Muslims. However, the majority of *bumiputera* in Sabah and Sarawak are non-Muslim. This situation is further complicated by other forms of cultural difference and, most important of all, economic difference. For instance, most of the Malays were peasants when independence came but the *bumiputera* of Sarawak and Sabah are a mixed lot, some urbanized, some peasants and some, like the Orang Asli in the Peninsula, were forest dwellers when Malaysia was formed. These specific material and cultural circumstances shaped the *bumiputera* politics within the peripheral Sabah and Sarawak.[33] This came quite early after the formation of Malaysia. It happened, first, in the Iban-dominated state of Sarawak. The state government, under its premier Stephen Kalong Ningkan, tried to assert its autonomy and this was perceived by the federal government as an attempt at separatism resulting in the imposition of emergency rule in the state in 1966. In Sabah, when its premier Donald Stephens tried to champion the cause of the Kadazan, this was also perceived by the central government as an attempt to seek an unacceptable level of autonomy. In 1967 he was replaced by Datu Mustapha, a Muslim Sulu chief and a leader of the Muslim Dusun.

These events set the tone of subsequent political relations between the states and federal government, not only between the Peninsula-based federal centre and the local states of Sarawak and Sabah but also within the

---

33. See footnote 12 for detailed reference on the relationship between the federal government and the states Sabah and Sarawak. In addition, see also Margaret Roff, 'The Rise and Demise of Kadazan Nationalism', in *Journal of Southeast Asian History*, vol. 10, no. 2, 1969, pp. 326–343; Margaret Roff, *Politics of Belonging: Political Change in Sabah and Sarawak*, Kuala Lumpur: Oxford University Press, 1974; Peter Searle, *Politics in Sarawak, 1970–1975: An Iban Perspective*, Kuala Lumpur: Oxford University Press, 1983; Jayum A. Jawan, *The Iban Factor in Sarawak Politics*, Serdang: Penerbit Universiti Pertanian Malaysia, 1993.

Peninsula. It was because of this contentious relationship that the *bumi-putera* of Sarawak and Sabah began to create their own visions of what Malaysia should be, which are quite different from those generated by the specific historical circumstances and ethnic configurations in Peninsular Malaysia. As a consequence, the use of *bumiputera* as an ethnic symbol in the attempt to create a kind of joint nationhood in Malaysia seemed to work in the opposite direction. The gap between the nationalist ideology, represented by *bumiputera*ism, and the social practice, the emergence of divergent versions of *bumiputera*ism, reinforces Anderson's point that any community which is based on wider links and not on face-to-face contact is an imagined one, hence constantly open to contestation. The rise of 'Kadazan nationalism' and 'Iban nationalism' in Malaysia is a testimony to this fact. It is the former which has been articulated most forcefully, especially as Sabah was ruled by the PBS, a Kadazan-controlled party, for more than a decade. In order to 'win' back Sabah, UMNO set up its own branch and division there and allowed for the first time non-Muslim *bumiputera* to become members, a kind of compromise on the principles of Malayness upon which UMNO has based its existence for the last four decades. Even though UMNO finally got to rule Sabah after the dramatic 1990 state elections, the 'fire' of Kadazan nationalism seems to be still burning. This was evidenced by the ability of the PBS to win a large number of parliamentary seats in Sabah in the 1995 elections.

WITHIN THE NON-BUMIPUTERA

Historically, the non-*bumiputera* communities have been exposed to the concepts of 'race' and 'nation', as understood in the British colonialist's sense, through their connections with their 'homelands'.[34] For instance, during the opening decades of the twentieth century the overseas Chinese, including those in British Malaya, were actively courted for their moral, and more importantly, material support by both Chinese revolutionaries and reformists. It was through such connections that by the 1920s and 1930s Sun Yat Sen's concept of *min-tsu*, a Mandarin translation of the Western concepts of 'race' and 'nation', came into circulation within the Chinese community in Malaya. It was adopted by the Chinese as a local discourse on ethnicity. This was not unrelated to the fact that the British colonial government itself had intro-

---

34. The best available general account of Malaysian history is Leonard Andaya and Barbara Andaya, *A History of Malaysia*, London: Macmillan, 1982. The following discussion on the political history of the non-*bumiputera* groups is based on the Andayas' description.

duced the concept 'race' in its censuses since 1871, which subsequently led
to its adoption by both the *bumiputera* and non-*bumiputera* groups.[35] These
were the circumstances within which the non-*bumiputera* began to shape
their own 'nations-of-intent'. For the purpose of this chapter, we shall
examine the Chinese case as an example because the community is
influential politically, not only in Peninsular Malaysia but also in Sarawak
and Sabah.[36] In fact, whenever Malaysianists discuss anything related to the
non-*bumiputera*, it is always the Chinese experience which is highlighted.

It has been argued that the influence of political events in mainland
China and circumstances within the colonial state of British Malaya since
early this century have made the Chinese, as a community, highly conscious
of safeguarding their cultural identity and in shaping the form and content
of possible nations suitable for encompassing the Chinese. However, the
Chinese have by no means been united on this score. For instance, the
Chinese-dominated Malayan Communist Party, formally established in
1930, was intent on replacing the colonial government with a 'Malayan
nation' in which a Malay person's loyalty to the nation was expected to be
higher than that to his Sultan and, as far as immigrants were concerned,
higher than loyalty to the homeland of his ancestors.[37] Even though the
MCP was finally disbanded in 1989, after having led a bloody guerrilla war
against the government for more than four decades, it has had a tremendous

---

35. For an excellent analysis of the colonial construction of 'race' as a category, through
the introduction of census, in British Malaya, see Charles Hirschman, 'The Making of
Race in Colonial Malaya', in *Sociological Forum*, vol. 2, no. 1, Spring, 1986, pp. 330–361.
See also Frank Dikötter, *The Discourse of Race in Modern China*, London: Hurst, 1992.

36. There have been numerous publications on overseas Chinese in Southeast Asia as
well as the Chinese in Malaysia. My present discussion is based on the following contribu-
tions: Wang Gungwu, 'The Study of Chinese Identities in Southeast Asia', in Jennifer
Cushman and Wang Gungwu (eds), *Changing Identities of the Southeast Asian Chinese since
World War II*, Hong Kong: Hong Kong University Press, 1988, pp. 1–22; Sharon Carstens,
'Chinese Publications and the Transformation of Chinese Culture in Singapore and
Malaysia', in Cushman and Wang Gungwu (eds), *Changing Identities*, pp. 75–95; Tan Chee
Beng, 'Nation-Building and Being Chinese in a Southeast Asian State: Malaysia', in Cush-
man and Wang Gungwu (eds), *Changing Identities*, pp. 139–164; Tan Liok Ee, *The Rhetoric
of Bangsa and Minzu: Community and Nation in Tension, the Malay Peninsula, 1900–1955*,
Working Paper 52, Centre of Southeast Studies, Monash University, Melbourne, 1988 and
her, 'Dongjiaozong and the Challenge to Cultural Hegemony 1951–1987', in Kahn and
Loh (eds), *Fragmented Vision*, pp. 181–201; Stephen Leong, 'Sources, Agencies and Manifestations of Overseas Chinese Nationalism in Malaya 1937–1941', doctoral dissertation,
University of California, Los Angeles, 1976; and Oong Hak Ching, 'British Policy and
Chinese Politics in Malaya', PhD thesis, University of Hull, 1992.

37. For a detailed analysis on the history of the MCP see Cheah Boon Kheng, *The
Masked Comrades: A Study of the Communist United Front in Malaya, 1945–1948*, Singapore: Times Book, 1979.

influence in shaping not only politics within the Chinese community but also in the wider Malaysian society long after its demise. Many laws originally introduced by the colonial government to curb the activities of the MCP have been retained by the post-colonial government even after the Cold War and the communist threat are gone. The infamous Internal Security Act (ISA), a rule which allows the authorities to detain any Malaysian without trial for an unspecified period, is one such law.

However, the more influential section of the Chinese community has, for over half a century now, been closely associated with Chinese education because education was viewed by the Chinese community as central to the construction and maintenance of Chinese identity, hence 'Chineseness'.[38] Admittedly, there were factions within this group. However, what bound them together for so long was the common vision of a nation in which the Chinese language, Chinese schools and Chinese culture would have a legitimate status. By implication, this vision is opposed to the official government position, which is based on the Malaysian Constitution, but the vision is still actively pursued by some factions within the Chinese community. For example, the Chinese educationists led an unsuccessful attempt (1967–78) to set up a Chinese-medium university, called Merdeka University. However, the vocational institute, called the Tunku Abdul Rahman College, which was also the brainchild of Chinese educationists, is thriving, with new branches coming up in Penang and Johor. It continues to receive substantial financial support from the government. More than 90 per cent of the students are Chinese and mostly from private Chinese secondary schools in Malaysia.

Since the Chinese community are numerically not really a minority in a traditional demographic sense, the importance and influence of the Chinese vision of nation must not be underrated. Besides, the community has economic clout. Many of its economic elites have successfully helped the rise of Malay corporate entrepreneurs and paved the way for successful Malaysian and Chinese joint ventures in the People's Republic of China (PRC), Taiwan and Hong Kong. A few have even been entrusted with managing important government-funded private companies. Thousands of Chinese Malaysian private students have successfully completed their tertiary education abroad and have come home to make critical contributions to Malaysia's economic success. Therefore, the strength of the Chinese view

---

38. A useful political history of Chinese education in Malaysia has been written by Tan Liok Ee, 'Politics of Chinese Education in Malaya, 1945–1961', PhD thesis, Universiti Malaya, 1985. See also her, 'Dongjiaozong and the Challenge to Cultural Hegemony', in Kahn and Loh (eds), *Fragmented Vision*, 1992, pp. 181–201.

and voice in the long run is not going to be diminished, but will rather be reinforced both politically and economically, despite claims of contrary trends.

UMNO, for instance, is becoming more and more dependent on Chinese voters for political support in provincial towns. It is not surprising that, with the emergence of the PRC as a potential economic giant in Asia in the next century, the *bumiputera*-dominated Malaysian government has become more willing to listen to Chinese demands. The recent 'Islam and Confucianism' dialogue organized by Malaysia's deputy prime minister Anwar Ibrahim is but one of the many signs of the 'softening' of attitude, if a rhetorical one, towards the Chinese community.[39]

Nations-of-Intent and Malaysian Social Science

The presence of the various nations-of-intent in Malaysia has had its impact on the construction of social scientific knowledge about Malaysia; hence it must not be dismissed out of hand. This is especially evident in the rise of the 'new' middle class in Malaysia, whose involvement in the process of 'mental production' has become increasingly significant. That they have played the role of 'backroom boys' as well as the 'main actors' in Malaysian politics and economy is abundantly clear but rarely examined critically.[40] In fact foreign scholars, observers and analysts, inevitably have been dragged,

---

39. The conference, held on 12 March 1995, was jointly organized by Universiti Malaya and Institut Kajian Dasar, Anwar's think-tank. It was well attended with a number of contributors from abroad. An analysis of the 1995 elections result reveals that UMNO has received strong support from the Chinese community. See footnote 17.

40. Nearly half of the past and present federal government cabinet ministers and many of the state chief ministers have been academics or senior researchers in government and private institutions: Rafidah Aziz (ex-lecturer, Universiti Malaya, or UM, now minister of international trade and industry); Dr Ting Chew Peh (ex-lecturer Universiti Kebangsaan Malaysia, or UKM, now minister of housing and local government); Dr Yusoff Nor (ex-lecturer UKM and ex-minister of public enterprise), Nafsiah Omar (ex-lecturer Universiti Pertanian Malaysia, ex-minister of national unity); Abdul Ghani Othman (ex-lecturer UM, ex-minister of sports and youth, and now chief minister, state of Johor), Dr Fong Chan Onn (ex-lecturer UM and now deputy minister of education); Dr Hamid Othman (ex-lecturer UKM, now deputy minister, prime minister's department); Dr Ibrahim Saad (ex-lecturer UKM, ex-deputy chief minister, Penang state, now deputy minister, prime minister's department); Dr Affifuddin Omar (ex-research director Muda Agricultural Development Authority and now deputy minister of finance); Dr Goh Cheng Teik (ex-lecturer UM, now, deputy minister of land and cooperative development); Dr M.Marimuthu (ex-lecturer UM, ex-deputy minister of health); and Dr Koh Tsu Koon (ex-lecturer Universiti Sains Malaysia and now chief minister, Penang state). About a dozen or so have become either members of parliament at the federal level or members of the state legislative assembly of a number of states in Peninsular Malaysia, Sabah and Sarawak.

directly and indirectly, into this 'ethnoscape' and nation-of-intent realm and complicity.

Like the political left in Malaysia, which finds that the 'ethnic question' is a thorny and unresolvable issue, the so-called 'radical scholars' (local and foreign) who study Malaysia also have to confront the unresolvable nation-of-intent-related 'ethnicity' issue.[41] As a consequence, it could be argued that social science knowledge about Malaysia has become highly ethnicized, even among them. By this I mean that knowledge, irrespective of philosophical and theoretical grounding, has been used directly or indirectly as an instrument to advocate an ethnic cause or to launch purportedly 'an objective, scientific critic' of an ethnic group or to justify the interest of an ethnic or sub-ethnic group.[42] It could also refer to knowledge that is structured according to a perceived ethnic division within which an academic analysis is framed, such as within the various nations-of-intent. For instance, there have been circumstances where Malaysianists, both local and foreign, have adopted a Marxist or Neo-Marxist approach to advance an openly chauvinistic position.[43]

Writings on the NEP and its implementation provide us with the best examples to date of how knowledge on Malaysia has been ethnicized. On the one hand, a number of non-*bumiputera* scholars opposed to the NEP have been writing 'scholarly' articles in international journals on the impact of this discriminatory policy on lower-class Malaysian Chinese and how it has made a few *bumiputera* extremely rich. On the other hand, a group of

41. For a brief account of the left in Malaysia and how they handle the 'ethnic question', see, Ikmal Said, 'Ethnic Perspectives of the Left', in Kahn and Loh (eds), *Fragmented Vision*, 1992, pp. 254–281.

42. See Norman Cigar, *Genocide in Bosnia: The Policy of 'Ethnic Cleansing'*, Houston: Texas A&M University Press, 1994, in which he examined in detail, partly through content analysis method, how Serbian academics became 'the intellectual instigators of ethnic cleansing' through the widely distributed 'academic' articles and pamphlets they wrote, together with Serbian writers and members of the Serbian Orthodox Church, on the illusory danger that Bosnian Muslim fundamentalists were planning a *jihad* against the Serbs hence the urgent need to free the Serbs of this danger through whatever means. This is, of course, an extreme example of ethnicized knowledge informed by a constructed nationalist agenda. In the Malaysian case, the ethnicized knowledge is presented in a more subtle manner informed by the various nations-of-intent.

43. Examples of such works are by Hua Wu Yin, *Class and Communialism in Malaysia*, London: Zed Press, 1983; Fatimah Halim (pseud. of Hing Ai Yun), 'The Transformation of the Malaysian State' in *Journal of Contemporary Asia*, vol. 20, no. 1, 1990, pp. 64–88; and B.N. Cham, 'Class and Communal Conflict in Malaysia', in *Journal of Contemporary Asia*, vol. 5, no. 4, 1975, pp. 446–461. For a recent survey on social science study of ethnic politics in Malaysia, see Francis Loh Koh Wah, 'Studying Ethnic Politics in Malaysia: From Plural Society to Political Economy to ...', a paper for the conference on 'Role and Orientation of Malaysian Social Science in the 21st Century', Kuala Lumpur, 26–27 August 1991.

bumiputera scholars has defended the NEP and published 'academic' pieces which argue that without the NEP the condition of the poor *bumiputera* would worsen and another racial riot occur as a consequence. They also ask, 'what's wrong with having more *bumiputera* millionaires?' No detailed and systematic studies have been carried out to show the role of the Malaysian Chinese in the commercial sector, or to what extent they have benefited from the NEP. For non-*bumiputera* scholars to describe the benefits that Chinese have received from the NEP would only weaken their 'academic' argument about the highly discriminatory nature of the policy. The 'nationalist' *bumiputera* scholars seem to find it a waste of time to study ethnic groups other than the *bumiputera*.

In this sense, writings on the NEP have inevitably shown symptoms of this tendency to ethnicized knowledge. Most of the ethnicized writings are about *bumiputera*, their faults and foibles. On the non-*bumiputera*, particularly on the Chinese, the writings tell us how they resist *bumiputera* dominance but not what some have gained in the NEP era. From a Western viewpoint, this is an example of what may be called 'academic dishonesty'. In the Malaysian context it could be seen as an 'academic' articulation, by Malaysianists, of the various ethnic groups' interests and nations-of-intent.

In other words, it is not uncommon in Malaysian social science discourse that even the best of the academic contributions written in the best Western academic tradition with the best of intentions function as an outlet for the discontented Malaysians they describe. This is an unfortunate situation but a reality that many Malaysian social scientists, of all ethnic backgrounds, and foreign scholars specializing on Malaysia, do not dare to admit. Inevitably, since many of these scholars have become 'backroom boys' to the various communal organizations and ethnic-based political parties, this ethnicized knowledge would further contribute towards the perpetuation of ethnic division in Malaysia.

However, despite the ethnicized tone of these contributions, it is a healthy sign for contemporary Malaysian society that brave Malaysian scholars, of all theoretical pursuasions and ethnic origins, are able to air their anti-'*bumiputera* establishment' views. For this reason alone the ethnicized contributions make interesting reading. Ironically, this has been the force which has created such a vibrant social scientific discourse amongst Malaysianists, local and foreign, thus far.

However, there are other power dimensions besides electoral power in contemporary Malaysia. A more balanced focus containing discussion of the attributes of powerful non-*bumiputera* and how the alliance of the elites across ethnic boundaries shapes Malaysian contemporary culture and politics would have mitigated, for example, the ethnicized flavour of much writing on Malaysian politics and culture. There have been serious attempts to redress this problem by a number of Malaysianists, such as by Chandra Muzaffar through his numerous publications published by Aliran, a social reform group, of which he was the founder and leader until recently. However, a recent debate regarding *Melayu Baru*, or the New Malay, within the *bumi-putera* community, shows that it is still informed by UMNO's nation-of-intent. The ongoing debate on 'national culture' is also highly ethnicized and framed within the various nations-of-intent discussed above.[44] The vexed question is, would the recent entry of 'post-modernist' or 'cultural' approaches on the Malaysian social science scene increase or defuse the ethnicized nature of the construction of knowledge about Malaysia? This is yet to be seen.

Conclusion

This brief essay has made an attempt to relocate the theme 'national identity' in a wider sociological context, namely, 'the modernization project' of developing countries, in which, besides the economic programme, the political programme of nation-building, hence the national identity issue, is a part. This conceptual recontextualization is necessary in view of the fact that many debates on 'nationalism', 'national identity' and 'nation-building', both within and outside academe, have been overtly 'political'. The Malaysian experience is offered here as an empirical example.

Many studies have advanced an argument that nationalist ideology often emerges as a reaction to industrialization and the fragmentation of society that it brings.[45] The state realises that, on the one hand, kinship ideology, feudalism and religion are no longer capable of organizing people, and yet, on the other, the relatively new industrial system of production urgently requires a kind of socio-cultural homogenization of the population

---

44. Two of Chandra Muzaffar's contributions published by Aliran publications are, *Challenges and Choices in Malaysian Politics and Society*, Penang: Aliran, 1989 and *The NEP: Development and Alternative Consciousness*, Penang: Aliran 1989. On Melayu Baru, see Rustam A. Sani, *Melayu Baru dan Bangsa Malaysia*. On national culture debate, see Kua Sia Soong, *National Culture*.

45. See, for instance, Ernest Gellner, *Nations and Nationalism*, Oxford: Blackwell, 1983, and his collection of essays in *Encounters with Nationalism*, Oxford: Blackwell, 1994. See, also, Ralph Grillo (ed.), *'Nation' and 'State' in Europe*, London: Academic Press, 1980, and John Breuilly, *Nationalism and the State*, (2nd ed.), Chicago: University of Chicago Press, 1993. See also Stein Tønnesson and Hans Antlöv's introduction to the present volume.

to prepare, on a large scale, a continuous pool of skilful workers. The success of the process of homogenization is dependent on the success of a mass education system, which is supposed to introduce 'national consciousness', and create cohesion and loyalty amongst individuals involved in a densely populated social system. A 'nationalist ideology' or 'nationalism' is often seen, in this context, as being able to fulfil these cultural and political require-ments for what is essentially a materialist objective.

It could be argued that a nationalist ideology is functional for the state for two main reasons; first, it recreates a sentiment of 'nationhood', that is, a feeling of wholeness and continuity with the past, and, second, it may come to terms with the negative consequences of modernity, particularly, the ruptured relationship between individual and society hence alienation result-ing from industrialization. 'Nationhood' begets 'national identity', which is both a political ideology and a faith for which previously people have been willing to sacrifice their lives. But, in the context of the newly emerging economies, such as Malaysia, would the state expect its citizens to die for the sake of achieving a statistical target of 'economic growth'? Herein lies the problem which the state faces in introducing a relatively new nationalist ideology in the post-Cold War era in countries such as Malaysia, that are solely motivated by a modernization project intent on transforming the country, through industrialization, into a developed modern nation.

The proclamation by the Malaysian state that there is an urgent need to have created a 'united Malaysian nation' with a *Bangsa Malaysia* identity by the year 2020, is a conscious effort on its part to foster a new 'nationalist ideology' to pre-empt its transformation to an industrialized developed status which, it believes, is now well on its way. Interestingly, the realization of this 'identity' has been put across by the state as the ultimate 'challenge' for all Malaysians; by implication, should this ideology introduced by the urban elites fail, the burden of the blame will fall on the mass of citizens. How-ever, the real challenge is to seek a middle ground or a compromise between an authority-defined nation, framed within the context of *bumiputera* domin-ance (as articulated by a particular group within the *bumiputera*, namely, UMNO), and the everyday ideas about nations-of-intent propagated by both the various *bumiputera* and non-*bumiputera* groups. Some of the latter have their social roots deep in the past and others in the recent post-colonial circumstances. The intervention by the 'new' middle class, in the form of perpetuating ethnicized social scientific knowledge framed in the nation-of-intent perspective, does not help this attempt to find a middle ground. The fact remains that irrespective of ethnic groups, what is being proposed and actively promoted has been a variety of nations-of-intent that could form Malaysia's future 'nationalist ideology' and 'national identity'.

The concept of nation-of-intent is analytically useful to understand the contradictions within the general discourse on 'nationalism', 'nationalist ideology' and 'nationhood' in the societies of emerging industrial economies such as in the East Asian region, for example, in Malaysia. It may also assist us to understand that particular discourse in a more positive light, separating analytically the authority-defined nation-of-intent from the everyday forms of the people at large, and how these two sets of nations-of-intent are articulated interests and how the state and people come to terms with that of the other.

For instance, in Malaysia today the main problem in the *bumiputera*-defined nation-of-intent called *Bangsa Malaysia* is that it has been perceived by non-*bumiputera* as being imbued with strong acculturationist, even assimilationist, tendencies and the latter prefer the state to adopt a more accommodative position, thus proposing a 'pluralized' nation, where no one single ethnic community predominates. Political, economic and demographic circumstances within Malaysia have allowed such a debate to proceed without creating open tension or enmity. Some could argue that perhaps such a debate is not possible in other countries with different historical and structural circumstances and could lead to conflict and bloodshed. However, I wish to argue that such a view, though partially valid, is too 'alarmist' and, in fact, echoes the position of the status quo within the state.

In the post-traditional social order, such as the one in Malaysia, when modern institutions and practices have already become 'traditions', 'pillars of authority' and 'measurement of social authenticity', when time and space have been transformed by globalization, creating macro large-scale systems and unleashing a host of contradictions at the micro-level, and when everyday 'transnationalist' existence continues to question and challenge the functionality of the state, it is impossible for the state and its authority-defined social reality to impose totally its presence on the more diffused and fragmented everyday social reality of the masses except in a draconian and authoritarian way. Within such a context, the contest may not be in the arena of *realpolitik* but at the discourse level, where concepts like nation-of-intent may become extremely useful not only to express dissent but also resistance in a subtle way.

Select Bibliography

The following bibliography contains mainly recent publications dealing explicitly with nationalism or national identity in Asia, but also some other general works which have particularly inspired the authors. Full references to other works cited will be found in the footnotes to each chapter.

Akzin, Benjamin, *State and Nation*, London: Hutchinson, 1964.

Alter, Joseph S., 'Somatic Nationalism: Indian Wrestling and Militant Hinduism', *Modern Asian Studies*, vol. 28, no. 3, 1994, pp. 557–588.

Amino Yoshihiko (trans. G. McCormack), 'Deconstructing "Japan"', *East Asian History*, no. 3, June 1992, pp. 121–142.

Anderson, Benedict R. O'G., *Language and Power: Exploring Political Cultures in Indonesia*, Ithaca: Cornell University Press, 1990.

——, *Imagined Communities: Reflections on the Origin and Spread of Nationalism*, London: Verso, (2nd rev. ed.) 1991.

Antlöv, Hans and Stein Tønnesson (eds), *Imperial Policy and Southeast Asian Nationalism, 1930-1957*, London: Curzon Press, 1995.

Ariffin Omar, *Bangsa Melayu: Malay Concepts of Democracy and Community 1945–1950*, Kuala Lumpur: Oxford University Press, 1993.

Balakrishnan, Gopal, 'The Nationalist Imagination', *New Left Review*, no. 211, 1995, pp. 56–69.

Befu, Harumi (ed.), *Cultural Nationalism in East Asia: Representation and Identity*, Berkeley: Institute of East Asian Studies, University of California, 1993.

Breckenridge, Carol A., and Peter van der Veer (eds), *Orientalism and the Post-colonial Predicament*, Philadelphia: University of Pennsylvania Press, 1994.

Breuilly, John, *Nationalism and the State*, Chicago: University of Chicago Press, (2nd ed.) 1993.

Brocheux, Pierre and Daniel Hémery, *Indochine: La colonisation ambiguë, 1858–1954*, Paris: La Découverte, 1995.

Brown, Delmer M., *Nationalism in Japan: an Introductory Historical Analysis*, Berkeley: University of California Press, 1955.

Burghart, Richard, 'The Concept of Nation-State in Nepal', *Journal of Asian Studies*, vol. 44, no. 1, 1984, pp. 101–124.

Chandler, David P., 'Maps for the Ancestors: Sacralized Topography and the Echoes of Angkor in Two Cambodian Texts', *Journal of the Siam Society*, vol. 64, part 2, July 1976, pp. 170–187.

Chatterjee, Partha, *Nationalist Thought and the Colonial World: a Derivative Discourse*, Minneapolis: University of Minnesota Press, (2nd ed.) 1993.

———, *The Nation and Its Fragments: Colonial and Postcolonial Histories*, Princeton: Princeton University Press, 1993.

Corpuz, O. D., *The Roots of the Filipino Nation* (2 vols), Quezon City: Aklahi Foundation, 1989.

Cushman, Jennifer and Wang Gungwu (eds), *Changing Identities of the Southeast Asian Chinese after World War II*, Hong Kong: Hong Kong University Press, 1988.

Dikötter, Frank, *The Discourse of Race in Modern China*, London: Hurst, 1992.

'Dimensions of Ethnic and Cultural Nationalism in Asia', special issue of the *Journal of Asian Studies*, vol. 53, no. 1, February 1994.

Duara, Prasenjit, 'Bifurcating Linear History: Nation and Histories in China and India', *Positions*, vol. 1, no. 3, 1993, pp. 779–804.

———, 'Deconstructing the Chinese Nation', *The Australian Journal of Chinese Affairs*, no. 30, 1993, pp. 1-28.

———, *Rescuing History from the Nation: Questioning Narratives of Modern China*, Chicago: University of Chicago Press, 1995.

Dumont, Louis, *Essays on Individualism: Modern Ideology in Anthropological Perspective*, Chicago: University of Chicago Press, 1986.

Eriksen, Thomas Hylland, *Ethnicity and Nationalism: Anthropological Perspectives*, London: Pluto Press, 1993.

Evans, Grant (ed.), *Asia's Cultural Mosaic: an Anthropological Introduction*, New York: Prentice Hall, 1993.

Fairbank, John K. (ed.), *The Chinese World Order*, Cambridge: Harvard University Press, 1968.

Fitzgerald, John, 'The Nationless State: the Search for a Nation in Modern Chinese Nationalism', *The Australian Journal of Chinese Affairs*, no. 33, 1995, pp. 75–104.

Friedman, Jonathan, *Cultural Identity and Global Process*, London: Sage, 1994.

Geertz, Clifford, *Negara: the Theatre State in Nineteenth Century Bali*, Princeton: Princeton University Press, 1980.

Gellner, Ernest, *Nations and Nationalism*, Oxford: Blackwell, 1983.

———, *Encounters with Nationalism*, Oxford: Blackwell, 1994.

Goscha, Christopher E., *Vietnam and Indochina: Contesting Concepts of Space, 1887–1954*, Copenhagen: NIAS Report no. 28, 1995.

Asian Forms of the Nation

——, 'L'Indochine repensée par les "Indochinois": Pham Quynh et les deux débats de 1931 sur l'immigration, le fédéralisme et la réalité de l'Indochine', *Revue française d'histoire d'outre mer*, forthcoming.

——, 'Quelques regards viêtnamiens sur la péninsule indochinoise pendant l'époque coloniale', *Bulletin de l'École Française d'Extrême-Orient*, forthcoming.

Greenfeld, Liah, *Nationalism: Five Roads to Modernity*, Cambridge: Harvard University Press, 1992.

Grosby, Steven, 'Territoriality: the Transcendental, Primordial Feature of Modern Societies', *Nations and Nationalism*, vol. 1, no. 2, 1995, pp. 143–162.

Harrison, Selig S. *The Widening Gulf: Asian Nationalism and American Policy*, New York: The Free Press, 1978.

Heine-Geldern, Robert, *Conceptions of State and Kingship in Southeast Asia*, Data Paper 18, Cornell Southeast Asia Program, Ithaca: Cornell University, 1956.

Heng Lai Ah, *Meanings of Multiethnicity: A Case-Study of Ethnicity and Ethnic Relations in Singapore*, Kuala Lumpur: Oxford University Press, 1995.

Henley, David E.F., 'Ethnographic Integration and Exclusion in Anticolonial Nationalism: Indonesia and Indochina', *Comparative Studies in Society and History*, vol. 37, no. 2, April 1995, pp. 286–324.

Hinton, Peter, 'Do the Karen Really Exist?', in John McKinnon and Wanat Bhruksasri (eds), *Highlanders of Thailand*, Singapore: Oxford University Press, 1986.

Hobsbawm, Eric, *Nations and Nationalism since 1780*, Cambridge: Cambridge University Press, 1990.

Hobsbawm, Eric and Terence Ranger (eds), *The Invention of Tradition*, Cambridge: Cambridge University Press, 1983.

Hoston, Germaine A., *The State, Identity, and the National Question in China and Japan*, Princeton: Princeton University Press, 1994.

Howell, David, 'Ainu Ethnicity and the Boundaries of the Early Modern Japanese State', *Past and Present*, no. 142, February 1994, pp. 69–93.

Johnson, Chalmers A., *Peasant Nationalism and Communist Power: the Emergence of Revolutionary China, 1937–1945*, Stanford: Stanford University Press (2nd rev. ed.) 1966.

Kahn, Joel S., and Francis Loh Kok Wah (eds), *Fragmented Vision: Culture and Politics in Contemporary Malaysia*, Sydney: Asian Studies Association of Australia in association with Allen & Unwin, 1992.

Kapferer, Bruce, *Legends of People, Myths of State: Violence, Intolerance, and Political Culture in Sri Lanka and Australia*, Washington: Smithsonian Institute Press, 1988.

Keyes, Charles, Laurel Kendall and Helen Hardacre (eds), *Asian Visions of Authority: Religion and the Modern States of East and Southeast Asia*, Honolulu: University of Hawaii Press, 1994.

Kopf, David, *The Brahmo Samaj and the Shaping of the Modern Indian Mind*, Princeton: Princeton University Press, 1979.

Kosaku Yoshino, *Cultural Nationalism in Contemporary Japan: a Sociological Enquiry*, London: Routledge, 1992.

Kumar, Ravinder, 'L'Inde: "Etat-Nation" ou "Etat-civilisation"?', *Hérodote*, no. 71, 1993, pp. 43–60.

Laitinen, Kauko, *Chinese Nationalism in the Late Qing Dynasty: Zhang Binglin as an Anti-Manchu Propagandist*, London: Curzon Press, 1990.

Leach, Edmund R., *Political Systems of Highland Burma. A Study of Kachin Political Structure*, London: Bells & Sons, 1964 [orig. 1954].

Levenson, Joseph, *Confucian China and Its Modern Fate: A Trilogy* (3 vols), Berkeley: University of California Press, 1968.

'The Living Tree: the Changing Meaning of Being Chinese Today', special issue of *Daedalus*, Spring 1991.

Mahathir Mohamad and Shintaro Ishihara, *The Voice of Asia: Two Leaders Discuss the Coming Century*, Tokyo: Kodansha International, 1995.

Maier, H.M.J., *In the Center of Authority: the Malay Hikayat Merong Mahawangsa*, Ithaca: Cornell University Southeast Asia Program, 1988.

Milner, Anthony, *The Invention of Politics in Colonial Malaya: Contesting Nationalism and the Expansion of the Public Sphere*, Cambridge: Cambridge University Press, 1994.

Morley, David and Kevin Robins, *Spaces of Identity: Global Media, Electronic Landscapes and Cultural Boundaries*, London: Routledge, 1995.

O'Hanlon, Rosalind and David Washbrook, 'After Orientalism: Culture, Criticism and Politics in the Third World', *Comparative Studies in Society and History*, vol. 34, 1992, pp. 141–167.

Ongkili, James, *Nation-Building in Malaysia, 1946-1974*, Kuala Lumpur: Oxford University Press, 1985.

Pandey, Gyanendra, *The Construction of Communalism in Colonial North India*, New Delhi: Oxford University Press, 1990.

Parekh, Bhikhu, 'Ethnocentricity of the Nationalist Discourse', *Nations and Nationalism*, vol. 1, no. 1, 1995, pp. 25–52.

Pollock, Sheldon, 'Ramayana and Political Imagination in India', *Journal of Asian Studies*, vol. 52, no. 2, 1993, pp. 261–297.

Prakash, Gyan, 'Subaltern Studies as Post Colonial Criticism', *American Historical Review*, vol. 99, 1994, pp. 1475–1490.

Pye, Lucian W., 'How China's Nationalism was Shanghaied', *The Australian Journal of Chinese Affairs*, no. 29, 1993, pp. 107–134.

Reynolds, Craig J. (ed.), *National Identity and Its Defenders*, Clayton, Victoria: Monash University, 1992.

Roff, William, *The Origins of Malay Nationalism*, Kuala Lumpur: University of Malaya Press, 1967.

Sack, Robert D., *Human Territoriality: Its Theory and History*, Cambridge: Cambridge University Press, 1986.

Seton-Watson, Hugh, *Nations and States: an Inquiry into the Origins of Nations and the Politics of Nationalism*, Boulder: Westview Press, 1977.

Shamsul A. B., *From British to Bumiputera Rule: Local Politics and Rural Development in Peninsular Malaysia*, Singapore: Institute of Southeast Asian Studies, 1986.

Smith, Anthony D., *Theories of Nationalism*, New York: Holmes & Meier, (2nd ed.) 1983.

——, *Ethnic Origins of Nations*, Oxford: Basil Blackwell, 1986.

——, *National Identity*, London: Penguin, 1991.

——, *Nations and Nationalism in a Global Era*, Cambridge: Polity Press, 1995.

——, 'Gastronomy or Geology? The Role of Nationalism in the Reconstruction of Nations', *Nations and Nationalism*, vol. 1, no. 1, 1995, pp. 3–23.

Stockwell, A.J., 'The White Man's Burden and Brown Humanity: Colonialism and Ethnicity in British Malaya', *Southeast Asian Journal of Social Science*, vol. 10, no. 1, 1982, pp. 44–68.

Tan Liok Ee, *The Rhetoric of Bangsa and Minzu: Community and Nation in Tension, the Malay Peninsula 1951–1987*, Working Paper 52, Centre of Southeast Asian Studies, Melbourne: Monash University, 1988.

Taylor, Robert H., 'Perceptions of Ethnicity in the Politics of Burma, *Southeast Asian Journal of Social Science*, vol. 10, no. 1, 1982, pp. 7–22.

——, *The State in Burma*, London: C. Hurst & Co., 1987.

Thongchai Winichakul, *Siam Mapped: a History of the Geo-Body of a Nation*, Honolulu: University of Hawaii Press, 1994.

Tønnesson, Stein and Hans Antlöv, *Nations-of-Intent in Southeast Asia: Indonesia, Vietnam and Malaya, 1945–1948*, London: Curzon Press, forthcoming.

Townsend, James, 'Chinese Nationalism', *The Australian Journal of Chinese Affairs*, no. 27, 1992, pp. 97–130.

Veer, Peter van der, *Religious Nationalism: Hindus and Muslims in India*, Berkeley: University of California Press, 1994.

Wang Gung-wu, 'Greater China and the Chinese Overseas', *China Quarterly*, no. 136, December 1993, pp. 926–948.

Wang Yeu-farn, 'The National Identity of the Southeast Asian Chinese', Stockholm: Centre for Pacific Asia Studies at Stockholm University, 1994.

Westerlund, David (ed.), *Questioning the Secular State: the Worldwide Resurgence of Religion in Politics*, Hong Kong: Hurst & Co, in print.

Wijeyewardene, G. (ed.), *Ethnic Groups Across National Boundaries in Mainland Southeast Asia*, Singapore: Institute of Southeast Asian Studies, 1990.

Woodward, David and J.B. Harley (eds), *The History of Cartography, vol. 2, book 2: Cartography in the Traditional East and Southeast Asian Societies*, Chicago: University of Chicago Press, 1994.

Index

List of Contributors

Hans Antlöv is a research fellow at the Nordic Institute of Asian Studies (NIAS) in Copenhagen. He recently initiated a Swedish network based at Göteborg University for studies in discourses and practices of democracy in Southeast Asia. His study of village power in Indonesia, *Exemplary Centre, Administrative Periphery*, has been published by NIAS/Curzon Press.

Graham E. Clarke is working at Oxford University's International Development Centre. As a social anthropologist he has worked extensively in the Himalayan and Central Asian Region. Recent publications include: 'Thinking through Nature in Highland Nepal', in O. Bruun and A. Kalland (eds), *Asian Perceptions of Nature* and 'The Movement of Population to the West of China: Tibet and Qinghai' in R. Foot and J. Brown (eds), *Migration: The Asian Experience*.

Christopher E. Goscha is an American researcher working in France on modern Thai and Vietnamese history. A longer treatment of the issues covered in Chapter 4 of the present volume, *Vietnam or Indochina? Contesting Concepts of Space in Vietnamese Nationalism, 1887–1954*, has been published by NIAS. Goscha is also the author, together with Thomas Engelbert, of *Falling Out of Touch: a Study on Vietnamese Communist Policy Towards an Emerging Cambodian Communist Movement, 1930-1975*.

Mikael Gravers is a senior lecturer in ethnography and social anthropology at Aarhus University in Denmark. His lengthy treatment of the scope and origins of xenophobia and ethnic strife in Burma, *Nationalism as Political Paranoia in Burma*, has been published by NIAS.

Torbjörn Lodén is Professor of Chinese Language and Culture at Stockholm University. His main fields of research are Chinese intellectual history, Confucianism and twentieth-century thought, and his publications include *Debatten om proletär litteratur i Kina 1928–1929* [The Debate about Proletarian Literature in China, 1928–1929].

Arild Engelsen Ruud is currently engaged at Oslo University's Department of History and the Centre for Development and the Environment (SUM), where from a historical and cultural viewpoint he is investigating bureaucratic practice in the district administration of West Bengal.

Tessa Morris-Suzuki is Professor in Pacific and Asian History at the Australian National University's Research School of Pacific and Asian Studies. Her research interests include questions of citizenship and ethnic identity, and the social effects of technological change. Among her publications is *The Technological Transformation of Japan*.

Niels Mulder works as a freelance social scientist specializing in comparative cultural analysis of contemporary Southeast Asian societies and continues to pursue his anthropological field research in the Philippines, Thailand and Java. Among his numerous publications are the widely-read *Inside Indonesian Society*, and *Inside Southeast Asian Society*.

Shamsul A.B. is Professor of Social Anthropology at the Universiti Kebangsaan Malaysia. He teaches, researches and has written extensively on culture and politics in Malaysia and especially issues of modernization, nation-building and identity construction. His best known book is *From British to Bumiputera Rule*.

Stein Tønnesson is a senior research fellow at NIAS, where till recently he headed the Institute's project on Southeast Asian nation building as research professor. The first publication from that project was Hans Antlöv and Stein Tønnesson (eds), *Imperial Policy and Southeast Asian Nationalism*. Among Tønnesson's earlier publications is *The Vietnamese Revolution of 1945*.

Peter van der Veer is Professor of Comparative Religion and Director of the Research Centre on Religion and Society at the University of Amsterdam. He has published several books including *Gods on Earth*, *Religious Nationalism* and *Conversion to Modernities*.

C.W. Watson lectures in Social Anthropology at the University of Kent, Canterbury. In addition to his work on modern Malaysian and Indonesian literature he has written on the Islamic dimensions of contemporary political debates in Malaysia and Indonesia. His most recent book (co-edited with R.F. Ellen) is *Understanding Witchcraft and Sorcery in Southeast Asia*.

Thongchai Winichakul is Associate Professor in History at the University of Wisconsin-Madison. His study, *Siam Mapped*, won the Harry Benda Award from the American Association of Asian Studies in 1995. He received an SSRC grant in 1992, and the Guggenheim Fellowship in 1994–95 to work on his next book, which deals with the history of historical knowledge in Siam.